The New ~~Dessert~~

MW00610346

STUDIES IN CONTINENTAL THOUGHT

John Sallis,
general editor

Consulting Editors

Robert Bernasconi
Rudolph Bernet
John D. Caputo
David Carr
Edward S. Casey
Hubert Dreyfus
Don Ihde
David Farrell Krell
Lenore Langsdorf
Alphonso Lingis

William L. McBride
J. N. Mohanty
Mary Rawlinson
Tom Rockmore
Calvin O. Schrag
†Reiner Schürmann
Charles E. Scott
Thomas Sheehan
Robert Sokolowski
Bruce W. Wilshire

David Wood

Photograph © Husserl-Archives Leuven,
courtesy Rudolf Bernet.

THE NEW HUSSERL

A Critical Reader

Edited by Donn Welton

INDIANA
University Press
Bloomington & Indianapolis

Publication of this book is made possible in part with
the assistance of a Challenge Grant from the National Endowment
for the Humanities, a federal agency that supports research,
education, and public programming in the humanities.

This book is a publication of

Indiana University Press
601 North Morton Street
Bloomington, IN 47404-3797 USA

http://iupress.indiana.edu

Telephone orders   800-842-6796
Fax orders   812-855-7931
Orders by e-mail   iuporder@indiana.edu

© 2003 by Indiana University Press

All rights reserved

No part of this book may be reproduced or utilized in any form or
by any means, electronic or mechanical, including photocopying and
recording, or by any information storage and retrieval system,
without permission in writing from the publisher. The Association of
American University Presses' Resolution on Permissions constitutes
the only exception to this prohibition.

The paper used in this publication meets the minimum requirements
of American National Standard for Information
Sciences—Permanence of Paper for Printed Library Materials, ANSI
Z39.48-1984.

Manufactured in the United States of America

Library of Congress Cataloging-in-Publication Data

The new Husserl : a critical reader / edited by Donn Welton.
    p.   cm. — (Studies in Continental thought)
    Includes bibliographical references and index.
ISBN 0-253-34238-4 (cloth) — ISBN 0-253-21601-X (paper)
1. Husserl, Edmund, 1859–1938. I. Welton, Donn. II. Series.
        B3279.H94N39 2003
        193—dc21

                                    2003002449

    1 2 3 4 5   08 07 06 05 04 03

*For Ludwig Landgrebe (1902–91),
a philosopher of his times,
a man of faith*

Contents

Discovering the New Husserl

WITH THE ONGOING publication of Husserl's lectures and working manuscripts from his middle and later periods, and with sustained studies of how his method and theories developed throughout the course of his thought, we are seeing a significant shift in the way the scope and the significance of Husserl's transcendental phenomenology are being interpreted and extended. The essays in this collection are an invitation to discover this "new Husserl."

Because of a surprising convergence between many deconstructive, analytic, and critical theory readings of Husserl, something like a standard picture emerged during the 1960s and 1970s and continues to hold sway today.[1] For this approach the first book of *Ideas* (1913) is taken as the definitive formulation of both the working method and the range of Husserl's transcendental phenomenology. The later works—and there were precious few published in comparison to the lecture and research manuscripts written—were understood either as elaborations upon this framework (*Formal and Transcendental Logic*), as a failed attempt to expand its scope through the integration of a theory of intersubjectivity (*Cartesian Meditations*), or as an effort to deal with such issues as paradigm shifts and cultural relativity that might prove an embarrassment to his efforts to make philosophy a "rigorous science" (*Crisis*). Toward the end, Husserl dimly perceived the threat to his program of transcendental analysis that his own later studies on what he called "genetic phenomenology" produced, so it is said, but these analyses were but fragments, never integrated into and harmonized with the canonical method of *Ideas I*. For the standard approach Husserl's lasting contributions are restricted to semantics, the logic of parts and whole, a structural account of intentionality, and the introduction of the notion of the life-world. To this several postmodern interpreters have added a second critical analysis that reduces Husserl to being a foil for developmental and genealogical accounts that attempt to overturn the very possibility of transcendental phenomenology.

The essays in the collection are shaped by a deep reading of not just the works published during Husserl's lifetime but also the countless lectures and working manuscripts he wrote, especially during his later Freiburg years.[2] They provide an alternative to the standard approach to Husserl by examining his method as a whole and by offering depth-probes into a number of issues, old and new, that occupied him during his exceptionally productive later period.

The opening two chapters by Klaus Held, first published in 1985–86 and now masterfully translated by Lanei Rodemeyer, offer what is arguably the best short introduction to Husserl "whole cloth." Attuned to the developments in Husserl's own thought, Held is able to take even the introductory reader from the early formulations of Husserl's *Logical Investigations* (1900–1901), to the important redefinition of the method as transcendental in *Ideas I* (1913), to his later studies of the life-world in a way that tracks the progressive unfolding of the original insights of phenomenology.[3] His analysis also provides a framework that situates the more focused studies that follow.

With an overview of the whole of Husserl's thought in hand, Part II presents internal developments in or offers further specifications of Husserl's groundbreaking theories of intentionality, types, and time-consciousness.

Clearly the theory of intentionality was Husserl's first decisive contribution to philosophy. Although Franz Brentano had reintroduced the concept into the philosophy of his day, it was Husserl's *Logical Investigations* that achieved the decisive breakthrough by connecting the idea of intentional content to a precise typology of acts. Studies of Husserl's theory of intentionality have been both sobered and strengthened by analytic readings of Husserl. But John Drummond suggests that by treating the noema as a mediating entity between acts and the objects to which they refer, a number of them lose the possibility of veridical reference, a doctrine close to Husserl. Attending to lecture manuscripts from the 1920s, his alternative account incorporates the notion of temporality and passive synthesis in a way missing from other discussions.

Dieter Lohmar offers the reader the first sustained study showing that Husserl's concept of type and Kant's notion of schema are functionally identical and that this notion is what carries the contested idea of a form of pre-predicative experience in Husserl. Using the resources of Husserl's genetic phenomenology, Lohmar also demonstrates that the claim of a circularity of types being produced through experience and yet experience being based on types can be overcome by attending to the fact that types are not concepts and that types undergo expansion and change on the basis of experience.

Intentional consciousness is temporal for Husserl. The account of time-consciousness in *On the Phenomenology of the Consciousness of Internal Time* (1928) was Husserl's first published attempt to study temporality. Yet this text consists mainly of lectures given in 1905 and does not reflect his reworking of the theory in what are known as the Bernauer manuscripts, composed between 1917 and 1918, and in the later C manuscripts, written between 1929 and 1935. Lanei Rodemeyer pays special attention to developments in his concept of protention, a side of time-consciousness that receives little attention in the earlier 1905 text, and suggests not just that it can handle the experience of novel situations but also that it supplies the founding temporal dimension of intentionality as a whole.

With the transformation of phenomenology into transcendental philosophy, a process begun after the *Logical Investigations* and given its first published formulation in *Ideas I*, his account of conscious acts was transposed into an analysis of transcendental subjectivity. Part III of this collection deals with three of the most pressing issues that attend this change.

Husserl's account of consciousness as consciousness-of seems to entail that anything that is brought to awareness is the result of an intentional act being directed toward it. And this implies that self-awareness, the cornerstone of his account of the self-evident nature of the existence of consciousness, is produced only by means of an act of reflection in which consciousness is made into object. But not only does this undercut the nature of consciousness, which is not an object, it also leads to the criticism that consciousness could be *self*-consciousness only as reflected upon and never in-itself. An essay by Dan Zahavi offers suggestive arguments against Heidegger, Tugendhat, Henrich, and Frank not only that Husserl has a notion of pre-reflective self-awareness but also that he offers a highly illuminating analysis of it.

David Carr adds much to this issue by concentrating more specifically on the status of consciousness as transcendental. He also works with the idea that the first and primary way that consciousness is present to itself is through self-awareness, but then studies the way in which the notion of reflection does function in a transcendental theory. One of the central difficulties with the notion of a transcendental self is that we arrive at it only through a set of rather complex methodological steps, suggesting that perhaps it is no more than a hypothetical construct produced by the need to provide a principle of unity to experience, and thus it does not really exist. Placing Husserl and Kant alongside each other, Carr offers a penetrating and lucid account of several crucial differences between the characterization of subjectivity as transcendental and the analysis of it as empirical. This, then, allows him to argue against the attempt by Dennett and others to reduce transcendental subjectivity to a piece of fiction.

The analysis of consciousness goes yet a step deeper when we ask how one places it in relation to the unconscious. The unconscious for Freud never directly manifests itself but is grasped only through gaps or improprieties in the materials that are conscious. But if the unconscious is always absent and never itself present, this confronts a transcendental phenomenology of consciousness with the task of encompassing it without making it into something that is not. Rudolf Bernet introduces the provocative thesis that we can discover how to thematize the unconscious in its own terms by turning to Husserl's account of intuitive presentifications, to phantasy, in particular.

The reliance upon a notion of self-awareness to secure the existence of consciousness and then transcendental subjectivity always runs the twofold risk of solipsism and, as a result, of dissolving the world into a web of subjective impressions. The two essays in Part IV respond to this risk, internal to any system of philosophy that gives priority to experience, by looking deeper into the concept of transcendental subjectivity and by pressing for a proper transcendental characterization of world.

Perhaps no concept of Husserl's has received more attention, in both philosophy and other disciplines, than that of the life-world. Since the second essay by Held deals with this extensively, the paper by Donn Welton attempts an appropriation rather than an exposition of the Husserlian concept of world. It suggests that to understand the world phenomenologically is to analyze it as horizon and that horizon is not a unitary structure but a highly differentiated triadic complex.

The complex issue of how one relates Husserl's concept of transcendental subjectivity to the notion of intersubjectivity has received a decisive breakthrough in the work of Dan Zahavi. By using manuscripts published in the three volumes of *Intersubjektivität,* he argues that Husserl's insistence on the absolute priority of the transcendental ego is compatible with his later account of transcendental intersubjectivity as the founding field. This later emphasis on intersubjectivity is what equips Husserlian phenomenology with a grounding structure commensurate with its treatment of the world as horizon and with a notion both of conventionality and of critique that gives phenomenology a purchase on phenomena.

The concluding two chapters of this volume rejoin the first two by focusing specifically on the question of phenomenological method.

In one of his very last discussions of his own phenomenology in 1934, four years before his death, Husserl said, "Everything I have written so far is only preparatory work; it is only the setting down of methods."[4] As several of the essays in this volume suggest, Husserl came to characterize his phenomenology in terms of a difference between static and genetic method. The second essay by Welton not only looks at the way the notion of genetic analysis emerges in Husserl's writings but also raises the question as to whether its relationship to static method is internal. It argues that while Husserl rejects the idea of a system, especially in the grand style of Hegel, static and genetic methods are systematically related to each other, and thus both are necessary components of his transcendental phenomenology.

The breakthrough to a genetic method brought a significant expansion of the scope of Husserl's phenomenology and, with it, of the kinds of issues that it was able to cover. Everything from the tacit features of perception to the historical transformations of cultural horizons was open to view. But there were yet other matters that seemed to push the method further, such as the notions of normality and normativity, birth and death, and the question of community. In a way that has opened new insight into the late Husserl, Anthony Steinbock suggests that this invites yet another expansion of the method, in the direction of what Husserl spoke of as the problem of generativity. He then invites us to follow this movement from the genetic to the generative.

The effort to capture a thinker as prolific and rich as Husserl in this collection leaves this editor with a keen sense of what space did not allow him to include. There is rich and important work being done by many others, and I am painfully aware of their absence. I can only hope that this collection serves as an invitation not just to the thought of Husserl but also to their efforts both to understand this marvelously complex thinker and to work with his ideas in philosophically fruitful ways.

Donn Welton
Stony Brook, New York

Notes

1. For a more detailed discussion of this convergence see Donn Welton, *The Other Husserl: The Horizons of Transcendental Phenomenology* (Bloomington: Indiana University Press, 2000), pp. 393–404.

2. The later period runs from 1916 to 1928, when he retired, and then to 1938, when he died. We now have thirty-five volumes in *Husserliana*, another ten volumes of correspondence, and yet another five volumes of *Husserliana Materialien*, with more on the way. Of the *Husserliana*, twenty-four volumes have been published from his whole career with twelve from the later period since the standard picture was codified (by around 1970). It is only as a result of the ongoing publication of the *Husserliana* that we have seen a progressive deepening of our understanding of Husserl's thought.

The effort to map an alternative to the standard picture did come early, most notably from Ludwig Landgrebe, to whom this collection is dedicated. See some of the essays collected in his *The Phenomenology of Edmund Husserl: Six Essays*, ed. with an introduction by Donn Welton (Ithaca: Cornell University Press, 1981). The best scholarship over the past thirty years has produced studies of a number of topics that have pushed us beyond the standard account, but only recently have we begun to understand the full scope of Husserl's phenomenological method as a whole.

3. As an aid to those who want to use this essay in connection with *The Essential Husserl: Basic Writings in Transcendental Phenomenology*, ed. Donn Welton (Bloomington: Indiana University Press, 1999), the citations in Held's essay also contain references to this reader.

4. Adelgundis Jaegerschmidt, "Conversations with Edmund Husserl, 1931–1938," *New Yearbook for Phenomenology and Phenomenological Philosophy* I (2001), 336.

Acknowledgments

THIS ANTHOLOGY IS very much indebted to two hardy souls who rendered valuable assistance with its production. In addition to co-translating one of the papers for the collection, Gina Zavota demonstrated exceptional precision with the editing of each of the essays and showed much insight in working through two of the pieces while they were still in draft form. Robb Eason secured copyright information, lent his critical eye to an analysis of drafts of some of the texts, and undertook the burden of reading the proofs of the entire collection. It goes without saying that this project would not have come to fruition without their hard labors.

The work of translating is crucial to the circulation of ideas but often goes unheralded. Let me pause to celebrate such labors. In addition to contributing an essay of her own, Lanei Rodemeyer has given us fluid and precise translations not just of one but of both the essays by Klaus Held. Julia Jansen joined forces with Gina Zavota in bringing the long essay by Dieter Lohmar into flowing English prose. And Christopher Jupp and Paul Crowe have mastered Rudolf Bernet's German essay, rendering it with both exactness and good English style.

Perhaps even less heralded are the labors of those at a press that shepherd a book through the approval and production process, but there are two to whom this volume is especially indebted. My appreciation goes to Janet Rabinowitch, the senior editor at Indiana University Press with a keen eye for quality, who had the insight to bring this project within the bounds of the feasible and the grace to deal with this sometimes irascible editor, and to Rebecca Tolen, who managed to be both patient and exceptionally helpful, and yet keep the project on schedule.

Reference List of Works by Edmund Husserl

Arithmetik

Philosophie der Arithmetik: Psychologische und logische Untersuchungen. Vol. 1. Halle-Saale: C. E. M. Pfeffer, 1891.

Arithmetik (Hua)

Philosophie der Arithmetik: Mit ergänzenden Texten (1890–1901). Ed. Lothar Eley. *Husserliana,* vol. 12. The Hague: Martinus Nijhoff, 1970.

Aufsätze I

Aufsätze und Rezensionen (1890–1910). Ed. Bernard Rang. *Husserliana,* vol. 22. The Hague: Martinus Nijhoff, 1979.

Aufsätze II

Aufsätze und Rezensionen (1911–1921). Ed. Thomas Nenon and Hans Rainer Sepp. *Husserliana,* vol. 25. Dordrecht: Kluwer, 1989.

Aufsätze III

Aufsätze und Vorträge (1922–1937). Ed. Thomas Nenon and Hans Rainer Sepp. *Husserliana,* vol. 27. Dordrecht: Kluwer, 1989.

Bedeutungslehre

Vorlesungen über Bedeutungslehre: Sommersemester 1908. Ed. Ursula Panzer. *Husserliana,* vol. 26. Dordrecht: Martinus Nijhoff, 1987.

Briefwechsel

Briefwechsel. Ed. Karl Schuhmann in collaboration with Elisabeth Schuhmann. *Husserliana Dokumente,* vol. 3. Dordrecht: Kluwer, 1994.

Cartesianische Meditationen

Cartesianische Meditationen und Pariser Vorträge. Ed. Stephen Strasser. *Husserliana,* vol. 1. The Hague: Martinus Nijhoff, 1963.

Cartesian Meditations

Cartesian Meditations: An Introduction to Phenomenology. Trans. Dorion Cairns. The Hague: Martinus Nijhoff, 1960.

Ding und Raum

Ding und Raum: Vorlesungen 1907. Ed. Ulrich Claesges. *Husserliana,* vol. 16. The Hague: Martinus Nijhoff, 1974.

Thing and Space

Thing and Space: Lectures of 1907. Trans. Richard Rojcewicz. Dordrecht: Kluwer, 1997.

Einleitung in die Logik

Einleitung in die Logik und Erkenntnistheorie:

	Vorlesungen 1906/1907. Ed. Ulrich Melle. *Husserliana,* vol. 24. The Hague: Martinus Nijhoff, 1984.
Erfahrung und Urteil	*Erfahrung und Urteil: Untersuchungen zur Genealogie der Logik.* Ed. L. Landgrebe. Prague: Academia-Verlag, 1938; Hamburg: Claasen, 1954.
Experience and Judgment	*Experience and Judgment: Investigations in a Genealogy of Logic.* Trans. James Churchill and Karl Ameriks. Evanston: Northwestern University Press, 1973.
Erste Philosophie I	*Erste Philosophie (1923/24),* Part I: *Kritische Ideengeschichte.* Ed. Rudolf Boehm. *Husserliana,* vol. 7. The Hague: Martinus Nijhoff, 1956.
Erste Philosophie II	*Erste Philosophie (1923/24),* Part II: *Theorie der phänomenologischen Reduktion.* Ed. Rudolf Boehm. *Husserliana,* vol. 8. The Hague: Martinus Nijhoff, 1959.
Ethik	*Vorlesungen über Ethik und Wertlehre, 1908–1914.* Ed. Ullrich Melle. *Husserliana,* vol. 28. Dordrecht: Kluwer, 1988.
Idee der Phänomenologie	*Die Idee der Phänomenologie: Fünf Vorlesungen.* 2nd ed. Ed. Walter Biemel. *Husserliana,* vol. 2. The Hague: Martinus Nijhoff, 1958.
Idea of Phenomenology	*The Idea of Phenomenology.* Trans. William Alston and George Nakhnikian. The Hague: Martinus Nijhoff, 1964.
Ideen I	*Ideen zu einer reinen Phänomenologie und phänomenologischen Philosophie,* Vol. 1: *Allgemeine Einführung in die reine Phänomenologie. Jahrbuch für Philosophie und phänomenologische Forschung,* Band 1. Halle a.d.S.: Niemeyer, 1913, 1–323.
Ideen I (Hua)	*Ideen zu einer reinen Phänomenologie und phänomenologischen Philosophie,* Band 1: *Allgemeine Einführung in die reine Phänomenologie,* Band 2: *Ergänzende Texte (1912–1929).* Ed. Karl Schuhmann. *Husserliana,* vols. 3a–b. The Hague: Martinus Nijhoff, 1976.
Ideas I	*Ideas Pertaining to a Pure Phenomenology and to a Phenomenological Philosophy,* Book 1: *Gen-*

eral Introduction to a Pure Phenomenology. Trans. F. Kersten. *Collected Works,* vol. 2. The Hague: Martinus Nijhoff, 1983.

Ideen II   *Ideen zu einer reinen Phänomenologie und phänomenologischen Philosophie,* Band 2: *Phänomenologische Untersuchungen zur Konstitution.* Ed. Marly Biemel. *Husserliana,* vol. 4. The Hague: Martinus Nijhoff, 1952.

Ideas II   *Ideas Pertaining to a Pure Phenomenology and to a Phenomenological Philosophy,* Book 2: *Studies in the Phenomenology of Constitution.* Trans. Richard Rojcewicz and Andre Schuwer. *Collected Works,* vol. 3. Dortrecht: Kluwer, 1989.

Ideen III   *Ideen zu einer reinen Phänomenologie und phänomenologischen Philosophie,* Band 3: *Die Phänomenologie und die Fundamente der Wissenschaften.* Ed. Marly Biemel. *Husserliana,* vol. 5. The Hague: Martinus Nijhoff, 1952.

Ideas III   *Ideas Pertaining to a Pure Phenomenology and to a Phenomenological Philosophy,* Book 3: *Phenomenology and the Foundations of the Sciences.* Trans. Ted Klein and William Pohl. *Collected Works,* vol. 1. The Hague: Martinus Nijhoff, 1980.

Intersubjektivität I   *Zur Phänomenologie der Intersubjektivität, Erster Teil: 1905–1920.* Ed. Iso Kern. *Husserliana,* vol. 13. The Hague: Martinus Nijhoff, 1973.

Intersubjektivität II   *Zur Phänomenologie der Intersubjektivität, Zweiter Teil: 1921–1928.* Ed. Iso Kern. *Husserliana,* vol. 14. The Hague: Martinus Nijhoff, 1973.

Intersubjektivität III   *Zur Phänomenologie der Intersubjektivität, Dritter Teil: 1929–1935.* Ed. Iso Kern. *Husserliana,* vol. 15. The Hague: Martinus Nijhoff, 1973.

Krisis   *Die Krisis der europäischen Wissenschaften und die transzendentale Phänomenologie: Eine Einleitung in die phänomenologische Philosophie.* Ed. Walter Biemel. *Husserliana,* vol. 6. The Hague: Martinus Nijhoff, 1954.

Crisis   *The Crisis of European Sciences and Transcendental Phenomenology: An Introduction to Phenome-*

nological Philosophy. Trans. David Carr. Evanston: Northwestern University Press, 1970.

Krisis (Ergänzung)   *Die Krisis der europäischen Wissenschaften und die transzendentale Phänomenologie: Ergänzungsband. Texte aus dem Nachlaß 1934–1937.* Ed. Reinhold Smid. *Husserliana,* vol. 29. Dordrecht: Kluwer, 1993.

Logik   *Formale und transzendentale Logik: Versuch einer Kritik der logischen Vernunft. Jahrbuch für Philosophie und phänomenologische Forschung,* Band 10. Halle a.d.S.: Niemeyer, 1929, v–xiii, 1–298.

Logic   *Formal and Transcendental Logic.* Trans. Dorion Cairns. The Hague: Martinus Nijhoff, 1969.

Logik (Hua)   *Formale und transzendentale Logik: Versuch einer Kritik der logischen Vernunft.* Ed. Paul Janssen. *Husserliana,* vol. 17. The Hague: Martinus Nijhoff, 1974.

Logische Untersuchungen (First Edition)   *Logische Untersuchungen.* 2 Bände. Halle: Max Niemeyer, 1900 and 1901.

Logische Untersuchungen   *Logische Untersuchungen.* 2nd rev. ed. 2 Bände. Halle: Max Niemeyer, 1913 and 1921.

Logische Untersuchungen (Hua)   *Logische Untersuchungen. Band II: Untersuchungen zur Phänomenologie und Theorie der Erkenntnis, I. Teil.* Ed. Ursula Panzer. *Husserliana,* vol. 19. The Hague: Martinus Nijhoff, 1984.

Logical Investigations   *Logical Investigations.* Trans. J. N. Findlay. 2 vols. New York: Humanities Press, 1970.

Passive Synthesis   *Analysen zur passiven Synthesis: Aus Vorlesungs- und Forschungsmanuskripten 1918–1926.* Ed. Margot Fleischer. *Husserliana,* vol. 11. The Hague: Martinus Nijhoff, 1966.

Phänomenologische Psychologie   *Phänomenologische Psychologie: Vorlesungen Sommersemester 1925.* Ed. Walter Biemel. *Husserliana,* vol. 9. The Hague: Martinus Nijhoff, 1968.

Phenomenological Psychology   *Phenomenological Psychology: Lectures, Summer Semester, 1925.* Trans. John Scanlon. The Hague: Martinus Nijhoff, 1977.

Phantasie   *Phantasie, Bildbewußtsein, Erinnerung: Zur Phänomenologie der anschaulichen Vergegenwärtigungen: Texte aus dem Nachlaß (1898–1925).*

Ed. Eduard Marbach. *Husserliana,* vol. 23. The Hague: Martinus Nijhoff, 1980.

Shorter Works

Husserl: Shorter Works. Ed. Peter McCormick and Frederick Elliston. Notre Dame, Ind.: University of Notre Dame Press, 1981.

Zeitbewusstsein

Zur Phänomenologie des inneren Zeitbewusstseins (1893–1917). Ed. Rudolf Boehm. *Husserliana,* vol. 10. The Hague: Martinus Nijhoff, 1966.

Time-Consciousness

On the Phenomenology of the Consciousness of Internal Time (1893–1917). Trans. John Brough. *Collected Works,* vol. 4. Dordrecht: Kluwer, 1991.

Convention on Citations
from Husserl's Works

Whenever available, references to both the original German text and the English translations are given. Sometime translations are not available; sometimes an author chooses to translate the text her- or himself even though a translation does exist. In order not to confuse these we use the following conventions:

1. If a citation from Husserl is given without comment, the translation has been made by the author of the essay.

   E.g., a reference that reads

   Krisis (Ergänzung), 179.

   means that the author of the essay is citing the German text on p. 179 and the translation is hers or his.

   A reference that reads

   Ideen I, 79; *Ideas I*, 93.

   means that the author is citing the German text on p. 79 (according to original pagination) *and* that the translation is the author's (even though the reference of the page in the English translation is given).

2. If the English translation is directly cited, the word *after* comes before the English title.

   E.g.,

   Ideen I, 79; after *Ideas I*, 93.

   means that the author is citing the German text on p. 79 (according to original pagination) *and* that she or he is quoting the existing English translation.

3. The phrase "modified [Eng. trans.]" means that the English translation is being reproduced but with certain changes by the author of the essay.

   E.g.,

   Ideen I, 79; modified *Ideas I*, 93.

   means that author is using the existing English translation but modifying it slightly.

PART I

The Scope of Husserl's Transcendental Phenomenology

1

Husserl's Phenomenological Method

Klaus Held

Translated by Lanei Rodemeyer

1. Husserl's Phenomenology Today

Edmund Husserl (1859–1938) was the founder of one of the major current movements in philosophy, phenomenology. It was especially significant for German philosophy during the first decades of the twentieth century and for French philosophy during the middle of the twentieth century. Fundamental philosophical works of our time, such as Max Scheler's *Formalism in Ethics and Non-formal Ethics of Values* (1913/16), Martin Heidegger's *Being and Time* (1927), Jean-Paul Sartre's *Being and Nothingness* (1943), and Maurice Merleau-Ponty's *Phenomenology of Perception* (1945) are programmatically considered phenomenological investigations.

Several phenomenological goals have been influential in other philosophies and academic areas not based in phenomenology, such as literary criticism or the social sciences, but especially in psychology. Today the influence of phenomenology extends well beyond the reaches of the German- and French-speaking world; here must point first to Latin America and Japan. But phenomenological ideas are also being discussed within the realm of Yugoslavia's unorthodox Marxism, in Czechoslovakia and Poland, in Italy, and increasingly in the area of Anglo-American thought, where at first a broad Husserlian influence was absent. Thus we could speak justifiably of a "worldwide phenomenological movement."

Experts consider Edmund Husserl, who launched this movement, to be one of the classical philosophers of the twentieth century. But little more than Husserl's name is known by the average person interested in philosophy—even in Germany. There is one main reason for this: Husserlian phenomenology may easily constitute the most important presupposition for the important early works of Heidegger and Sartre (mentioned above), but because Husserl was Jewish, his later writings could no longer appear in the Third Reich. Thus continued analysis of Husserl's thought was interrupted, whereas in the 1950s and 1960s, Heidegger and Sartre were again discussed intensely—both inside and outside of the German university.

The silence with regard to Husserl in Germany's "period of economic miracles" remains a disgraceful posthumous triumph of National Socialism, even if we must concede two things. First, from the beginning, the dry diction of Husserl, the "armchair philosopher," hardly offered as much for public debate as the handy formulations offered by existentialism. Second, the complete edition of Husserl's writings, which have been historically critically edited since 1950, unfortunately did not appear in Germany.[1]

In the second half of the 1960s and in the 1970s, one heard even less mention of Husserlian phenomenology, as interests returned strongly to Heidegger's later philosophy, to existentialism, and to Gadamer's hermeneutics (which also shared important goals with phenomenology). In addition, "Critical Theory" in the Frankfurt School, linguistic analysis following the later Wittgenstein, so-called French structuralism, and academic theory and history appeared with alternating intensity in the foreground of not only professional but also public interests. The name Husserl has only resurfaced more frequently in recent decades—even in discussions outside of the university—because the main concept of his unfinished later philosophy, the "life-world,"[2] increasingly draws attention.

2. Life and Work

There is nothing "spectacular" to tell about the inconspicuous scholarly life of Edmund Husserl. He was born on 8 April 1859, in Prossnitz in Moravia. From 1876 until 1882 he studied mathematics and philosophy, first in Leipzig and then in Berlin. His graduation in mathematics, in the winter semester of 1882–83, was followed closely by in-depth philosophical study under Franz Brentano in Vienna. In Halle, Husserl graduated with his habilitation, entitled "On the Concept of Number: Psychological Analyses." He remained there to teach as a university instructor from 1887 to 1901. In 1900–1901 Husserl published his first main work, *Logical Investigations* (in two volumes), with which he established his phenomenology. Because of this work, he was called to take a position as associate professor in Göttingen. He was only made full professor there when he was forty-seven, in 1906. Then from 1916 until he retired in 1928—to be succeeded by Martin Heidegger—Husserl was chair of philosophy at Freiburg in Breisgau. He died there on 27 April 1938.[3]

A circle of friends and students already formed around Husserl when he was in Göttingen, called the "Göttingen School" of Phenomenology. The School was soon joined by a philosophical movement native to Munich. Together with two Munich philosophers, Moritz Geiger and Alexander Pfänder, as well as his student from Göttingen Adolf Reinach (who later fell in World War I) and Max Scheler (who was then lecturing in Berlin), Husserl founded his *Yearbook for Philosophy and Phenomenological Research* in 1913, which became a reservoir of works in phenomenological research. In this yearbook appeared not only the above-mentioned works of Scheler and Heidegger, but also other outstanding philosophical works up through the 1930s. Edith Stein was one of the names that became especially well known, although also known independently of the *Yearbook;* she was Husserl's first assistant, a Jew who converted to the Catholic church, later became a Carmelite, and eventually died in a concentration camp. Other famous names include Roman Ingarden, an influential Polish philosopher; Jan Patocka, a noted Czechoslovakian philosopher who later became known as the speaker of the human rights declaration "Charta 77"; and Aron Gurwitsch and Alfred Schütz, both of whom lectured in the United States after the Second World War.

Husserl started off his yearbook with a programmatic work, *Ideas Pertaining to a Pure Phenomenology and to a Phenomenological Philosophy,* which was supposed to come out in three volumes, but of which only the first was published during his lifetime.

With *Ideas I,* which was his second main work—published thirteen years after *Logical Investigations*—Husserl took a turn in his phenomenology, one which his companions in Göttingen and Munich could not accept. We will return later to the old and new forms of phenomenology: the "study of essence" of the earlier period and the transcendental-philosophical stamp of Husserlian thought in his Freiburg period.

Once again, a long time passed before Husserl allowed more important works of his to appear. In 1928 he prevailed upon Heidegger to publish a text made up of parts of old lectures and research manuscripts, put together by Edith Stein, the now renowned *Lectures on the Phenomenology of Inner Time-Consciousness.* In 1929 Husserl himself published a new introductory text, *Formal and Transcendental Logic.* He then expanded two longer lectures, which he had presented at the Sorbonne in Paris in 1929, into an introduction to phenomenology; these appeared in French in 1931 under the title *Cartesian Meditations.* The German version was not published until 1950, as volume 1 of the *Husserliana* edition. Finally, in 1936 Husserl was able to publish—only outside of Germany—one more part of his last work, which was once again to be a new introduction to phenomenology: *The Crisis of European Sciences and Transcendental Phenomenology.* The completed work did not appear until 1954, as volume 6 of the *Husserliana.* An arrangement of research manuscripts, put together by Husserl's former assistant Ludwig Landgrebe, was likewise only able to appear outside of Germany; under assignment from Husserl, Landgrebe worked on and published *Experience and Judgment* in 1938.

Excluding *Logical Investigations* and *Lectures on the Phenomenology of Inner Time-Consciousness,* only programmatic introductory texts appeared during Husserl's lifetime, and these—as mentioned—were sometimes unfinished works, one of them not even in German. Husserl's actual work, however, did not concentrate on such introductions, but rather on concrete phenomenological analyses. Husserl wrote as he was thinking. Day after day, working untiringly from 1890 to 1938, he filled around 45,000 pages with his analyses, written in Gabelsberger stenography. Neither his creative power nor his unconditional devotion to the subject were broken, even when the Nazis forbade him to set foot in the university. After Husserl's death, the danger arose that his research manuscripts, the actual product of his life's work, might fall into the hands of the Nazis. A Belgian Franciscan monk, Hermann Leo Van Breda, rescued Husserl's posthumous work in a daring move before it could be seized by the National Socialists.[4] In 1939 Van Breda founded a Husserl-Archive at the University of Leuven in Belgium. Since 1950, working together with another Husserl-Archive founded later at the University of Cologne, the Leuven archive has been publishing the aforementioned *Husserliana* edition. This historical and critical complete edition includes those works already published by Husserl himself or which he intended to publish, his most important unpublished course lectures, presentations, and essays, and—as appendices or as individual volumes—thematically grouped selections from Husserl's research manuscripts.

One cannot penetrate Husserl's world and thinking without effort. For this reason, the reader might welcome some guidance. Husserl's *Encyclopedia Britannica* article is recommended for those who seek a short and easily readable conception of phenomenology from his own pen. His foundational introduction to phenomenology in *Ideas I*, "The Fundamental Phenomenological Outlook," goes a bit deeper. His text on perception in his writings on "passive synthesis" contains a short outline of an especially typical concrete phenomenological analysis, although his most famous detailed analyses can be found in his texts on "inner time-consciousness" and "intersubjectivity." Finally, certain later texts offer access to Husserl's problematic of the "life-world," which we mentioned earlier.

Those who wish to study Husserl more intensely, beyond these recommended selections, should first read Husserl's main programmatic introductory works from 1913, 1931, and 1936: *Ideas I, Cartesian Meditations,* and *Crisis.* Husserl's two lectures from 1907 and 1925 (*Husserliana,* volumes 2 and 9) are also appropriate introductions. One piece that Husserl wrote in 1911, *Philosophy as a Strict Science,* is characteristic of the pathos evident when phenomenology was just beginning; Husserl caused quite a sensation with this work, and its title became a controversial phrase in twentieth-century philosophy. The lecture *First Philosophy,* from 1923–24, is especially informative for a more intensive struggle with the fundamental problematic of transcendental phenomenology. If one wishes to study more concrete analyses, then, aside from the texts already mentioned, the second volume of *Logical Investigations* is indispensable. The following *Husserliana* volumes contain other analyses of issues that, relatively speaking, are fairly approachable: the second book of *Ideas Pertaining to a Pure Phenomenology and to a Phenomenological Philosophy* (volume 4); *Thing and Space* (volume 16, from a lecture course in 1907); *Analyses to a Passive Synthesis* (volume 9, from texts written between 1918 and 1926); and the first text ("Fantasy and Image-Consciousness") in *Fantasy, Image-Consciousness, Recollection* (volume 23, from a lecture course in 1904–5). In addition, I should include the aforementioned joint work from Husserl and Landgrebe, *Experience and Judgment.*

3. The Basic Problematic of Phenomenology

The title "The Phenomenological Method" reveals the motif for which phenomenology originally became famous. Husserl's primary demand was for a new philosophical method. By "philosophical method" we mean a way, a procedure, that leads to a recognition of truth. The way to such a recognition is designated through its goal, and Husserl formulates this goal programmatically in his aforementioned paper from 1911, *Philosophy as a Strict Science*. Here Husserl turns against the conception of philosophy disseminated at the turn of the last century, that philosophy is not a science but rather a "worldview." In so doing, he fights against the relegation of philosophy to philosophical "historicism," the idea that the only task basically remaining for philosophy is to write its own history. By rehabilitating the scientific character of philosophy, though, Husserl did not intend that philosophy be reduced to scientific theory, as certain influential schools wished during his lifetime—and wish again today. He also did not mean for philosophy to conform to the methods of the modern natural sciences.

Husserl's actual goal was for a radically unprejudiced knowledge, which was in no way a new ideal for philosophy. By freeing itself of prejudice, philosophy has wanted to distinguish itself from simple opinion since ancient times. As Plato originally formulated it: *epistēmē*, true knowledge, should take the place of *doxa*, opinion. Opinion falls short of true knowledge in two ways. First, certain vacillations which are "due to the situation" always underlie opinions. True knowledge should be free from subjective biases in changing lived situations, and in this sense, it should be "objective" and lasting. Second, whenever we just have an opinion, we are making an unfulfilled knowledge claim. For example, when someone says, "I think it is too hot in Italy in August," or "I think that the Pythagorean theorem is provable," that person is saying, My point of view could be verified by my driving to Italy in the summer, or by my actually carrying out the proof of the theorem. In this way, simple opinion refers through its meaning to situations in which what is meant would be proved, fulfilled, confirmed. Such situations bring us close to the issue or the matter at hand, which is only given to us "from a distance," so to speak, through opinions.

In this respect, we carry opinion over into true knowledge by moving ourselves into specific experiences or general events that bring us as close as is necessary to the matter at hand. As we pointed out above, however, true knowledge requires first of all that it be lasting and objective—meaning that knowledge must be independent of its respective lived situations. Thus, when we want to determine true knowledge by distinguishing it from opinion, we are faced with a certain tension between the requirement of objectivity and that of getting close to the matter at hand. We could basically say that this tension is

unleashed by Husserl's philosophy, and yet at the same time, it is held in sus-
pense. Husserl strove for an unprejudiced "strict science" where this tension
would not be dissolved by simply choosing one side or the other.

The claim that one must be close to the matter at hand takes precedence
over the call for objectivity in one way: I can only talk about an issue—whether
it is objective or just my opinion—because I assume that, in principle, I can
realize the possibility of experiencing it through some kind of closeness, which
is to say, through "intuition" or "bodily." Without this possibility, I would not
know about the issue at all; it would not even exist for me. So in every situation, I know that whatever I encounter in my experiences or thoughts refers to
situations in which the experienced event or thought originally—Husserl says,
"originarily"—arose or could appear within the compass of my experiences and
thinking. However an issue may appear, each appearance of something relates
back or ahead to its *being originarily given* for me, and, in the last analysis, it
obtains its sensible content from that originary moment.

In the situation of an originary appearance, *I* take up the relation to the
issue; it appears *for me* as something experienceable, livable, or knowable on the
world's stage. In this sense, as Husserl says, everything that appears originarily
has the character of being *subject-relative;* in other words, an object can appear
only when it presents itself to a subject in a specific situation. On the other
hand, objective knowledge requires that it not be bound to changing subjective
situations; that which is objectively known cannot just be subjectively relative—
"for me"—rather, it must be "in itself," that is, it must exist independently of
a relation to subjects and their situated experiences. But since every experience and thought is based upon situations of originary appearance, then even
the knowledge of objects—no matter how "in itself" an object may seem—
presupposes subjectively situated types of originary givenness.

At this point we can already recognize the philosophical question, arising
out of these considerations, which reveals the inner beginnings of Husserl's
philosophizing: how are the *manners of givenness* of objects, in which we comprehend them as things in themselves, that is, as objectively existing, connected
back to originary, subject-relative manners of givenness? A correspondence, a
correlation, whose concrete character depends upon the type of object in play,
exists between the in-itself-ness of objects and their subjective, situated manners
of givenness. Sticking to the above examples: a country's climate is given originally to me in a completely different way than the content of a mathematical
theorem, and the originary ways that these two issues appear are not interchangeable.

The two sides of this correlation are inextricable from one another: the
object-in-the-How-of-its-givenness—the "*noema*" as Husserl says in *Ideas I*—
corresponds to the *noesis,*[5] the accompanying manifold of actualized experiences
and knowledge through which a specific type of object originarily appears to
me, and only can appear to me; I cannot, as it were, push this manifold aside
and then look at the object. This correspondence between type of object and

manner of givenness is a rule that can be formulated "*a priori,*" meaning it can be formulated with unconditional universality, before any experience. *The objects in the How of their appearances* with their associated manners of givenness are the "phenomena," the "appearances," that "phenomenology" deals with, and from which it obtained its name. In the Husserlian sense, phenomena are nothing other than the existing things which are "in themselves" in the world, but only in such a way that they show themselves in their respective situatedness and as subjectively "for-me."

That the question regarding the *correlation* between objective thing and originary subjective manner of givenness shaped the inner beginning of Husserl's thinking is confirmed at one point in the *Crisis,* where Husserl reflects upon his life's work:

> The fact naively taken for granted, that we see each thing and the world in general as they appear to us, concealed, as we recognize, a great horizon of remarkable truths which never entered, in their uniqueness and in their systematic connectedness, into the purview of philosophy. The correlation of the world (the world of which we always speak) and subjective manners of givenness never aroused in philosophy a philosophical awe (that is, before the first breakthrough of "transcendental phenomenology" in the *Logical Investigations*), even though it was resoundingly present in pre-Socratic philosophy and sophistry—although here only as a motive for skeptical argumentation. This correlation never aroused its own philosophical interest that might have made it the topic of an appropriate scientific attitude. We remained trapped in what was taken for granted, that is, that each thing appears differently for each person.[6]

And in one annotation, Husserl uses a tone of personal confession that is exceptional for him:

> The first breakthrough of this universal a priori of correlation between an object of experience and its manners of givenness (about 1898, while I was working through my *Logical Investigations*) shook me so deeply that, since then, my entire life's work has been dominated by the task of systematically working out this a priori of correlation.[7]

That which we have called "closeness to the matter at hand," "closeness to the issue," or *originarity* has been known for a long time in the philosophical tradition as a foundation or norm of philosophical knowledge: philosophers call it evidence. Husserl takes up this concept because he also consistently applies this idea—that of referring each world-experience to originary manners of givenness—to philosophical knowledge itself. Even phenomenology draws upon the original "bodily" appearance of that about which it makes claims. Without insight ("*intuitio,*" "intuition"), which "makes things clear" through its closeness to the matter at hand and thus its factuality ("evidence"), philosophical thought remains an empty reasoning and construing. Husserl contrasts such conceptual play with phenomenological representation, with description based on evidence. Kant's observation is still always valid: "Concepts without intuition are empty." For this reason, Husserl formulates the "*principle of all principles*" for all philosophy in *Ideas I,* namely that

> every originarily given intuition is a rightful source of knowledge, that everything that presents itself to us originarily in "intuition" (in its bodily reality, as it were) is simply to be taken as that which it gives itself to be—but also only within the bounds in which it gives itself.[8]

Through this principle, Husserl claims, "no conceivable theory can lead us astray. We should realize that each theory could draw its truth only from originary givenness."[9]

Philosophy should assert no more and no less than what is possible for it on the basis of *originary, given intuition.* Evidence becomes a model for philosophical knowledge, but this is because such knowledge itself is ruled by a dependence upon and reference to the originarity of each experience. The appearance of the world in manners of givenness is, in this sense, grounded in evidence. Insofar as this appearance makes up the main theme of phenomenological philosophy, we could offer this formula: phenomenology as method is the attempt to provide evidence for evidence. Here evidence becomes the foundation of the way to philosophical knowledge *and* its object. Husserl was himself aware of how the concept of evidence became centrally important in a way it never had been in philosophy before, as we can see in his chapter "Psychologism and the Transcendental Foundation of Logic" in his *Formal and Transcendental Logic.*

The methodical, fundamental demand for evidence and the task of "investigating correlation" are two sides of one and the same foundational claim. For this reason, it is not enough for phenomenology to make general statements about the universal *a priori* of correlation between objects and their manners of givenness. If such statements are not to remain distant from the matter at hand because of their generality, then they themselves must rest upon concrete investigation, investigation of the specific manners of appearance of different types of objects. The philosopher must, as Husserl said on occasion, be prepared to exchange the big bills of his universal themes into the small change of detailed analyses that are close to the issue. In this way, philosophy as phenomenological method becomes "working philosophy"—this, too, is a phrase coined by Husserl.

4. The Refutation of Psychologism[10]

The method that leads to philosophy's goal of being a strict science is, for Husserl, the investigation into correlation as grounded in concrete evidence. How did this method develop?

Husserl's thinking found its stride in his *Logical Investigations,* and he became thereby renowned. The first volume, the *Prolegomena to a Pure Logic* (hereafter *Prolegomena*), caused a particular sensation; these prolegomena were devoted primarily to the critique of *psychologism,* an approach that, at that time, had widely dominated philosophy. Husserl had himself still tended toward this position in his habilitation work, "On the Concept of Number." In fact, his subtitle was characteristic of this approach: "Psychological Analyses." More than anything else, the critique of the mathematician and philosopher Gottlob Frege gave Husserl the impetus to develop his ideas, which in turn led to his classical refutation of psychologism in the *Prolegomena.* Psychologism had many faces, but in view of the main problem of Husserlian thought, which we just mentioned above, we can say here that the basic tendency of psychologism consisted in dissolving the tension in understanding truth one-sidedly in favor of subjectively situated achievements.

Husserl's focus in the *Logical Investigations* was laying the foundation of logic as a normative "scientific teaching"—today we would say "scientific theory"—because, for him, logic was fundamental for scientific knowledge in general. True knowledge shows itself to be independent of situations, especially in the "objectively valid" logical structures that establish thinking and, further, in "objectively valid" norms of all other types that guide human activity. Such norms are universal laws. But where is the "place" that universals exist, especially the laws of logic? We can make these laws an object of our thought, but do they possess an independent being over against that thinking? Psychologism answers no. According to this position, logical laws are nothing more than a natural regulation of the psychic processes we call "thinking"—just like there are laws of nature for processes in the material world.

Husserl refuted this conception in the *Prolegomena* so convincingly that psychologism could then simply be filed away into the archives of the history of philosophy. Today we consider the untenability of psychologism self-evident because of Husserl's reasoning, but the fact that this refutation was actually (at that time) in no way self-evident can already be seen in the large number of authors with which Husserl takes issue. Indeed, his text includes numerous annotations referring to these authors.

Husserl, originally a mathematician, explains the untenable consequences of psychologism as applied to the laws of thought through a comparison with the functioning of a calculator[11] (which today has been superseded by the computer). The mechanics of a calculator—or the electronics of a computer (i.e., hardware)—follows a completely different set of laws (namely, physical laws) than the chains of symbols that one calculates with the machine (i.e., software). Psychologism cannot explain this difference. It replaces the question about the right kind of thinking with what is essentially a scientific, empirical description of thought processes—for example (in the terms of today's clinical psychology), the structure of the neuro-physiological circuits in our brain.

Basically, a double meaning of the concept of "thought" is sacrificed by psychologism. Thought is the universality of the standardizing logical laws in our thinking; that is, "thought" is understood as that which we think when we carry out our thinking. But we can also understand "thought" to mean the carrying out of thinking as a psychic operation. Psychologism reduces the universal being of thought to the factual, conscious processes of thinking. In this way, psychologism explains logic on the basis of psychology, raising it to the level of science instead of philosophy. Contrary to this, Husserl points out that the universality that standardizes our thinking is valid, independent of the factual and empirically comprehensible changes in subjective knowledge situations; it has existence that is "objective," "in itself."

Afterward, this idea of thought—independently of Husserl—asserted itself through the development of logic, becoming modern "symbolic" or "mathematical" logic. At the same time, one side of the problematic went unnoticed, one which would become ever more prominent in the development of Husserl's main claim. That which is objectively valid, which exists in itself, is only accessible to us—*as* independent of factual, subjective constitution—through our going back to its corresponding subject-relative originary manners of givenness. This also applies to the laws of logic. They do not hover in some pedantic platonic heaven of ideas, but rather are bound back to the situated experience of their being carried out in thought. If we detach these laws from situations, then logic becomes a setting up of systems of rules, rules which can no longer be anything more than technical specifications for the setting up of true statements; they would be without any attachment to the content of lived situations in which a person can originarily convince herself whether something is true or false. We thereby relinquish these subjective manners of givenness to empirical psychology. Thus we come to a "division of labor" between empirical psychology and logic, where we understand "logic" as a pure technique of setting up calculations. The problem of *one* truth, which Husserl had still seen, disintegrates, namely, how to work through the tension between that which is objectively-universally in itself and that which is for me in situated manners of givenness.

Given this development, Husserl later had to defend himself against a one-sided objectivist interpretation of his early critique of psychologism. In addition to dealing with this later interpretation of his *Prolegomena*, Husserl also had to take a position against a development within the very movement which he himself had launched. When Husserl's critique of psychologism rescued an objectivity (*Gegenständlichkeit*) that subsists objectively in itself, it was perceived as such a liberation that Husserl's first followers viewed his achievement as consisting almost exclusively in recovering philosophy's orientation toward the object. They understood phenomenology to be a "*turning toward the object*," and they made his maxim "*to the things themselves*" into their battle cry. Adhering to this maxim was supposed to free philosophy from its modern bent toward subjectivism. An anti-subjective objectivism emerged which, more or less, considered itself capable of tackling, without further support, "validities" or "essences," be they logical, mathematical, ethical, or otherwise.

Husserl himself in no way understood his anti-psychologism to be anti-subjective in this sense, not only according to his later work *Formal and Tran-*

scendental Logic, in which he looks back and interprets his own earlier think-ing, but also already in the fifth and the sixth of his *Logical Investigations,* his position becoming finally clear in his *Ideas* of 1913. Husserl, too, wanted to go "to the things themselves." "The things themselves," though, only ap-pear originarily in the subjective processes or achievements of intuitive self-givenness. These achievements take place in human consciousness. Thus, in the first decade of this century, *consciousness* had already become the field of re-search in Husserlian phenomenology, but this program was only announced explicitly in his 1913 *Ideas.*

5. Phenomenology as a Study of Essence[12]

What protects phenomenology—which understands itself as an exploration of consciousness—from falling back into psychologism? Here we must first mention one of Husserl's central concepts: the intentionality of consciousness.

Husserl first discovered the philosophical implications of the *a priori* of correlation when he considered theoretical judgment; at the time, he was con-cerned with laying the groundwork for logic in his *Logical Investigations.* He never completely lost sight of this more philosophical problematic, and, in 1929, he explicitly took it up again in his *Formal and Transcendental Logic.* Already in the first decade of this century, though, he had extended his investigation of correlation to all experiental consciousness. Everything that we can talk about sensibly must be accessible to us in some specific kind of originary given-ness. Not only in the case of theoretical knowing, but also in the case of all "*acts*"—in perceiving, feeling, desiring, aspiring, loving, believing, practical ap-praising, etc.—that toward which we refer (with the respective activities of consciousness) appears either "bodily intuited" for us (in the manner of "self-givenness") or in such a way that consciousness must be dependent upon or referred to such "*fulfillment*" or "*verification*," even though it is not actually realized at that moment.

In this sense, consciousness, in all its variety, is concerned with an "*object*" in the broadest sense of the word: a pole toward which certain activities of consciousness refer. To every perceiving there is something perceived, to every thinking something thought, to every loving something loved; every act has something as its focus. Husserl was able to latch this onto the theory of inten-tionality developed by his mentor in philosophy, Franz Brentano—who himself recovered a scholastic idea. Consciousness is "intentional," which means that, in every one of its acts, consciousness is *consciousness-of-something.*

The coinage "Consciousness is consciousness-of-something" has become, since Husserl, commonplace in philosophy. Put this way, it neither contains anything new when compared with how Descartes or the German Idealists al-ready conceived consciousness, nor does it express what was special about Husserl's teaching about consciousness. Specific to Husserl, first of all, is the idea that consciousness depends upon and refers to originary manners of givenness, that is, to "evidence" in the very broad meaning of the term about which we spoke earlier. If consciousness were not a referring consciousness, possessing the capacity, the "ability" (*Vermögen*) to bring the empty, indirect, indefinite "intended" to fulfillment, then it would not have any intentionally given object. In order to be able to be consciousness-of-something at all, consciousness must know of its own potential (*Möglichkeit*)—Husserl coins a striking conceptual term here, "potentiability" (*Vermöglichkeit*)—to allow the related "something" to appear in intuition. Consciousness's intending of an object is, therefore, not a static relation-to-something, but instead is animated with its tendency toward originarity; Husserl uses the words "intention" and "intending" throughout his works in a way similar to our daily usage, indicating a purposeful striving. Intentional consciousness is, in all its forms, focused on finding satisfaction in the intuited self-having of lived experience. Consciousness wants to go toward evidence; that is what forms its goal, its telos. In this sense, all conscious life—as Husserl would say in his later work—rests under the rule of a "teleology."

The idea of the *a priori* of correlation, the second specification of Husserl's concept of intentionality, is closely connected with this characterization of consciousness: Consciousness cannot be imagined as an empty beach, with the ocean washing random objects ashore. It is not a container indifferent to what fills it. Rather, consciousness is made up of various acts whose character is determined by a corresponding type of objectivity, an objectivity that appears exclusively to consciousness in the manners of givenness appropriate to it. This is independent of whether the related object is factually there or not. For example, even when I only imagine the existence of a perceived thing in a visual perception, the type of conscious activity (in this case, seeing perspectivally) is still determined by the object (in this case, the object-in-space). As these acts are nothing without the objects *of which* they are conscious, we can say that intentional consciousness carries a relation to the object in itself. With the concept of intentionality, the classical problem of the modern "theory of knowledge"—how a consciousness which is at first world-less could take up a relationship with an "outer world" that lies beyond itself—is basically brought to a close.

The treatment of consciousness as intentional no longer permits the objectivity subsisting in its own right and standing over against the activities of consciousness to be dissolved psychologically into these activities because the character of the act is determined precisely by this standing-over-against. In addition, and even more importantly, this takes place independently of whether the intentionally intended object is factually there or not. The character of the activities of consciousness is not dependent on the empirically given objects that happen to be there, but instead on "*Essence,*" that is, on the universal determination of types of objectivities. Thus there are areas of objectivities, "*regions of being,*" as Husserl says, that are differentiated according to the special characteristics of their being, their "*Eidos,*" that is, the mental view that they offer in a corresponding originary intuition. *Eidetic* objective determination corresponds, according to the *a priori* of correlation, to a universal, eidetic condition of the intentional acts that are related to the objectivity in question.

Because these acts and their objectivities can be characterized independently of empirically determinable facts, their correlation, as has already been indicated, is an *a priori;* the multitude of types of objects and their manners of givenness comes to philosophical research as a field of knowledge that comes "before" external experience. As Husserl argues, phenomenology does not make facts its topic—that is, its topic is not individual situations that are ascertainable by individual persons in their intentional experience and their objectivities. Phenomenology abstracts from contingent, factual conscious processes and objects, directing its view toward the essential laws that determine the construction of these acts and the regions of being that appear in them. These laws include, first of all, *necessity,* that is, no single case of intentional life can escape them; and second, *universality,* that is, they include all individual cases. Husserl calls this activity of going back from the factual qualities of intentional lived experiences and their objects to the eidetic determination which underlies them—and for which the factual qualities are merely interchangeable examples —*eidetic reduction.*

Psychologism denied the existence of a certain type of universality— that of the normalizing logical laws of thinking—by interpreting it as a quasi-natural law that governs our thought processes. With Husserl's refutation of psychologism, universality gained a new prominence in philosophy. The "turn to the object," which was celebrated due to Husserl's efforts, was understood above all as the rescue of the objectivity of universality. Within phenomenological research, the theme of universality became primarily understood as eidetic universality. For Husserl's associates from Göttingen and Munich, this exploration of the eidetic state of objective regions and their related intentional acts constituted the phenomenological project. Phenomenology, in its first years, became known primarily as a method of essential knowledge, due to these phenomenologists' subtle analyses of essences. The phenomenological method meant, as the phenomenologists from Göttingen and Munich stressed emphatically, pressing forward to the originary mental intuition, a "bringing into view," the "*ideation*" of eidetic circumstances, striving toward an "*insight into essence,*" and, in this sense, attaining "the things themselves."

Husserl always included the eidetic reduction among his methodical instruments. It is not by accident that the *Ideas*—with which Husserl launched his *Yearbook,* the body of publications shared by all phenomenologists—begins with the chapter "Fact and Essence." In this study of essence, the first consequence of his refutation of psychologism, Husserl continued to overlap with the Göttingen and Munich schools of phenomenology. But in the next part of *Ideas I,* "The Fundamental Phenomenological Outlook," there was a separation of minds. Here Husserl drew radical consequences from his thematization of intentional consciousness, consequences which went far beyond a phenomenology of essence. In fact, to his friends from Göttingen and Munich, he seemed to be sliding back into modern subjectivism.

One consequence of this step was that, in the 1920s, there was a critical examination of his study of insight into essence. For example, if we are required to search for the subjective conditions of an appearance in consciousness—that is, for the originary manners of givenness—for every objectively existing thing, then this should also apply to the givenness of eidetic situations. Thus phenomenology imagined its task to be the development of a phenomenology of its own way of knowing, of intuiting essences, and Husserl tried to work through this project in his teaching of "*eidetic variation.*" This teaching first became accessible with the publication of *Experience and Judgment,* which Landgrebe edited; in these investigations, Husserl takes up some of the programmatic promises made in his *Formal and Transcendental Logic.*

All areas of study—even the empirical—focus on universal statements. Empiricists attain such universality by way of the particular and the factual; using observation and experiment, they establish universality through induction, that is, through universalizing the results of observation in methodical steps. The empirical universalities which are gained in this manner remain "comparative," as Kant puts it, because the universal statements attained are only relatively the most universal, to be compared with the provisional results taken along the way of this process of universalization. This means that a comparative universal always remains open to revision. By contrast, the universality of necessary eidetic determinations comprises from the very beginning—"*a priori*"—every possible thinkable situation; neither can it nor does it ever need to be revised. The theory of eidetic variation explains how this unconditional universality of thinking comes to be originarily given.

Just like the consciousness assumed by those scholars who were led astray by empiricism, phenomenological consciousness, which comprehends essential universals, must also be based on individual cases. That which is empirical—experience—rests finally in perception. But an empirical investigator can only universalize in inductive steps because he is bound to the examples of factual perception; he has to wait to see what facts show themselves in perception. A phenomenologist of essence, on the other hand, can attain unconditional universalities precisely because she is not dependent upon such waiting for perceived factual events. When she bases her conclusions on individual exemplary situations, she does not have to perceive them. Consciousness that is not bound to the factual perception of individual situations is called fantasy; such consciousness can think up all sorts of examples for itself.

In fantasy, we have the possibility of imagining an intentional, lived experience or some given object in that experience over and over; according to Husserl, we can arbitrarily "run through the variants" of its determinations, always differently, in free variation. But in this arbitrary consciousness, the universality of essence can end up as originary givenness. In other words, when we run through the variants of an object, we can pay attention to its limits, that is, how far we can go before the imagined object or its comprehending act becomes something else, before it loses its identity. In this way, certain identical determinations jump out from all these conceivable situations, certain invariant determinations from this variation of examples—and it is precisely these determinations which make up the essence of the act or object in question. Thus we consider the essence of a thing originarily in "eidetic variation" by reflecting on its limits while thinking through it in our fantasy.

Obviously, one question remains open in this theory: those limits which are discovered by consciousness while running through the variants are clearly already given to it. Consciousness does not invent these limits. Rather, it bumps into them; they are the boundaries beyond which such a running through of the variants cannot go. What sets such boundaries for fantasy in its free play? What engages varying consciousness in such a way that reflection can bring the invariants in it forward? Husserl did not answer these crucial questions in his theory of eidetic variation. One possible solution to this problem— which we do not find in Husserl, however—could be this: essence as invariant brings forward, in objectified form, the rules according to which the referential interconnections (*Verweisungszusammenhänge*) of horizonal consciousness are structured.[13] We will explain horizonal consciousness in the following sections.[14]

6. World-Belief and Epochē

In a certain sense, phenomenology, when taken as a method of insight into essence, still remains in front of the gates of philosophy. Philosophy has been understood since the very beginning as a knowledge of the whole. For this reason, Aristotle characterized philosophy as the study that views existence with respect to what is common to everything that exists: being.[15] Husserl simply calls this whole the "world." Because he is concerned with establishing a radical lack of bias, philosophy for Husserl must be knowledge of this world as whole; as long as our knowledge remains limited only to individually knowable sections, we continue to face the danger that unrecognized prejudices will remain in the regions of being within the world that are as yet unknown. For this reason, Husserl must again take up the most basic question of a philosophy which seeks the whole.

Because it can be used, and was used, to light the way from partial regions of the world (i.e., specific regions of being and their related types of acts) to their eidetic determinations, this insight into essence as such is still not a general knowledge of the world in the sense of a whole. The determinations of regions of being are not yet the determinations of existence-as-a-whole, or in other words, of the proper object of philosophy. If phenomenology is to be a radically unbiased philosophical method, then Husserl has to ask whether and how phenomenology could make world-knowledge possible.

Because he strove for such a lack of bias, Husserl obtained his concept of philosophical truth by contrasting it to natural opinion. For this reason, the next question for him was: might people in natural, pre-philosophical life already have something to do with the whole as such, or is it philosophical knowledge which first opens for them an access to the "world"? Husserl's fundamental answer was: people already have a consciousness of the world before any philosophy. For this reason, that which changes through philosophy can only be an *attitude* toward the world. According to this, the question, "How can the whole of the world become a topic for phenomenology?" is given the following wording: "How does the '*natural attitude*' of people lead to a new, philosophical attitude?"

The question to be asked before the last one mentioned, however, is: Why do people have consciousness of the world already before any philosophical knowledge? Going from his idea of correlation, Husserl characterized the natural attitude in the following way. The objects in my world are encountered in manners of givenness that are contingent upon their situations. A perceived thing, like this table here, for example, can appear to me only in such a way that it shows me one side at a time. In order to see the "entire" table, I must go around it, and in this way it is given to me irrevocably "perspectivally." But when I actualize any one of these perspectival views—one of the table's *adumbrations,* as Husserl says—as a manner of givenness, it is clear to me at the same time that the being of the table is not exhausted in this one aspect, which it offers me at this moment. "More" is intended with the object than that which happens to appear in its manner of givenness.[16] In my intentional, lived experience, I ascribe an existence to the object which transcends its changing givenness, its difference from situation to situation. These perspectival adumbrations are subject-relative. The existence of the object, on the other hand—according to my understandable belief—transcends its subjectively situated appearance; it exists "in itself," "objectively." In this way, an existential judgment about objects constantly—tacitly, so to speak—invades consciousness in the natural attitude, saying: they *are,* that is, objects have an existence that is independent of both subject and situation.

In normal cases, intentional lived experience takes its object as existing; in this sense, it contains a "*positing of being.*" The relation of people in the natural attitude to objects is their understandable belief in the existence of objects. This "*belief of being*" relates, first of all, to the individual objects of individual intentional, lived experiences. If we look at it closer, though, we see that this belief encompasses the whole of all such objects, that is, the "world."

Intentional consciousness constantly posits being; in other words, certain objects or their characteristics are taken as existing. This "*validity of being,*" however, is something fundamentally unstable. Intentional, living consciousness keeps moving forward in its search for the fulfillment and verification of its intentions which are, more or less, "vague" or "empty." At the same time, it is always the case that some objects, which consciousness has taken as existing or constituted as such and such up to that point, prove suddenly and inevitably to be nonexistent, or at least constituted in some other way. Thus, time and again we have to "*cancel*" certain validities of being. Through transferring our indefinite pre-intentions to originary manners of givenness, we gain not only fulfillments or verifications but also "*disappointments.*" One fundamental conviction remains untouched throughout, however: the belief that the world exists as the *ground* upon which we, in a way, place all objects. Every disappointment always leads, namely, only to a "not like this, but some other way," never to a complete nothingness. Thus the world's existence remains intact, as "*ultimately valid*," even when we must set aside the existence and the particular manner of being of this or that object. Husserl calls this belief of being related to the world the *general thesis of the natural attitude.*

This inexpressible conviction of the being of the world accompanies every single consciousness of an object. In addition to this, the possibility of turning my attention to other objects from the object given at this moment belongs to every intentional, lived experience. For example, in the case of perceiving the front side of the table here, I am conscious of the fact that I can go around it and see its back side; I can let my gaze wander around the room in which it stands; then I can glance out of the window of this room and discover even further objects; and so on. My concrete, intentional, lived experience thus traces out for me a certain margin of possibilities from which I can, step by step, always thematize more objects. While I might make use of these margins freely, I do not do so in a completely arbitrary fashion. *How* I can thematize further is governed by a regulation with which I am inexpressibly acquainted. Accordingly, I have a consciousness which refers from one experienced object to ever further objects.

Husserl called this acquaintance with regulated referential interconnections —by which I can proceed with my concrete experience—*horizonal consciousness,* and he called these margins of possible experience which are thereby opened *horizons.* Husserl took up and broadened the daily meaning of the word "horizon." In a comprehensive sense, a horizon is my circle of vision, the circumference which is around me (as the center of orientation for my world), and it shifts according to my change in position. As the margin of my possibilities of experience, the horizon is something subjective; I may find these "potentialities" to be already there, but they are there in such a way that *I* am the one who has control over them: I have the consciousness "I can . . ." Because it is within my full power, my "capability," to follow the referential interconnections in any direction I choose, Husserl is able to characterize horizonal consciousness —using a concept we already mentioned above—as a consciousness of my "potentiabilities."

Belonging to our potentiability is a consciousness that can always proceed further in its thematizing of new objects, that is, a consciousness of an endless "and so on." We are confident, as we mentioned above, that our intentional, lived experience will never run up against complete nothingness—even when individual experiences of disappointment cancel the validity of individual objects—because of the strength of this consciousness. Thus we have, in the endlessness of horizonal consciousness, the assurance of a final horizon that cannot be canceled; a *horizon for all horizons* opens up: the world.

With this determination of the world as the *universal horizon,* the concept of the general thesis becomes concrete. In the same way that manners of givenness belong to an individual object, the consciousness of this individual object is embedded in a *world-belief.* The object, that toward which my acts are directed, the pole of my attentiveness, is something identical, as opposed to the manifold of its manners of givenness (i.e., its changing adumbrations), through which it is able to present itself to me. Similarly, the world is something identical, persevering, as opposed to the individual, lived experiences of objects. The validity of being of objects might be confirmed or weakened in originary givenness, but the one world remains as ultimately valid.

The natural attitude of people is this general thesis, world-belief. But how does this relationship to the world get carried over into a new, philosophical relationship? Husserl points out that the analysis of the appearance of objects in manners of givenness already requires a shift in attitude. In the intentional, lived experiences that we carry out in the natural attitude, objects are our "*theme.*" We already somehow know that objects can appear to us only in manners of givenness—for example, perceived objects can appear only in "adumbrations"—but, normally, we never direct our attention to this situated-subjective appearing, or if we do, then only sporadically. Thus this appearing-in-manners-of-givenness is carried out *unthematically.* Husserl says: It "*functions*" as a medium through which we relate to the object that exists for us. In this functioning, situated-subjective appearing remains in the shadows of our attention—to the benefit of the light in which the object, taken as existing, presents itself. Similarly to manners of givenness, world-belief also functions unthematically. When we follow the referential interconnections of horizonal consciousness in some direction, we are only thematically interested in the objects and types of objects that we run into along the way. We never thematize our belief that, in spite of individual experiences of disappointment, our intentional, lived experience will never completely disappear into nothingness.

Thus, intentional consciousness in the natural attitude is, as Husserl formulates it, "infatuated" with thematic objects. It "*just-lives*"—this, too, an expression characteristic of Husserl—in its devotion to objects taken as existing. The functionings of manners of givenness and of the horizon of the world—the latter remains fundamentally unthematic in the natural attitude—then become themes of phenomenological analysis. With this, however, the phenomenologist no longer just-lives. Both the direction of her attention and her interest in the validity of the being of objects are broken. The intentional "gaze" of the phenomenologist no longer focuses on objects taken as existing, but rather on objects in the How of their unthematic appearance and in the embedding of this appearance in horizonal consciousness. In this way, the phenomenologist's gaze is bent back upon the subjective aspect, first, of the actualization of manners of givenness, and second, of a horizonal referential consciousness. In short: phenomenological analysis has the quality of *reflection*.

Reflection is based upon a position that requires that the phenomenologist free herself from her infatuation, from her belief in the being of thematic objects. Instead of swimming in the stream of just-living, she rises above it; she no longer carries out her interest in the existence of intended objects, and instead becomes an *"uninterested"* or *"disinterested observer."* She holds herself out of the relationship that takes place between herself as a naturally experiencing person and the objects appearing as existent to such a person. She places this relationship *in brackets,* so to speak, and observes the intentional life that is now within the brackets from outside. Perhaps I should briefly mention an explanatory analogy: the jostling, bustling life of just-living is put behind an "observation window," as it were; although we, as observers, cannot stop living—we must continue to do so necessarily—we also cannot make any more assumptions about this just-living as we study it, and thus it is "neutralized" for us.

In just-living, consciousness takes a position on the existence of the objects it encounters: as long as a being is valid and is not canceled, consciousness grants, affirms existence; if it becomes invalid or somehow questionable, consciousness switches over to negation or to some position toward existence that lies between affirmation and negation, to "maybe," "perhaps," or something similar. The disinterested, reflecting observer must refrain from any of this kind of position-taking. She lets such things be, holding them in abeyance, because if she were not to do this, she would remain infatuated with the being of objects, and that which is unthematic in the natural attitude—that is, the manners of givenness and horizonal consciousness—could not make it into view.

This *abstention from* every type of *position-taking,* this *neutrality* compared with all of its possible modifications, Husserl calls *"epoché,"* a concept taken from ancient skepticism. This description literally means "to stop" or "to hold oneself back," in this case, from taking a position on existence. This position of the epoché is the new position sought with regard to the world, the position through which philosophy distinguishes itself from the natural attitude. The discovery of this position contains the answer to how the phenomenological method can become philosophy, which means, how it can become a thematization of the whole. The whole of the world—where the "world" is understood as the horizon of all horizons—is that which is absolutely unthematic for the natural attitude. Thus it is the epoché that first makes possible the transposition from a phenomenology of "insight into essence" into a strict unbiased *philosophical* method.

7. The Phenomenological Reduction[17]

The regions of being, whose eidetic determinations are brought to light by insight into essence, consist of types and species of being—using the terminology of the philosophical tradition. Those determinations which relate to the whole of existence overall "transcend" and go beyond the determinations of types and species. In scholasticism they were called "transcendentals." Pre-Kantian thinking, because it was a study of transcendentals, was itself already a *transcendental philosophy*. In order to correspond with this pre-Kantian transcendental philosophy, phenomenology cannot limit itself to being a study of the essences of the specific regions of being and their corresponding intentional, lived experiences. Kant then gave a new meaning to the concept of *"transcendental"* in that he described "all knowledge," as that "which has to do not only with objects, but rather with our way of knowing objects, insofar as this way of knowing might be *a priori* possible."[18] At this point, philosophy becomes universal knowledge because it makes existence in general its topic, through the *a priori* relation of being to consciousness.

In the "Fundamental Phenomenological Outlook" of *Ideas I*, Husserl sets up phenomenology in the tradition of transcendental philosophy as it was established by Kant. He can do this because the phenomenological investigation into correlation coincides with both conditions of Kant's definition: On the basis of the position established by reflection under the epochē, phenomenology views objects in the How of their appearing for intentional consciousness. In other words, phenomenology does not ask directly and ₒimply about these objects, but rather about their "way of being known." And, as a method of insight into essence, phenomenology sets forth that which is *a priori* in this relation to consciousness. But how does *consciousness* now move into the focal point of phenomenology? In other words, how does phenomenology become transcendental philosophy in the Kantian sense?

One kind of epochē is possible, one which limits itself to neutralizing our position on existence in individual, intentional, lived experiences. The world as a whole does not yet come into view, however, through such a partial abstention from our "belief in being." The epochē must become *universal* if the phenomenological method is to become philosophy. It cannot allow any position with regard to existence to remain untouched. But a difficult problem arises here: even the claims that phenomenology makes about the intentional appearance of objects take a position on existence. By making judgments about appearance-in-manners-of-givenness, these manners of givenness are taken as existing. But if phenomenology were to refrain from making these claims about existence as well, then it could make no more claims at all. The universal epochē bases itself on a renunciation of every claim to knowledge, and thus of philosophy as *science;* it had this very same function in ancient skepticism. Phenomenology as a science therefore must make a sustainable claim from a region that is an exception to the epochē.

Phenomenological claims refer to intentional acts of consciousness. For this reason, the region that we seek can only be consciousness. But how can retaining the validity of being for consciousness be consistent with the "air-tightness" of the universal epochē? The universal epochē is the abstention from the general thesis of the natural attitude; it neutralizes the validity of the *world*. If the being of consciousness were the same kind as the being of the objects in the world (to which the natural belief in the world relates), then it would be impossible for phenomenological philosophy to assign being to consciousness. Accordingly, the being of consciousness must be of a fundamentally different kind than that of objects in the world. This thesis at first appears surprising, because, according to our pre-philosophical belief, consciousness is based in people, and they, for their part, are a component of the world. Thus it must be shown that intentional consciousness, contrary to how it appears naturally, does not belong to the world; in its way of being, it is not "mundane," as Husserl says.

At the same time, a second project presents itself: if the world is the whole in general, then there is nothing "next to" or "outside of" it, because the whole in general is itself defined as having nothing external, nothing other to it. Hegel called this Totality. Accordingly, it is impossible that consciousness be something "next to" or "other than" the world; in other words, it must be identical with the world. This thesis can be put into concrete form in only one way that would be phenomenologically meaningful: the world is the whole of all intentionally appearing objects. In the natural attitude, people distinguish objective existence, the being-in-itself of objects, from their subject-relative appearance in relation to consciousness, their manners of givenness. The being-in-itself of objects is that aspect of objects' existence of which people in the natural attitude are convinced, namely, that objects are subject-irrelative, unrelated to consciousness. The identity of the world and consciousness, however, can mean only that the being-in-itself of the world is nothing other than its intentional appearing-for-consciousness, which goes against the belief of its being in the natural attitude.

With this thesis, Husserl presents phenomenology as a variety of modern idealism. It is in this idealistic position, though, that we find the actual difference between the phenomenological-philosophical position and the natural attitude. The latter maintains, as an unthematic world-belief, that the being of the world and the objects in it are independent of their appearance in consciousness. The concrete form of this natural conviction is that this appearance remains unthematic. The natural attitude leads only to the being-in-itself of objects, that they are independent of consciousness and subject-irrelative, and not to the subject-relative givenness of objects. This attitude is the basic position of "just-living." Contrary to this, the phenomenologist who is researching correlations relates this existence, which is supposedly independent of consciousness and not subject-relative, to subject-relative appearances. And further: he leads this existence back to such appearance (as its foundation).

Husserl calls this leading back the *phenomenological reduction*. It is nothing other than the radical universalizing of the epochē. Whereas in the universal epochē the being of the world is robbed of its validity, this being now reveals itself as appearing-for-consciousness. With this reduction, the phenomenological method becomes transcendental in the sense of the tradition established by Kant. In the eidetic investigation of correlations, objects are already viewed in the How of their appearance for consciousness, but the matter of their existence may still remain open. Only with the phenomenological reduction is the being of objects clarified *as* being-conscious. Insofar as the phenomenological reduction is understood as a radically universalized epochē and insofar as it amounts to an idealistic position, Husserl calls it *transcendental-phenomenological* in his later notes to his *Ideas I,* as well as in his projects in the 1920s.

This transcendental position of looking for the foundation of existence by going back to the actualization of appearances by subjective consciousness was rejected by Husserl's friends from Göttingen and Munich as a relapse into subjectivism. They limited themselves to what Husserl called the eidetic reduction, disregarding facts in favor of eidetic universality. This reduction, too, contains a type of epochē, a holding-in-suspense of the assumption of factual existence: essential circumstances exist independently of whether there are specific factual situations or not. According to Husserl, though, we must distinguish sharply between the phenomenological and the eidetic reduction because the phenomenological reduction is the consequence of the epochē (the abstention from *every* position on existence), and because I can also apply the epochē to factual, individual, lived experiences without examining their eidetic structures. The reduction of objectivities in general to my consciousness (that which allows for their appearance) is very different from a reduction of facts to their essences.

Those critics of Husserl from within phenomenology saw an impoverishment in his transcendental-phenomenological reduction. According to them, relating back to consciousness cuts philosophy off from the richness of objective existence; the call "to the things themselves" thus atrophies in a new subjectivism. But this was a misunderstanding of the concept of reduction. The phenomenological reduction is hardly "reductionistic." Not taking part in the belief that objects exist independently of consciousness, the belief of the natural attitude, does not mean that we no longer pay attention to objects. On the contrary, it is only through reflection that the matter of objects allows itself to be analyzed in such a way that we can see, unreduced, how it presents itself originarily to consciousness, and it is only through the epochē and the phenomenological reduction that reflection opens itself unconditionally to the analysis of originary manners of givenness. Transcendental phenomenology does not disregard the world in favor of consciousness; rather, its interest arises precisely *in* its illumination of the phenomena that make up our consciousness of the world. In fact, the transcendental phenomenologist is interested in consciousness only as the site of the appearance of the world.

8. The Way to the Reduction[19]

Given the conclusions we have just made, two projects arise—if the phenomenological method is to become philosophy. First of all, Husserl must prove that intentional consciousness is not mundane, or in other words, that it exists in a different way than the objects of the world. Second, he must really carry the transcendental-phenomenological reduction through, meaning he must follow a conceptual path by which we discover that the presumed being-in-itself of objects is nothing other than subject-relative appearance. Husserl formulated this way to the reduction in his "Fundamental Outlook" in *Ideas I* in a manner that, along the way, also provided the first proof we mentioned. Later, however, Husserl was no longer satisfied with this proof. For this reason, beginning in the 1920s, he intensely sought a more convincing way to the reduction.

If we first disregard Husserl's questionable proof that consciousness is not mundane, however, then we see that he does justify his phenomenological idealism in the "Fundamental Outlook" with the following considerations. The conviction that the being of the world is independent of consciousness is part of the belief of being in the natural attitude; this attitude also assumes that objects in the world are subject-irrelative, that is, they exceed their appearance-in-manners-of-givenness and thus are transcendent. The genuine phenomenological question must then be: how does intentional consciousness carry out this lived experience of transcendence in its originary form? How does the conviction that objects and the world are "more" than that which is given in each situational appearance originally arise?

Husserl's typical example for our experience of an object is the perception of a thing.[20] In actualizing the momentary adumbrations of this table here, for example, my consciousness is also co-conscious of horizonal potentiabilities, which are further perceptions. The momentary manners of givenness (for example, the view of the front side of this table) refer me through their own sensible content to potential experiences in which more of the table, or beyond it, more of the world in general, would become given. In this sense, we can say that, in each experience of an object there lie "*motivations*" which lead beyond it. Crucial here is the difference between what is given at this moment and that which is experienceable through the actualization of motivated potentiabilities. Every object is known as something existent on the basis of this difference, where its being is not absorbed into the manner of givenness that then happens to be actualized. The fact that the being of an object itself exceeds my direct (momentary) perceptual experience of its being is my originary experience of the transcendence of objects and the world.

This transcendence does not immediately mean that the object is totally unrelated to consciousness, but rather the opposite; it means that, while that which is transcendent may not itself be presently given to consciousness, in principle a motivated transition to its actual appearance already lies, to some extent, in the referential interconnection of potentiabilities. In short, the originary form of the lived experience of transcendence is the fact that the experience of an object is embedded in horizonal consciousness. Objective transcendence may originarily emerge in its not being related to consciousness directly, but this is just the reverse side of a latent relation to consciousness, one which can be revealed through motivations. Here, "relation to consciousness" means situated-subjective appearance. In fact, this is how each transcendent being proves to be appearance.

This proof, however, is subject to an ambiguity. According to the explanation we have given, that which transcendent objects "exceed" is the link of their appearance to the situation of the manners-of-givenness that happen to be actualized. The "transcendence" of which Husserl speaks is understood as originarily exceeding whatever the situation happens to be. However, Husserl understands appearance-in-manners-of-givenness not only with relation to the situation but also with relation to the subject. Further, "subjective" means based in consciousness. Therefore, Husserl must interpret the transcendence of a situation also as exceeding consciousness.

Such an interpretation, however, presupposes that consciousness already exists on its own before it is exceeded, because only that which is already something in itself can be transcended. Consciousness must possess such definite characteristics that its being exceeded is intrinsic to it in advance. At first, consciousness relates to those characteristics which are "immanent" to it; its basic character is its inner relation to itself. Transcendence then consists in consciousness's relating to something other than its own inner self, thus reaching out to "givennesses" which are not immanent. In this sense, Husserl distinguishes the *transcendent* objects of the world from the *immanent* givennesses of consciousness. Through this, however, the proof that consciousness is not mundane, which we have set aside until now, gains central meaning for the reduction: Husserl must now explain in what way this "immanence"—which is exceeded by the transcendence of mundane objects—exists.

In his "Fundamental Outlook" in *Ideas I,* Husserl clarifies how consciousness is not mundane through a comparison: He chooses material, spatial things as an example for transcendent objects-in-the-world. The way things exist is revealed, according to the universal *a priori* of correlation, in the way that they appear originarily. The same goes for the way consciousness exists: consciousness is the whole of all intentional, lived experiences. These lived experiences emerge concretely in my actualizing the manners of givenness through which an object appears to consciousness; in our example of the perception of a thing, these are the *adumbrations* through which the thing comes to be given. These adumbrations, which are unthematic in the natural attitude, are made thematic in reflection; in such reflection, we can make adumbrations originarily present in intuition, and in this sense we can innerly "perceive" our consciousness. Through a comparison of the outer perception of things with the reflexive, inner perception of their unthematic adumbrations, the difference between the manner of being of consciousness and that of mundane objects must come to light.

The result of such a comparison is this: whereas a (mundane) thing only comes to be given through adumbrations, this is not the case for its reflectively perceived adumbrations. The manners of givenness which are unthematically actualized in perception, for example, are not once again given through unthematic manners of givenness in reflection; they do not appear to reflecting consciousness as subject-*relative* in adumbrations, but rather as *absolute*. Consciousness is thus given to itself in reflection as free of adumbrations. According to the *a priori* of correlation, the way whatever is given exists corresponds to its manner of givenness. Therefore, consciousness possesses absolute existence as opposed to the subject-relative existence possessed by the objects in the world.

In order to illustrate the absoluteness of consciousness, Husserl makes use of the classical methodological doubt found in Descartes's *Meditations*. According to Descartes, I can doubt the existence of everything conceivable, but not the existence of my self, insofar as and as long as I conceive. The existence of my ability to conceive—the existence of consciousness—is the indubitable remainder which cannot be questioned, even by a general, comprehensive doubt. This is similar to Husserl's position: because mundane objects are given as subject-relative, their validity of being can be canceled out at any time; to be subject-relative entails the possibility of error. In principle, because we can be mistaken, it is imaginable that our entire belief in the world could collapse. On the other hand, the validity of the being of consciousness, because of its absolute givenness, is unable to be canceled, and thus it is absolute.

Even if the existence of the entire world were to lose its validity, and, in this sense, the world were to be "destroyed" for consciousness, something would be left over: absolute consciousness as a "*residuum of the destruction of the world.*" Phenomenological reflection affirms this residuum. As this reflection looks deep into consciousness-as-absolute, it discovers manners of givenness as a part of what is "immanent" to it. These are contained as indubitable "*reell,*" or immanent, pieces in the stream of intentional, lived experiences. From these, we must distinguish the objects in the world as "*real,*" which possess only an insecure transcendent existence and which are beyond the stream of lived experience immanent to consciousness.

This is where the method of the reduction begins to cause the distinct paths within traditional Cartesian dualism—the paths of consciousness and "outer world"—to converge. In the long run, such a dualism did not satisfy Husserl for several reasons. We will mention only three here. First, it results in a confusing interplay between the concepts of "immanent" and "transcendent." Insofar as the transcendent existence of the world is traced back to its appearance in manners of givenness, which are immanent, this transcendence of objective existence proves to be immanent. But can it be reasonably understood with the term "transcendence" if it is really "immanent transcendence"?

Second, this paradox of a consciousness which exceeds itself and yet remains in itself also contradicts the very spirit of the investigation of correlations at its most basic level. Husserl's concept of intentionality basically settles the classical Cartesian problematic of what is "inner" versus "outer" with regard to consciousness. This problematic returns, however, because Husserl over-interprets the subjective character of "manners of givenness." Because they are naturally unthematized, manners of givenness are undoubtedly subjective insofar as they can be brought to light only through reflection. But for Husserl, they are also subjective in the sense that they can be carried out only inside consciousness. This is a one-sided interpretation, though. Certainly, manners of givenness are the way in which intentional consciousness carries out its lived experiences, but in the same stroke these are appearances-*of*-something; in other words, they are manners of self-revelation, of existing things presenting themselves. If we were to apply the Cartesian question, asking whether we should add these lived experiences to the category of consciousness's "outer" or "inner" world, then we could not appropriately comprehend their richness. Lived experiences break down this dualism; they are the In-between, that which originally opens the dimension of intentional appearance within which consciousness and the world have already met—before any subject-object rift.[21] Husserl discovered this In-between through resolving this subject-object rift by understanding truth in a way that was not one-sided; he was thereby the first to push open the door to entirely new possibilities in thought for twentieth-century philosophy.

Third, the Cartesian proof that consciousness is not mundane, in *Ideas I,* also contravenes the method of the epochē. In the beginning of his "Fundamental Outlook," Husserl explicitly separates this method from Cartesian doubt. According to Husserl, Descartes also sought a way to suspend the natural attitude. Descartes believed that the way to do this would be methodically to set up a universal negation in opposition to the natural, positive position on existence. But negation is still a variety of position-taking. The natural attitude can only be overcome through setting aside *all* possible positions, that is, through the epochē. Husserl, however, covertly retracted this insightful aspect of his critique of Descartes when he considered the possibility that extreme disillusion could call the existence of the world into question, and when he explained that non-mundane consciousness is the "residuum of the destruction of the world." Thus consciousness for Husserl—as with Descartes, basically—joins the remainder of affirmable being which survives the negation of the world.

When Husserl engaged Descartes again much later, in his *Cartesian Meditations,* he did criticize him on this point, saying that consciousness for Descartes was still "a little leftover piece of the world."[22] As long as consciousness is still a piece of the world whose existence is affirmed in the natural attitude, it does not distinguish itself from mundane objects in the way it exists. This accusation also affects Husserl's "Fundamental Phenomenological Outlook." Thus Husserl, after *Ideas I,* was pressed to clarify the phenomenological conception of consciousness from the perspective of his method. In the 1920s, Husserl conceived a way to the reduction, documented in his article in the *Encyclopedia Britannica,* which went through "*phenomenological psychology.*" This way prefigures transcendental phenomenology, in which consciousness is still understood as mundane, that is, as the soul that retains the character of a being-in-the-world. The whole world of objects is already reduced to the How of its pure intentional appearance, and yet phenomenology remains mundane here, that is, it remains a pre-philosophical science that is trapped in a belief in the world. As such, it is no different from non-empirical psychology, no different from the science which establishes the identifiable essential structures of all lived experiences through eidetic reduction in such a way that they can be analyzed in the reflective inner examination of the epochē. According to Husserl, this introspective-eidetic psychology has a double function. First, it is the *a priori* foundation of all empirical psychology; psychology today, which is almost completely run as a pure natural science and which believes it can get by without any introspective-eidetic foundations, is groundless and will thus eventually falter, according to Husserl. Second, phenomenological psychology is the first step to transcendental phenomenology. The former already contains the latter in its entirety, but only as mundane. According to Husserl, all we need is an "indicative change," whereby consciousness will be grasped as transcendental instead of mundane, in order to transfer this new type of psychology into transcendental philosophy.

Wherein lies this indicative change? Consciousness, as we have occasionally pointed out, is the stream of intentional, lived experiences, and thus Husserl also spoke of the "*stream of experiences.*" In this stream, all of my lived experiences are unified, and this unity is known to me because I describe all of my lived experiences as "mine." That they are "mine" means that they belong to "me," "I" am the one who actualizes them. Thus I am—as the "*performing-ego,*" as Husserl calls it—the basis of all of my experiences' belonging together, that is, of the unity of my stream of consciousness. In my intentional, lived experiences, I am directed toward objects-in-the-world, but I can also make my own ego an object of my reflection. Through such objectification, the ego in the natural attitude appears to itself as something existing in the world. In fact, this objectification is a making-worldly: I apprehend myself sociologically as role player, in experimental psychology as an experimental subject, and so on.

During such self-objectification, this act of making-worldly withdraws itself somewhat: I myself as performing-ego—as I, the one who carries out each experience of objectification—remain to some extent on this side of the objectification, as the performer. Understood in this way as performing-ego, I am basically a being that is not mundane; I am "*pure ego,*" as Husserl says. Here "pure" means "unable to be captured by any objectification that makes-worldly." Apprehending consciousness no longer as mundane, but instead as transcendental, means considering this pure performing-ego. Husserl therefore also calls it the "*transcendental ego.*"[23] The transcendental ego in us is nothing other than the mundane ego; phenomenological reflection is in no way a literal division of consciousness. It is just a reminder that, in the final moment, I am a being that is not completely absorbed into any objectification, thereby preserving my freedom and responsibility. In whatever way Husserl might have thought out the method of realizing this indicative change in the transition from phenomenological psychology to transcendental phenomenology, it is clear that his primary concern was considering myself in my free responsibility.[24]

Husserl did not follow the concrete way to the reduction in his reflections on method that we just problematized. The "reduction" or "leading back" of existence from objects and the world to their intentional appearance can only mean explaining this existence on the basis of appearance. The fact that certain types of objects are taken as existing in-themselves by consciousness must be made comprehensible through their appearance in related manners of givenness. Given that consciousness transcends originary situated-subjective givennesses in a motivated way, then the integral nature of the world must be constructed through its eidetically distinguishable regions of objects. This construction of the world out of consciousness's motivated achievements of transcendence is called "*constitution*" by Husserl.[25] The actual project of investigating correlations in transcendental phenomenology, then, is analyzing the constitution of different categories of objects.

As a method of eidetic and transcendental-phenomenological reduction, phenomenology developed into one of the very few comprehensive systematic projects of twentieth-century philosophy. In spite of its questionable aspects—a few of which we have just indicated—this project is an essential link between classical German transcendental philosophy and those new departures characteristic of the twentieth century, such as existentialism, the philosophy of Being, hermeneutics, academic theory, and linguistic analysis, all of which are somewhat linked to phenomenology. For this reason it is worthwhile to follow the way Husserl's phenomenology has gone as a method in order to "reconstruct" systematically the transition from the age of Idealism to our epoch. Only in this way can we assess, in a somewhat authoritative manner, the far-reaching effects and consequences of the endeavors of contemporary philosophy. In another respect the study of Husserlian texts is attractive insofar as working through the investigation of constitution in concrete analyses enriches our philosophical understanding of people's experience of the world from many different angles.

Notes

This essay was first published as Klaus Held, "Einleitung," in *Edmund Husserl: Die Phänomenologische Methode, Ausgewählte Texte* (Stuttgart: Philipp Reclam), I: 5–51.

    1. This comment does not at all detract from the merit deserved by the Nijhoff publishers in the Netherlands for their work with regard to Husserl.

    2. On the problem of the life-world see Section 7 of the next essay in this volume. Husserl's discussion of this is found in *Krisis; Crisis,* §§8, 9, 33, 34, *Beilage II* (Appendix 5);

and the texts in *The Essential Husserl: Basic Writings in Transcendental Phenomenology*, ed. Donn Welton (Bloomington: Indiana University Press, 1999), §§20 and 21. So as to facilitate access to the texts under discussion, references will be given not only to Husserl's individual works but also to any corresponding selections found in *The Essential Husserl*.

3. For more about Husserl's life, see K. Schuhmann, *Husserl-Chronik: Denk-und Lebensweg Husserls. Husserliana Dokumente*, vol. 1 (The Hague: Martinus Nijhoff, 1977).

4. Cf. H. L. Van Breda, "Die Rettung von Husserls Nachlaß und die Gründung des Husserl-Archivs," in *Husserl und das Denken der Neuzeit*, ed. H. L. Van Breda and J. Taminiaux (The Hague: Nijhoff, 1959), 42ff.

5. More in-depth explanations of these concepts can be found in Section 2 of the next essay in this volume.

6. *Krisis*, 168; *Crisis*, 165.

7. *Krisis*, 169; *Crisis*, 166.

8. *Ideen I*, 43–44; *Ideas I*, 44; italics deleted.

9. *Ideen I*, 44; *Ideas I*, 44.

10. *The Essential Husserl*, §1.

11. Cf. Husserl, *Prolegomena, Logische Untersuchungen*, I, 68; *Logical Investigations*, 103.

12. *The Essential Husserl*, §§7, 14, 15.

13. This plausible thesis can be found in U. Claesges, *Edmund Husserls Theorie der Raumkonstitution* (The Hague: Nijhoff, 1964), 29ff.

14. See Section 6 of the next essay in this volume as well.

15. Cf. Aristotle, *Metaphysics*, 1003a.

16. For a more exact analysis of all these relations, cf. Section 2 of the next essay in this volume; *Analysen zur passiven Synthesis*, 3–24; and *The Essential Husserl*, §12.

17. *The Essential Husserl*, §5.

18. Kant, *Critique of Pure Reason*, B 25.

19. *The Essential Husserl*, §19. See also §§20 and 21.

20. For a more exact analysis of the perception of a thing cf. Section 2 of the next essay in this volume; *Analysen zur passiven Synthesis*, 3–24; and *The Essential Husserl*, §12.

21. This whole problematic is taken up again in a more concrete form in Section 3 of the next essay in this volume.

22. Husserl, *Cartesianische Meditationen*, 63; *Cartesian Meditations*, 24.

23. For a closer look at this whole problematic, cf. Section 4 of the next essay in this volume.

24. Cf. the last section of the next essay in this volume.

25. For a closer look at this concept, cf. Section 1 of the next essay in this volume.

2

Husserl's Phenomenology of the Life-World

Klaus Held
Translated by Lanei Rodemeyer

1. The Problem of Constitution

Founded by Edmund Husserl, phenomenology in many ways enriched, and to some degree substantially influenced, philosophy—and many other academic areas—in the first three decades of the twentieth century. Husserl's last work, *The Crisis of European Sciences and Transcendental Phenomenology,* composed in 1936 just two years before his death, created new waves, the effects of which are still being felt today. In this work Husserl focuses primarily on introducing the concept of the life-world. Many people today seek a model of the world that represents a place where they could feel at home, where they could "live" in the fullest sense of the word. This searching might be brought about, for example, by our shock over the conditions of the environment, revealed to us by some disaster, or our discomfort with regard to a society whose rational organization and management is ever more pervasive. Thus this key term from Husserl, "*life-world,*" appears increasingly in both scholarly circles and public discussions. In order that these contributions be given a more sturdy foundation, we should reconstruct the conceptual context from which the term "life-world" arose to become a central philosophical concept.

Husserl's consideration of the life-world includes a radical critique of the spirit of the modern sciences. Remarkably, this critique is not fundamentally hostile toward science. On the contrary, Husserl's objective is to revive philosophy both as a *science* and as the basis of scientific work in general. In this way, his return to the life-world could be helpful in protecting today's sciences and civilizations, which are noticeably self-involved, from the romantic movements of younger generations, movements that demand we return to a safe, pre-scientific and pre-technical world. Because of this self-involved attitude, the tension between the "two cultures" in the modern world resurfaces, a tension that has been discussed since the 1960s in connection with the theses of Charles Snow, the English romantic and scientist.[1] Modern existence seems to be split between the soulless life of a scientifically and technically rational world, with all of its specializations, and the full existence of a historical-personal world with its cultural manifestations. This division is also mirrored in the vacillation of contemporary philosophy between the successors of two traditions, now called "analytic" and "continental." There have been many attempts to connect the analytic and scientifically oriented thinking, which arose from modern empiricism and positivism, with the transcendental-philosophical, dialectical, existential, or hermeneutic successors of the early European traditions.

Husserl's thought possesses an affinity toward both sides, and for this reason it is predestined to play the role of mediator between these "two cultures." Because of his education as a mathematician in the intellectual world of the end of the nineteenth century, the analytical philosophical tradition is reflected in Husserl's work. Similar to the positivism of his day, Husserl's thought integrates the search for a "natural concept of the world"—which for him culminates in his later theory of the life-world—with the attempt to provide a foundation for the sciences. It is not by accident that we see increasing attempts in recent times to build a bridge between analytic philosophy, which is predominant in Anglo-American circles, and Husserl's phenomenology. On the other hand, however, we can also view the transcendental-philosophical context of Husserl's later analyses of the life-world as a bastion against our loss of history, or at least our careless approach to the tradition of classical philosophy, an approach which, in part, arises through a scientific-theoretically oriented, analytical philosophy. Due to this more historical side of Husserl's work, the problematic of the life-world has an inner connection to existential-hermeneutic philosophy, a connection developed through continued analysis of Husserl in the works of Heidegger, Sartre, Gadamer, and others. For similar reasons, the concept of the life-world has recently gained special significance in the social philosophy of Habermas, whose work belongs to the tradition of leftist Hegelianism.

The title of the first essay in this volume, "Husserl's Phenomenological Method," referred to the claim with which phenomenology originally arose: phenomenology wanted to be a radically new philosophical method that strives toward freedom from prejudice. But neither for Husserl, nor for any of the other great phenomenologists (i.e., Scheler, Heidegger, Sartre, Merleau-Ponty, to name just the most important figures) did phenomenology remain merely a method; it became a philosophy. In other words, according to Aristotle's ancient definition, phenomenology turned into an interrogation of all that is with respect to its being. As a philosophy, phenomenology becomes "constitutive analysis" in Husserl's work; "being" takes on the character of an objectivity (*Gegenständlichkeit*) constituted in consciousness. What this means will be clarified in the following sections, all of which are dedicated to the problem of constitution.

Reduced to the simplest formula, all constitutive analyses serve to clarify the way and manner in which the world appears to people; the basic theme of the phenomenological investigation of constitution is the world taken as appearance, as "phenomena." As Husserl's thinking developed in his last years, he was led to define the appearing world as the life-world. The "life-world" is nothing other than the "world" that had always been the focus of Husserl's thinking about constitution—but now, of course, with an importantly en- riched meaning, which we will discuss in a moment.

The connection between "constitution" and "life-world" is indicated in our title "Husserl's Phenomenology of the Life-World." In this way, the title of the first essay in this volume, "Husserl's Phenomenological Method," reminds us of the starting point of Husserl's philosophical path, while the title "Hus- serl's Phenomenology of the Life-World" reminds us of its end—an end that, because of the abiding question of the life-world, is still at work today.

With his constitutive analyses, Husserl furnishes us with concrete evidence for the idealist position that his phenomenology leads to.[2] In the *natural atti- tude,* which is the position people take with regard to the world prior to phe- nomenology, the world and the objects in it count as something *objective,* as entities existing in themselves; in other words, as things existing without any relation to consciousness. This existence of the objective world, understood here as unrelated to the subject, is differentiated from its being given for human consciousness, from its "appearance" as "subject-relative." Husserl's phenome- nological idealism traces the existence of the world that is supposedly indepen- dent of consciousness back to its appearance to and for consciousness. Husserl does not justify this *"reduction"* with some kind of universal arguments— which would be expected, given the history of modern philosophy. Rather he shows, through detailed individual analyses, how human consciousness goes from different types of objectivities to the conviction of their existing in them- selves in their respective categories.

After more careful examination, we see that the "appearance" of objects arises in the following way: every object is known by me as something identical —as *one* object—but it presents itself to me in its many ways of being given, ways which vary subjectively according to the situation. If we had only the succession of these subjective-situated *manners of givenness* in consciousness, then no world with identical and persisting objects would appear to us, objects of whose subsistence in-themselves we are unquestionably and obviously con- vinced in our natural attitude. Objects exist "in themselves," that is, they are more than, or are not exhausted by, that which is momentarily given as situa- tionally relative to the subject. The object strikes me as something that has existence beyond this manifold of momentary manners of givenness; in this sense, the object *transcends* such multiplicity. There must, however, be a basis for my grasping the object as transcendent. Further, this basis can only be mo- tivated by subjective-situated appearances. Our analysis of this *motivation* with regard to different types of objectivities describes the general project of the investigation of constitution.

In the natural attitude, human interest is directed toward objects. The manners of givenness through which objects must appear remain unnoticed; they are usually never thematized, and if they are, then only sporadically. In order to bring these manners of givenness to light, bringing them out of the concealment of their unthematic existence, we specifically need phenomenological *reflection*, whose *method* we discussed in the first essay in this volume. This reflection shows that all manners of givenness can be divided into two large groups. On the one hand, an object can be given to me in such a way that I also have consciousness of a reference to and a dependence on other manners of givenness that are possible for me, manners of givenness in which the object would be present to me in intuited closeness. On the other hand, an object can just appear to me in this very closeness, which Husserl describes as *originarity.* All presentations that are not close to the matter at hand—in other words, all vague, somehow hidden or distorted, or indefinite presentations which are more or less empty of content—tend toward "fulfilling" themselves in the *originary manners of givenness* of the object in question, because their (unfulfilled) experienced content does not satisfy consciousness. Meanwhile, this currently given experienced content already indicates possibilities through which, by realizing them, consciousness can attain fulfillment. According to Husserl, consciousness is *intentional,* that is, it is directed toward objects. Inseparable from this "being-directed" is an intention toward fulfillment, because only originarily fulfilled experiences provide consciousness with original objects that have a definite factual content; without the possibility of fulfillment, there would be no consciousness of objects at all.

For this reason, our analyses of constitution must begin with those originary manners of givenness that motivate consciousness to encounter objects. Phenomenology describes how originarily experiencing consciousness "makes" a set of objects construct themselves in such a way that they appear to consciousness as something existing in themselves. This activity of construction, which is performed by consciousness and made visible through analysis, is called "*constitution*" by Husserl, appropriating a concept from the neo-Kantians at the turn of the century. Constitutive analysis reveals how the actualizing of originary manners of givenness motivates consciousness to *transcend* the situated moments of these manners of givenness in the direction of definite types of objectivities, thus attaining its belief in their existence (its "*world-belief*"). For this reason, Husserl describes his phenomenology, among other things, as *transcendental philosophy,* because it explains this transcending as an analytic of constitution.[3]

Constitutive analyses always relate to a specific realm of objects. They show how the existence of objects belonging to a specific type or species of existing things comes about in the related activities of consciousness. The general essential structures of such realms of objects—for example, objects of perception, numbers, linguistic meanings, norms of justice, ethical values, etc.—make up the "guiding thread" for these analyses. These essential structures become known through the method of the "*eidetic reduction*" (i.e., related to the eidos, the essence), where we abstain from facts in order to pay attention to their universal determinations.[4]

In order to avoid having an unsystematic collection of individual analyses,

Husserl began by classifying existence generally into three comprehensive regions: the material nature of things in space, animal (ensouled, living) nature, and the spiritual-personal world. He did this in the second volume of his *Ideas,* which was not published during his lifetime. The basic determinations of the being of these regions are developed in theories through which the existence of these types of objects is specified.[5] At the same time, these "regional ontologies" comprise the *a priori* presuppositions by which the various individual sciences differentiate themselves from each other.

The investigation of constitution is presented through an abundance of projects whose organization results from the idea that all types of intentional, lived experiences point to each other through their reference to originarity. In other words, in each consciousness there is not only a reference forward, toward future or possible originarity—insofar as a closeness to the matter at hand is still lacking—but there is also a reference to originarity already experienced—insofar as consciousness has already attained a closeness to the issue and thus to the matter itself. Consciousness refers back from its factual content to other intentional, lived experiences, without which consciousness would itself not be possible. In this way, a lived experience is "founded" by others. This idea of *foundation* became quite influential in the systematic ordering of Husserlian constitutive analyses, gaining a fundamental methodological significance in the whole phenomenological movement.

The idea of foundation led Husserl to the assumption that, because it is presupposed in all other types of lived experiences, the perception of things in space should be taken as the basic example and ground for intentional, lived experience in general. No matter how I relate to whatever I encounter—through feeling, or willing, or practical activity—I always presuppose its existence. Using a practical object or loving another person would not be possible without the experience that that which appears usable or lovable is actually there. This certainty of existence, however, is provided by elementary sensory perception. In the relation between sensory perception and the rest of my intentional, lived experiences we find a type of one-sided "foundational relation": the other intentional, lived experiences are not possible without perception, whereas perception is possible without them. Because of this, in *Ideas II,* the region of being whose objects are given in sensible perception—in other words, material nature—becomes the most fundamental domain of objects.

This thinking through *foundational relations* leads us to the idea that the intentionally experienced world is, in a certain way, built in layers. This idea of layers has actually been further developed, independently of phenomenology, through the work of Nicolai Hartmann. For Husserl, both perception, taken as establishing what is present, and the objectivity given in it make up the supporting layer in the construction of world experience. This whole theory is later emphatically opposed both by Heidegger's presentation of daily human praxis in *Being and Time,* where the "present-at-hand" (what is presently there) is given a secondary position to the "ready-to-hand" (what is readily there), and by Scheler, with his analyses of sympathetic and love relationships.

Admittedly, perception is the basic experience in the constitution of the real world for Husserl. This does not mean, however, that perception for its part might not be founded by intentional, lived experiences that lie even deeper. In fact, consciousness already constitutes objectivities, even in such lived experiences where we are not yet dealing with material objects in space or with the living and personal world in "higher level" regions of being. Those activities of constitution that are situated under the realm of perception according to the ordered construction of foundation, though, will continue to be our topic.

2. Perception as the Model of Constitution[6]

The fact that the order of foundation does not begin with sensory perception does not change the fact that this type of lived experience represents the most exemplary case of intentional consciousness for Husserl in general. The reason for this lies in his conception of originarity. Not only are intentional lived experiences (which become the object of phenomenological knowledge) related to originary manners of givenness, but also phenomenological knowledge itself is a form of intentional lived experience and thus is referred to and directed toward originarity as well. Husserl calls originary givenness in philosophical knowledge *evidence*.[7] Its character is *intuition*, in which I observe objects, or rather, certain universal essential relations, free of interest and involvement.[8] This definition is surreptitiously carried over to Husserl's understanding of originarity in general. For him, originarity means intuited givenness. An intentional lived experience, however, where we originally and literally carry out intuition, is the visual perception of a thing. Thus Husserl gathers from this typical case the determinations that then become standard, either directly or indirectly, for all of his constitutive analyses.

The perception of a thing is intuition, insofar as the thing shows itself to me in the presence of Here and Now. Intuition means having something present for Husserl, where "*presenting*" (*Gegenwärtigung*) is distinguished from the many possibilities of "re-presenting" (*Ver-gegenwärtigung*), such as, for example, memory or imagination. In such intuited having-present of perception, however, it becomes clear that the thing in view is in no way present in every respect. This observation actually always reawakened Husserl's astonishment and somehow colored all of his concrete constitutive analyses. What is astonishing in each observation is this: a thing—for example, this table here—may present its front side to me, but its back side and other aspects remain presently hidden from me; in spite of this, "the thing," that is, the perceived object as a whole, is known to me.

Through more careful consideration, we realize that this *one* intuition, in which this *one* thing is given to me, contains a multitude of manners of givenness which Husserl calls "*adumbrations*" in the case of perceived things. From among all the adumbrations, those which are actually carried out show me the thing as "really" intuited, and the others for their part are known to me as potentialities (*Möglichkeiten*), potentialities which *can* be carried over into real intuition. I make use of these potentialities as I would something that lies within my power; for this reason, Husserl calls them "*potentiabilities*" (*Vermöglichkeiten*). The actualized adumbrations point, on the basis of their own sensible content—for example, to every front side there also belongs a backside —to potentiabilities. Husserl calls this playing field of what can be perceived, opened up to me by the referential interconnection of potentiabilities, their "*horizon*."

Clearly, I can only say that I perceive "the thing," that is, this table here, when I also am anticipating horizonal co-given potentiabilities. But with this, my attention directs itself toward the thing and not at all toward the potentiabilities as possible manners of givenness. The latter remain *unthematic*, because my *theme* is the object itself. My experience of perception forges ahead in such a way that I keep taking up unthematic potentiabilities, thereby learning either further determinations of the thematic thing itself (the "inner horizon") or other objects and object relations (the "outer horizon"). In essence, the intuition of a thing is in itself always an *anticipation* of readily available, horizonal— in other words, not actually intuited—manners of givenness.

Through such anticipation, a thing is known to me as something whose existence *transcends* what happens to be currently given, and in this sense, it exists "in itself," "*objectively*." Constitutive analyses, though, are meant to explain this apprehension of objects as existing in themselves; for this reason, Husserl must pay attention to the moments in which such anticipation is in play. Thus he distinguished these moments in his foundational work on the phenomenological method—in the first volume of *Ideas I*—developing terminology for them.

Current, unthematic adumbrations make up the springboard, so to speak, for anticipation. The fact that adumbrations are unthematic means that I do not encounter them as objects. Because they do not face me as objects, Husserl makes the following problematic conclusion: they must be something that is contained within what I carry out subjectively. For example, if a thing appears to me with the color "brown," this color belongs to the thing as something objective (*Gegenständliches*); "in" me, however, as a "*reell*" moment,[9] the non-objective brown-sensation underlies this objective givenness.

At first, Husserl described such sensory contents as "data," that is, as inner givennesses that appear in consciousness on the basis of impressions—produced by the external stimulations of the sense organs. Behind this whole conception lies the tradition of the sensualist theory of knowledge, going back to British empiricism. But the concept of "*sensory data*" is already misleading because it gives the impression that we are dealing with something like inner objects. Sensory contents, however, as components of unthematic manners of givenness, are not objects at all. The residual effects of sensualism in Husserl's theory of perception will return as one of our topics in the next section.

Sensations, as "*reell*" moments of consciousness, are in themselves not yet related to objectivities. They have a non-objective content, but this content "functions" unthematically as the groundwork from which consciousness can direct itself toward objects; only through sensation is the objective world's wealth of colors, tastes, figures, and smells accessible to perceiving consciousness. In sensation, the material for the appearance of the world lies ready, we could say. But this material—Husserl uses the corresponding Greek expression "*hylē*" ("stuff")—must first be made usable for the appearance of certain objects, their qualities and relations, for consciousness. This takes place when the manifold of sensory content is objectified and is *apprehended* as belonging to the unity of an object. That which is sensed is taken, "*apperceived,*" in such a way that an objectivity "presents" itself in it.[10] Husserl calls this "forming" or "animation" of "hyletic material," of "primary apprehended content," *noesis,* freely using an ancient Greek term which describes the carrying out of observation and attending to. The perceived thing is constituted through the noetic formation of the hylē in apperception.

Currently given sensory content thus gives us the beginning of apperception. But through apperception, consciousness extends over and beyond itself, letting "the thing" appear in it. In this way, consciousness anticipates the possibility of experiencing a thing as a whole. In my actualized given sensory content, the thing never presents itself with all of the aspects that it could ever offer me; it shows itself—if we can understand the concept of "*perspective*" in a very broad sense and not as limited to spatial consciousness—always and only through a one-sided perspective. Through its one-sidedness, each perspective, each adumbration, refers to others that I am not presently actualizing, but that are known to me as co-present possibilities. In my intuition of the front side of a house, for example, the backside, which I could see if I wanted, is co-present to me. Husserl calls this having-co-present in presentation "*appresentation.*"

In appresentations, the potentiabilities of further experience lie ready for consciousness. Appresentation thus opens up playing fields of potentiabilities, that is, of horizons. Because appresentations belong to apperception, apperception establishes horizons for consciousness. The constitution of an object through apperception does not only cause an object to be given for consciousness, but it also allows horizons to come into being. Constitution is this development of horizons.

Because the object is embedded in a horizon, it always carries an excess of sensory content for consciousness as compared to those manners of givenness through which it is currently appearing. On the basis of this excess, which is motivated through appresentations in apperception, the object is taken by consciousness in the natural attitude as existing in itself, as transcendent. The phenomenologist, however, as an uninvolved, reflecting observer does not buy into this view of transcendence when she encounters an object. This does not mean that she denies this view; she merely refrains from taking any position with regard to existence.[11] She observes the object purely in the way it appears to perceiving consciousness in its manners of givenness. That which is understood as "the object in the How of its intentional appearance"—distinguished from the object that encounters our natural, unreflecting consciousness as something existing in itself—Husserl calls *noema,* corresponding to the noesis.

The concept of "noema" can have a double meaning, however. Apperception consists in the hyletic manifold's being gathered up and applied to *one* object. This unifying activity Husserl calls "synthesis," along with Kant. As the focal point of the unification of many manners of givenness, the noema is nothing more than that which faces me, a pole to which consciousness relates and about which it assembles its own manifold. Husserl calls the object understood in this way the "noematic core." This is the object taken as the simple "carrier" of its qualities and other determinations, which is then abstracted from this whole allocation. The noematic core is the object considered abstractly, as a determinable unity. But if we take the word "object" in its fullest sense, then we understand it with *all* of its determinations as they appear to consciousness through the manifold manners of givenness. The "core" taken *with* the whole fullness of its determinations is called the "noematic sense." This is the concrete object-in-the-How-of-its-intentional-appearance. It is this object-in-the-How that comes to be given to consciousness through the activity of constitution. For this reason, Husserl can also define constitution as *sense-giving* or sense-endowment.

Sense-giving is apperception; consciousness interprets and "animates" some primary content that is already at its disposal in such a way that it is thereby convinced that, in this content, an objectively existing object is revealing itself. In processing this hyletic multitude, constitution is an *"achievement."* With this achievement, consciousness transcends itself; it surpasses its own *"reell"* moments—the hylē and the carrying out of noetic apprehensions—going toward *"real"* objects which encounter it as noema.

3. The Primary Elements of Perception[12]

The understanding of constitution that we just outlined contains a double distinction: on the one hand, we distinguish *reell* given things, which are immanent to consciousness, from real given things, which are transcendent; on the other hand, we distinguish the content of apprehension (hylē) from the apprehension itself (apperception). In the first distinction, a dualism harkening back to Descartes—between the inner world of consciousness and the outer world of material objects—returns again in Husserl's thinking, a dualism which by its very nature has nothing to do with a phenomenology of intentional lived experiences.[13] This Cartesian dualism is already overcome in the beginning of phenomenology, with Husserl's fundamental discovery of the In-between-dimension of appearing-in-manners-of-givenness. The sensualist interpretation of sensation to which we referred, with its differentiation between inner sensory data and outer stimulation is only a later variety of Cartesianism, and for this reason it is phenomenologically untenable. Insofar as the second distinction we mentioned above (between the content of apprehension and apprehension itself) presupposes Cartesian dualism and sensualism, it, too, cannot be phenomenologically upheld. In Husserl's later "genetic phenomenology," which we will treat more carefully in a moment, however, this second distinction gains a new, non-Cartesian meaning. Husserl was himself quite critical of his own Cartesianism, but he did not always follow through on this critique. He developed an ambivalent position toward his form-content scheme of the constitution of the apprehension. Occasionally it appears as if he rejected this distinction entirely because of its Cartesian and sensualist presuppositions, but then he works with it again in a way that is largely independent of this tradition.

Husserl clearly distanced himself from the sensualist understanding of sensations in his later work, especially through his works on *kinaestheses*. The elementary domain of lived experiences, sensation, was taken traditionally as a sphere of "undergoing," of *passivity*. According to this understanding, sensory impressions come over us, without our having anything to say about it. Prejudiced by Cartesianism, Husserl first thought these impressions did not yet have a relation to the material existing in the transcendent world, since they were received purely passively and taken as immanent to consciousness. It was the *activity* of apperception that was supposed to furnish the hylē with worldliness, relating consciousness to the world. In order to escape an unphenomenological Cartesian dualism, Husserl had to resolve this dichotomy between purely passively pre-given stuff and the activities performed upon it, proving that sensation is worldly from the beginning because it is always already related to doing, that is, it contains an elementary activity.

In the case of sensation, consciousness is hardly a passive receiving station. If I reflect upon my own sensing, I notice that I can only have all of the sensed impressions that I have because I am doing things in my living body. In order to cause certain aspects of my objective surroundings to be given for me—aspects such as color, form, temperature, weight, etc.—I have to move my eyes, my head, my hands, etc. Sensory perception ("perception" in Greek is "*aisthesis*") and the movement of my living body ("movement" in Greek is "*kinesis*") create here an indissoluble unity. This unity brings the concept of "*kinaesthesis*" to the fore, a concept which Husserl took over from the literature of his contemporaries in psychology in order to give it central meaning in his own theory of perception.

The fact that sensation takes place kinesthetically could traditionally be overlooked because kinaestheses are tied to manners of givenness and thus are carried out unthematically. They become visible only through phenomenological reflection, when it is directed inward and followed through carefully. Even the idea that sensations might be triggered externally through impressions could only come about if one did not observe these sensations through inner reflection. Sensations thus appeared as effects that were caused by external stimuli. But if I describe sensation purely in the way that it presents itself to me in reflection, then such a relation of cause-and-effect reveals nothing.

One might think that the sensualist tradition turned out to be right, as kinesthetic movements take place in a passively mechanical way, without my conscious involvement. This may be true for normal cases, as we usually carry out our kinesthetic motion without noticing, through habit, but in the cases where our perceptive movement is disrupted or hindered, we become aware of our own capability (in Husserl's terms, our potentiability) to navigate actively. This whole theory of kinaestheses is quite meaningful for an entire realm of progressive phenomenological-psychological research being done in the area of the body; Husserl's constitutive analyses opened the door to these investigations with his discovery of activities in passivity. From among Husserl's successors, Maurice Merleau-Ponty provides us with the greatest wealth of observations in this field, in his work entitled *Phenomenology of Perception.*

Kinesthetic consciousness is only one of the achievements of constitution that consciousness must have already accomplished if perception is to take place at all. Like Kant, Husserl asks about the "conditions of possibility of experience" in his transcendental philosophy, and similar to Kant, he comes across consciousness of space and the fact that perceived things are embedded in a causal interrelation that links them all together. Beyond this, though, Husserl discovers further founding layers that Kant had not yet seen or had only indicated, all of which are accessible through phenomenological description.

According to Husserl, an especially characteristic proto-level of perception, which is closely related to kinaestheses, is the constitution of *"fields of sense."* If sensation were merely a wholly passive reception of impressions, then we could assume—with the sensualist tradition—that the received impressions were individual, simple data in themselves, that they were like indivisible flakes snowing into consciousness. Sensation would thus give an originally dotted picture of the world: spots everywhere, surfaceless units that could only be objectively conceived as surfaces through apperception. But as the passive experience of sensation is soaked through with activity from the very beginning, then the content that arises out of such sensation must also correspond to this activity. As we saw with the activity of apperception in the perception of things, activity means synthesis, the bringing together of multiplicity into one unity. Thus, in sensation, fields and forms appear from the very beginning; Husserl calls them configurations. Complexes of color with certain contours present themselves in our vision, for example, before any apperception of individual things with their multiple qualities and reciprocal relations. Here Husserl's antisensualist self-critique took a path similar to Cézanne's impressionist pointillism, whose painting introduced a new experience of surface color forms. This illumination of our assumptions regarding perception through phenomenology also touches on Gestalt psychology, which arose in the twentieth century.

Husserl calls the active passivity of consciousness, to which the fields of sense owe their unity, "*association*," another concept taken from the empirical tradition. With this term, though, he names a further constitutive assumption in perception. Stressing that his definition is contrary to the empirical conception of the term, Husserl explains that we should not take the term association to mean some sort of blind mechanism. That would be to understand the experience of sensation (without my conscious involvement) in the same way as some processes in material nature that are subject to mechanical rules. Rather, association is already a process of sense formation. Association originarily arises when something reminds me of something else, for example, when a specific smell reminds me of an apartment I once visited. The connecting link between the two given things, through which consciousness of one calls up consciousness of the other, can be, for example, a similarity between the two, but it can also be another "connecting point." Through "something reminds me of something" a *pairing* of two given things in consciousness first arises. Through reflection we see that association is not a blind mechanism, because I can recreate and understand through which connecting point(s) a pairing originally arose in consciousness.

4. Time-Consciousness[14]

Even deeper than association, something else occurs in the founding construction of consciousness which invariably brings about the *formal* continuity of consciousness in an elementary way. This synthesis, "inner time-consciousness," is plainly *the* fundamental level of constitution. In speech, "time-consciousness" means "consciousness *of* time." But this "of" is misleading, because it gives the impression that we are dealing with a consciousness that has made time as an object its theme. Strictly speaking, though, we find such an objectively directed consciousness only starting at the level of the perception of things. Nevertheless, we know "time" pre-objectively; in fact, according to Husserl, time is that which is first known overall with regard to the order of foundation. Consciousness is a stream of lived experiences, in other words, a flowing manifold. But these many different types of lived experiences are all known to me as "my experiences." Through their all belonging to "me," these experiences all belong together, and thus they form a unity. This synthetic unity of the diversity of the *stream of lived experiences* is, according to Husserl, temporality. Temporality makes up the form of how consciousness exists, and, strangely enough, it does this in such a way that consciousness simultaneously innerly "knows" this as its own form. This is "inner time-consciousness."

All Husserlian constitutive analyses are guided by the basic goal of explaining how objectivity (*Objektivität*), "being in-itself," arises for consciousness. This also applies for analyses of time. For this reason, Husserl takes up the problem of time in a completely different way than the other two great theorists of time in the twentieth century, Bergson and Heidegger. In Husserl's eyes, perceived things are the typical case of objectivity. Starting at this point, he sees that, for a whole series of reasons, material objects are able to appear to us as existing things that transcend our subjective actualization of their manners of givenness. The main reason for this follows from the fact that, on the one hand, all manners of givenness are subject to temporal succession because they are situated in my flow of consciousness; on the other hand, perceived things have an objective existence for consciousness primarily because they are themselves free from this succession of their manners of givenness. In other words, perceived things belong immovably to a specific time. Because of this immovability, the duration of these objects' existence is measurable and datable. Thus the fact that they exist in themselves follows fundamentally from the fact that these objects are present at a determinable point in time, or over a succession of such points in *"objective time."*

Husserl's analysis of time must be viewed from the problem with which he started out: how is this "objective time" constituted for consciousness? Thus his first question is this: how does such time become known originarily? We imagine objective time as a straight line. Every point on this line is a now, a present. With this image, we take all of the nows to be equal. But this does not correspond with our originary experience of time. There is originally always *one* now that has priority for my consciousness: the present, that is, the hour, the day, the year, in which I am currently living. We arrange the rest of the nows into certain relations with the current present: they are earlier, that is, they belong to the past, or they will come later, in the future. The past or future nows further organize themselves according to their greater or lesser distance from the current now. In this way, originarily experienced time is always oriented with the current present as its central reference.

The manners of givenness of time oriented in this way are remembrance and expectation. Through them, I "re-present" the past and the future, that is, the "surroundings" of the current present that are temporally closer or further away. I can only "re-present" these dimensions of my temporal horizon, though, because I or someone else has once experienced, or will experience, them in their current present. In this way, the manners of givenness of "remembrance" and "expectation" are related back to their manners of givenness as "presenting." Like all manners of givenness, those of the temporal dimension are also carried out subjectively. They appear in the stream of consciousness. This stream, however, is itself a temporal succession of intentional lived experiences. If a lived experience has taken place, then, from that point on, it retains an immovable position in the past of my *stream of consciousness*. In this way, the positions in time that are past become in-themselves for my consciousness, prior to any objectivity of perceived objects in objective time. The fact that a given thing exists in itself rests upon its embeddedness in a horizon of potentiabilities. Knowing this, we can now ask the question that launches the entire theory of constitution: through which achievements of consciousness does the elementary "objectivity" of these temporal positions of my stream of consciousness take place? In other words, how does the pre-objective conscious-ness of my consciousness's temporal horizon, that is, "inner time-consciousness," develop through the fact that I possess the potentiability of remembering hav-ing actualized certain lived experiences, and through this, remembering the contents of these experiences?

In answering this question, it is quite helpful to Husserl that time-consciousness is an especially striking example of how "distant" intentional experiences refer to and depend on originary experience. The "re-presentation" of the past and the future through remembrance and expectation refers in its own way to lived experiences, where what we now "re-present" was once, or will be, immediately given as present. "Yesterday" is an elapsed "today," "right away" is an impending "now," etc. Accordingly, present consciousness is origi-nary time-consciousness, and thus the first project for constitutive analysis is to ferret out within this dimension any types of manners of givenness that are unthematic for consciousness in the natural attitude—manners of givenness that motivate my conviction that it is possible to "re-present" lived experiences that we have actualized in the past and thereby to organize them in an irre-versible succession of temporal positions.

The unthematic manners of givenness we seek come to light when we re-flect and pay attention to the fact that present consciousness is in no way con-sciousness in a "now," lacking extension, taken as a punctual incision between past and future, but instead, consciousness has a certain extension in itself—an extension which is variable according to the experience. I experience the "pres-ent" concretely as the space of time of a soccer game, of writing a letter, of listening to a melody, etc. Within this extended present, there is a peak of ac-tualization which Husserl calls the *primordial impression,* which is then sur-rounded by a "halo" of just-having-been and just-coming. That which just-has-been is immediately still-present to me in its slipping away. I retain it *in* its fading, unthematically, that is, without my attention being directed specifically toward this holding-on-while-slipping-away. Similarly, that which is just enter-ing the now is also co-present. Only in this way, for example, are the beginning and end of a sentence present to us over and beyond the actually spoken sounds we hear in the flow of speaking, allowing us to hold on to a train of thought. Two unthematically functioning manners of givenness, *retention* and *proten-tion,* make this possible, stretching present consciousness so that it has a certain width, so to speak.

Retention develops our ability to "re-present" explicitly that which has passed in the following way. My momentary retention sinks—such is the origi-nary form of the continuous "flowing" of time—into the least distant past, and the now which was just actually taking place becomes a new retention. In this new, immediately actualized retention, however, the prior retention also remains immediately co-present, and so on. This interlocking of retentions into one another goes on continually, so that a "comet's tail of retentions" arises. This chain of retentions is thus preserved beyond the limit of current present consciousness, like something that has sunk down beneath the surface, and this makes it possible for me to rediscover what took place in the past through re-presentation. Husserl calls this explicit re-presentation "recollection," in order to differentiate it clearly from the immediate and early form of remembrance, namely, retention. When I recollect, I "wake up" what has sunk down—we might call them "sedimented presents"—and I am able to locate them in the past because I have a "sleeping," unthematically functioning consciousness of the chain of retentions from their place in the past up to the present, and I can refer to this consciousness. With this potentiability, my past-horizon is constituted as an accumulation of my past experiences that is linked to my present. The same goes for the development of my future-horizon. In this way, consciousness acquires its inner temporal horizon and thus a pre-objective, formal basis for the objectivity of all things.

Consciousness of the objective time of perceived objects is thus based upon this foundation, although this consciousness cannot come about without the contribution of the rest of the achievements of constitution that support perception, to which we already referred. In addition, the "living" and the "spiritual-personal" regions of being are brought to givenness by consciousness on further levels of constitution. On all levels, constitution carries itself out as synthesis, that is, as the unifying of multiplicity. Primordial synthesis is "transitional synthesis," known to me unthematically in every presenting while the chain of retentions continually push on. Pre-objectively, I am aware of the sliding, sinking away of what is retained as well as of its complement, the continual coming-upon me of what is protended, and I experience how every present stretches through this transitional period into a "field of presence." The consciousness that protention, primordial impression, and retention are inseparably bound together in this transition period of the extended present is the first consciousness of unity-in-multiplicity, and thus it is the primordial form of any synthesis that I may carry out. The originary constitution of the form of time in inner time-consciousness is repeated and modified on every level of constitution, a process which Husserl occasionally calls "temporalizing." Given this, Husserl explains programmatically in his later work, the *Crisis*, that "all constitution, of every type and level of existence, is a temporalizing."[15] In this way, the analysis of the original development of time has a meaning that surpasses all else for Husserl.

Husserl explicitly showed later in his life that all achievements of synthesis are modifications of the primordial synthesis of time-consciousness; he exemplified this especially with reference to those essential facts with which phenomenology was especially interested because of its own method.[16]

Essences, as universal objects, appear to us in the natural attitude as timeless, as beyond time. But if we look at their originary manners of givenness in eidetic variation more carefully, this supposed being-beyond-temporality proves actually to be a special type of temporality. If we relate essential universalities back to our experience of time, then they exist "everywhere and nowhere."

This means that, on the one hand, we can produce the idea of universals at any time in our consciousness, and we can repeat this production in any random now ("everywhere"). In this sense, essential universals are "*ideal*" objects, because the contrary of the ideal, namely, real things, are "*real*" in that they are located once and for all in the datable succession of presents in objective time. On the other hand, the flip side of this ideality is that universal objects are "irreal," meaning that they have no position or duration in objective time ("nowhere"). In this way, even the supposed timelessness of universals relates back through its manners of givenness to the temporality of consciousness.[17]

In the second chapter of his analyses of inner time-consciousness, a certain problematic thrusts Husserl into a dimension even deeper than the constitution of the inner time-horizon outlined above. We are dealing here with the most difficult—although the most fascinating—problematic of Husserl's phenomenology, one which repeatedly captivated him, from his early analyses of time into his last years.

Consciousness owes its unity to the ego, which allows me to recognize all of my lived experiences as "mine." In reflection, I can direct my attention to my own ego, making it my theme, making it an object facing me—and this is precisely the work of transcendental phenomenology. Meanwhile, however, I— the I who is reflecting—remain always and irremovably on this side of this objective representation (*Vergegenständlichung*).[18] Thus there is a "primordial ego" that can never be objectified. In fact, because this primordial ego is not at all an objectivity, the character of phenomenology is finally established as transcendental philosophy. The ego can only reflect on itself, though, because it already "knows" of itself as "primordial ego" before any explicit reflection. This pre-objective self-consciousness, however, is nothing other than time-consciousness in the primordial form of its originarity: I slip away from myself into the past in every moment of my conscious life, and yet at the same time, I am constantly retentionally aware of myself. This primordial retention is the most original synthesis. In this synthesis I have always already identified myself with myself—prior to any type of objectification—and simultaneously, I have also always already gained the first distance from myself. Through this pre-objective self-identification, my primordial ego, on the one hand, is something unchanging, that is, it is standing and remaining; on the other hand, through this pre-objective self-distancing, it is something living and streaming, that is, something that can become something different in comparison to what it was before. Thus my ego, in its deepest dimension, is a living being, wherein "standing" and "streaming" are one.

Husserl calls this dimension the "*living present*" in his unpublished research manuscripts dealing with this topic, written in the 1930s. In his texts on the *Phenomenology of Inner Time-Consciousness,* composed two decades earlier, he admits that "the names are still missing" for these deepest connections between ego and time. His questioning back toward the living present, arising at this late point in his life, was for Husserl the last and most radical step of the "phenomenological reduction" through which phenomenology proves itself as transcendental philosophy. In his *Critique of Pure Reason,* Kant described the origin of time as the hidden "art of the human soul" which is inaccessible to us. Husserl decided to take the risk, trying to unravel the secret of time through his analyses of the living present.

5. Intersubjectivity[19]

Given the "objectivity" of things in the perceived, material world, consciousness has not yet reached objectivity (*Objektivität*) in the narrower, common sense of the word. In today's everyday speech as well as in scientific discussions, objectivity means valid for everyone: such objectivity is taken to be the form of knowledge that is most worth striving for—especially in our day and age when we believe so strongly in the sciences. That which is objective in the sense emphasized here is that which, when apprehended, is independent of all situations as they are experienced by different, experiencing subjects. In Husserl's terms, something objective is that which always appears the same in the "intersubjective" multiplicity of its manners of givenness. Objectivity understood in this way presupposes *intersubjectivity,* that is, the interrelation of subjects among themselves. For this reason, an explanation of this type of objectivity first requires an analysis of the constitution of intersubjectivity.

One might mistake the goal of this constitutive analysis if one hoped for a phenomenological description of the different forms of community, such as friendship, family, society, state, and so on. What mainly interests Husserl here is the possibility of objectivity: how can objects appear to different people in the same way in spite of people's different experiential situations? Asked more radically: how can we explain the fact that not only does every individual consciousness have an experiential world that is exclusively its own, but together they also possess an experienced world that is common to them all, that is, a universal horizon that surrounds their subjective horizons?

This question gains exceptional meaning for Husserl because only by answering it can he prevent phenomenology from faltering. As a transcendental philosophy, phenomenology supports itself upon a methodical procedure of reflection. But I can only reflect as an individual. I describe the appearance of the world experienced by me in the manners of givenness actualized by me. But these analyses could only be carried out in egocentric form, with the one being addressed always only being myself, if it were impossible for us to come to an understanding through referring to common objects. Importantly, these common objects include the themes of phenomenological investigation. Transcendental phenomenology as science, which I not only carry out "solipsistically," alone by myself, but also together with many others, is thus held back as long as I, through constitutive analyses, cannot account for how an "objective" (in the narrower sense) world common to all of us is possible.

I take the objects of our shared world—as I take all given things that are in some sense in-themselves—to be objective because they transcend the situatedness of their manners of givenness. For this reason, Husserl must ask, through what type of transcendence does an objective thing—in the strongest sense of the word—constitute itself? When we speak here of situatedness, we mean being situated in the differentness of each individual subject's experience of the world. The limitation to our individual experiences in our subjective worlds is released through the transcendence of objects. In order to track down how this transcendence originally and originarily comes to be for consciousness, Husserl must begin methodically from the lived, experienced horizon of a person who has never heard anything from other subjects and their view of the world.

Thus Husserl begins his analysis with this thought-experiment: I refrain from all those determinations that maintain our shared world as experienced not only by me, but also by many people. Through this abstraction, one experiential horizon is left over wherein everything appears exclusively to me with the determinations that can only have been obtained out of my own intentional lived experiences. Husserl describes this abstractively reduced world as primordial,[20] taken from the Latin word *"primordium"* ("origin"); the methodical operation which carves out my "sphere of ownness" he describes as the *primordial reduction.*

From the perspective of the primordial world, the objective world-for-everyone reveals additional determinations that transcend primordiality and that return us to the fact that my world is also experienced by others. Husserl calls that which exceeds the primordial world "foreign," or "ego-foreign." This foreignness is primarily made up of the characteristics of the world that are obtained by other people. But these other subjects also transcend my primordial world. Thus they, too, are something foreign, and they are, according to Husserl's thesis, that which is first and originarily experienced as ego-foreign in the order of foundation. He argues that, by virtue of the fact that my world is co-experienced by subjects who transcend my primordial sphere, the world obtains the characteristic that it is a shared world with contents that are taken as objective for everyone.

This argumentation is questionable. From a phenomenological standpoint, there is more reason to believe that people originarily exist as forgetting themselves in our shared world, and that they first encounter themselves as a different or even a foreign person emerging from this sense of commonality. This is Heidegger's conception in *Being and Time.* On the other hand, Husserl's analyses on this topic become interesting for those who are interested in what phenomenology has to say with regard to the foundations and forms of shared human life. From this perspective, Husserl's claims might inspire social philosophers, even though social relations were not his main concern. In this area, the work of Alfred Schutz has become quite well known. Schutz's analysis of Husserl had an important result, though. The key term "life-world" has been extensively interpreted since then as "social life-world"—a meaning that Husserl definitely did not consider originally. "Life-world" was for Husserl, as we will see, a scientific-critical, not a social-philosophical, concept. Since then, the social-philosophical aspect of this concept has become central to the thought of Jürgen Habermas.

What motivates me to transcend my primordial sphere toward what is first foreign to me, that is, to other subjects, toward another subject? In order to resolve this constitutive problem, Husserl refers consistently, first, to the basic difference between originary and non-originary consciousness, and second, to the fundamental, lived experience of perception. In every perception, as we have already mentioned, that which is presently given, the "presented," refers me unthematically to what is co-present, "appresented," motivating me to envision the latter along with the former. Now, if it is possible that I am motivated in my primordial world toward the transcendence of this world, then this can only happen by my appresenting something not present in something that is primordially present. This present is the body of the other person, a body which, from within my primordiality, I do not yet know is the living body of another person. This body motivates me to appresent the other person appearing immediately within it, in its transcendence. In this way, a body that appears in my primordial world is apprehended as the living body of another person. This apperception is the first step of the constitution of intersubjectivity. According to Husserl, all experiences of living together in a shared world, and all forms of socialization, are built upon this first step.

Based upon what we have said so far, the fundamental task for Husserl's theory of intersubjectivity is to differentiate the appresentation of our experience of foreign egos from the appresentation of our normal perception of things (where our perception of things does not exceed my sphere of ownness), thus bringing out the special features of foreign-ego appresentation. It is a very subtle, but also highly problematic, analysis.

We will have to satisfy ourselves here with drawing our attention to certain crucial points of this theory. One of the first of such points is Husserl's recourse to his theory of association. The motivation to transcend my primordial sphere derives from the peculiar way another body appears; through its "demeanor," it reminds me of my own body. This "something reminds me of something" is the basic form of association, which Husserl calls "pairing."

Through other bodies, I can be reminded of my own, because my body is at the same time my "living body" (*Leib*). I have a pre-objective consciousness of my living body—and herein lies a second essential point—mainly because I carry out kinesthetic movements with it through perceiving. Meanwhile, my material living body is always known to me as something that is "here"; in my living body, I am always "here." This lived-bodily Here wanders along with me, so to speak, wherever I might go, thus creating an absolute point of reference for my spatial orientation, one which I can never give up. Compared to my material living body, I encounter every other body as "there."[21]

This associative consciousness relating the similarity of these two bodies, in which mine dwells "here" and the other "there," awakens in me two possible conceptions; in Husserl's terms, two potentialities are motivated in me. First, I can imagine in real expectation that I could go over there sometime in the *future* where the other body *now* is located, and that I could have recourse to the same demeanor then as she does now; of course, I am located presently with my material living body "here" and not "there." Second, I can put myself into the demeanor of the other person *now* already—not really, but in fantasy—and imagine that I was there. In this way, I am already there presently, even if it is only fictively, in the form of an "as if."

Both possible conceptions, the real and the fictive, can now work together —this is a salient point in Husserl's analyses, one which he did not make very clear himself. Both potentialities begin to complement each other mutually only at the point when the body that really appears "there" not just incidentally, but continually, reminds me of my own living-bodily behavior through its demeanor. It is only through fantasy that the possibility arises for me to recognize a being similar to myself behind the demeanor of that body. Of course, I would never realize that another, foreign consciousness is appearing over there on the basis of fantasy alone. In other words, I cannot recognize an ego that is different from me and with which I can never become identical only through fantasy. In fiction, I can always only create other presentations of my *self;* I can only imagine modifications of my own self. But I also have the capability of picturing my being "there" as a real possibility in my future, and therefore, through the real difference that exists now between the Here of my living-body and the There of that body, I become aware that there is a real difference between my ego and the ego in that body there, which through my fantasy had appeared as a modification of my ego. In this way, the ego in that body there is transformed for me from a simple, fictive modification of my self into a real "other," a "foreign" ego, that is, into a being similar to me, into whom I may think myself in my understanding, with whom I may "*empathize,*" but with whom I am not identical.

In this way, a new apperception arises through a blending of my real consciousness of difference (connected to the difference between Here and There) with the modification of my ego in fantasy. On the basis, first, of the pairing association of both bodies' demeanors, and second, of my consciousness as living-body, I conceive the demeanor of the other body as the appearance of a foreign ego. In this way, the being of another person is constituted for me originarily.

In the other body (which I encounter as something presented "there"), the other person (for whom that body is her living-body) is co-present to me. This appresentation differentiates itself fundamentally from any appresentation in primordial perception in that I never have the possibility (potentiality) of making that co-present manner of givenness into one which is actualized by me: in fact, co-presence is the condition in which any body there is given to me as the living-body of another ego. I can never become that other ego. In other words, the other body can never be given to me as my own living-body. This means that the other body can never become my absolute Here for me, that is, it will always be "there." Thus in the final analysis, the subjects of Husserl's theory of intersubjectivity encounter each other as "others" because their existence in the world is bound to the absolute Here of each individual's living-body, and because these living-bodies—as the bodies that belong to them—can never occupy the same There at the same time. Herein lies the originary source of "the experience of foreign egos."

6. Genetic Phenomenology and the Origin of Modern Science[22]

The study of constitution, which we have been presenting, is basically made up of several theories. Each one of these theories is related to a layer of foundation, or rather, a region of being. Through this, however, the appearance of the world, the whole of existence, that into which phenomenology as transcendental philosophy inquires, disintegrates into the appearance of different domains of objects. But Husserl's actual objective is to understand how our natural belief in the being of the *world* is constituted. The whole of the world is hardly the sum of all self-contained groups of objects; rather, it is the *universal horizon* of all horizons. This means that it is simply the comprehensive realm of my potentiabilities that are all interconnected through referential relations. After drafting *Ideas I,* Husserl envisioned his project: to producing a whole systematic interrelation between the individual theories of constitution, a system that would explain ever more clearly how all the horizons of intentional consciousness are unified in one world-consciousness.

We already mentioned this claim to combine all the theories of constitution in Section 3. As long as Husserl proceeded from the assumption of passive, pre-given sensational data which was both immanent to consciousness and worldless (allowing consciousness's relation to the world to be established as an activity built upon passivity), however, he could not assertively expand his analysis from the constitution of objects to one of world constitution. For this reason, he had to give up the idea of two levels of consciousness, passivity and activity (based on Kant's distinction between receptivity and spontaneity), and he had to show, first, that the passive pre-conditions of perception already contain activity—which we have already discussed here—and, second, that all active, apperceptive achievements for their part are subsumed by passivity.

In his later works Husserl calls these active achievements "*primordial foundation.*" A primordial foundation takes place when consciousness—not that of some individual, but that of a speech- or culture-community (however we define it)—surpasses its prior objective horizon, moving on to a new type of objectivity, for example, when a new tool is invented. All objects of human culture have been constituted at one time through such an object-forming achievement of primordial foundation. With every primordial foundation, consciousness acquires the potentiability to come back at any time to this new type of objectivity; in other words, the experience of the object in question becomes habit. This *"habitualization,"* or also *"sedimentation,"* is a passive process, meaning it is not a process that can be actively set in motion by me as the actualizer. In fact, the creative act of primordial foundation normally falls into the world of the forgotten. Our habits become unthematically familiar with the potentiability of experiencing different types of objects. This means, however, that, through the passive habitualization of primordial foundation, a horizon develops in which consciousness can live without continually having to re-actualize the original emergence of this horizon in its active primordial foundation.

With this, the theory of constitution acquires a whole new dimension. Inner history, or *"genesis,"* where horizonal consciousness develops and enriches itself, becomes its main theme. This theory of genetic constitution divides itself into two main areas. Not every horizon can be based upon the habitualization of a primordial foundation, because then every primordial foundation would presuppose that the objective horizon which it is transcending (in order to go toward a new objectivity) goes back to a primordial foundation, and that this does the same, and so on. As such, the questioning back to past primordial foundations would be infinite, which is impossible. There must be certain horizons that consciousness "always already" has at its disposal, that is, horizons that have never been founded at one specific time through an active, apperceptive achievement. Therefore, the activity of primordial founding presupposes a *passive genesis* of elementary horizons. This genesis has no beginning that sets it up in the inner history of consciousness; rather, it takes place at all times. The constitutional events that are "underneath" the level of perception are involved in this genesis, especially the original development of time in the "living present," "association," and kinesthetic consciousness. All of these passive processes, which are continually in motion, already prefigure activity. For this reason, there is a smooth transition from passive genesis to the second area with which the theory of genetic constitution is concerned, *the active genesis* of primordial foundation. This activity, for its part, remains surrounded by passivity by means of the "secondary passivity" of habitualization.

Only at this point, with the phenomenology of active and passive genesis, do we find a phenomenology that systematically unifies all constitutional events to one whole interrelation; this discovery further engenders the idea that consciousness does not constitute isolated objects but, instead, constitutes horizons and thereby the world. Therefore, the phenomenological method finally becomes transcendental philosophy only through an inquiry into the whole of existence with regard to its appearing for consciousness.

The discovery of this dimension of conscious history through the theory of genetic constitution made it possible for Husserl to reintroduce his phenomenology in his last works, in a different way. In the *Crisis,* he presents transcendental phenomenology as the only applicable diagnosis of the crisis of the senses that arose through the modern "scientizing" of our world and lives. This diagnosis presupposes a corresponding "medical history": Husserl conceives all of modern science to be the result of a series of primordial foundations in the history of science and philosophy, the last of which—and most relevant for us—was the institution of the modern, mathematically based, natural sciences.

Every primordial foundation, as the active constitution of a new objectivity, exceeds an unthematic, familiar horizon of objects. With this surfaces the "belief of being" maintained by a consciousness which lives in the natural attitude: objects are ascribed objective existence, that is, they appear as irrelative to unthematic manners of givenness, and thus as irrelative to the horizonal consciousness in which these manners of givenness are embedded. With the primordial foundation of the cultural image of "philosophy and science," the whole of the world was objectified, becoming a theme of research for the first time in human history. Through the method of the modern natural sciences, the modern ideal of unconditional scientific objectivity then arose through a new primordial foundation: anything scientifically valid should be free from all relativity, itself due to subjective givenness. Thus, the scientifically identifiable world existing in itself is understood as radically disconnected from all subjective experiential horizons.

This ideal of objectivity is hardly self-evident, however. Rather, it is the product of an achievement of our apprehension that came along with the primordial foundation of modern science. For example, we can compare the attitudes of ancient and medieval scientists toward the world to today's attitude. Ancient science was understood as *"theoria,"* meaning it was understood as a mental intuition which observed that which is knowable without any thought to how it could be used, that is, observing it in how it shows itself *from itself.* The relation of the modern scientist to his object of study—which in most cases was nature itself—was appropriately characterized by Kant through a famous comparison made in his *Critique of Pure Reason.*[23] the modern researcher definitely lets nature teach him, but not like a "student who simply recites everything that the instructor wants," but instead like a "judge who requires the witnesses to answer the questions he submits to them." This image of "requiring the witnesses" is intended to describe the modern researcher's methodical and ordered placement of the conditions of his observation. Experimentation that uses such conditions of observation bestows a technical character upon research from the very beginning. Thus a technical spirit rules in modern science even before it actually uses technology. This spirit is that of success, the effectiveness of its methods. A technique is successful when the object of study is caused to show more of itself than it would have shown on its own.

Because such a methodical, modern theory forces objects to reveal themselves, it necessarily gives us confidence that, in principle, nothing can escape the clutches of research any longer. This does not mean that everything has already been investigated, but that, basically, everything appears investigat*able* in the optimism of this science. The investigative process may well extend into eternity, but it is carried by the conviction that every object, with the help of the appropriate methods, *can* be brought to reveal itself. In this sense the unified spirit of investigation taken up by all individual sciences is related generally to the sum of all objects. The world becomes a theme for all of modern science, but here the "world" is understood as the totality of objects. The world as thematized by transcendental phenomenology, on the contrary, is the universal horizon, meaning the realm of all our potentiabilities of experiencing objects as organized through referential interconnections. Husserl's thesis is the following: in the theory of the pre-modern period, the world may well have appeared as the totality of objects—as it does in the modern period—but it also retained its horizonal character at the same time.

The fact that the world was still understood as horizon in pre-modern science comes to light in that the pre-given conditions under which objects reveal themselves were not touched. This means that, in pre-modern science, the embeddedness of objects in their related experiential horizons was preserved. The canon of these ancient sciences resulted because they reflected the horizons of pre-scientific life. For example, algebra arose because there was a lot of counting and calculating already in everyday situations and occupations. This is similar for geometry, medicine, jurisprudence, etc. In fact, these old names still express their link back to lived horizons: before any philosophy and science, one had to measure (*geometrein*) the land, search for the remedy (*medicina*) for sickness, form the lawfully ordered relations to others with wisdom (*prudentia*), etc.

These ancient sciences, with their links to horizons, connect to the pre-scientific "practical arts" of humankind, to the art of measuring, of healing, etc. The Greeks called such knowledge, this knowing how to do something upon which such arts were based, *téchne*. With the radical suspension of this link to our horizons, though, this practice in scientific learning must render itself independent *as* a practice. Because it is indifferent to pre-given horizons, modern science can only be regulated by itself. In this sense, it becomes a "simple" *téchne,* as Husserl says. This "simple" means that we no longer know how to do things through our tie to horizons—in the Greek sense of the term *téchne*—but instead we operate in an immanent, "technical" way—in the modern sense of the word—one that is based on its own effectiveness.

Pre-modern science could only set up *finite* projects because of their horizonality. "Horizon" literally means "boundary line," "limit." A horizon may not determine everything that will in fact come forward with regard to objects, but it does determine what *can* arise in it in general. The limitations of scientific areas of study and the corresponding finiteness of their projects in early science resulted from the limits that were indicated by horizons. When we loosen our tie to horizons—with the final goal of completely breaking that tie—then any pre-given boundaries (taken from our pre-scientific life-praxis), which would divide the sciences into manageable quantities, would fall away. This is why today the door is wide open to unlimited specializing in the sciences. The entire realm of the sciences in general, as well as their individual projects, rid themselves of the limits set for them by our tie to horizons. Such limitless science can set itself the goal of investigating all of existence in its infinity, an infinity that transcends all partial horizons.

Husserl shows how the methods of modern research, which are indifferent to horizons, arise from a pre-modern science that is tied to horizons by showing how the modern study of nature has been mathematized. Husserl interprets this mathematization as the radical suspension of our ability to intuit natural knowledge of the world. This suspension is only possible, however, because a tension between intuitability and unintuitability already exists in our natural knowledge of the world—a tension we already discussed in our section on perception.

Our experience of the world is thus doubled: By actualizing unthematic manners of givenness, intentional consciousness relies upon the referential interconnection of its potentialities (likewise unthematically familiar), because every manner of givenness is embedded in this referential interconnection. In actualizing originary manners of givenness, though, consciousness experiences intuitability. In this way, the world is intuited by consciousness as it moves through unthematic referential interconnections. The world appears to consciousness "*perspectivally*"—in the broad sense of the term to which we already referred—through horizons and manners of givenness. Consciousness constantly "de-perspectivizes" the perspectivity of its experience of the world by anticipating "the thing," the whole object, in the entirety of its manners of givenness. Every consciousness of an identical object, every objectification understood in this way, is this de-perspectivizing. The de-perspectivizing anticipation of the identity of a thing cannot be intuition, however, because "the thing" is never entirely given to consciousness. Thus the world—as the whole of anticipated identities—cannot be experienced through intuition. In the *Crisis,* Husserl calls such a constant de-perspectivizing through the anticipation of identities the "*inductivity*" of living, saying that people are guided by their anticipation of identities, that is, the world, and thus they can—at least roughly—predict and plan how their experience will proceed. The mathematization of modern science has its final root, according to Husserl's thesis, in an acceleration of this pre-scientific inductivity.

In the natural attitude, the world as the horizon of all horizons is simply unthematic; in other words, the universal horizon eludes all objectivating thematization. The belief—unthematic and self-evident—that the world exists in itself becomes concrete through our belief in the objective being of individual objects, objects toward which consciousness directs its attention with its de-perspectivizing anticipation of identity. As philosophy and science emerge, the world itself becomes thematic, that is, that which is basically unintuited becomes objectified. The identity of the world existing in itself, upon which natural consciousness unthematically places its confidence through its random knowledge of objects—without ever catching up to them in objectification—now becomes the object of an anticipation that transcends all natural inductivity. Insofar as this anticipated identity of object and world could never really be given in intuition, it is something ideal. In this sense, Husserl can label both the object and the world as *ideas*. Every *téchne,* though, as a pre-scientific knowing how to do something in the world, refers to specific objects, and thus is guided by anticipations of their identity. In this way, natural, inductive foresight lives from the anticipation of ideas in the "practical arts."

As long as the sciences did not give up their link back to the horizons of a pre-scientific *téchne,* the thematization of the world as an idea in philosophy and science could not yet deploy its full explosive power. When we remove the limits of the sciences, though, their object, the world, appears in its endlessness. Thus the world becomes an *"infinite idea"* for modern science. Unfortunately, this objectification of the world as infinite idea then rubs off onto the process of our scientific understanding of objects. The process becomes *"idealized."* Natural foresight becomes scientific "induction." In modern science, this inductive anticipation of the identity of objects—which hovers before us as an idea—bursts all the boundaries set by our link to pre-given horizons. All possible anticipations become, as Husserl says, "thought as if we had already run through them." In concrete scientific praxis, *"idealization"* consists in the mathematization of nature that characterizes modern natural science.

The methodical research of modern science, which is persistently placed upon mathematical foundations, becomes an approach to the world as an "infinite idea" that can never end; this means that it acquires the character of unending progress. This presupposes, though, that "the world" that science approaches in its progress exists prior to this progress and independent of it. Through this, however, the world (as science's "infinite idea") appears as an object that is free from all embeddedness in horizons. Our natural "belief of being" thus works itself into an extreme in modern science: in the being-in-itself of the world, all trace of any reference to the subject and the perspectivity of its world-experience is extinguished. This radical liberation of scientific knowledge from any limitation by subject-relative manners of givenness, this unconditional "objectivity," becomes our highest norm.

7. The Life-World and the Critique of Objectivism[24]

As far as the basic foundational concepts of modern science are concerned, the world is conceived as an infinite idea. Due to the passive sedimentation of all apperceptions, this foundational concept, like all primordial foundations, becomes commonplace. As a result the historical-conscious origin of this ideal of objectivity is forgotten. In other words, the norm calling for unconditional objectivity becomes self-evident, and the epistemological position called *"objectivism"* arises. But this position leads to a crisis of meaning in modern science, and further, to a crisis of life in a world ruled by science.

This radically neutralized world, stripped of its horizons, is something inhuman. Freedom is actually what is most human for Husserl, where freedom is understood as the responsibility that I possess as a transcendental primordial ego, unable to be captured by any objectification. I am responsible for my activity, and activity means seizing possibilities. Furthermore, possibilities are possibilities-in-the-world, that is, they lie ready as the potentiabilities of horizonal consciousness. In this way, horizons are the playing fields of experience, opened in and through someone's activity; they are inseparable from people as responsible, active subjects. The attempt of modern research to separate the being of the world radically from its horizonal-perspectival appearance, however, necessarily leads to our losing the connection between research and responsible activity. Modern research, which is understood as an unending process of methodical-technical steps meant to force the world (as infinite idea) into unending self-revelation, becomes an independent activity, exempt of responsibility. Therefore, the legitimacy of modern research becomes, alarmingly, based only on itself. The "crisis of European sciences" of which Husserl speaks in the title of his late work is the loss of meaning that results from such a purely subject-irrelative world that, if it really were to exist, would abolish all human responsibility.

This discomforting aspect of life in a totally scientific world has grown since Husserl. At the same time, we cannot see any way out of this crisis because the origin of objectivism has been forgotten. We do not recognize that even the world as an infinite idea, which is supposedly entirely subject-irrelative, is just the correlate of a specific, historically based epistemological position. Husserl exposes this forgottenness in the *Crisis*, reminding us that the belief in a totally de-perspectivized world, one which exists absolutely in itself, can only be primordially founded by transcending a comprehensive, albeit unthematic, subject-relative horizon.

Husserl calls this comprehensive horizon the "*life-world*," differentiating it from the world as a general object of scientific research and especially from the modern world as characterized by science. The modern scientific world refers back to the pre-scientific life-world through its sense of being an absolutely subject-irrelative world, which it acquired through its primordial foundation; without such a contrast to the subject-relative world, the ground would fall out from underneath this absolute world. Accordingly, the modern transcendence of what is scientifically objective remains tied to subjective activity; even this transcendence cannot escape the universal correlation between objectivity and its subjective-situated appearing in manners of givenness. The scientific world, which supposedly exceeds the subject-relativity of the life-world's horizons, is still caught in the tow of this subject-relativity. In other words, the objects of science are sense-formations that owe their existence to the subjective achievements of a particular theoretical and logical praxis—and this praxis itself belongs to life in the life-world.

Husserl shows that the modern praxis of research is embedded in the life of the life-world through two circumstances. Both are trivial observations, but they gain a meaning that is far from trivial if we consider their background, where epistemic praxis is reconstructed as an idealization and mathematization of natural induction.

The first observation: in order to conduct his scientific praxis, the modern researcher requires various means that are given to him through intuition. For example, he uses instruments of measure with some kind of graduation marks that he needs to read, in which case he relies upon his immediate visual impressions. Or he speaks with other researchers or reads their articles. In every situation, he is convinced that what he is immediately seeing or hearing exists as something. Like every "belief of being," this belief is based upon the researcher's indisputable, yet self-evident, presupposition: if necessary, I could convince myself of the being of that which I am encountering through my immediate experience of these instruments by actualizing the appropriate originary manners of givenness. But the fact that we can actualize these horizonal possibilities at any time remains unthematic; only that which is known—without being directly intuited—is thematic. The fact that we have these potential intuitions at our disposal is something so self-evident that even the observation we just mentioned, which reminds us of this obvious situation, sounds trivial. This triviality, however, merely reflects the fact that the intuited world—in which the modern researcher lives and moves and which he clearly presupposes—has the character of being unthematic.[25]

Husserl first introduces the concept of "life-world" in the *Crisis* as a title for this unthematic, intuited world. He points out that the researcher, in his praxis of gaining knowledge, remains irrevocably in a situation where he has to rely upon intuited manners of givenness; but, insofar as this is the case, the known horizon of intuitability creates, in these intuited manners of givenness, the ground upon which the researcher bases his research. In this sense, as Husserl says, the life-world is the *"ground of intuition."* Although the modern scientist deals with a world that transcends all the intuited horizons found in the natural praxis of gaining knowledge (because he considers the scientific world to be infinite), his knowledge remains connected back to a world that appears in these intuited horizons which are not included by scientific praxis. This world is the life-world.

Now we turn to the second circumstance that reveals the rootedness of the modern praxis of research in the life of the life-world. To be exact, while we only make use of objects in our pre-scientific praxis on the basis of our anticipations of identity which transcend intuition, it is horizonal consciousness which actually makes it possible for us to handle these objects as if they were given to us as immediately intuited. This means that these objects belong, for their part, to a horizonal, unthematic reserve of our potential experiences. This even applies to the objects that are only available to us because we have used modern, mathematized science—an unintuited knowledge—for the industrial manufacture of technical products. For this reason, Husserl's observation seems trivial. We operate the light switch or turn on the television, and we avail ourselves of these behavioral possibilities without ever having to thematize what these objects actually are, taken as scientific, technical objects. This is possible in principle because all the results of any anticipation of identity that is de-perspectivized and that transcends intuition—and thereby all objects gained through scientific idealization—sink down into the reserve of unthematic, horizonal, pregiven possibilities of our praxis. Here the idea of "sedimentation" from the genetic theory of constitution comes into play. That which has been de-perspectivized through every activity of idealization "re-perspectivizes" itself, becoming a component of the world that appears in the horizons of intuition of our non-scientific praxis. Husserl describes this process in the *Crisis* as a "*streaming-in*" into the life-world.[26] Streaming-in shows that the methodological praxis of knowledge remains embedded in non-scientific praxis; otherwise, its results, along with this very methodological praxis, could not move into the horizon of a non-scientific praxis as unthematically familiar, becoming applicable in and on this foundation.

With the theory of streaming-in, a new aspect of the life-world is revealed. In its basic meaning as intuited world, "life-world" can be used as a term of contrast to the unintuited world of science. As a consequence of genetic sedimentation, however, the objectified results of any praxis that transcends intuition—and this includes those results of modern technological praxis based upon idealization—flow into the intuitable horizons of non-scientific praxis. The transformed world that appears unthematically in these horizons is also the life-world. Thus "life-world" loses its character as a contrasting concept. The universal horizon, not only for pre-scientific praxis (which is bound to its horizons and thus is bound to intuition), but also for the praxis of gaining knowledge in modern research (which radically transcends intuition), is the life-world. This means that, in this sense, the life-world in its "universal concretion," as Husserl says, is nothing other than a comprehensive world, the universal horizon to which the "belief of being" of the natural attitude refers. Of course, this concept of the world is essentially richer compared to its earlier formulation; the world of the natural attitude is now a world that enriches itself historically through the praxis that takes place in it and its sedimentation, through "streaming-in." It is the concrete, historical world.

Philosophy, according to its own traditional understanding of itself, is that which asks about the whole of being in general. But because modern science, through its methodically controlled individual investigations, thematizes the world as infinite idea, and thus thematizes the whole of being, one could get the impression that philosophy has become superfluous. The specialized individual sciences seem to take this question away from philosophy and to answer it more effectively than the philosophical tradition. For his last introduction to transcendental philosophy, however, Husserl chooses in the *Crisis* to criticize this position of modern science. His critique shows that the theme of philosophy is the world as a subject-relative, universal horizon that enriches itself historically, that is, as the life-world. The world understood in this way is forgotten in the modern praxis of objectivistic research. Transcendental philosophy, however, is based upon reflection; it is a consideration of the responsible subject to whom the world appears. Therefore, while an attitude toward the world that is dominated by science will forget not only the subject-relativity of horizonal consciousness but also the subject itself, philosophy reveals itself as necessary even today because the responsibility of active subjects must be kept alive. Further, philosophy is possible because we can prove, through the theory of genetic horizonal constitution, that objectivistic science relates back to and is dependent upon life-worldly experience.

Just because we have lifted the veil of forgetfulness of the life-world from modern science does not mean for Husserl that we must give up our efforts toward scientific knowledge in general. Rather, with a phenomenological "*science of the life-world*," the demand for unbiased world-knowledge—which was primordially founded with the origin of philosophy and science—should reach fulfillment. With the passing of time, the objectivism of modern science distorted and relativized this demand. Objectivism infringes upon science's original ideal of being unbiased by causing us to forget the subjective genesis of all horizons; in other words, by favoring the objective side of knowledge, science becomes an aggressively one-sided understanding of truth.[27] With the primordial foundation of science's intention to obtain unbiased world-knowledge, according to Husserl, a norm for knowledge was set up that became valid for all of humanity. As the "officials of humanity," philosophers who think transcendental-phenomenologically give an account of the extent to which philosophical-scientific thinking has lived up to the intention behind its primordial foundation. And in this historical-phenomenological comparison between science's original intentions and their fulfillment up until now, humanity realizes its rational responsibility to itself.

Notes

This essay is a translation of Klaus Held, "Einleitung," in *Edmund Husserl: Phänomenologie der Lebenswelt, Ausgewählte Texte* (Stuttgart: Reclam, 1986), 5–53.

1. Cf. *Literarische und naturwissenschaftliche Intelligenz. Dialog über die "zwei Kulturen*," ed. H. Kreuzer (Stuttgart: Klett, 1969).

2. For a better understanding of the concepts that are presented in a rather condensed manner over the next few pages, see especially Sections 6–8 of the first essay in this volume, where I provide a more comprehensive discussion.

3. For more on the concept of "transcendental," see Section 7 of the first essay in this volume.

4. For a closer look at this method, turn to Section 5 of the first essay in this volume, as well as the section "Fact and Essence" in *Ideen I*, part I, chap. 1; *Erfahrung und Urteil*, §§86–89; and *The Essential Husserl*, §15.

5. With regard to the classification of "regional ontologies," cf. the entire structure of *Ideen II*.

6. *The Essential Husserl*, §6.

7. Cf. Section 3 of the first essay in this volume as well as *Formal and Transcendental Logic*, §§8 and 56–67; *The Essential Husserl*, 238–39, 259–72.

8. Cf. Section 6 of the first essay in this volume.

9. Cf. Section 8 of the first essay in this volume as well as §41 of *Ideen II*; *The Essential Husserl*, 70–72.

10. Cf. §41 of *Ideen I* as well.

11. For a closer look at the method of the "epochē" see Section 6 of the first essay in this volume as well as §§31 and 32 of *Ideen I*; *The Essential Husserl*, 63–65.

12. *The Essential Husserl*, §§10 and 12.

13. Cf. Section 8 of the first essay in this volume.

14. *The Essential Husserl*, §11.

15. Husserl, *Krisis*, p. 172; *Crisis*, p. 169.

16. Cf. Section 5 of the first essay in this volume as well as the section "Fact and Essence," *Ideen I*, part I, chap. 1; *Erfahrung und Urteil*, §§86–89; and *The Essential Husserl*, 292–99.

17. Cf. Husserl, *Erfahrung und Urteil*, 303ff.; *Experience and Judgment*, 253ff.

18. With regard to the following, cf. Section 8 of the first essay in this volume.

19. *The Essential Husserl*, §§9 and 10.

20. Husserl says "primordinal" at least as often as he says "primordial" in his numerous analyses on intersubjectivity, but "primordinal" is not correct according to the Latin origin of the word. Thus we will always be using the term "primordial."

21. With regard to the whole theory of body (*Körper*) and living-body (*Leib*), cf. *Ideen II*, 143ff.; *Ideas II*, 151ff.; *The Essential Husserl*, 175ff.

22. *The Essential Husserl*, §§17, 18, and 20.

23. Cf. Kant, *Critique of Pure Reason*, B XIII.

24. *The Essential Husserl*, §21.

25. Cf. Husserl, *Krisis*, 452f.

26. Cf. Husserl, *Krisis*, 115, 141, annotations 213 and 466; *Crisis*, 113, 138.

27. Cf. Section 3 of the first essay in this volume.

PART II

Intentionality, Types, and Time

3

The Structure of Intentionality

John J. Drummond

WHEN FRANZ BRENTANO revived the scholastic term "intentionality" to identify the distinguishing characteristic of psychic phenomena, he departed from an unmistakable and obvious fact of our experience: "in presentation something is presented, in judgement something is affirmed or denied, in love loved, in hate hated, in desire desired, and so on."[1] But this fact of the directedness of experience to an object is no less remarkable and mysterious for being unmistakable and obvious.

We ordinarily think of the knower and the known as two, as externally related to one another in the world. At the same time, however, we recognize that the object is in some sense given "in" the experience, that the experience in some sense grasps hold of and "possesses" its object, that the knowing "contains" what is known. From this perspective, the experience and its object are not externally related but internally united. How is it that our experiences—occurrences in subjects existing in the world—"contain" objects existentially distinct from themselves? What notion of "contents" can make sense of this self-transcending and object-containing nature of experience?

This question is complicated further by additional questions about veridicality and truth. Experience can appear to "go beyond itself" and "reach" an object, yet actually fail to do so in two ways: (1) sometimes our experiences "contain" objects that appear other than they actually are, and (2) sometimes our experiences "contain" or "reach" objects that do not actually exist.[2] So even if one were to account satisfactorily for how experience can transcend itself and truly apprehend an object, there is the difficulty presented by the fact that some experiences only appear to transcend themselves in this way. We must, therefore, come to understand not only how knowledge can "reach its object reliably," how it can be "in agreement" with its object, but how it can fail to do so. What notion of "contents" can make sense of the transcending character of experience such that we can distinguish truthful from non-truthful experiences?

Experience, then, appears as a riddle[3] and subjectivity as a paradox.[4] In experiencing objects in the world around us, consciousness transcends itself and achieves an objectivity shared with other conscious beings who exist in the world with us. The conscious subject is both subject *of* the world and subject *in* the world. Husserl's phenomenology is an attempt to solve this riddle and resolve this paradox, and his analyses of intentionality—both of the general structures of intentional consciousness and of particular kinds of experiences—are rich in detail and fruitful for continued study.

1. Real and Intentional Contents

Husserl's first detailed treatment of intentionality appears in the first edition of the *Logical Investigations* of 1900,[5] where he distinguishes between "the real [*reellen*] or phenomenological (descriptive-psychological) content of an act and its intentional content."[6] In other writings he identifies two real (*reell*) constituents in an act: the intentional apprehension and its sensuous contents.[7] Husserl isolates these constituents by means of imaginative variations. In considering perceptual acts, Husserl first imaginatively varies a perception such that the perceptual apprehension and its objective correlate remain constant but the object now *appears* differently; such changes in appearance, Husserl claims, are attributable to changes in the fullness and vivacity of the sensuous contents.[8] Examples of such perceptual variations occur in situations wherein an object is seen in varying illuminations or seen first through a mist and then not.[9] Such changes, according to Husserl, occasion correlative changes in the complex of sensations. Hence, "many perceptions essentially differentiated by their complex of sensations are and can be perceptions of one and the same object."[10] Husserl also varies the perception such that the sensuous complex remains the same but the perceptual apprehension and, correlatively, the perceived object change. Thus, "the same complex of sensation-contents can ground different perceptions, perceptions of different objects."[11] The example used to illustrate this case is a perception that undergoes modal variations and passes over into a new perception. For example, the perception of a person comes to be doubted in which case the perception might pass over into that of a mannequin.[12] What is really seen—clothing, hair, color, shape, and the like—remains the same, but the identical sensation-contents presenting these are subjected to different interpretations in the two perceptual apprehensions.

If A represents the apprehension, C the contents, and O the perceived object, then, beginning with the case $A_1(C_a) \rightarrow O_1$, the preceding variations yield the following results: $A_1(C_b) \rightarrow O_1$ and $A_2(C_a) \rightarrow O_2$. A consideration of the three schemata yields the conclusion that the determination of the object is a function of the perceptual apprehension or, alternately, that the sensations are neutral with respect to the object. However, such neutrality must not be understood as indeterminacy; the sensation-contents function as "presenting contents" in the perception of an individual, qualified spatial object.[13] They present the sensible features of the object and are "animated" by the apprehension, thereby bringing an object with its sensible properties to presentation.[14]

Husserl in the first edition of the *Investigations* also identifies three senses of "intentional content": (1) the intentional object of the act, (2) the matter of the act, and (3) the intentional essence of the act.[15] The matter of the act determines the *manner* in which the object is intended in the act, and it stands opposed to the quality of the act, that is, to that which makes the act the kind of act—for example, perceptual, memorial, judgmental—it is.[16] The act-matter is the "content which stamps [the act] as presenting this, judging that, etc."[17] and as "the sense of the objective apprehension."[18] The matter, in other words, determines the reference to this particular object and in a certain manner, precisely as such and such.[19] An act can have this intentional content in common with acts of different qualities; a perception and a memory, for example, can share the same matter. When acts of different qualities have a common matter, "the intentional objectivity is the same in the different acts."[20] Since the matter of the act determines a presentation as *this* presentation of the object, it is not enough to say merely that the object *which* is intended is identical in such acts; we must say also that in acts sharing a common matter the object is presented in identically the same manner. For example, my seeing my key in the ignition and my seeing it on the table, although qualitatively the same, are materially different: one presents the key as in the ignition, the other as on the table. On the other hand, my judging that the key is on the table presents the "key's being on the table" as judged; my wishing that the key be on the table presents the "key's being on the table" as wished. In these acts, the "content" or matter of the presentation is the same, but *how* this content is presented still differs; in one case the state of affairs is judged, in the other wished. This difference in the *how* of the presentation of an identical content is attributable to the different act-qualities, whereas the identity of the object intended (the key) and of the manner of its being intended (as on the table) is attributable to the fact that they share a common matter. The object as intended, then, manifests both these determinations: it is determined in a particular manner (*Weise*) and with a qualitative how (*Wie*) of presentation.

Husserl calls the combination of the matter and quality of an act its "intentional essence." The real content of the act is not exhausted, however, by the intentional essence.[21] Two acts might be identical with respect to both quality and matter and yet differ. Such would occur, for example, when viewing a blue and gray, striped necktie first under fluorescent lights while shopping, then in ordinary light. The object as intended in our perception occurring in ordinary daylight, that is, the perceived tie as striped blue and gray, is identical with the object as intended when we view it under fluorescent lighting in a department store. However, the fluorescent lighting varies the appearance of the colors, and, consequently, the perceptions vary descriptively. This variation Husserl attributes to a change in the sensuous contents of the act.[22] The variation introduced through the change of sensuous matter, however, is inessential. We continue to see the same object determined in the same manner with the same "how" of presentation. The intentional essence, in other words, characterizes the intention as this intention without completely specifying an act as this act. In the distinction between intentional essence and sensuous content, we find on the side of intentional content an echo of the distinction between the really contained apprehension and its sensuous contents.

Husserl claims in the first edition of the *Investigations* that the really contained apprehension is the instantiation of an intentional essence. He is led to this claim by the framework established by the distinction between real and intentional contents. The *Investigations* contains a descriptive, psychological account of the manner in which an act intends an object, but this account is developed by reference to the act's *intentional* contents, specifically its matter and intentional essence. But, on the first edition's own terms, the intentional contents are not—as noted earlier—to be included in the descriptive or phenomenological contents of the act and, by extension, not to be included in a phenomenological description. Something really contained in the act must determine its intentionality. However, in order to avoid the perils of psychologism, the objective content or objective sense of the act cannot be understood as a psychological reality. Husserl avoids psychologism, then, by making the really contained apprehension the instantiation of an essence that is not itself a psychological essence. The intentional essence is just such an essence.

By virtue of instantiating an intentional essence an act of a certain quality is directed toward an object in a certain manner.[23] Individual experiences are differentiated by their sensuous matter and, psychologically, by their subjects and whatever causal and associative factors are at work (or play) in that subject's experience. The quality and matter of the act serve as both the real contents and the intentional contents of an act. As instantiated, they are the real contents *by* which *this* act is directed to an object. As essential, they are intentional contents that transcend any particular subjective or psychological realities and are thereby capable of grounding an *intersubjective* awareness of an *objectivity*.

The claim that something must be common in different acts of a single subject or in the acts of different subjects, all of which are directed to the same object in the same manner, requires postulating an essential act-matter to underlie the commonality only to the extent that one is barred from appealing to the intentional object of the experience. The identity of content in these acts could be explained just as easily—and perhaps more plausibly—in terms of the identity of the intentional object itself. If we can appeal to the intentional content as matter and intentional essence to give an account of intentionality, why not simply appeal to the intentional content as intentional object to provide such an account? Such an appeal would, however, fly in the face of Husserl's caution in the first edition of the *Investigations* against using the expression "intentional content" to refer to the intentional object.[24]

2. The Phenomenological Reduction

In the second edition of the *Logical Investigations* (1913), there is a crucial change in the treatment of intentionality, a change whose significance is barely noted in the *Investigations* themselves and that reflects a train of thought finding its first detailed statement in the simultaneously published *Ideas I*. Whereas Husserl had in the first edition distinguished *between* the real or phenomenological content of an act and its intentional content, he now distinguishes *within* the phenomenological content of an act between its real and intentional contents.[25] In the first edition, only the real content—that is, the phenomenological or, as he also calls it, the "descriptive-psychological content"—of an act could be included in descriptions that remain faithful to the Brentanian commitment to a descriptive psychology. This accounts for the double-character of matter and essence as real and intentional contents as well as the doubling of sensible properties in the "blue"-content presenting the blue of the object. However, the intentional content that in the first edition was *outside* the bounds of a descriptive psychology is now in the second edition *within* the bounds of a phenomenological description, and the entire account of intentional content can now be recast in a new light. Husserl confirms this understanding in a footnote that refers us to the detailed account of the intentional correlation presented in *Ideas I*.[26]

Since Husserl's reformulated distinction in the second edition of the *Investigations* inclines us toward including the intentional object within the phenomenological contents of the act and since the language of "matter" and "intentional essence" is almost completely absent from *Ideas I*, we should try to understand the sense in which the intentional object can be included within what can be described phenomenologically. In the *Investigations'* discussion of the first sense of intentional content as intentional object, Husserl actually makes two distinctions. The first distinguishes "the object, such *as it is intended*, and the object pure and simple, *which* is intended,"[27] whereas the second distinguishes "the objectivity [*Gegenständlichkeit*] to which an act, taken fully and wholly, directs itself and the objects [*Gegenständen*] to which the different partial acts, which make up that act, direct themselves."[28]

The second distinction is a part-whole distinction on the side of the intentional object between the full and partial objects, a distinction which includes a reference to a correlative part-whole distinction on the side of the act between the full act and the partial experiences composing the full experience. The first distinction, on the other hand, is a distinction between an identical object and the various ways in which it might appear or be intended. The second distinction, therefore, underlies the first, because the combining in single acts of the abstract partial objects and the combining in complex acts of both abstract and concrete partial objects determine the manner in which the object is intended; this combining presents a completed view of the object, of the key as in the ignition or as being on the table. The object determinately intended, that is, the object as intended, is then distinguished from the identical object which is the object of this full intention as well as many others.

Husserl recognized the ambiguities in speaking of intentional contents and the intentional object, and this is why he had cautioned us against using the expression "intentional content" to refer to the intentional object. But in exercising this caution Husserl does not say that the intentional object is not a part or aspect of the intentional content of the act. He says that referring to it as the "intentional content" of an experience is ambiguous and to be avoided because the expression "intentional content" refers to both the contents *to* which the act is directed (the intentional object) and the contents *by* which the act is directed to this object (the instantiated intentional essence). Husserl does not, properly speaking, distinguish between the intentional content and the object of the act but only between the intentional content as object and the intentional content in other senses.[29] And while it is true that Husserl in the *Investigations* says he will not use the term "intentional content" to refer to the object of an intentional experience, he says this not because it is wrong to do so, but because it is ambiguous.

The change between the first and second editions of the *Investigations* is a consequence of Husserl's introduction in *The Idea of Phenomenology* and subsequent development, especially in *Ideas I,* of a decisive methodological innovation, namely, the "phenomenological reduction." It can be characterized most briefly and simply as the suspension of our participation in the general thesis characteristic of what Husserl calls the "natural attitude."[30] The natural attitude takes for granted the existence of the world to whose objects our ordinary experiences are directed. Even when we have doubts about the qualities or existence of the particular object intended, we continue to accept the existence of the *world* to which conscious experience is in general directed. The reduction, then, is the suspension of our participation in this naïve acceptance characteristic of the natural attitude. The reduction does not deny (and then require, *à la* Descartes, reestablishing) the existence of the world. It does not exclude from our continued attention either the objects of our experience or the world as both the totality of objects and the background in and against which particular objects appear. The reduction transforms neither the world nor its objects. The reduction instead transforms our *activity* by suspending our participation in the positing characteristic of our natural experiences.

We live in the natural attitude; we philosophize in a different attitude, a reflective attitude. We enter the philosophical attitude through the phenomenological reduction. In the philosophical reflection made possible by the reduction, we consider objects in their relation to acts of consciousness, precisely as objects of an intentional consciousness, just as they are intended. By virtue of the performance of the phenomenological reduction, our philosophical attention turns to the correlation between consciousness and the world in general and to the correlation between particular acts of consciousness and their intended objects. In the performance of the reduction objects are presented to us as presumptive existents that are the correlates of experiences having certain interests, concerns, and thetic characteristics. These presumptive existents are thereby presented as objects having a certain significance for us.

This, then, is the true sense of the "re-duction": it *leads* our attention *back* from the straightforwardly intended object of the natural attitude to the act in which the object is intended in a determinate manner. We continue to attend, now philosophically, to our ordinary experiences and their ordinary objects, to our ordinary interests and concerns and the ways in which objects can be significant relative to them. The two notions of the phenomenological reduction and of intentionality are inseparable in Husserl's mature thought, for the performance of the reduction is just the means by which we shift our attention to the intentional correlation that Husserl's account of the structure of intentionality is meant to describe.

For this descriptive purpose Husserl adopts in *Ideas I* a technical terminology—the terminology of "noesis" and "noema"—meant to indicate that we are talking about acts and their intended objects from a philosophical, rather than a natural, perspective. But in employing this technical language, Husserl introduces no new existents; he merely transforms the way in which we attend to acts and objects. The noesis is the act philosophically considered; the noema is the intended objectivity philosophically considered, just as it is intended with its significance for us, in relation to our animating interests and concerns, and with certain thetic characteristics.

3. The Noesis–Noema Correlation

Before the introduction of the reduction, the concrete transcendent objectivity as intended was not considered a part of the phenomenological content of the experience, and the notion of an immanent, intentional objectivity was rejected as incorrect. Husserl, consequently, needed to explain the object *as it appears* exclusively in terms of the act and its real contents. After the formulation of the notion of the reduction, however, the object which is intended remains within the scope of that upon which we phenomenologically reflect, although with its index changed. The object *which* is intended is considered *just as* it is intended in the act. This new view is stated in his reformulation of the distinction between real and intentional contents, or, in the language of *Ideas I*, in the distinction between the noesis and the noema. Unfortunately, Husserl's reformulation of the notion of intentional content as the noema does not remove all ambiguity from the notion of intentional content.

The whole upon which Husserl now reflects is the intentional correlation itself, that is, the intending act with its intentional correlate. Husserl uses the term "noesis" to refer to those features really (*reell*) or immanently contained in the act *by virtue of which* the act is intentionally directed to an object, that is, those moments of the act which "bear in themselves what is specific to intentionality."[31] For example, the perceptual apprehension of an object, but not the sensation-contents which the apprehension animates, belongs to the perceptual noesis. Husserl uses the term "noema" to refer to the intentional correlate of the act, but he explicates the noema in multiple ways. These varied explanations have generated much controversy about how best to interpret the noema. I shall not enter into all the details of this controversy here, but shall try in what follows to take all the ambiguities into account.[32]

Husserl characterizes the noema at once as (1) the intended as intended and (2) a sense: "Perception, for example, has its noema, most basically its perceptual sense, that is, the *perceived as perceived.*"[33] How is it that the noema can be both a sense and the intended objectivity itself? Husserl distinguishes three moments in the noema: the thetic characteristic (the noematic correlate of the act-quality), the noematic sense (the assimilation of act-matter into the newly conceived intentional content), and the determinable X (the "innermost moment" of the noema).[34] Husserl used the image of a core to distinguish the noematic sense from the full noema (the union of noematic sense and thetic character). To get to the core, however, we have to work *through* the outer covering and disclose the core lying *within.* In a similar manner, Husserl now identifies what we might think of as the core of the core, an innermost moment which we disclose only by working *through* the core (the noematic sense) to uncover the determinable X lying *within* it. Hence, Husserl can characterize the noema both as (1′) that *in* which we find the identical object itself and (2′) that *through* which the act intends an object. The language of "through" does not posit an instrumental entity ontologically distinct from the intended object. The noema is not a mediating species or entity that takes us through *and beyond* the sense to the object. We instead go "through" the noematic sense by *penetrating* it and finding its "innermost moment," the objective something to which the act is directed: "we become attentive to the fact that, with talk about the relation (and specifically the direction) of consciousness to its objective something, we are referred to an *innermost* moment of the noema. It is not the just designated core, but something which, so to speak, makes up the necessary central point of the core and functions as 'bearer' for noematic peculiarities specifically belonging to the core, namely for the noematically modified properties of the 'meant as meant.'"[35]

The intended objectivity is contained within the noema just as it is intended, and the determinable X is that object considered formally, apart from its determinations. As such, it is capable of providing a principle of identity by virtue of which a variety of noematic phases or concrete noemata, all intending the same object in different manners, can truly be said to intend an identical object: "Several act-noemata have here, throughout, *different cores,* yet such that, in spite of this, they merge in a *being identical,* into a unity in which the 'something,' the determinable which lies in each core, is known as identical."[36] It is this "identical" lying *within* the noema that is the something known, the intended object. This interpretation of the noema, then, allows for Husserl's discussion of the object as presented *through* the noema or sense as well as *in* the noema. Furthermore, this interpretation of the noema also allows us to understand how Husserl can describe both the noema as a sense (the object considered insofar as it is significant for us) and the intended object itself just as it is intended in the act (i.e., with just that significance for us).

There are, then, four points that summarize Husserl's characterizations of the noema: (1) the noema is a sense (although in what Husserl calls an "extended signification" to indicate that he is referring to a notion of sense [*Sinn*] broader than linguistic meaning [*Bedeutung*]); (2) the noema is the intended object just as intended; (3) the noema is that through which consciousness relates itself to its intended object; and (4) the "objective something" to which consciousness is directed, that is, the intended object itself, is the "innermost moment" within the noema.

Arguments for the ontological distinctness of the intended object and the noema find their best evidence in Husserl's admission that in our descriptions of objects and our descriptions of noemata we predicate of them different properties. Thus, in a famous text—and one of the clearest to which those who view the noema as a mediator between the act and intended object can appeal—Husserl says:

> The *tree pure and simple,* the physical thing belonging to nature, is anything but [*nichts weniger*] this *perceived tree as perceived* which, as perceptual sense, inseparably belongs to the perception. The tree simpliciter can burn up, be resolved into its chemical elements, etc. But the sense—the sense of *this* perception, something belonging necessarily to its essence—cannot burn up; it has no chemical elements, no forces, no real [*realen*] properties.[37]

We must immediately note that in reading this passage the notion of sense cannot properly be understood as it was in the first edition of the *Investigations*. The sense or meaning is the intentional correlate of the act, not an intentional essence instantiated in it. The noema cannot be an ideal species mediating the relation between the act and its intended object or, as Føllesdal would have it, "like a Peircean type, which is instantiated in various individual acts."[38] Nowhere in *Ideas I* do we find the language of sense as an instantiated species or as a token. Instead we find the noema's relation to the noesis characterized by the language of "correlation" and "parallelism,"[39] and the multiplicity of acts with the same thetic character directed to an identical objectivity in the same determinate manner characterized by the language of the "sameness" of noematic content. This sameness of noematic content, however, is now to be understood not as the sameness of a universal species or type, but as the identity of a non-really (*irreell*) but intentionally contained object. Indeed, at the level of the determinable X within the full noema, this sameness of content is, as we have seen, explicitly characterized as the "identical."[40]

Moreover, nothing Husserl says in distinguishing the object which is intended from the object as intended suggests an *ontological* difference between the intended and intentional objects, as Smith and McIntyre would have it. While they (1) recognize that Husserl has (a) abandoned a species-theory of meaning and (b) assimilated the notion of act-matter to the notion of noema, they, (2) attributing to Husserl a real distinction between intended object and matter, conclude that Husserl intends an ontological distinction between the object intended and the intentional object (i.e., the object as intended or the noema). The noema, they argue, is the intentional correlate of the act but not itself the intended object; it is a mediator between the act and its intended object. But this misunderstands Husserl's notion of the reduction: our refocusing attention on the intended object just as intended does not disclose any new entities but views the straightforwardly intended object in a new way. Finally, their interpretation fails to account adequately for Husserl's discussion of the determinable X within the noematic core or sense. They view the determinable X along the lines of a demonstrative pronoun. However, demonstrative pronouns do not themselves differentiate and pick out particular objects as their referents; demonstrative reference depends upon context and, most important, it depends upon the content available in that context to the experiencing agent. The demonstrative pronoun itself, however, as an indexical, must remain purely formal, but, while the determinable X is formal, it cannot be—and, as we shall see later, is not—purely formal.

Mediator-theories of intentionality—whether they view the noema as a mediating species (Føllesdal) or a mediating abstract particular (Smith and McIntyre)—fail, for they transform the fundamental datum of the intentionality of conscious experience into something no longer fundamental. To claim that an act is intentional because it instantiates a meaning-species or because it has an intentional object—a sense—that refers to an object is to locate directedness to an object first and foremost in the sense. Mediator-theories make the act intentional by virtue of an intensional entity whose (referential) direction to an objectivity is prior to the intentionality of the acts containing the intensional entity. Mediator-theories, in other words, replace the intentionality of acts with the different relation of the intensionality of sense, making the intentional directedness of an experience a function of the intensional directedness (referentiality) of a meaning. For Husserl, however, meaning and reference flow from the act. Intentionality belongs first and foremost to conscious acts: acts intend objects as significant. The claim that our experience is intentional means that a meaning-intending experience meaningfully directs us to an object. Only by virtue of this is the meaning or sense referred to the object.

The "burning tree" text quoted above is exceptional in the strength of its denial of an identity between the worldly object intended by the act and the perceived as perceived, that is, the perceptual sense. We must agree that the object as perceived in *this* perception remains for our reflective consideration *as a sense*, even when the perception has ceased because the act has changed or because the object is no longer available for perception. However, this does not require an ontological distinction. Indeed, my recognition that the tree I saw disappeared in the fire itself depends upon certain phenomenal continuities uniting the manifold of perceptual and memorial noemata such that I can recognize that *in* them the same tree is intended. Moreover, the point that the quoted text makes about the differences in predicables between objects themselves and noemata is maintained—and must be maintained—even when one asserts that the noema is the intended object itself just as it is intended. One does not predicate of the perceived object as perceived, that is, the perceptual appearance of the object upon which we reflect philosophically, what one predicates of the perceived object straightforwardly experienced, because the kinds of consideration given to the two necessarily differ.[41]

4. Temporality and Horizons

Our consideration of noematic content to this point has incorporated the distinction between the object which is intended and the object as intended. We must also incorporate, however, Husserl's distinction between the full objectivity and the partial objects. But there are two perspectives from which this distinction can be considered. The first perspective considers the whole and its parts without relation to time, for example, the state of affairs about which I judge can be considered as the whole comprising the concrete (the material thing) and abstract objects (e.g., the thing's shape) that I bring into a relation in making the judgment. This perspective leads to an analysis of the stratification involved in complex noemata and is an extension of the sort of analysis we have seen in distinguishing the full noema, the noematic sense, and the determinable X. The second perspective considers the whole and its parts in relation to time, for example, the complete perceptual noema can be considered as the whole comprising the noemata of all the phases of a temporally extended perception. This perspective leads to an analysis of the dynamic character of our experience, the ongoing revisions of our intentions, and their satisfaction or disappointment in subsequent phases of an experience or in different experiences.

We see examples of both perspectives in Husserl's detailed account of the perception of an identical material thing in space. In the perception of a material thing he distinguishes an ordered stratification involving two levels: (1) the phantom, that is, the object of simple sensible encounter, and (2) the substantial thing itself with its causal and material properties.[42] The level of the substantial, material thing is grounded in the phantom, for causal properties can be given only in a causation which presupposes the existence of an object that causally affects another object or is affected by another. Such an object must, in principle, be capable of being given as a sensibly qualified, spatio-temporal identity. For a thing to be experienced as causally affecting another thing or as affected by another it must, in other words, already be experienced as a thing in a narrower sense, in the sense of a sensible existent or phantom.[43]

Any attempt to analyze the (partial) experience of a phantom, however, reveals that the temporality of experience is already presupposed in those analyses that focus simply on the stratification present in the intended object. In other words, any account of an experienced objectivity rests upon a number of distinctions presupposing Husserl's analysis of the temporal structure of all conscious experience. The first and most important of these distinctions is that between genuine and non-genuine appearances.[44] The material thing appearing in perception is always given from this or that side or under this or that aspect. However, the perceptual object is not merely the side or aspect appearing in any given momentary perceptual phase. The presently appearing side or aspect is inseparable from the complete object itself. The givenness of the object (rather than just the side or aspect) requires a supplementation of the momentary appearance. There is necessarily and in principle in the perception of a material object a co-presence of seen and unseen sides or aspects of the object.[45] Simple perception grasps its correlate not as a side-of-the-whole, but as an object, one of whose sides and aspects is seen while the others are unseen.

From the noetic point of view, a perceptual phase entails an entire perceptual system by virtue of the structure belonging to any phase of experience, a structure that accounts for the temporality of our experience.[46] This structure has three moments: primal impression, retention, and protention. The primal impression intends the genuine appearance of the object; it is the presenting (*Gegenwärtigung*) of a side or an aspect of the material thing through sensation-contents. The non-genuine appearance, on the other hand, is not presentation through sensation-contents.[47] Rather, the non-genuine appearance is the making present or re-presenting (*Vergegenwärtigung*) of an unseen side or aspect by virtue of perceptual retention or perceptual protention. This non-genuine appearance is the necessary supplement to the genuine presentation through sensations. Thus, while the impressional moment in a perception presents the actually seen side through sensation-contents, its retentional moment makes present to the perceiver the already, but no longer, seen sides or aspects of the object, and its protentional moment makes present the not yet seen, but possibly about to be seen, sides or aspects. Alternately, the genuine appearance is the presenting through sensation-contents of the momentarily appearing side of the house against a background, while the non-genuine appearances are the making present of the remaining sides of the house as well as that part of the background hidden by the genuinely appearing side of the house.[48]

The view that the non-genuine appearance is the making present of unseen sides without the presence of sensation-contents does not entail the view that this making present is accomplished through memorial or imaginative presentations. If the front of a house were presented sensuously in a perceptual phase while the back of the house were made present in a memorial or imaginative phase, there would no longer be any unity within the perceptual act itself. In other words, if perceptual retention and perceptual protention were memorial and imaginative presentations, there would no longer be a *perception* of the whole house.[49] Furthermore, if we consider an imaginative presentation of the house, the distinction between genuine and non-genuine appearances again arises. The front of the house is genuinely presented through the contents proper to imaginative presentations, *viz.,* the phantasm, while the other sides of the house are non-genuinely made present without the presence of a phantasm. Here, if it is argued that these non-genuine appearances are imaginative presentations through phantasms, the distinction between genuine and non-genuine appearances collapses.[50] Both perceptual and imaginative presentations contain within themselves genuine and non-genuine appearances. Thus, the difference between genuine and non-genuine appearances cannot be explained in terms of a distinction between perception and imagination.

Husserl instead claims that a concrete perceptual phase animating sensation-contents is a complex of full and empty intentions.[51] The filled intention—primal impression—animates sensation-contents in bringing to awareness a genuine appearance of a side or aspect of the object, while the empty intentions that are devoid of contents—retention and protention—bring into our perceptual awareness the non-genuine appearances that complete the presentation of the perceived object.[52] Retention holds on to those appearances previously presented through sensation-contents, whereas protention tends toward fulfillment, becoming actually fulfilled only when the appropriate sensation-contents are present for animation in the course of the temporally extended perceptual process.[53]

The temporal structure of the perceptual act, then, grounds the distinction between the genuinely and non-genuinely appearing sides or aspects of the object, and the temporal duration of the act is filled also by bodily activities motivating the emptying of filled intentions and the filling of empty ones. But this temporal structure of consciousness is not alone sufficient to account for the awareness of an identical object; it, too, is too formal. The perceptual act must be explained in such a way as to account for the material determination of the object. Husserl's account of association—a continuation, he says, of the theory of time-consciousness[54]—fills the gap between the formality of the analyses of intentionality and the materiality of the manifold appearances.

Association involves the interplay of awakening, recollection, and anticipation. The individual is affected by some phenomenon which rises to prominence in the momentary phase of consciousness. As the genuinely experienced phenomenon passes over into retention it is replaced by a new genuinely experienced phenomenon. The conscious agent continues to be affected by the original appearance, but now only retentively and non-genuinely. As the experiential phase which had directly intended a particular appearance of the object sinks farther and farther into the past, it, by virtue of retention, remains connected with the presently experienced impressional appearance, and, thus, the appearance continues to affect the ego, although the degree of its affection is lessened.[55] Affection "goes along"[56] the retentive connections; there is a gradation of affection within the momentary phase of consciousness ordered according to the degree to which the content of an appearance is still retained within the living present and the degree to which it has slipped from consciousness. The impressional affection of consciousness awakens these retained appearances of the object, appearances which had previously and impressionally affected the ego, and this awakening reinforces the affective force of the retained appearances.[57]

Husserl calls this the "near synthesis" of association, but it does not exhaust the sphere of associative synthesis. The affection of the impressional phenomenon also awakens past experiences that have sunk back into the past to a degree that they have been forgotten, to a degree that they are no longer retained within the present. The present phase of experience recalls these forgotten but newly reawakened experiences into the present and reproduces their content therein so as to constitute the objectivity as an identity presented in a phenomenal manifold. This, Husserl maintains, is the most genuine sense of association,[58] the "distant" or reproductive association in which no longer retained experiences are restored to the retentive sphere of the present such that past appearances of the objectivity become once again affective, attracting the attention of the conscious agent, and thereby contributing to the present constitution of the experienced objectivity.[59] Associative recollection—like the retentions in which it is grounded—must be distinguished from memory in the ordinary sense; it does not involve, as memory does, a change in the index of the objective time of the object. Recollection, insofar as it is an associative moment of a present experience, is involved in my awareness of an objectivity as I experience it now, although it contributes elements of meaning not directly experienced in the present.

Distant awakening, recollection, and reproduction in the present are association in its most genuine sense, an association of what is not present and not retained in the present with what is present. They are the associative making-present or re-presenting (*Vergegenwärtigung*) of what has passed beyond the present. Upon such association, however, is founded another level of association, *viz.*, an analogizing protention or anticipation.[60] Within the concrete present, intentionality is directed not only to the impressional present and the past but to the future as well. This direction to the future is found in protention. Founded upon it, in turn, is the moment of anticipation contained within any experience. Such anticipation, however, presupposes certain unities or similarities of encounter.[61] Anticipation is founded upon what is genuinely given in the primal impression and the non-genuine appearances associated with it, including both the affectively reinforced retentions within the living present and the recollection and reproduction of awakened empty retentions.[62] Future manifestations of the experienced objectivity are anticipated on the basis of their similarity with what has already been experienced in the past.[63] Protention, in other words, is a modification of retention and recollection.[64] It modifies retention and recollection in such a way that if in given circumstances in the past someone has experienced *P*, then given similar circumstances in the present, he or she can anticipate *P* again.[65] Just as recollection does not thematize the temporal determination of the object as past, so anticipation does not thematize the temporal determination of the object as future. Anticipation, while directed to the future course of my experience, is a moment of my present experience and its direction to a present objectivity.

These associative syntheses are necessary conditions for the presentation of identical objects.[66] It is only through awakening, reproduction, recollection, and protentive anticipation that other appearances of an identical objectivity are made present to consciousness in its present phase. It is through association, in other words, that a consciousness of the manifold arises, and it is only when this consciousness arises that the consciousness of an identical object variously appearing can arise. It is only through association, therefore, that the present, concrete phase of an experience intends an objectivity as the identity given in a manifold of appearances, which manifold is made up of an impressional appearance, the awakened, recollected, and reproduced appearances associated therewith, and the protentively anticipated appearances based thereon. And it is only in such a manifold that the object is presented as an object to which the conscious agent can again and again return and repeatedly experience.[67]

Intersecting the distinction between full and empty intentions is the distinction between determined and undetermined intentions.[68] The intention of a house, for example, might indeterminately intend a house as made of unspecified materials, as having a color, and as having multiple stories, but without further determining our sense of the house. The determined intention, on the other hand, might intend a three-storied, red brick townhouse with a peaked, slate roof, and so on.

The distinction between genuine and non-genuine appearances and that between undetermined and determined intentions only intersect; they cannot be reduced to one another. An empty intention tending toward fulfillment may be either determined or undetermined. If it is determined, the fulfilling perception is not at the same time a determining perception. If it is undetermined, then the fulfilling perception is not merely fulfilling but also determining. To the essence of the undetermined intention, therefore, belongs determinability in continued encounters with the object.[69] Such determinability has as its ideal limit full determination. The determined intention in fact, however, is always to some extent undetermined, and it can always be more fully determined; for example, a perception of my own house which notices some particular quality or feature never before noticed is a determining perception. Husserl refers to this continuing process of determination as "more precise determination."[70]

Interpreted from the noematic standpoint, the distinction between genuine and non-genuine appearances is the distinction between the genuinely given and its horizons. The horizons are what transcends the genuinely given in any momentary presentation of the object. The noematic correlate of a perception is the object, whereas the genuine noematic correlate of a perceptual phase is a side or aspect of the object. The fact that what is genuinely given is only a side or aspect of the object indicates that the genuinely given side refers beyond itself to other sides and aspects of the same object. This referring beyond is the horizon of what is genuinely given. More specifically, this horizon is the "inner" horizon of the genuinely given. The genuinely given side or aspect refers to other non-genuinely given sides or aspects of the same object. There is also an "outer" horizon, *viz.*, the background against which an object is given, the surrounding in which it is given.[71]

The horizonal structure of the noematic correlate is founded upon the structure of the perceptual apprehension as a complex of full and empty intentions. What is referred to in the inner horizons of the given is emptily intended in the perceptual phase. This empty intending is, in turn, based on the moments of perceptual retention and perceptual protention. When the front of a house is perceived, it is expected, as was the case in past perceptions of houses, that if the percipient were to walk around the house, he or she would see the back of the house.[72] We here see the importance of Husserl's discussions of bodily activity in perception. Husserl claims that there is a correlation between a series of kinaesthetic sensations in which we are aware of our own bodily movements and a series of presenting sensations through which different sides and aspects of the perceived object are shown in an ordered progression correlative to the progression of our bodily movements.[73] The awareness of an identical object is necessarily mediated by the movements of the body,[74] for it is only through such activity that the manifold of appearances in and through which one and the same object is given as identical is generated. Most significantly, these bodily activities bring about the awareness of an object with its own position in space and its own bodily enclosedness.[75] As we approach an object, for example, it takes up a larger portion of our visual field, and as we retreat from it, it takes a smaller part of the visual field; these indicate that the object has its own fixed position in space. As we walk around an object, part of the appearance first presenting an object disappears from the field and is replaced by another part of the appearance that previously had been a neighbor of the first part. Such phenomenal ordering in the changing appearances—along with ordered phenomenal changes in the outer horizon of the object—indicates the presence of an identical object throughout the flow of appearances.

The determinable X is the way in which Husserl in the purely static account of *Ideas I* points us toward both (1) a genetic account that takes into account the temporality of consciousness and (2) an identity-in-manifolds analysis of the relation between the object and its noematic presentations. *Ideas I* is misleading insofar as in its analyses the identical object and the X appear as purely formal notions. As later texts reveal and as we have discussed, they are in fact not purely formal; they are dynamic concepts imprisoned by *Ideas I* in the straightjacket of a static analysis. Once we take the determinable X outside the limits of a purely static analysis, the determinability of the X should be understood as the object's capacity to come to a more precise determination in the course of a temporally extended experience.[76] The X as an identity can be understood, however, only against the manifold in which it manifests itself and in the light of the tendency toward fulfillment we find in conscious life. The determinable *X*, therefore, is both a formal and a teleological characterization of the identical object.

The tendency toward complete and precise determination of the perceived object must, however, be limited in some way if our perceptual expectations are ever to be genuinely satisfied, for we can never fully experience the infinite manifold of appearances in which an object can be presented. The limiting factor is the practical interest at work in our perception and governing our perceptual life at the moment.[77] The practical interest limits the goal of precise determination to those features relevant to our interest in the object, and, at the same time, limits the degree of precision necessary in order for those interests to be satisfied. Our practical interests, then, call forth certain qualities for attention and require that the object be given such that we can best experience those qualities to the degree necessary to satisfy our interests in the object.[78]

The identically intended object, then, is what reveals itself in systematic alterations from one noematic presentation to the next. There is an ordered and continuous series of changes involving both similarity and dissimilarity such that we can attribute identity to an object manifesting itself within the manifold of varying noemata. In our straightforward experiencing of objects, this identity is an identity in and through time, in and through apparent change, in and through real change, in and through relations (e.g., spatial or causal relations) with other objects, in and through various valuations, uses, and so forth.

5. Horizonal Reference

The account of the perceived object as an identity presented in a manifold of sensible appearances, of real and apparent changes, of causal relations, and so forth reveals the complex character of the presentation even of individual objects. The noematic manifold is systematically interwoven in a manner that correlates with the retentional/impressional/protentional structure of consciousness and that is grounded in the impressional contents of consciousness. Our experiences have horizons; they intend in their inner horizons other sides and aspects of the experienced object and in their outer horizons a background (e.g., of other objects) or a context (e.g., a theoretical context) against or in which the object presently intended is located. Noetic phases with their noematic content are associationally related such that the horizons of the impressionally given contribute to our present apprehension of an object. This fact, in turn, allows us to disclose the significance of the second aspect of the claim that the object is presented in and *through* the noematic sense and thereby to clarify the notion of intentional reference.

To posit something as an identity is to posit a certain relation among apparently different things. The recognition of an object as identically the same is possible only given a certain relation among multiple appearances, multiple noematic phases. The inner horizons, grounded in associative recollection and protentive anticipation, bring that multiplicity of temporally differentiated noematic phases to presence at once and as an identical object. The noema presenting the object differs abstractly from the act's intended object—it is an abstract phase of the intended object's concrete presentation—and by virtue of a difference in the way we attend to the object. We attend straightforwardly to the object; we attend phenomenologically to the noema, that is, (a) we attend to the object in relation to the act intending the object, and (b) we attend to that object just as intended in the act. The noematic sense, as a moment of the full noema, refers to the identical, intended object not simply by virtue of its relation to a determinable X within it, but by virtue of its horizonal connections with the manifold of noemata presenting that same object. Reference goes "through" the noematic sense of a particular phase of consciousness to the "identical" within it by virtue of its horizonal connections with the manifold of noemata presenting one and the same object.

This complex nature of the presentation even of simple objects enables us to understand failures of reference. Husserl's notion of fulfillment posits a "coincidence" or "covering" or "congruence" (*Deckung*) between empty and full intentions such that we recognize the identity of what was emptily (absently) intended and what is intuitively present. In the truthful encounter with things, this congruence is present; in non-truthful encounters, it is not. In truthful encounters, the thing is the identical in the manifold of presence and absence; in non-truthful encounters, an identification of what is present with what was absently intended cannot be achieved. Intending non-existent objects and intending objects as other than they are can be understood only by contrast with our truthfully intending existent objects. Acts intending non-existent objects or intending objects as other than they are refer through their inner, outer, or intersubjective horizons to actualities in contrast with which we understand these non-existent objectivities as well as non-veridicality or falsity. Some of the partial intentions composing the concrete act, in other words, refer to actualities, while other partial intentions do not. Concrete acts involving objectless or mistaken or fictional reference, then, refer horizonally to actualities—ultimately, to the world—but refer to their direct object in a non-veridical or false manner that over the course of an experience can, but does not always, correct itself.[79] For example, my understanding of an actual person might attribute to her qualities she does not possess. Nevertheless, my intention, by virtue of its association with other understandings and presentations of the same person, grasps an actual, identical object, even though this particular manifestation of that person is non-veridical. We can see here the enormous fruitfulness of Husserl's account of intentionality: he is able to escape the modern, skeptical, psychologistic problematic, but at the same time he is able to handle the problem of appearances, of non-veridicality and falsity, of absence and non-existence.

6. Founding and Founded Acts

I have, largely for the sake of convenience, limited my examples to perceptual intentionality. But convenience was not the only reason for this limitation. Husserl believes that all acts are either "objectifying acts" or based thereon and that perception is the fundamental objectifying act. This has led some to charge Husserl with granting an unwarranted privilege to cognitive acts, but I do not think that Husserl's claim about objectifying acts is best read in the context of a distinction between cognitive and other kinds of experience, say, between the cognitive and the practical or between the cognitive and the axiological. We have seen, for example, that Husserl recognizes that even in perception there is always a practical interest in the world or an object governing to some degree the course of the unfolding perception. Instead, we should understand Husserl's claim about objectifying acts in the light of his distinction between founding and founded acts.

To say that an act is founded upon another means that it (a) presupposes that other act as necessary and (b) builds itself upon that other act's matter or noematic sense so as to form a unity with it. Founded acts can also be objectifying; judging a state of affairs would be an example of a higher-order objectifying act. But founded acts can also be "non-objectifying," although this term is somewhat problematic. Practical or axiological intentions, for example, when their specifically practical and axiological moments are abstracted and isolated, are "non-objectifying," since they present only an aspect of an object but do not present that object in its own right. However, practical and axiological intentions are necessarily founded on objectifying acts. In their concrete occurrence, therefore, they include an objectifying act as a part and thereby intend an objectivity with an additional practical or axiological significance. Founded acts have essentially the same intentional structures at work as do founding ones. In order only to sketch the intentionality of higher acts and the intentional processes by which they come about, let us look very briefly at the examples of judgment and valuation.

To judge is to grasp intentionally a state of affairs. As such, judging involves a syntactical achievement in which we come to an awareness of a categorially articulated objectivity. The object's categorial determinations are not available originally to simple perception but become available only in continued inspections of the object—in what Husserl calls "explicative" and "relational" contemplation of the object[80]—and the predicative and associative activities based thereon. The object about which we judge is already given, for example, in a perception or remembrance, and in judging we distinguish features or parts or relations belonging to the object and make them the object of a special regard. We then explicitly intend higher-order objectivities by explicitly identifying the features, parts, or relations as belonging to the object, that is, by articulating, say, relations of attribution, possession, causation, or subsumption. The act of judging, therefore, is directed toward the object so as to grasp it with respect to some categorial form or other. These categorial forms are, consequently, objective or ontological forms mirrored by the logical forms belonging to the senses in and through which we intend the categorically articulated objectivities.[81]

In this straightforward judging of the natural attitude, we remain turned toward the objects about which we judge and to their properties and relations, and, in general, to the judged states of affairs themselves. We are not aware of any logical reality that we might call the judgment itself or the proposition. However, a change of focus is possible, Husserl tells us, such that we focus on the judgment *qua* judgment rather than the objectivity judged. We judge now at a second level, the logical level at which we make judgments about judgments.[82]

In the verification motivated by our critical concerns, the individual when directly presented with the objectivity can run through the articulations posited in the judgment and recognize that the object is in fact as it was supposed to be. Husserl says that this involves an "*identifying coincidence* between the object (and ultimately the whole judgment-complex, the state-of-affairs) which was no doubt something previously believed and what now—in the evident believing which fulfills the cognitive intention—is given as it is itself, the fulfilling actuality."[83] In the evidence which confirms a supposition, that is, in the experience which, so to speak, presents the state of affairs "in person," in its "bodily" actuality, there is an identity existing between the supposed objectivity merely as supposed—the judgment or proposition in the logical sense—and the supposed objectivity in its actuality. The latter, Husserl is clear, is in the case of the true judgment the *positum* to which the straightforward judging is directed, that is, it is the state of affairs intended in the judgment. The supposed state of affairs just as supposed is, however, in the case of the verified or true judgment, identical with this. The difference between the intended state of affairs itself and the judgmental or propositional sense is the *attitude* we take toward the state of affairs: in the natural attitude with its straightforward direction to objects we focus upon the state of affairs itself, whereas in the critical attitude or logical attitude we focus on the proposition. In the phenomenological attitude we take one further step and focus on the judgmental noema, the state of affairs in its relation to the judging act.

We see a different example of this founding relation at work in evaluations and evaluative judgments. According to Husserl, the valuable properties of things are disclosed by the feelings or emotions. The experience of an object having value presupposes a cognitive experience of the object and involves a moment of feeling which builds itself upon and unites itself with this cognition.[84] More precisely, we should say that the value-properties belonging to the object or state of affairs are founded on what Husserl calls that object's "logical" properties (i.e., the sort predicated in simple, unmodalized, categorical propositions). A constellation of logical properties is such as to arouse a feeling,[85] and the value-properties are the correlates specifically of this moment of feeling or emotion in the concrete valuing act. Since this feeling or emotion is the affective response to cognized properties, our emotional apprehension of the object, our valuing it, incorporates the underlying cognitive content.

Moreover, my valuing experiences can—and often do—move beyond this moment of feeling. On the one hand, we develop the experience at a higher level of understanding by explicitly judging the object or state of affairs as valuable. This judgment incorporates both the cognitive and evaluative moments underlying it. On the basis of my affective response to the object or state of affairs, I understand its value and can, by virtue of the cognitive content incorporated into the experience of value, provide objective reasons for thinking it valuable.[86] Additionally, my affective response can motivate an explicit desire for the object or a desire to transform some state of affairs so that I might enjoy the object or realize the desired state of affairs; the affective response and recognition of the object or state of affairs as good motivates an intention to act. The combination of the practical judgment and the intention to act is the deliberate intention.

There is, as with any judgment, a tendency toward confirmation of the judgment of value or the deliberate intention that goes beyond the statement of reasons; we seek, as it were, sound judgments. The judgment tends, in other words, toward a fulfilling intention. In the case of the deliberate intention, fulfillment or disappointment is found in the action. The evidence that the object is in fact good is found in the direct experience of it as good, for example, in its use or consumption or realization and in the attendant satisfaction of our emotions, desires, and understanding of value.[87] We are not, of course, infallible in valuing an object; hence, neither is fulfillment in an evidential experience infallible. The emotions, and the desires grounded in them, must be cultivated and refined, and this includes ensuring that the beliefs cognitively contained in the emotions are themselves true. Nevertheless, in such evidential insights, I do gain objective evidence, confirming or disconfirming evidence, about the value-property I have attributed to the object.[88]

The value of things can be apprehended hypothetically as well. For example, there need not be an actual desire or emotion operative in order to recognize the value of an object. The value of a thing can be apprehended in an experience which includes an "as if" feeling; our understanding can recognize the value as befitting the object relative to certain attitudes, emotions, or desires that some other person has or that any person might have. Alternately, since the cultivated emotions assist us in recognizing what is valuable and morally salient in various situations, we can recognize that an object would be valuable *were* it to have certain cognizable properties. But the full concreteness of the evaluative intention is realized when our actual emotions and desires are in play.

There is, no doubt, much more to be said about judging and valuing acts.

But these examples are sufficient to make us realize the fruitfulness of the notion of intentionality and the power of intentional analysis to illuminate the
enormous richness of our mental life. We can glimpse in the intricacies of intentional life the remarkable powers of mind to disclose and consider objects.
We can understand both how these disclosures and considerations can occur
and how they can be truthful or erroneous.

Notes

1. Franz Brentano, *Psychologie vom empirischen Standpunkt. Erster Band,* ed. O. Kraus
(Hamburg: Felix Meiner Verlag, 1955), 124; after Eng. trans., *Psychology from an Empirical
Standpoint,* ed. O. Kraus, trans. L. McAlister (New York: Humanities Press, 1973), 88.
2. Husserl's account of intentionality clearly takes its place both in the epistemological
debates characterizing modern philosophy—debates in which the object of consciousness had
been reduced to a psychological content and the logical laws governing our knowledge of
objects had been reduced to empirical, psychological laws—and in a more particular debate
among Brentano's students concerning what Bolzano called "objectless presentations."
    With respect to the modern debate, Husserl believes that Cartesian doubt severs the
world from our reflection upon our own ideas, but it also reveals that our ideas have a content
apart from any relation to a presumed world. Any idea, then, can be considered under two
aspects: from the point of view of its "formal reality" as a mode of mental substance and
from the point of view of its "objective reality" as having a content, as about something; cf.
René Descartes, *Meditations on First Philosophy in Which the Existence of God and the Distinction of the Soul from the Body Are Demonstrated,* 3rd ed., trans. Donald A. Cress (Indianapolis:
Hackett, 1993), 27-28. The relation of this content to the world is explained by Descartes in
both causal and representational terms (*Meditations,* 27ff., 47ff.), terms accepted by Locke—
at least with respect to primary qualities (cf. John Locke, *An Essay Concerning Human Understanding* [2 vols., New York: Dover, 1959], I: 122-24, 168-82)—but rejected by Berkeley
on the grounds that causal and representational accounts presuppose the very knowledge of
existent objects called into question by the argument from illusion (cf. George Berkeley, *Of
the Principles of Human Knowledge,* first part, ¶¶1-21, in *Berkeley: Essay, Principles, Dialogues
with Selections from Other Writings,* ed. Mary Whiton Calkins [New York: Charles Scribner's
Sons, 1957]). The outcome of such a line of argument is the claim that appearances are subjective, that is, psychological contents having no ontological status independent of their being
a part of the experience. The transcendence of experience and the so-called object is inexplicable except as an imaginative or transcendental projection of what belongs to the subject.
So, for example, Hume claims that appearances are psychological entities (impressions and
ideas) and that the sense of a continuously and distinctly existing object is an "imaginative
fiction," a projection occasioned by imaginative propensities to complete and perfect experienced regularities; cf. David Hume, *A Treatise Concerning Human Nature,* 2nd ed., ed. L. A.
Selby-Bigge, rev. ed. P. H. Nidditch (Oxford: Clarendon Press, 1978), 198-209. Similarly, for
Kant the phenomenal object is a complex of representations that are organized by consciousness in a rule-governed way; cf. Immanuel Kant, *Critique of Pure Reason,* trans. Norman

Kemp Smith (New York: St. Martin's Press, 1965), 125–28, 134–38, 144–45, 156–57, 164–65. Husserl thinks that both Hume and Kant are guilty of forms of psychologism, that is, the view that the objects of experience and the rules and categories that govern them are reducible to the mental entities and the rules and categories that govern them. Hume, according to Husserl, is guilty of an empirical psychologism, whereas Kant is guilty of a transcendental psychologism.

With regard to the second debate, the possibility of objectless presentations seemed a scandal for any philosopher wanting to assert the thesis of intentionality (cf. Bernard Bolzano, *Wissenschaftslehre: Versuch einer ausführlichen und großtenteils neuen Darstellung der Logik mit steter Rücksicht auf deren bisherige Bearbeiter* [Sulzbach: J. E. v. Seidel, 1837], I: 304). Bolzano had claimed that every presentation or mental act has its "presented," but he distinguishes between two senses of "the presented": the presentation-as-such (what he also called the "objective presentation") and the object of presentation (*Wissenschaftslehre*, ¶49). An object-less presentation contains an objective presentation or content but no object of presentation. The notion of "objective presentation" or "objective content" is not dissimilar from what we find in G. E. Moore's response to the modern epistemological arguments concerning illusion and hallucination; cf. G. E. Moore, "The Refutation of Idealism," in *Twentieth-Century Philosophy: The Analytic Tradition,* ed. Morris Weitz (New York: Free Press, 1966), 15–34, and "A Defense of Common Sense," ibid., 119ff. Moore claims that the objects of sensation or sense-data are not inseparable parts of a sentient experience but an objective content not identical with the object itself.

Brentano denied Bolzano's view that some presentations lack objects even while admitting that some acts intend non-existent objects. He claimed that the intentional object is a special sort of immanent object to which our acts are directed even in those cases where there is no actual existent. Brentano's students Meinong (Alexius Meinong, "Über Gegenstände höherer Ordnung und deren Verhältnis zur inneren Wahrnehmung," in *Abhandlungen zur Erkenntnistheorie und Gegenstandstheorie,* ed. R. Haller, *Alexius Meinong Gesamtausgabe* [Graz: Akademische Druck- u. Verlangsanstalt, 1971], cf., e.g., II: 381), Twardowski (Kasimir Twardowski, *Zur Lehre vom Inhalt und Gegenstand der Vorstellungen* [Vienna: A. Hölder, 1894]; trans. as *On the Content and Object of Presentations: A Psychological Investigation,* trans. R. Grossman [The Hague: Martinus Nijhoff, 1977]; cf., e.g., 2), and Husserl rejected Brentano's account of the intentional object as an immanent objectivity. They shared the view that the language of "immanent objectivity" was too psychologistic in character, threatening to reduce—as the empiricists had done—what Bolzano had rightly recognized as the logical content of the presentation to a real part of the presenting act itself, and each sought in his own way to respond to Bolzano's problem. For an account of these efforts, cf. John J. Drummond, "From Intentionality to Intensionality and Back," *Études phénoménologiques* 27–28 (1998): 89–126. The form that these debates took means that Husserl's first attempts to define intentionality were centered around a distinction in the kinds of "contents" belonging to experience.

3. *Idee der Phänomenologie,* 20; *Idea of Phenomenology,* 17.

4. *Krisis,* 184; *Crisis,* 181.

5. Edmund Husserl, *Logische Untersuchungen. Erster Band: Prolegomena zur reinen Logik,* ed. Elmar Holenstein, *Husserliana* XVIII (The Hague: Martinus Nijhoff, 1975); *Logische Untersuchungen. Zweiter Band. Erster Teil: Untersuchungen zur Phänomenologie und Theorie der Erkenntnis,* ed. Ursula Panzer, *Husserliana* (The Hague: Martinus Nijhoff, 1984); and *Logische Untersuchungen. Zweiter Band. Zweiter Teil: Untersuchungen Zur Phänomenologie und Theorie der Erkenntnis,* ed. Ursula Panzer, *Husserliana* XIX/2 (The Hague: Martinus Nijhoff, 1984); *Logical Investigations.* The *Investigations* were first published in 1900–1901. The Prolegomena and the first five investigations were revised somewhat for a second edition in 1913,

the Sixth Investigation in 1921. For ease of accessibility, in addition to the references to the *Husserliana* pagination and the English translation, I shall include in square brackets references to the pagination of the first and second editions as published by Niemeyer.

6. *Logische Untersuchungen (Hua)* II/1, 411 [*Logische Untersuchungen (First Edition)*, 374]; *Logical Investigations*, 576.

7. *Ding und Raum*, 45; *Thing and Space*, 39. This same distinction is made in a number of places and in a number of forms. Cf., e.g., *Logische Untersuchungen (Hua)* II/1, 433 [*Logische Untersuchungen (First Edition)*, 393–94/*Logische Untersuchungen*, 419]; *Logical Investigations*, 591, where the distinction is drawn, as we shall see below, between the intentional essence and its sensuous contents; cf. also *Ideen I (Hua)*, §85, where the distinction is drawn between the intentional form (apprehension) and sensible hylē. Husserl also calls the intentional form the "noesis"; cf. *Ideen I (Hua)*, 194 [*Ideen*, 174]; *Ideas I*, 205 (again, for ease of accessibility, I provide in square brackets the pagination for the original German edition).

8. *Logische Untersuchungen (Hua)* II/1, 433 [*Logische Untersuchungen (First Edition)*, 393–94/*Logische Untersuchungen*, 419]; *Logical Investigations*, 591.

9. For examples such as these, cf. *Logische Untersuchungen (Hua)* II/1, 433 [*Logische Untersuchungen (First Edition)*, 394/*Logische Untersuchungen*, 419]; *Logical Investigations*, 591; and *Ideen II*, 41; *Ideas II*, 44.

10. *Ding und Raum*, 45; *Thing and Space*, 39.

11. *Ding und Raum*, 45, *Thing and Space*, 39; cf. also *Ideen II*, 41; *Ideas II*, 44.

12. Cf. *Ding und Raum*, 45; *Thing and Space*, 39; cf. also *Erfahrung und Urteil*, 99–100; *Experience and Judgement*, 92.

13. *Ding und Raum*, 46; *Thing and Space*, 39–40. The notion of sensation-contents has been criticized from a phenomenological point of view. Aron Gurwitsch (*The Field of Consciousness* [Pittsburgh: Duquesne University Press, 1964], 71–96, 168–84, 265–73) criticizes the claim that there are neutral sensation-contents contained in perception. John Drummond (*Husserlian Intentionality and Non-foundational Realism: Noema and Object* [Dordrecht: Kluwer, 1990], 144–46; and "On the Nature of Perceptual Appearances, Or Is Husserl an Aristotelian?" *The New Scholasticism* 52 [1978]: 1–22) admits the presence of a sensuous dimension as one of the psycho-physical conditions operative in perception, but he criticizes the notion of sensation-contents as "presenting" objective determinations of the object.

14. *Ding und Raum*, 46; *Thing and Space*, 39–40.

15. Cf. *Logische Untersuchungen (Hua)* II/1, 413ff. [*Logische Untersuchungen*, 375ff.]; *Logical Investigations*, 578ff.

16. There are no major differences between the first and second editions in their discussions of the notion of intentional content. What difference does exist centers on the second sense: the matter and quality of the act are more clearly identified as intentional matter and the intentional quality of the act. This, no doubt, also reflects the fact that Husserl now recognizes that the intentional content of the act can be included within a phenomenological description. Hence, identifying the matter and quality as intentional no longer runs the risk of eliminating references to matter and quality from a phenomenological description.

17. *Logische Untersuchungen (Hua)* II/1, 425–26 [*Logische Untersuchungen (First Edition)*, 386/*Logische Untersuchungen*, 411]; *Logical Investigations*, 586.

18. *Logische Untersuchungen (Hua)* II/1, 430 [*Logische Untersuchungen (First Edition)*, 390/*Logische Untersuchungen*, 416]; *Logical Investigations*, 589.

19. *Logische Untersuchungen (Hua)* II/1, 429 [*Logische Untersuchungen (First Edition)*, 390/*Logische Untersuchungen*, 415]; *Logical Investigations*, 589.

20. *Logische Untersuchungen (Hua)* II/1, 427 [*Logische Untersuchungen (First Edition)*, 387/*Logische Untersuchungen*, 412]; *Logical Investigations*, 587.

21. *Logische Untersuchungen (Hua)* II/1, 431 [*Logische Untersuchungen (First Edi-*

tion), 392 / *Logische Untersuchungen,* 417]; *Logical Investigations,* 590; Husserl, *Logische Untersuchungen (Hua)* II/2, 620 [*Logische Untersuchungen (First Edition),* 562 / *Logische Untersuchungen,* 90]; *Logical Investigations,* 740.

22. *Logische Untersuchungen (Hua)* II/1, 433–34 [*Logische Untersuchungen (First Edition),* 394 / *Logische Untersuchungen,* 419]; *Logical Investigations,* 591–92.

23. That this is Husserl's view is confirmed by the fact that Husserl claims that the "semantic" essence of acts which give meaning to expressions, that is, the correlate on the side of the act of the ideal meaning of the expression, coincides with their intentional essence (cf. *Logische Untersuchungen (Hua)* II/1, 435 [*Logische Untersuchungen (First Edition),* 395 / *Logische Untersuchungen,* 421]; *Logical Investigations,* 592–93). Just as the meaning of a particular expressive act is the instantiation of a meaning-essence (cf. *Logische Untersuchungen (Hua)* II/1, 106 [*Logische Untersuchungen (First Edition),* 100 / *Logische Untersuchungen,* 100]; *Logical Investigations,* 330), so too, the particular meaning-giving act is an instantiation of an intentional essence which determines *in specie* the meaning of the expression. And, by extension, any particular act is an instantiation of an intentional essence that determines *in specie* the object as intended in a determinate manner and as the object of a certain kind of act.

For discussions of Husserl's view that the meanings present in individual acts of meaning are instantiations of meaning-essences, cf. Dallas Willard, "The Paradox of Logical Psychologism: Husserl's Way Out," in *Husserl: Expositions and Appraisals,* ed. F. A. Elliston and P. McCormick (Notre Dame, Ind.: University of Notre Dame Press, 1977), 10–17; and J. N. Mohanty, "Husserl's Thesis of the Ideality of Meanings," in *Readings on Husserl's Logical Investigations,* ed. J. N. Mohanty (The Hague: Martinus Nijhoff, 1977), 76–82. Smith and McIntyre also take the view that in the first edition of the *Investigations* the real content of an individual act is an instantiation of the act's intentional essence, that is, that the relationship between the act's ideal, intentional content (where "intentional content" does not refer to the intentional object of the act) and its real content is the relationship of instantiation rather than the relationship of possession of a common, abstract part; cf. David Woodruff Smith and Ronald McIntyre, *Husserl and Intentionality: A Study of Mind, Meaning, and Language* (Dordrecht: Reidel, 1984), 116f. While this view of meaning can be argued for the first edition of the *Logische Untersuchungen (Hua),* it is already in flux by the time of the publication of the second edition; indeed, in *Ideen I,* Husserl essentially discards the language of intentional essence, and its inclusion in the second edition of the *Logische Untersuchungen (Hua)* is largely a consequence of Husserl's decision not to rework the *Logische Untersuchungen (Hua)* in their entirety. As Husserl's views mature, there is no longer a need to describe ideal or intentional content in terms of "species" or "essences"; in its place will come the language of "*irreell,*" the "ir-real," which is also ideal or abstract. Furthermore, this abstract component of an intentional experience can be shared by various acts because it is intentional as the objective correlate of these acts rather than as their essence.

24. Cf. *Logische Untersuchungen (Hua)* II/1, 416 [*Logische Untersuchungen (First Edition),* 378]; *Logical Investigations,* 580. It is only, as we shall shortly see, after the formulation of the notion of the reduction that Husserl includes the intentional contents within the phenomenological contents of the act and, therefore, only after the formulation of the notion of the reduction that Husserl can include the intentional object, the intended object itself just as intended, within the phenomenological contents of the act. Cf. *Logische Untersuchungen (Hua)* II/1, 411n [*Logische Untersuchungen,* 398n]; *Logical Investigations,* 576n; *Ideen I (Hua),* 202–5, 295–97 [*Ideen,* 180–83, 265–66]; *Ideas I,* 213–16, 307–8. Cf. also Drummond, *Husserlian Intentionality and Non-foundational Realism,* 34ff. Moreover, any such appeal to the intentional object would have to avoid attributing a special ontological character to the object; otherwise we would merely return to a Brentanian theory of intentionality or encoun-

ter ontological problems of the sort faced by Meinong and Twardowski; cf. Drummond, "From Intentionality to Intensionality and Back," 89-126, 94-108.

25. *Logische Untersuchungen (Hua)* II/1, 411 [*Logische Untersuchungen*, 397]; *Logical Investigations*, 576.

26. *Logische Untersuchungen (Hua)* II/1, 411n [*Logische Untersuchungen*, 397n]; *Logical Investigations*, 576n.

27. *Logische Untersuchungen (Hua)* II/1, 414 [*Logische Untersuchungen*, 400]; *Logical Investigations*, 578.

28. *Logische Untersuchungen (Hua)* II/1, 415 [*Logische Untersuchungen*, 401]; *Logical Investigations*, 579.

29. Smith and McIntyre, *Husserl and Intentionality*, 108, claim that the distinction is between the intentional object and the intentional contents.

30. *Ideen I (Hua)*, 61 [*Ideen I*, 52-53]; *Ideas I*, 56-57.

31. *Ideen I (Hua)*, 192 [*Ideen I*, 172]; modified *Ideas I*, 203.

32. This controversy was first characterized by Hubert Dreyfus ("The Perceptual Noema: Gurwitsch's Crucial Contribution," in *Life-World and Consciousness: Essays for Aron Gurwitsch*, ed. L. Embree [Evanston, Ill.: Northwestern University Press, 1972], 135; revised and reprinted as "Husserl's Perceptual Noema," in *Husserl, Intentionality, and Cognitive Science*, ed. H. Dreyfus [Cambridge, Mass.: MIT Press, 1984], 98) as a debate between those who view the perceptual noema as a percept and those who view it as a concept. But the debate was not limited to a debate about the perceptual noema, and it came to be more broadly characterized as one between content-theories of intentionality (and of the noema) and object-theories, or between mediator-theories and object-theories, or between the Fregean interpretation and the non-Fregean interpretation, or between propositional and transcendental readings, or between West Coast and East Coast readings (or yet others!).

The issue arises in the variety of expressions Husserl uses to explain his doctrine of the noema. On the one hand, he speaks of the noema as the intended objectivity as intended, and on the other, he speaks of the noema as or including a sense. The boundaries of the interpretational debate were first defined by the competing interpretations of Aron Gurwitsch and Dagfinn Føllesdal.

Gurwitsch, while recognizing that the noema is also a sense, emphasizes the noema or intentional object as the intended objectivity itself simply as intended (cf. *The Field of Consciousness*, esp. 228-79; "Husserl's Theory of Intentionality in Historical Perspective," in *Phenomenology and Existentialism*, ed. E. N. Lee and M. Mandelbaum [Baltimore: Johns Hopkins University Press, 1967], 24-57; and "Phenomenology of Thematics and the Pure Ego: Studies of the Relation between Gestalt Theory and Phenomenology," "Some Aspects and Developments of Gestalt Psychology," "On the Intentionality of Consciousness," and "Contributions to the Phenomenological Theory of Perception," all in *Studies in Phenomenology and Psychology* [Evanston, Ill.: Northwestern University Press, 1966], 175-286, 3-55, 124-40, 332-49). This identification of the object which is intended with the object as intended, that is, with the noema as sense, raises the questions of how to explicate, first, the difference and, second, the relation between the object intended and the object as intended. Gurwitsch's responses to these questions were united in his claim that the intended object itself is a whole of noematic parts or presentational moments or senses.

Føllesdal, on the other hand, emphasizes the noema as sense, as an abstract intensional entity which semantically mediates the act's reference to the object ("Husserl's Notion of Noema," *Journal of Philosophy* 66 [1969]: 680-87; reprinted in Dreyfus, ed., *Husserl, Intentionality, and Cognitive Science*, 73-80; cf. also "Noema and Meaning in Husserl," *Philosophy and Phenomenological Research* 50 [Supplement, 1990]: 263-71). Thus, intentional directedness is analyzed as a triadic relation. To iterate the formulation proposed by Smith and McIntyre, the act entertains a noema (i.e., a sense) and thereby prescribes an intended object which might or might not actually exist; cf. *Husserl and Intentionality,* 143. An act's entertaining a sense refers the subject of the act to an object in a determinate way in much the same way that a word's expressing a sense refers the speaker (or author) and audience to an object in a determinate way. The sense is a determinate manner of presenting.

Some authors have adopted an irenic approach to the controversy. See, e.g., J. N. Mohanty, *Husserl and Frege* (Bloomington: Indiana University Press, 1982), 70–79; and "Intentionality and Noema," in *The Possibility of Transcendental Philosophy* (Dordrecht: Martinus Nijhoff, 1985), esp. 201–2. Cf. also Donn Welton, *The Origins of Meaning: A Critical Study of the Thresholds of Husserlian Phenomenology* (The Hague: Martinus Nijhoff, 1983), §§4.1, 5.4, 6.4, and chap. 7; and Mary Jeanne Larrabee, "The Noema in Husserl's Phenomenology," *Husserl Studies* 3 (1986): 209–30.

For a brief overview of the controversy, cf. John J. Drummond, "Noema," in *The Encyclopedia of Phenomenology,* ed. Lester Embree et al. (Dordrecht: Kluwer, 1997), 494–99. For criticisms of both Gurwitsch and Føllesdal, as well as of the irenic approach, cf. John J. Drummond, "A Critique of Gurwitsch's 'Phenomenological Phenomenalism,'" *Southern Journal of Philosophy* 18 (1980): 9–21; Drummond, *Husserlian Intentionality and Non-foundational Realism,* esp. chaps. 4–5; John J. Drummond, "An Abstract Consideration: De-ontologizing the Noema," in *Phenomenology of the Noema,* ed. John J. Drummond and Lester Embree (Dordrecht: Kluwer, 1992), 89–109; and Drummond, "From Intentionality to Intensionality and Back," 89–126.

33. *Ideen I (Hua),* 203 [*Ideen I,* 182]; *Ideas I,* 214.

34. *Ideen I (Hua),* 206, 297–304 [*Ideen I,* 185, 266–73]; *Ideas I,* 217–18, 309–16.

35. *Ideen I (Hua),* 299 [*Ideen I,* 268–69]; modified *Ideas I,* 311.

36. *Ideen I (Hua),* 302 [*Ideen I,* 271]; modified *Ideas I,* 314.

37. *Ideen I (Hua),* 205 [*Ideen I,* 184]; modified *Ideas I,* 216.

38. Føllesdal, "Noema and Meaning in Husserl," 271.

39. Cf., e.g., *Ideen I (Hua),* §§88, 90–91, 98.

40. Cf. *Ideen I (Hua),* §131.

41. Richard Holmes also answers claims in favor of the Fregean interpretation supported by appeals to this text; cf. his "An Explication of Husserl's Theory of the Noema," *Research in Phenomenology* 5 (1975): 149–52.

42. *Ding und Raum,* 341–46; *Thing and Space,* 297–302.

43. *Ding und Raum,* 343; *Thing and Space,* 299; cf. also *Ideen I (Hua),* 370 [*Ideen I,* 316]; *Ideas I,* 363; and *Passiven Synthesis,* 23.

44. *Ding und Raum,* 49–54; *Thing and Space,* 42–46.

45. *Ding und Raum,* 51; *Thing and Space,* 43; *Passiven Synthesis,* 4.

46. I cannot here explore the details of Husserl's account of the temporality of consciousness. For such an account, see John Brough, "The Emergence of an Absolute Consciousness in Husserl's Early Writings on Time-Consciousness," *Man and World* 5 (1972): 298–326; and his "Translator's Introduction" to *Time-Consciousness,* xi–lvii.

47. I take the view that Husserl believes that only the impressional moment animates contents to be an implication of his rejection of the apprehension/contents-of-apprehension schema in his discussions of time-consciousness; cf. Brough, "The Emergence of Absolute Consciousness," 311–13, and his "Translator's Introduction," xliii–xlviii.

48. *Ding und Raum,* 49–50, 55; *Thing and Space,* 42–43, 47.

49. *Ding und Raum,* 55–56; *Thing and Space,* 47–48.

50. *Ding und Raum,* 56; *Thing and Space,* 48.

51. *Ding und Raum,* 57; *Thing and Space,* 48.

52. *Ding und Raum,* 57; *Thing and Space,* 48.

53. *Passiven Synthesis,* 8.

54. *Passiven Synthesis,* 118.

55. *Passiven Synthesis,* 165.

56. *Passiven Synthesis,* 164.

57. *Passiven Synthesis,* 176, 420.

58. *Passiven Synthesis,* 119.

59. *Passiven Synthesis,* 178.

60. *Passiven Synthesis,* 119.

61. *Passiven Synthesis,* 185.

62. *Passiven Synthesis,* 187.

63. *Passiven Synthesis,* 187.

64. *Passiven Synthesis,* 187, 289–90.

65. *Passiven Synthesis,* 187–88; cf. also *Ideen II,* 223; *Ideas II,* 235.

66. *Passiven Synthesis,* 175.

67. *Passiven Synthesis,* 110, 112–16, 120, 180.

68. *Ding und Raum,* 58; *Thing and Space,* 49.

69. *Ding und Raum,* 59; *Thing and Space,* 49–50.

70. *Passiven Synthesis,* 8–9.

71. *Passiven Synthesis,* 6.

72. *Passiven Synthesis,* 7.

73. While I do not deny the presence of kinaesthetic awareness of our bodily activities, the correlation crucial to understanding perception is not the correlation between two real (*reell*) sequences of sensations, but the correlation between (a) bodily activities and processes and (b) the flow of appearances presenting an identical object; cf. John Drummond, "On Seeing *a* Material Thing *in* Space: The Role of Kinaesthesis in Visual Perception," *Philosophy and Phenomenological Research* 40 (1979–80): 19–32.

74. *Ding und Raum,* 170; *Thing and Space,* 143–44.

75. Drummond, "On Seeing *a* Material Thing *in* Space," esp. 27–31.

76. Cf., e.g., *Ding und Raum,* §27ff; *Passiven Synthesis,* 5, 20–22.

77. *Ding und Raum,* 134; *Thing and Space,* 111.

78. Cf. John Drummond, "Objects' Optimal Appearances and the Immediate Awareness of Space in Vision," *Man and World* 16 (1983): 177–205.

79. Space does not permit a full exploration of the details of this notion of "horizonal reference." For a fuller account, see Drummond, *Husserlian Intentionality and Nonfoundational Realism,* §39; and Drummond, "From Intentionality to Intensionality and Back," 117–25.

80. Cf. *Erfahrung und Urteil,* §§22–46.

81. *Logik (Hua),* 120; *Logic,* 115.

82. *Logik (Hua),* 117; *Logic,* 112.

83. *Logik (Hua),* 128; modified *Logic,* 123.

84. *Ideen II,* 8–11; *Ideas II,* 10–13.

85. *Ideen II,* 10; *Ideas II,* 12.

86. *Ethik,* 252.

87. Husserl describes, by analogy with categorial intuitions, the experiences fulfilling value-judgments as "axiological" intuitions; cf. *Ideen II,* 9; *Ideas II,* 10.

88. *Ethik,* 26.

4

Husserl's Type and Kant's Schemata

Systematic Reasons for Their Correlation or Identity

Dieter Lohmar
Translated by Julia Jansen and Gina Zavota

THE GOAL OF this investigation is to show that the Kantian concept of *schema* and the Husserlian concept of *type* are functionally almost identical. Their mutual function is to guide the synthetic unification of the intuitively given in the perception of objects.

First, I will briefly describe the systematic place occupied by the function I ascribe to both Kant's *schema* and Husserl's *type*. Second, I will give a brief exposition and interpretation of the function of Kant's schemata. In particular, I will clarify the specific involvement of this function in the constitution of objects. Third, I will explicate Husserl's concept of the type and its relation to Kant's schemata—the type is here understood as a specific form of prepredicative experience. Finally, an important systematic objection must be dealt with, namely, the rejection of the type as a fundamental object-constituting function.

1. The Function of the Schema

First, I would like to outline briefly the systematic place of the function that both schema and type fulfill. This place is perception, or more precisely, the process of apprehension of sensuously[1] given intuitions as the presentation of objects. Let me begin with a simple example. I see a yellow flower in a meadow. I see its stem and its leaves. The initially simple-sounding question is: How do I know that this stem and these leaves belong to this flower, that they together form one objective unity? The question seems to be all too easy because the answer is all too easy: Don't you see it? The stem begins directly under the blossom, the leaves are attached to the stem. Thus, the spatial contact alone clearly shows their connection. But is it really that easy? We now notice the grass around the flower, and we have to admit that it also touches the flower. If it were only a question of spatial proximity, then this grass would also be considered part of the flower, possibly part of its stem. How do we ultimately know, then, that the grass closest to the flower is not its foliage? How do we know that a stem normally grows from the ground up and not sideways? Somehow we know all this. However, it is becoming clear that we do not know how we know it.

Apparently, we know it somehow "from experience." For, as the flower in the meadow shows us, it is not sufficient to simply take a closer look in order to answer the following decisive question: *What in sensibility belongs to a seen object and what does not?* This question seems, however, to be the central systematic question with regard to perception, that is, with regard to that process through which we *select* from what is sensuously given to us that which will represent the object for us. Not even this selection, however, exhausts the entire perceptual activity, for in perceiving we "assert"—by constituting an objective sense—that certain "parts," which present themselves as considerably different and which can even belong to different sensuous fields, belong together in *one object.* The yellow color thus belongs to the green stem, the sweet scent belongs to the yellow flower. Once again it becomes cear that this activity, which one must correctly call a *synthesis,* requires some sort of grounding, that is, a kind of knowledge that would ensure its possibility.

Kant's claim that such a purposeful combination, or synthesis, is indispensable in order to have objects at all is, in the eyes of many phenomenologists, likely to be the result of his inclination for construction, to which Husserl testifies on many occasions.[2] Does Kant's thesis not imply that our sensibility provides us with nothing more than a chaos of sensations, an unconnected hotchpotch of sense data? However, let us now consider from a phenomenological standpoint which activities are necessary in order to have an object in intuition. To conduct such an investigation we must engage in an analysis of the process of apprehension (*Auffassung*) or apperception (*Apperzeption*). Husserl himself analyzes some important aspects of the apprehension of sense data "as something" in the Fifth Logical Investigation, but he largely ignores the necessary synthetic processes, as well as the empirically grounded guiding mechanism of these syntheses.[3] Only the genetic-phenomenological concept of the type can fill this lack.

I see a student in the second row of the classroom. What can Kant's thesis that in intuition there lies nothing but an unconnected compilation of intuitive presentations, a "chaos of sensations," mean in this situation? Kant claims that our synthetic activity must, by means of concepts, introduce coherence, order, and unity into this chaos. At first sight, this seems implausible. When we see "something," we do not encounter a "chaos of sensations." So what does Kant mean? All he asserts is that the synthesis of the intuitively given must have already been achieved by the time we see objects. Thus, we have to ask once again, What does it mean to say "I see a student"? More precisely, what must I have already done before I can see the student?

My eyes are moving, my glance is moving around within the visual field. One moment I see a head, then an arm, another arm, hands, a table. But the situation seems to resemble that of the yellow flower in the meadow: there are other heads, hands, tables, etc. We have obviously discovered the first problem. How do I know that this head and these arms belong together? As with the flower, one could argue that I simply see that they belong together. After all, they are very close to one another. What tells me, then, that the equally close table does not belong to the head? Further, how do I know that the feet sticking out from under the table do belong to the very same person? How do I know that the voice I am hearing belongs to this moving mouth?—Solving these problems requires a function that, if you will, "tells" me what a person sitting behind a table approximately looks like and what belongs to him.

At this point I should pause to reflect for a moment upon the naive character of this description. We cannot simply take for granted that things like "arms," "legs," or "heads" are lying ready at hand in sensibility like the parts of a puzzle, waiting to be put together. On the contrary, we can presuppose that only insofar as we apprehend a whole, for example, the sensibly given person, can we apprehend the parts as something distinctive, for example, as a head or a leg. The same holds for the next lower level: eyes, nose, hair, and mouth do not lie in sensibility in order to be put together as a face, etc. The iteration of the problem of synthesis on ever lower levels shows, on the one hand, that the apprehension of an object is a unified process. Only through retrospective reflection do we locate artificial levels that are not to be found in the living process.

On the other hand, however, it is a specific achievement of phenomenological analysis to be able to thematize different levels of the synthesis. We can ask, for example, whether the search for a first level does not constantly point to ever lower levels of syntheses that threaten to trap us in an infinite regress. Yet we could also attempt to demonstrate that while there is a sequence of levels pointing "downward," there are also elements of sensibility which, in a certain sense, come together "by themselves." This "by themselves" is, of course, not to be understood literally, for only the subject can perform unifying syntheses, that is, syntheses guided by the material of sensibility itself, although not guided conceptually. In his analysis of the unifying of what is "sensuously prominent" (*sinnliche Abgehobenheiten*) in *Passive Synthesis,* Husserl argues for this second, non-conceptual synthesis.[4]

Kant, on the contrary, does not conceive of the possibility of limiting the necessary "downwards" syntheses. Even a line, or something like a part of an outline, shows itself, according to Kant, only because we have already synthetically unified something in intuition by means of concepts. Thus he says in the *Critique of Pure Reason:* "We cannot think a line without *drawing* it in thought.

We cannot think a circle without *describing* it."[5] Everything, therefore, that contributes to the assemblage of a thing sensibly showing itself (for example, a part of an outline) must have been put into sensibility by the understanding according to some concept. This is why Kant can write that the understanding by no means finds in sensibility "such a combination of the manifold; rather, the understanding *produces* it."[6]

One could argue that Kant wants to declare all of us geometers, who each day secretly construct the objects we perceive, producing the elements of the perceived objects (e.g., outlines) using the material of intuition. This production would occur by means of mathematical and geometrical concepts, and also by means of pure concepts of the understanding. However, one must not criticize Kant for consistently thinking his position through to its conclusions, and thereby allowing for theses that clearly run contrary to our own experience. For it is obvious (although there is no way to monitor the activity) that we do not incessantly "construct," let alone with discursive concepts. Kant himself was well aware of this problem.

Kant ascribes to the concept the function of guiding the synthesis. However—and this is an important aspect of his theory—the concept functions in this case in a manner that makes it possible to successfully assemble the elements of sensibility into an object. Using the purely discursive form of the concept "student," that is, "animal of the species *homo sapiens sapiens,* male, roughly twenty years old, shoulder-length hair, glasses, etc.," one would never reach the goal of object constitution. Two arguments confirm this impossibility. First, all these concepts can be further dissolved into partial concepts, leading to an infinite regress. Second, it is hard to comprehend how such a purely discursive concept, which can always be broken down into further discursive concepts, could ever acquire a meaningful relation to sensible intuition. If one holds that purely discursive concepts could achieve such a relation, one must also claim that the understanding can apply concepts to the sensibly given simply by literally "running around" (*discurrere*) in itself. But on this point Kant is unambiguous: intuition and concept are both necessary for cognition. Thus, Kant is particularly aware of the problem of the application of discursive concepts, and his theory of the schema of a concept is an attempt to solve this problem in an appropriate fashion.

Kant realizes that we need something that is, in a certain way, "closer" to intuitions than the collection of purely discursive, linguistically graspable characteristics determining the concept "student." He offers a solution to this problem by claiming that we do not only have the concept "student" in its just mentioned discursive form, but also as a *schema*. A schema is, according to the chapter on schematisms in the *Critique of Pure Reason,* something like a "sensible" concept of an object.[7] But to speak of a "sensible" is merely to describe a goal; nothing is said about how to reach that goal. A different characterization seems more helpful: The schema is a rule according to which we can produce all images and aspects of an object. It could be compared to the presentation of a shape (or of an outline). When I say that I know the shape of a person, then I mean by shape something general, which cannot be restricted to a sitting person or standing person, but which is equally appropriate for all possible positions and all possible people. I know by means of a schema that to this student must belong one head and a right and a left arm, at what angle they must be attached to the torso, that the table does not belong to him but the feet do, etc. The schema of "head" or "face," then, is the rule by means of which I can find and put together those sensible elements which belong to a face.

It was Kant's opinion that the schema of a concept is in a certain way equal with the *concept* itself. He also speaks of a "schematization" of concepts. The "schematism of the pure understanding" is the manner in which the concept, which is only a collection of discursive characteristics, can become a schema.[8] Kant was clear about the fact that only schematized concepts can be applied to intuitions. This is not only true for pure concepts of the understanding, but also for pure mathematical and geometrical, and even for empirical, concepts. Since Kant was mainly interested in the *a priori* conditions of object constitution, he only peripherally dealt with schemata of empirical concepts, such as "dog." According to Kant, the connection between concept and schema remains one of the darkest secrets of human nature ("a secret art residing in the depths of the human soul"),[9] one we can only approach step by step. Ultimately, in Kant the concept of the schema remains in many ways obscure and impenetrable.

Certainly, there are, dispersed throughout Kant's writings, some indications of how the schema of an empirical concept, for example, the schema of a person, may come about in a sequence of experiences in which people are actually intuitively given. However, this empirical-genetic aspect of his discovery of schemata, that is, the generation of schemata through homogeneous experiences of objects that are in some sense similar, never really interested Kant very much. His intention was merely to uncover the a priori conditions of cognition. In Kant's opinion, the empirical-genetic dimension of the problem was a matter of psychology. His main task he believed to be the uncovering of the non-empirical, that is, *a priori,* factors of cognition.[10]

In order to arrive at an appropriate theory of the genesis and the precise function of schemata, however, we have to begin with precisely the empirical questions and investigate how a schema can arise from experiences of the same type that are in some way "similar" to each other. However, this investigation is impossible under the presuppositions of Kantian transcendental philosophy, especially if one understands Kant's critical philosophy dogmatically—that is, as a previously given doctrine not to be further perfected. The possibility of a more appropriate theory of something like schemata presents itself when one understands Kant's criticism as a method, one which could be fruitfully combined with other theories of consciousness, also understood as methods. Only with Husserl's phenomenology and, in particular, with its later *genetic* manifestation, will it be possible to inquire into the genesis of schemata.

2. Kant's Theory of the Schema

In this section I will investigate what exactly schemata are in Kant, and why they are needed. One could immediately object that enough commentaries on the concept of the schema have already been published. Therefore, it is important to point out the special standpoint of my analysis. Kant developed his theory of schemata primarily in order to respond to a very specific question: In what way are pure concepts of the understanding applicable to intuitions? As mentioned above, Kant's main interest was in the *a priori* conditions of cognition, which he located in the pure concepts of the understanding. Pure concepts of the understanding (e.g., causality or substance), however, cannot stem from sensibility, because they contain elements which are, in principle, incapable of being fulfilled in experience, such as the presentation of a necessary connection between events, which is implied by the concept of causality. We might experience the necessity of a connection—that is, the fact that it always exists— in some cases, but never in all. Since categories cannot be derived from intuition, it is for Kant especially important, but also especially difficult, to show how they can be applied to intuitions at all.

Husserl's phenomenology, on the contrary, is exclusively concerned with concepts arising from experience and, at times, from a supplementary idealization. Thus, the comparison between the Kantian schema and the Husserlian type cannot be performed through pure concepts of the understanding. In order to compare the functions of the schema and the type, we must restrict ourselves to the realm of empirical concepts, such as "house" or "dog." This, in turn, calls for a rereading of Kant's theory of schemata with a new interest, namely, in the possibility and application of schemata of empirical concepts. Such a project certainly harbors some serious difficulties, since we are concentrating on a Kantian achievement on which Kant himself did not focus. Nevertheless, it will be shown that Kant's description of the function of schemata was in many respects oriented around the case of an empirical concept.

In the first sentence of the schematism chapter in the *Critique of Pure Reason*, Kant formulates the essential characteristic of a legitimate subsumption of an object under a concept: The concept must be "homogeneous" (*gleichartig*) with the presented object, that is, it must contain all the characteristics that we present in the object.[11] This "presenting" initially only means "thinking," for in the case of analytical judgments, we only have to exactly know the concept (e.g., "bachelor") in order to apply a predicate to the object ("a bachelor is unmarried"). Predication on the grounds of an intuitive givenness is, however, included by Kant's formulation, meaning that I may legitimately apply a concept p to an intuitively given object S if all the characteristics that p encompasses conceptually are intuitively given in S.[12] Yet we have already discussed that the manner in which such characteristics or partial concepts can be contained in intuition has to be regarded as a systematic problem.

With regard to concepts of the understanding, their application to intuitions entails a particular difficulty, for these categories contain sensible elements that are, in principle, not to be found in intuition and experience, for example, the necessity of a connection between events. At least for pure concepts of the understanding, there must exist, if only for that reason, a kind of "mediation," a modification of the concept or the category, which can be applied to intuitions. Kant calls this "mediating presentation" the schema. The schema is a "third thing" between pure concepts of the understanding and intuition. In order for the application to intuitions to be possible, the schema "must be homogeneous with the category, on the one hand, and with the appearance, on the other hand."[13] On the one hand, then, schemata must stem from the power of understanding and thus be "intellectual";[14] on the other hand, they must be sensible, that is, homogeneous with sensibility.[15] Since pure concepts of the understanding—as transcendental conditions of objectivity in general—must be applied to all objects, the schemata of categories cannot contain any determinations other than temporal ones, that is, transcendental determinations of temporality.

Kant specifies the character of schemata further by showing the relation between schema and image. On the one hand, the schema is "a universal procedure of the imagination for providing a concept with its image."[16] On the other hand, Kant distinguishes carefully between schema and image. Schemata are "rules of synthesis," "rules for determining our intuition,"[17] "methods for presenting a concept in an image," or, as already mentioned, "universal procedures of the imagination for providing a concept with its image."[18] However, whereas the image is "a product of the productive imagination's empirical ability,"[19] the schema is a product of the "pure and a priori imagination."[20] According to the paradigm of geometrical construction (triangle), the schema, for example, the prescription for the construction of a triangle, is a rule for the production of an intuitive exhibition (*Darstellung*) of the concept. Such a rule is not restricted to a determinate image with determinate measures and contents. The "universality" of the concept is preserved in the schema, which is nothing but the schematized form of the concept. Schemata are rules for the synthesizing activity of the imagination with intuitive material. With their aid one *could* produce all possible images of an object *ad infinitum*.

Due to the rule-like character of schemata, Kant prefers to illustrate them by means of purely geometrical concepts. The schema of a triangle, as the "rule for the production of an image of all possible singular instances of this concept," can be equated with the prescription for its construction. To every possible intuition of a triangle belongs an act of construction, by means of which the pure, productive imagination produces an intuitive exhibition of the concept. The imagination thus synthesizes the manifold in pure intuition according to the rule of construction.[21]

Although the case of geometrical construction is much simpler than the cognitive achievement of the recognition of a person, for example, highly simplified, the model of geometrical construction remains helpful. Kant wants to show that in geometrical construction we find the same "formative synthesis" that also enables us to apprehend an everyday object by means of an empirical concept.[22] Whether we construct a geometrical object or apprehend intuitively given objects, we must, for example, "know" where the object "continues," with which other sensible elements it is "connected," etc.

Certainly, the model of geometrical construction has its limits. It contains peculiarities that are not to be found in all schemata, let alone in all empirical concepts. For example, there exists no necessity (as in the case of empirical concepts) to "assimilate" the guiding function of the schemata in apprehension to what is sensibly given (e.g., to apply the schema of a standing cow to a cow that is lying in the grass). In the case of geometrical constructions the intuitive aspect is freely produced. This glance at the schemata of empirical concepts shows the empirical core of the guiding function of schemata, but it also becomes clear that we sometimes have to "perspectivally modify" the schemata of empirical concepts of things (e.g., cows) in an appropriate way so that they become applicable to the given intuition. Thus, the activity of the imagination in its mediating function between intuition and concept must also come into play on the "conceptual" side.

Schemata of empirical concepts are, therefore, rules by means of which we can "draw" different forms of what is conceptually intended. The concept "dog" accordingly "signifies a rule whereby my imagination can trace the shape of such a four-footed animal in a general way, i.e., without being limited to any single and particular shape."[23] The rules meant here cannot, however, stem from the pure productive imagination *a priori*. As rules for drawing figures of empirical concepts (dog, horse), they must refer back to achievements of the empirical, reproductive imagination.

How must we imagine the concrete use of "rule-like" schemata in the process of perception? At this point, a passage in the transcendental deduction[24] provides some explanation. Schemata *guide* the combination (synthesis) of intuitions, which are "sporadically" and "individually" given by sensibility, toward an exhibition of a unitary object. This synthesis is performed "directly on perceptions."[25] We can, in fact, illustrate it with the example of the flower mentioned earlier. The flower has a blossom, a stem, and leaves. Every perception of an object contains elements which, regarded separately, can be understood as partial perceptions. These elements become interconnected, something which they cannot do in the senses,[26] only through the synthesis of the imagination. This becomes particularly clear in the case of a synthetic combination of intuitions from different sense-fields; the scent of the flower, for example, can be combined with its visual appearance. In apprehension, the imagination is supposed to "bring the manifold of intuition to an [or, one] image";[27] that is, it must connect the sum total of the elements of intuition that can exhibit an aspect of the object.

The necessity of synthetic combination is also illustrated by the following example. When we look out of a window divided by a wooden frame, we see fragments of shapes, for example, a tree branch separated from the corresponding trunk by the beam running across the window. In this case, we cannot say whether the trunk fragment and the branch fragment belong together if we do not know what the object about which we want to think *is*. The branch must be conceived in its relation to the trunk and vice versa. I interpret the former as a continuation of the latter, although their spatial connection in sensibility is interrupted (by the window frame). I test, so to speak, whether I can, by means of a schema, imagine the branch as a possible continuation of the trunk; if so, I then legitimately posit the branch-fragment as an actual continuation. According to Kant, one could thus say that the function of apprehension is to combine the impressions that are given by intuition into more or less loosely assembled images.[28]

Sometimes the synthesis of an object according to a schema necessarily transcends the sensibly given, thus adding something in thought that can never be given in sensibility. This supplementing function we find in the fundamental, object-constituting categories, for example, substance as permanent ground for properties. It is also in play, however, in everyday human apperception, to which we ascribe a subjective dimension of experience (i.e., consciousness), although this dimension can never be given in sensibility. In all cases, the connection of the given (e.g., "impressions")[29] requires a guiding rule in order to prevent it from collecting a mere "pile of presentations devoid of any rules." The fundamental model of apperception is a model of an activity of synthesis regulated by schemata.

Kant's example of the perception of a house exemplifies the way in which temporally successive synthetic activities can nonetheless constitute one permanent object.[30] In the process of "running through" the perceived object with my eyes, sensibly present elements are spontaneously combined into one shape in thought. Only through this synthesis does what is sensibly given acquire the character of fragments of a shape. When I perceive a house, "the order in the perceptions' successions"[31] can be different in different instances. I can, for example, "start from the house's top and end at the bottom, but they could also start from below and end above; and they could likewise apprehend the manifold of the empirical intuition by proceeding either to the right or to the left."[32] Kant avoids here the use of empirical concepts (roof, floor, window, door, etc.), which could denote pieces of the house, in order to avoid the false impression that these elements, or fragments, are given in intuition as "complete" objects. This is not the case, for only in the apprehension of something determinate can these elements become parts of that determinate something. In the process of apprehension, they are only points of reference, which can be located at the top, at the bottom, to the right, or to the left. Only when I integrate the exhibiting (*darstellende*) elements into one apprehension of a house, do they become *parts* of a house; and only then can I, in reflective retrospection, call them "roof," "door," "window," etc. The whole and all its parts receive their objective sense in one unitary act. In the apprehension of a house, the combination and the conceptual determination of the elements occur simultaneously. Kant refers metaphorically to the idea of the "image" (*Bild*) to characterize the schematically guided activity in perception, which assembles the object out of given intuitive elements as in a collage: "I draw, as it were, the house's shape."[33]

Once more we must return to the mutability of schemata, which we pointed out in connection with the example of the cow lying in the grass. Even if we "know" by way of a schema what we want to see, we still need something like a "rule appropriate to the specific circumstances of the event of perception." This "assimilated schema" enables us to draw—in order to stay with the image of the image—every position and angle (to our senses) possible of that which we expect to see. Apparently, it mainly consists of a necessary perspectival assimilation to our point of view and to the position of that which we see. If we have a starting point, we have to know, for example, in which direction or with which inclination to "continue" or, at least, how we could possibly continue; otherwise, we could not combine what we expect to combine. In other words, we could not see what we expect to see by means of the schema.

The perspectival distortion and the alteration of the shape due to an alteration in the object's position must, so to speak, be compensated for. Objects of external perception are, due to their "different positions in relation to [our] senses,"[34] always given in a certain perspective. Nevertheless, we can also recognize a house from the side, or see a sitting person or a cow in the grass. When a movable body alters its position, its mode of appearances, for example, its outline, changes as well. A sitting person has a different outline than a standing person. If I still perceive her as a person, then I have to see her as a sitting person. Thus, I must "know" what a sitting person looks like, and, moreover, I have to apply this knowledge in some way in the course of perception.

It is crucial to understand that the alteration of the schema which enables the perception of a sitting person does not only imply an alteration of the actual "paths" my "wandering glance" takes on the side of sensibility. The assimilation of the schema also means that my "wandering glance" orients itself according to a different "hiking map," which is appropriate for the altered shape. Thus the imagination also has the task of perspectivally distorting or correcting the shape expected by virtue of the schema, that is, in whatever perspective and position. Only on the basis of such flexible expectations is it possible to test whether the intuitively given elements can be seen (combined) as a position or perspectival aspect of the expected object. This achievement of the imagination does not affect the side of sensibility but the side of the expected, that is, in a certain sense the side of the schema. It is a method of perspectival correction (*Umzeichnung*) and positional alteration of the expected objects.

In the case of a mere perspectival correction of a shape, the relation between the parts of the corrected shape and their angles remains the same. Geometrically speaking, we have a shape-preserving *affinity-transformation*, like the transformations we perform when we rotate or stretch geometrical objects while preserving their angles. All possible shape-preserving corrections, therefore, belong to the same class. However, this class does not only contain all possible perspectival aspects of the same object, but also all possible positions such objects can occupy. The positional variation could also be understood geometrically, although there are limits to the geometrical paradigm, for the knowledge of possible positions of, for example, the human body also depends on empirical data, such as which joints can be bent or turned and which ones cannot. Here at the very latest, we become suspicious: All this specialized knowledge is necessary in order to see a person who is sitting or bending over?

One may justifiably object that at least we do not know that we have such complex knowledge. Naturally, then, it might be difficult to convince us of its existence. We could just as well claim to be brilliant artists who, by means of some "knowledge" slumbering in our schemata, can draw all possible shapes and positions of a person. Most of us know, however, that we cannot do this; I, at least, certainly cannot.

And yet, the proof that we have such knowledge in principle is astonishingly simple. We must merely distinguish between the ability to actually draw or paint such a shape and the ability to judge such a drawing. For the sake of brevity, I will call the former the "ability to draw" (*Zeichnungsfähigkeit*) (or "ability to produce," *facultas faciendi*) and the latter the "ability to judge" (*Beurteilungsfähigkeit*) (*facultas judicandi*). Our ability to judge implies that we "know" how a human shape presents itself in all possible positions and perspectives, and that we can thus judge any possible drawing. This ability is common to all of us. For example, when we watch a painter at work, we immediately notice when an outline is too broad, when an arm or a leg is too long or has an "impossible" angle. We can immediately say whether something about the proportion or the position of the body parts in the drawing is "incorrect." What most of us lack is the trained ability to draw an imagined or seen shape. The artistic ability to draw requires talent and a great deal of practice, whereas to exercise our ability to judge, with which we are concerned here, we only need to have and apply schemata.

In our "knowledge" of the different possible positions of human bodies, the empirical core of schemata of everyday concepts shows itself once again. We are now able to work out the dependence of these schemata on our previous experiences in greater detail. For this purpose, I will analyze some of Kant's attempts to characterize schemata of empirical concepts. Kant initially defines the schema of an empirical concept, in this case "dog," as "a rule whereby my imagination can trace the shape of such a four-footed animal in a general way."[35] This characterization can be transferred to all empirical concepts of external objects. The schema of the concept "poodle" is a rule whereby we can draw all possible variants, positions, and perspectives of a poodle. The generality of this "tracing" (*Verzeichnung*) lies in the fact that I can draw a sitting, running, or lying poodle in different perspectives. The "procedure of the understanding with respect to these schemata" includes, as we have seen, two different kinds of rules: (1) Rules for the production of different shapes (e.g., that of a poodle), and (2) rules for the shape-preserving correction of shapes (e.g., transformation into a different position or perspective). The schema, then, does not limit me to "any single and particular shape offered to me by experience, or even to all possible images that I can exhibit *in concreto*."[36] Since a rule for the production of certain shapes is *qua* rule general, it cannot be identified with a determinate image. It remains a proto-image (*vor-bildlich*),[37] making its presence felt only through its guidance of our combinatory activity.

How do we acquire schemata? With regards to a priori concepts, Kant can legitimately claim that their schemata must be *a priori* as well, that is, they must stem from the understanding alone. With regard to empirical concepts, however, he would have to concede that their schemata must be derived from experience. I can learn to distinguish a dog from a cow only on the basis of experience. We know from the mistakes children make that we frequently have to say "this is not a 'bow-wow'" so that they learn to distinguish cows and dogs. Schemata of empirical concepts, therefore, must somehow gather experiences we have had in intuitively given cases. However, as we have stressed repeatedly, Kant was not interested in the empirico-genetic aspect of schemata.

A further peculiarity of schemata would have probably disquieted Kant more seriously. If we acquire schemata of empirical concepts through experience, then they are dependent upon experience and therefore subject to change. A simple example would be the concept "dog," which also contains a certain idea of the size of animal to be expected. If we live in a country where there are no small dogs, such as beagles or poodles, but only large ones, then our schema will have to change as soon as we see such small dogs, and vice versa.[38] But we should not expect theories from Kant in a field in which he was not interested.

We encounter one model that helps us understand how schemata are dependent upon experience in Kant's exposition of the genesis of a standard idea (*Normalidee*). For the purpose of detecting the standard idea of a beautiful man, the imagination piles up a great number of images. Where the most characteristics overlap, that is, in the "darkest" spot in the pile, we find the characteristics of the beautiful man in general.[39]

Moreover, schemata have an important function with regard to the temporal combination of events; causality, for example, is such a fundamental schema. Kant was specifically interested in pure concepts of the understanding, since they exhibit *a priori* conditions of objectivity. For example, he understands the schema of causality as a rule that objectively determines temporal relations between events. The schema of causality is a rule whereby something "real . . . whenever it is posited" is always followed by something else.[40] "Always" is here synonymous with the necessity which we co-conceive when we think of certain events as causally connected. An apple disconnected from the branch falls downwards—that is, with necessity, in all cases, "always."

The necessity that characterizes all objective cognition is, according to Kant, identical with the necessity arising from the category of substance. Taken as a schema, substance means "permanence of the real in time"[41] and refers to a lasting connection between the permanent substantial bearer of qualities and the qualities. "Permanent" is again synonymous with "always" and signifies that the connection presented is objective, that is, that it is in some way "necessary." In other words, it outlasts the momentary intuitive connection between thing and qualities and persists. This persistence is an element of everyday object constitution. When we say "the book is green," we mean that there is a connection between the book and its color which does not merely exist for a moment and then disintegrate, but which persists for a certain period of time.

In order to conclude, let's return once more to the perception of objects, which we can then apply to the perception of sequences of events. The condition for the legitimate application of an empirical concept is provided by a positive answer to the following question: Could I produce from intuition the exposition (*Darstellung*) of an object that I want to perceive? Do I arrive at an exhibition of the object's shape through some sort of exhibition—simultaneously motivated and limited by the fragments present—that conforms to the rules of "drawing"? Kant writes that "when I turn the empirical intuition of a house into a perception by apprehending the intuition's manifold," then "I draw, as it were, the house's shape."[42] "Drawing" (*zeichnen*) or "tracing" (*nachzeichnen*) the shape of a house always implies an orientation around an empirical concept. I am not actually drawing the shape; for in standard perception we merely combine the given material of the prominent features in intuition (*anschauliche Abgehobenheiten*).[43]

The legitimate subsumption of an object under a concept requires that the concept contain the characteristics that are intuitively given in the object to be subsumed. We can understand this containment preliminarily as the congruity of the conceptual characteristics with the intuition as regards their content. However, this model of plain congruence is too simplified to be appropriate to the matter at hand. There *is* no shape of an object in sensibility previous to the regulated intervention of the imagination. The sensible elements first have to be gathered and combined; only by being successfully combined do they become fragments *of* something. I must use the schema to examine whether it is possible to form a definitive shape out of the prominent features given in intuition.

3. Husserl's Theory of the Type

Husserl did not take up Kant's concept of the schema productively, although it certainly could have been put to use in a phenomenological conception of object-constitution. In his later, genetic phenomenology, however, Husserl developed his notion of the pre-conceptual type, which plays the same role as the schema in Kant. Nonetheless, it would be incorrect to claim that Husserl just "reinvented the wheel," for Husserl's analysis of the function of the type is placed in a very different methodological context. The fact that our concepts are grounded on, and develop through, our previous experiences is a starting point for genetic phenomenology.

Kant determined the concept of the *a priori* as "prior to and independent from all experience." Hence, for Kant no function genetically developed from experience can be considered a transcendental condition of objectivity, for all transcendental conditions of the possibility of having objects (*Gegenstandshabe*) are *a priori*. All genetic questions are, for Kant, *a posteriori* and therefore matters of psychology. Husserl, by contrast, understands the concept of the *a priori* in the sense of "intuition of essences" (*Wesensschau*) and "ideational abstraction" (*ideierende Abstraktion*), which he later methodologically specifies as "eidetic variation" (*eidetische Variation*).[44] Therefore, he is able—if only in his genetic phenomenology—to understand a function formed in experience, such as the *type*, as an *a priori* element of constitution. A type is generated through a series of homogeneous experiences and can then guide our synthetic combination of the singular, intuitively given elements of an object. The type is thus a transcendental condition for the possibility for the constitution of objects. While the fundamental difference between the two thinkers' conceptions of the *a priori* must be noted, a far-reaching analogy between the functions of Kant's schemata and Husserl's types can also be made.

An object's type functions mainly in perception. The typifying apperception of objects is an indispensable and constantly operating function which is based on the empirical sediments (*Erfahrungsniederschläge*) the subject acquires.[45] We apprehend in advance (*im voraus*) everything which affects us not as merely determinable in principle, but as already determined. This determination has the sense of "being-familiar-in-advance" (*Im-Voraus-bekannt-sein*). We always apperceive, as Husserl puts it, the unknown in the mode of the known, the unfamiliar in the mode of the familiar.[46] The function of the type of an empirical concept (e.g., dog) in the case of apperception consists in that of an intentional *fore-prehension* (*Vorgriff*). This *fore-prehension* allows us to expect something determinate (e.g., a part, future behavior, or a quality) within a fluid variability. Our expectation is thus, on the one hand, already determined with respect to content. On the other hand, however, it remains flexible in order to "adapt" to the respective intuition, for example, through perspectival correction.

I will now attempt to approach the thesis of the functional equivalence of schema and type. For this purpose I will characterize the type from three different angles. First, I will give an exposition of the specific pre-conceptual generality of the type and its gradations. I will then examine the genesis of the type, and, finally, I will describe the process of "awakenings" (*Weckungen*) of certain types and the rivalry between typifying apperceptions. A detailed investigation of the specific function of the type within apperception is also needed. It will become clear that the type, in a manner similar to that of Kant's schema, has the task of guiding the combinatory formation of an intuitive exhibition (*Darstellung*) out of the material given through the senses. Only by virtue of this guidance is it possible to perceive a unitary object and to combine its exhibiting elements. The type thus turns out to be the basis for the possibility of apperception. Moreover, the type must be distinguished from general empirical concepts, which are applied in predicative subsumption.

There are different levels of generality in typifying apperception. There are very general typifying apperceptions which contain a large field of heterogeneous objects, such as the type "animal" with its numerous subtypes. Conversely, there is also a successive limitation of typifying expectations. For example, I can see an animal and then notice that it is a dog or, even more precisely, a German shepherd. On closer inspection, I perceive perhaps a dog familiar to me (even that would still be a typifying anticipation). It is possible, then, to have a type of an individual thing. Into the other direction, namely, the expansion of generality, the most general type is defined by expecting an object to be a substrate of determinations, as something explicable in general.[47] This most general typification is then narrowed down to specific types like thing, animal, man, artifact, etc.[48]

The gradations from the type of the "general something" (*Etwas-überhaupt*) down to the type of the individual thing start with a "totality of typifications,"[49] which belongs to the world-horizon as a whole, and which is then further differentiated more and more into different specific types. The concept "conifer" has a greater extension than "fir." Similarly, one could speak of the "extension" and the "level of generality" of a type.[50] With regards to this generality, the lowest generality is the completely self-same individual, the "this," the individual concretum. As soon as we leave the exceptional case of complete identity (putting aside the alteration of position and perspectival givenness), we notice that between individuals of one type there can be a weaker or stronger similarity: "With the transition from the similar to the similar a coincidence appears which is still not a complete coincidence. The similar members which have overlapped one another are *divergent*."[51] The levels of similarity are, on the one hand, conditioned by the similarity itself (a quality difficult to reduce to other characteristics),[52] that is, by the "proximity" of the similarity of each moment. On the other hand, the levels are conditioned by the number of similar moments, or by the "degree of approximation to total similarity."[53]

In the explication of a perceived object, which follows an initial perception of the whole (*Gesamtwahrnehmung*), the indeterminate and general empty anticipations are successively filled out.[54] One could say that the initial perception of the whole begins with the most general type allowed by what is given. With each step of the explication, the typical expectation "narrows," until it finally reaches a particular specific type. Proceeding from a very general type (general something, substrate of determinations, real thing), the typifying anticipations change simultaneously with the successive narrowing of the type involved in the explication. The horizon of typifying anticipations "is constantly in motion; with every new step of intuitive apprehension, new delineations of the object result, more precise determinations and corrections of what is anticipated."[55] The type helps, as it were, in two respects: it "tells" us what in sensibility belongs to the object and what does not, and it draws our attention to ever new particularities which a case of such a type will have. Hence, the type also determines our expectations; I expect the scent of a flower, for example, even when I see it, at first, only from afar.

What is anticipated in typification is, however, only determined as "indeterminate and general."[56] In expectation, a certain "realm [*Spielraum*] of possibilities"[57] is given, since different intuitions can fulfill the same typical expectation; for example, different colors fulfill the typical expectation of surface coloring.[58] We can understand this specific indeterminateness of the type as an "'extension' of the indeterminate generality of anticipation."[59] In a certain sense, the type, like Kant's schemata, must have such a latitude or realm (*Spielraum*). The type enables us to apprehend different objects as exemplars of the same type.

The specific indeterminateness of the type also makes it possible to comprehend different modes of presentation (adumbrations, perspectival exhibitions) of the same object. Hence, even the type of an individual thing must display a "vague,"[60] indeterminate generality[61] that leaves much room for an *affinity-transformation* of the unknown into the known. Like the schema of an empirical concept, the type must also encompass different perspectival exhibitions of an object. Thus, the type never has a completely determined sense, but only a "frame of empty reference."[62]

The perception of an unfamiliar object, which commences with the most general group of types (*Typik*) and is progressively narrowed down in the explication of concretely given objects, results in the constitution of a new object type. "With each new kind of object constituted for the first time (genetically speaking) a new type of object is permanently prescribed, in terms of which other objects similar to it will be apprehended in advance."[63] The constitution of a new type is an everyday situation not only for children, but for adults as well. Adults also acquire new types of individual objects every day, for example, of particular people. With this new type "other objects similar to it" can be apprehended, namely, as objects of this type.[64] The constitution of a new type also creates a new possibility for action; I can apprehend other objects as modifications of similarity of the object known to me. With further experience I can expand this habituality. I can then apprehend an object as a modified member of a group of objects linked by a coincidence of similarities. In this sense one can interpret the type as a combination of a plurality of objects which resemble each other. It would then be possible to understand the type of a singular thing as the combination of a group of exhibitions of the same object. Each member of the group could be converted into all the others by means of *affinity or similarity-transformations.*[65] The similarity is the empirical ground for a combination of familiar cases into a group. At the same time, each individual member of the group expands the realm of what we expect in our typifying apperception. Accordingly, Husserl writes that the typifying apperception of a dog is based on what we have already experienced with regards to a certain group of (similar) individuals, "inasmuch as we have already had previous and frequent experience of 'similar' animals, of 'dogs.'"[66] He thus stresses once again that the empirical basis of the type, that is, the instituting (*Stiftung*) of a new type, always comprises only a finite number of objective experiences. The same holds for the expansion and consolidation of a type through further applications. In view of this finite group of experienced objects, one could understand the type as a form of family resemblance.

But where does this connection between the objects in one group "lie"? Where, if you will, is it "situated"? Generally speaking, without touching on the mode of being "situated," we can say that the connection "lies" in the subject. The experiencing subject achieves the connection, maintains it over time, and modifies it according to further experiences. A further question presents itself here, for the metaphor of "lying in" does not yet determine "how" the connection within a series of object experiences is achieved by, and "in," the subject.

Before we turn to the problem of where the connection is situated, however, we must clarify that the reference to a finite number of experiences of individual objects in the case of the type is fundamentally different from the unlimited generality of a universal concept. According to its sense, namely, the sense it acquires through experience, the type does not point to a universal conceptual generality. Thus, it is not to be equated with either a general concept or an empirical concept. The type does not refer to a general core; instead the individual object is thought of as a member of a finite resemblance group. No reference to a general core is made prior to the use of a universal concept.[67]

The constitution of empirical general concepts is nonetheless based on typifying apperception. Yet it goes beyond the givenness of individual objects (or groups of objects) by requiring a reference to something universal.[68] The typifying apperception is genetically more fundamental than the general concept and is its foundation: "on the basis of this reference we can always constitute a general concept 'dog.'"[69] Types are passively pre-constituted in a sequence of perceptual experiences. In using them, we notice "prescriptions of familiarity" that are made manifest in concretely determined expectations: "When we see a dog, we immediately anticipate its additional modes of behavior: its typical way of eating, playing, running, jumping, and so on."[70] In typifying apperception, these expectations are transferred to the object presently given in intuition. We see the intuitive appearance of these typical expectation as if "in advance."[71] Each apprehended typified thing can then lead us to the general concept belonging to its type. Nonetheless, in typifying apperception a singular thing always remains a singular thing (as a singular element of a group of similar objects). On the basis of the typifying apperception we can then form a general concept.[72] As soon as we are attuned to the generality meant by the concept, then each typical characteristic, "each part, each particular moment in an object, furnishes us something to apprehend conceptually as general."[73] The group of types belonging to a dog thus prescribes further experiences, and so if we proceed in our thought-experiment to ever new cases, the presumptive idea of "dogs in general"[74] eventually arises. The typifying apperception of an object as dog remains the point of departure. Husserl even calls it, in this context, the "actual concept": "Thus, superseding the *actual concept,* specifically acquired in actual experience, a *presumptive idea* arises, *the idea of a universal.*"[75]

In a manuscript which was partially used for the print copy of *Experience and Judgment,* there are some helpful passages that were not included in the final version which explain the relationship between the type (the "concrete essence") and the general concept (the "general essence"):

> Thus, the apprehension of general objects (general essences) already presupposes the apprehension of concrete essences, more precisely: concrete essences must have already been singled out [*ausgesondert*] so that a general essence can be "seen out of" [*herausgeschaut*] them. Concrete essences need no "comparison." They reach originary givenness by being singled out [*Aussonderung*], but not by simultaneously bringing to view [*Zusammenschauen*] particulars and not by "seeing" [*Herausschauen*] or "intending" [*Herausmeinen*] the general "out of" them. Concrete essences are not species.[76]

In typifying apperception, individual objects are intended simultaneously as concrete individuals and as members of a finite group of similar objects. A consciousness of the identical generality (of the species) in the many similar elements can emerge only on the basis of typical similarity. "First, there must be consciousness of similarity—or likeness—(this is not identity), and then a higher level of identification can erect itself on this ground: The *ens simil* [*itudinis*], the identical in the similar as such. E.g., the general [concept] 'color.'"[77] The two differ with regard to their intentions. On the one hand, I can turn to the one common identicality, that is, the general, in different individuals. On the other hand, I can focus on something concrete and single it out from the individual object insofar as I simply notice, by typifying, its similarity to other objects.[78]

In types and in the prescriptions awakened by types, we can find sediments of parts of that experience which we acquired through the explication of objects. Explicatory coincidence (*Deckung*) mainly results in an augmentation (*Bereicherung*) of an object's sense. At the same time, the type of the same object is also augmented and modified; "new typical determinations and familiarities are established."[79] On a higher level, the same holds for empirical concepts. Through the continuous experience of new cases of objects to which empirical concepts are applied, "empirical concepts are changed by the continual admission of new attributes."[80]

In the process of specifying and correcting concepts, elements which can only be constituted intersubjectively, for example, scientific theories and other people's knowledge, are also integrated. I learn from my teachers that, although it looks like a fish, a whale is a mammal and breathes through lungs.[81] Scientific concepts are thus constituted within a community. Consequently, we arrive at the problem of how far "downward" the influence of intersubjective constitution reaches. In particular, we need to raise the question of whether the fundamental types remain completely independent from such linguistically mediated corrections. Is it perhaps not the case that only sensibly-intuitive "outward analogy"[82] is at work in typifying apperception?

Everyday experience offers a wide range of vaguely determined types, such as grass, shrubbery, tree, etc. Most of the time, our experience gathers the rather obvious characteristics in order to form relations of similarity and types. A whale can thus be typified as a "fish," even though it belongs to the class of mammals. The "outward analogy," which includes shape, motion, and lifestyle, suffices for everyday purposes. Husserl calls these types "prescientific" or "non-essential" and distinguishes them from the "essential types" of the natural sciences.[83]

After these general analyses, we return to the systematic question of how the contents of the type are contained "in" it and "in" the subject. We begin our response with an investigation of the manner in which the content of the type reveals itself to us. For this purpose, Husserl attempts to explain the difficult interpenetration of typically awakened expectations and their fulfillment in intuition, which in retrospect proves the legitimacy of the typifying *fore-prehension* (*Vorgriff*).[84] Typifying apperception prescribes, on the one hand, an indeterminately general "style of explications to be realized, with explicates corresponding to them";[85] in the simplest case, we continue to perceive the object in the same mode. On the other hand, typifying apperception already lets us expect determinate qualities of the object, if only in the mode of fluid motion. Often, the expected remains expected within a framework of vague similarity.[86] The anticipating *fore-prehension* can, however, also imply a clearly indicative, determinate expectation. "When we see a dog, we immediately anticipate its additional modes of behavior: its typical way of eating, playing, running, jumping, and so on."[87] The typifying apperception allows us to see as if "in advance" what we cannot actually see yet. "We do not actually see its teeth; but although we have never seen this dog, we know in advance how its teeth will look."[88] This prescription is transferred by analogy from an object already perceived to the object presently grasped in typifying apperception. What is seen as if "in advance" may or may not show itself in further experience, that is, the typifying apperception may or may not sustain itself.[89] In the process of successively sustaining itself in intuition (the fulfillment of expectations) and of seamlessly narrowing down the type into specific types, the typifying apperception attains a pre-predicative right. Insofar as typical expectations apperceptively pre-ceive (*vorgreifen*) something which we expect to see, the type directs the regard of apperception (the perceiving regard) to those moments that make the given object into a case of that very type. In order to confirm or disappoint our typical expectation, we must, as it were, "look up" whether what is apperceived as a dog "runs like a dog," "eats like a dog," and has the shape of a dog.[90]

The typifying apperception can be followed by a predicative subsumption. To that end, what was "put together" into an intuitive exhibition of the object—a combination made possible by the type in apperception—needs to be voluntarily "run through" again in an active explication. The categorical intention then reaches through the individually given to a general object (the "to be an A"). The expectations awakened by the concept will then coincide with the intuitively fulfilled intentions. In typifying intuition, the specific concepts contained in a concept—Husserl even calls them "typical attributes"[91]—show themselves in this manner as "present" in the object. On the basis of these coinciding syntheses, it is possible to make a predicative judgment, for example, "This is a dog."

A further systematic question concerning the analysis of the function of types in perception must be raised, namely, how does what is given in intuition prompt a specific type to operate, that is, to be applied in perception? The first aspect of this investigation must be an examination of how a specific type is "awakened." This awakening happens by association. It is important to emphasize that this association, in which "this recalls that,"[92] is a special kind of association. The *awakening association* does not connect intentional objects with other objects; rather, it awakens specific types, which then enable us to perform a certain action, namely, the apperception, or at least the attempted apperception, of what is given in intuition as an object.

The application of a type is indeed comparable to an action. Actions too must be learnt; in fact, in everyday experience we continuously increase our repertoire of actions while the acquisition of new skills is hardly noticeable. We would not tell our friends with pride that we now know how to cook spaghetti, where our car's spare tire is located, or how to change the printer cartridge. However, all these actions establish permanent habitualities, of which, prompted perhaps by details of this first action, we can again become conscious and which can again result in action. When I see a car at the side of the road with a flat tire, when I read a text in which not all the letters are well printed, or when my children scream "Spaghetti!"—in all these cases such an awakening of everyday habitualities takes place. Our ability to see objects by means of a type is also a habituality. However, the "I can" of a passively constituted typifying apperception is situated on a level of constitution and activity that is far deeper than that of a conscious action.

The emergence of specific types through specific moments given in intuition is dependent upon perceptual experience. Types configure and alter themselves through the experience of each subject. The specification and correction of a typifying apperception leaves behind a "habitual possession," a "habitual knowledge."[93] Once a subject has made a specific intuitive constellation into a typifyingly apperceived object, its (perceptual) experience always includes some augmentation and modification of a familiar type. From then on, on the other hand, the experiencing subject always "sees," or apperceives, the concrete object with its augmentation. On the other hand, it also knows from that time onward that "this kind of intuitive constellation" (e.g., a bolt of lightning, a patch of fog, or the rustling of a mouse in the grass) can be a case of such a type. The augmentation is made manifest in the mode of expectation of certain elements which the perceptual interest then "wants"[94] to bring to intuition. With the constitution of a new type or the correction of a type that is already familiar, we have acquired permanent experience. We have also acquired a permanent connection between certain intuitive constellations (e.g., the rustling in the grass) and certain types, which lies ready for a further "awakening." Thus, we have found in the change of types, which is grounded in experience, one of the forms of the "preservation" of pre-predicative experience.[95] Once a type (e.g., "flower") is established and experientially determined, it allows for "a new flower making its appearance [to be] recognized on the basis of associative awakening of the type 'flower,'" that is "without an intuitive recollection of the earlier cases of comparison being necessary."[96]

The case of competition between different types in the process of apperception is particularly elucidating. It is certainly possible for competing types to be awakened in the course of experience, since the awakening takes place by association.[97] A new type emerges "on the basis of the associatively awakened relation of the likeness of one object with other objects" without the recollection of previously perceived objects being necessary.[98] An alteration of the type (or a competition between different types) can, therefore, be brought to the fore by "details" that initially seemed insignificant. Such "details" then associatively awaken a different, previously experienced type in which they occur as elements or which they had accidentally accompanied. The previously mentioned model of the "narrowing down" of typifying apperception—the explication which proceeds toward ever more specific types, which further and further approximate to what is given in intuition—must therefore not be understood as entirely unambiguous and mechanical. An apparently unambiguous "narrowing down" can once again become more diversified, either through further determination in the course of the experience itself (e.g., the red ball that suddenly appears green) or through associative awakening of a different type (e.g., in Husserl's famous example of a change in apprehension from "doll" to "woman"). In this case, several competing apprehensions are opposed to one another.

When different typifying apperceptions compete, the type's function of guiding the explicating regard (in apprehension) becomes particularly obvious. Husserl describes this guidance as dependent upon the series of types effective at the moment, which directs the regard "toward especially impressive qualities, by means of which an object of precisely this determinate type, or this individual object, is distinguished from other objects of like or similar types."[99] We see, for example, the typical shape of a dog, its typical movements, etc., and focus on what distinguishes it as a collie or German shepherd. [100]

In the Fifth Logical Investigation, Husserl considers the example of a wax figure in a panopticum, which represents a charming woman who is waving at us. [101] Initially we see a woman, but then we become aware of the illusion and realize that it is nothing more than a wax doll. The illusion is the result of two "perceptive apprehensions permeating each other," [102] of the competition between two intuitively fulfilled acts of perception containing different material, or different objective senses. Such a permeation of acts, that carry different material on the basis of the same sensuous presence, is possible only "in the form of conflict," although the intentions coincide "according to a certain tenor [*Erscheinungsgehalt*] of appearance." [103] The intentional content (*Inhalt*) "real woman" competes with the intentional content "real doll." Natural-looking colors and movements lend support for the "woman waving at us," while a certain mechanical movement speaks for the "moving doll," etc. Only when the contest is decided, based on a clearly predominant "tendency of perception (tendency of belief)," can I judge: It is not a woman, but only a doll. [104]

Let us now introduce the genetic concept of the type. The expectations contained in the type guide the perceiving regard, which in the case of a vacillating intuition "wanders" from one source of the intuition to the other. This "wandering regard" follows the current intuition. For example, when I see a doll, I focus on its fixed stare, and I notice the rattling of its mechanical movements; I am almost waiting for further jerking motions, and I carefully register the stereotypical image of its movements. My regard is constantly and with increasing attention directed to a spot on its sleeve, which is so unnaturally compressed by the incessant movement that no human arm could possibly be inside it. However, when I see not the doll but the woman, I repeatedly look into her eyes, which "look back at me." I notice the vividness of her movements, the naturalness of her comportment, her reactions to changes in the environment, etc. Thus, I notice only details which can designate a living body or a non-living thing, depending on the respective direction of the apprehension. Yet the difference is not resolved in the difference of direction, for in intuition different moments "show themselves" as well, depending on what I see and with which sensuous horizons I see it.

All information (*Kenntnisse*) about similar qualities of concrete objects belonging to a particular type—acquired in the course of experiential history—is the habitual possession of individuals. During the process of typifying apperception, it gives rise to certain expectations. Nonetheless, the content of the type and the resulting expectations differ according to the specific person and experience. Consequently, an experienced person (as well as an experienced dog) expects burning heat from an oven, whereas a child does not. The corresponding perceptual interest then attempts to bring these concrete expectations to an intuitive fulfillment. In the process of a type-regulated apperception, an exhibition (*Darstellung*) of the typically expected object is put together from what is sensibly present—as far as what is present allows.

At this pivotal point, Husserl's description of the function of the type comes remarkably close to Kant's exposition of the role of schemata of empirical concepts in apprehension (and in the subsumption of an intuitively given object under an empirical concept). [105] However, Husserl does not stress the necessity of combinatory synthesis as Kant does. Kant, in turn, believes that even the "smallest" unit of any possible synthesis must itself be guided by concepts. Even a line does not simply "show itself"; rather, we must produce it by gathering and combining what is intuitively given according to the concept of a line. For Kant, sensibility is a "turmoil," a "chaos," as long as the understanding does not intervene and regulate it through concepts. Husserl, however, departs from Kant at this point, for he believes that there are in sensibility so-called "prominent features" (*Abgehobenheiten*), which stand out (*abheben*) in "passive synthesis" in contrast to homogeneous and heterogeneous realms in the field of intuition. For example, a section of an outline can stand out in sensibility without the synthetic *unification* (*Vereinheitlichung*) (a "passive synthesis" is still a synthesis) having a concept of this line or needing to apply such a concept. Obviously, Kant and Husserl—despite their proximity regarding the function of types and schemata—*do not agree on the extent of order (Ordnungsgrad) in what is sensuously given.* [106]

4. The Problem of the "Beginning of Experience" and the Expansion and Impoverishment of Basic Types

Let us assume that the guiding function of schemata (in Kant) and the type's guidance of the regard in typifying apperception (in Husserl) are largely analogous. It would seem, then, that a vicious circle arises within the structure of the conditions of perception in the Husserlian (but not the Kantian) conception. The typifying apperception is based on past experience of previously constituted objects, but this experience is itself based on the object-constituting achievement of the type. A methodologically sound phenomenology can calmly confront this problem, however, for such an apparently irresolvable mixture of genetically later and earlier achievements is easily approachable through genetic phenomenological analysis. Such a structure of conditions, however, could appear circular and aporetic when viewed from a Kantian standpoint. Kant avoids the problem of circularity by means of the powerful presupposition of pure concepts of the understanding, which are always already introduced *a priori* (i.e., prior to all experience) by the understanding.

Let us provisionally intensify the Kantian suspicion of circularity. It is directed against the claim that by uncovering the object-constituting function of the type (or the schema) we have already found the last ground for the possibility (*letzte Ermöglichungsgrund*) of perception and cognition. The circle can be described as follows: Each type at work in experience presupposes previous experience, but since the type is at the same time supposed to be object-constituting, it must have been operating in that previous experience as a constitutive element as well. If we want to avoid this circle, then it seems that only one solution remains: for the possibility of experience, we must presuppose concepts (like the Kantian categories) that are already at our disposal before all experience. [107]

I will now attempt to show that this objection is somewhat hasty, namely, for two reasons. On the one hand, the type—understood as a concept-like function—is typically assessed "too highly," namely, as a concept of an object that already contains the sense-elements accidence and substance and perhaps also causality. On the other hand, the objection neglects the mutability of the type; in other words, it overlooks the important role of the expansion of types in experience and their impoverishment in intersubjective correction.

We must not put the fundamental constitutive types on a level that is "too high," for there are—as we will see—extremely rudimentary, but at the same time fundamental, types of events (*Ereignistypen*) which do not yet contain the notion of substance and its properties. In its most minimal form, a type consists of a synthetic connection between simple "impressions": for example, between two impressions that have occurred together in my experience several times in a regular manner and have thereby entered into an associative connection. In order to avoid the misrepresentation of this "event" as an objectively temporal event in a possible causal chain, we should instead speak of a complex of sensations (*Empfindungskomplexion*) or of a sensuous unity (*Empfindungseinheit*).

Let us consider an example. The experiential history of almost all people begins with sensations like the characteristic taste of mother's milk and the warmth which is regularly connected with it. One is not likely to claim that an object in the sense of a conceived substrate with its properties is constituted through the connection between the two sensations. However, these sensations constitute a permanent synthetic unity by virtue of their reference to each other. We can refer back to this unity in further experiences through typifying apperception of the same lived experience. Either presentation can awaken the other as expectation and guide the constitution of the lived experience on the basis of the given sensations.

Yet the type can always incorporate further presentations into the synthetic unity, such as the warmth of the skin, the mother's touch, her voice, etc. In the regular co-appearance of sensations, the type of a certain event develops (event is here understood as the synthetic unity of sensations, not as an element of a possibly causally connected chain of events). The more presentations the type incorporates, the more differentiated it becomes and the more content it gains. Conversely, the type also loses some elements in the process of impoverishment, a process to which we will return in a moment. At some point in the process of differentiation, a transition occurs from a fundamental type of an event to the type of an object, which can be detached from my subjective experience (*mein Erleben*). It thus becomes apparent that the type which, regarded as a concept, can constitute objects detachable from my subjective experience is in no way the most fundamental form of the type. At this point, however, many questions of genetic analysis appear which demand further investigation.

If we must then assume that the first concept-like functions (which, following Husserl, we call types) simply consist of the interrelation of two sensations, then the question arises as to how we can arrive at complex concepts like "dog" or "person." In order to respond, one has to keep in mind the two different directions of type-alteration mentioned above. The first can be called *expansion*. In expansion, the type continuously incorporates new characteristics, only, of course, those characteristics present in sensations which accompany the original connection. To this extent, we can regard types—and also their expansion—as primordially established (*urgestiftet*) through experience.

We become acquainted with wine, for example, though its fluidity and its weight, and we are pleased by its scent, its taste, and its red color. In our subject, these three sensations are associatively connected with each other. Whenever we are given the first two sensations, we also expect the third, the red color. Now, "experienced" people know that not all wines are red. Thus it becomes clear that the process of type-expansion is, on the one hand, hasty and, on the other hand, radically subjective.

How then can I correct such hasty expansions? The subjectivity of the type, in the sense of an experiential and personal relativity, can be overcome only by further experience and communication. If, with our subjective type of wine (wine = red wine), we even want to perceive white wine as wine, then we can, for example, have a conversation with other people about the fact that they believe that white wine is also wine. On the basis of intersubjective guidance, we must then, so to speak, "free" our type from the element of red color. We can interpret this process as an *impoverishment* of the type through intersubjective communication. Since in conversation we use concepts for types, a mutual intersubjective correction of word usage and types occurs. Only in this way is a common intersubjective use of empirical concepts possible.

One can hardly overestimate the readiness of a type to be expanded; types are downright voracious. The alteration of our types, however, is usually hidden within everyday trivialities. I will mention a few such trivial examples that illustrate the expansion of types through experiences, which in turn result in new associative connection within the type. For example, if we coincidentally had a mild headache while getting acquainted with red wine (not afterwards, which one can also experience sometimes), then it is possible that we will add this sensation to the type of red wine and thus find it less pleasant than other people do. If we then—perhaps for entirely unrelated reasons—feel nauseous, we might connect this nausea associatively with the sensations the wine is delivering to us and regard wine from then on as undrinkable (at least for us). These subjective elements of types, which are due to the accidental circumstances at the time, can be detected only in conversations with others. Perhaps they persuade us to give red wine another chance. [108] Everyone has probably had similar experiences. Sometimes we are aware of the subjectivity of the connection of sensations in the type; in this case, we may be able to rationally control it. For example, a person who was once bitten by a dog might be afraid of dogs her entire life. However, she is aware of this connection and recounts her experience almost as a sort of explanation for her—from the perspective of others—unmotivated fear. One could object that these examples are too trivial and commonplace; however, the expansion and impoverishment of types take place precisely in everyday experience.

The experiences I have had with certain objects, such as houses, previous to the present perception of an unfamiliar house are made manifest in *typical expectations*. The type contains these experiences, so to speak, in the form of concrete expectations. The respective concrete type is, therefore, not a concept-like function *a priori* (in the Kantian sense as "prior to all experience"). Nevertheless, the function of the type, that is, the guiding of the synthesis of intuition that we must perform in perception, is *a priori* (in the Husserlian sense of an essential necessity [*Wesensnotwendigkeit*]). Every perception of something must put together given sensations, and this synthesis requires guidance.

Here we encounter once again the above-mentioned problem of the "beginning," that is, the systematic difficulty of where to take the functions that guide the synthesis if not from previous experience. How the "first" experience is possible remains obscure, since it always already presupposes experience. However, this formulation of the problem neglects the formation of rudimentary types, which can consist solely of the associative connection between two sensations. Such "objects" think neither the substance-accidence connection nor causality. Therefore, the basic types in their further expansion and impoverishment invalidate the objection of Kantian philosophy. They refute the claim that the only way to avoid the problem of the beginning of experience is by means of pure concepts of the understanding immanent in reason.

Notes

1. [Trans.: Kantian literature largely uses "sensible," whereas "sensuous" is prevalent in Husserlian texts. This tendency is reflected in our translation, although we use both terms interchangeably.]

2. On Husserl's knowledge and judgment of Kant's epistemology see Iso Kern, *Husserl und Kant. Eine Untersuchung über Husserls Verhältnis zu Kant und zum Neukantianismus* (The Hague: Martinus Nijhoff, 1964).

3. In the Fifth Logical Investigation, apprehension is explained by Husserl as the activity that "interprets" the sensibly given real contents as an exhibition (*Darstellung*) of an

object. The real contents are what is directly given to the senses in an intuition. In the attempt to give a provisional approximation, we could speak of sense data instead of real contents, although this could lead to many misinterpretations. On the one hand, the term "sense data" is strongly affiliated with the tradition of empiricism. On the other hand, one could be tempted by the idea that real contents already mean something like constituted objects, which need "interpretation." Probably in order to avoid this misunderstanding, Husserl omits almost all uses of the word "interpretation" in the second edition of the *Logical Investigations*. An understanding of real contents as given and, simultaneously, self-sustaining objects would be utterly false, for real contents form only a dependent moment of the full intentional act. Thus, only in reflection can they be understood as independent objects. We have real contents always only as exhibiting (*darstellende*) moments of intentional objects. In Husserl's words, we never see red data, but we always already see a red rose. We always already have a phenomenon, understood as an intentional object, that presents itself to us in real contents, that is, in a certain mode of apprehension and with a certain quality of positing (*Setzungsqualität*).

In the Fifth Investigation, Husserl also investigates several important aspects of perception that are contained in intentional apprehension. *What* a certain constellation of real contents is apprehended *as,* Husserl emphasizes, depends on the subject and its achievement. In certain places Husserl calls such a constellation the summation (*Belauf*) of sensations (cf. *Logische Untersuchungen* (*Hua*), I, XXX). Consistently, he points out the possibility of a change in apprehension with the respective real contents remaining the same, and even identifies it as one of the most important features of apprehension. Everybody knows the example of the charming woman in the Panopticum who is, perhaps even in alternating apprehensions, at one point apprehended as an actual human being, at another as a wax doll. The alteration in the mode of apprehension must be considered as well. Husserl's fundamental distinction between intuitive, pictorial, and symbolic apprehensions implies the possibility of different apprehensions based on identical real contents. The pictured "A" can be apprehended intuitively as a black figure, pictorially as a pictorial presentation of a house, tent, or roof, and symbolically as the sign "A" with which, for example, the word "automobile" begins. Likewise Husserl draws attention to the fact that it is possible to apprehend one and the same object while the real contents are constantly changing (e.g., when I walk around one object).

Nonetheless, Husserl's account has serious shortcomings. For example, he does not explain what leads the synthetic contraction of the elements in intuition. He also fails to show how we "know" what belongs to the perceived object and what does not. Without the concept of the type Husserl is unable to provide an answer to these questions.

I have referred to these necessary investigations, which, to my knowledge, were not executed by Husserl himself, in the essay "Grundzüge eines Synthesis-Modells der Auffassung. Kant und Husserl über den Ordnungsgrad sinnlicher Vorgegebenheiten und die Elemente einer Phänomenologie der Auffassung," *Husserl Studies* 10 (1993): 111–41.

4. Cf. mainly the investigations in the *Lectures about Genetic Logic* (winter 1920/21), which were later published under the title *Analyses of Passive Synthesis* as *Hua* XI. The third part of these lectures is expected to be published soon as a supplementary volume to *Hua* XI.

5. B154. All translations of the *Critique of Pure Reason* are taken from I. Kant, *Critique of Pure Reason,* unified edition, trans. Werner S. Pluhar, intro. by Patricia Kitcher (Indianapolis: Hackett, 1996).

6. B155.

7. A146/B186.

8. Cf. I. Kant, Academy Edition, AA4, 98.

9. B180.

10. "*A priori*" is here to be understood in the Kantian sense as "before all experience."

11. The first sentence says: "Whenever an object is subsumed under a concept, the pre-

sentation of the object must be *homogeneous* [*gleichartig*] with the concept; i.e., the concept must contain what is presented in the object that is to be subsumed under it. For this is precisely what we mean by the expression that an object is contained *under* a concept" (A137/B176).

12. Schemata, therefore, can be understood as a kind of criterion. Their fulfillment must be provided by intuition in order to legitimatize the subsumption of what is intuitively given under a concept. According to this conception, the schema would be a kind of sequence of characteristics that must be fulfilled by intuition in order for a predication (e.g., "This is a tree") to be legitimate. Only the presence of the demanded characteristics permits the application of the concept. Thus, in this view, schemata formulate the conditions for the application of concepts to intuitions. I have already discussed this implication of a characteristic-theoretical conception elsewhere (cf. *Erfahrung und kategoriales Denken. Hume, Kant und Husserl über vorprädikative Erfahrung und prädikative Erkenntnis* [Dordrecht: Kluwer, 1998], chap. II, 4).

13. A138/B177.

14. A138/B177.

15. In the first paragraphs, Kant uses the concept of homogeneity (*Gleichartigkeit*) in four different aspects which I can only point to here. Cf. my "Kants Schemata als Anwendungsbedingungen von Kategorien auf Anschauungen. Zum Begriff der Gleichartigkeit im Schematismuskapitel der 'Kritik der reinen Vernunft,'" *Zeitschrift für philosophische Forschung* 54 (1991): 77–92.

16. A140/B180f.

17. A141/B180.

18. A140/B180. This formulation is probably one of the rare occasions when Kant uses "image" (*Bild*) in a metaphorical sense. He means a synthetic exposition (*Darstellung*) of an object out of given intuitions, which we would rather call a "collage." Accordingly, apprehension is that phase of perception in which the imagination "brings the manifold of intuition to an image" (A120). As will be shown, this synthesis is guided by the schema. (For an understanding of this function, the footnote on A120 proves helpful.)

19. A141/B181.

20. A142/B181.

21. We cannot deal with Kant's concept of "pure intuition" in detail.

22. Consistently, Kant writes that "the formative synthesis whereby we construct a triangle in imagination is entirely the same synthesis that we perform in apprehending an appearance in order to frame an experiential concept of it" (A224/B271). Apprehension is the "running through" and "gathering" of the elements of intuition that can exhibit (*darstellen*) the object for us.

23. A141/B180.

24. A120f.

25. A120.

26. Cf. A120.

27. A120.

28. A120n.

29. A120n.

30. The emphasis on the necessary temporal sequence in perceptions of complex objects is intended. Kant uses the example of the house to explicate the necessity of temporal allocations in apprehension in connection with the application of categories of relation (cf. A192f./B237f.).

31. A192/B237.

32. A192f./B237f.

33. B162.
34. A45f./B63.
35. A141/B180.
36. A141/B180.
37. [Trans.: The German *vor-bildlich* refers to both the quality of "preceding an image" and to a paradigmatic character, as in *Vorbild*, "raw model," "prototype."]
38. We can further demonstrate the mutability of schemata by means of yet another systematic example: There must be schemata for individuals as well. For example, there must be a schema for my friend Peter who intuitively reveals himself to me in many different modes. All these different modes require a schema for "seeing Peter," which would have to go beyond the schema "person" and be specifically directed to this individual. This schema would have to change over time, however, because Peter could get gray hair or shave off his beard. Kant would have probably hesitated to presuppose a schema for an individual, mainly because he always conceived the schema as a schematized concept. The concept of a singular (*conceptus singularis*) is, according to Kant, impossible, since a concept is necessarily general and must be valid for many different objects. We can thus conclude that there can be no schema of a singular object.
39. Cf. I. Kant, *Critique of Judgment*, trans. Werner S. Pluhar, with a foreword by Mary J. Gregor (Indianapolis: Hackett, 1987), AA, 233f. K. Düsing has also pointed out the similarity between this procedure and the formation of a schema by the imagination ("Schema und Einbildungskraft in Kants 'Kritik der reinen Vernunft'," in *Aufklärung und Skepsis*, ed. L. Kreimendahl [Stuttgart: Fromman-Holzboog, 1995], 52f.).
40. A144/B183.
41. A144/B183.
42. B162.
43. I do not consider the capacity for self-affection in the present paper. Self-affection is the peculiar ability of the mind to affect its own sensibility in conformity with the object which is perceived through schemata. This means that we insert sensations into sensibility that do not come "from the outside" but "from ourselves." A very common form of self-affection is the sensation we have when we watch somebody biting into a lemon or enduring pain. In these cases, our sensation approximately resembles the sensation of that person; it is not, however, identical with it. This capacity for self-affection plays a very significant role in object constitution. Kant thematizes the constitutive function of self-affection under a variety of different names, such as poetic imagination, self-affection, figurative synthesis, and *synthesis speciosa*. You will find a more precise exposition of the role of self-affection in Lohmar, *Kategoriales Denken*, chap. II, 10–11, as well as in the rather historical essay "Traum-Subjekt und Wahrnehmungs-Subjekt. Über die Beiträge von Leibniz und Kant zur Aufdeckung des Phänomenbereichs der Selbstaffektion," in *Alter* 6 (1998): 475–501. Within a more methodological framework I treat this topic in "Vier Thesen zur Selbstaffektion," which will be published in the volume on the conference of the Deutsche Gesellschaft für phänomenologische Forschung, "Die Sichtbarkeit des Unsichtbaren," held in 1998 in Leuven.
44. It is impossible for me to provide here a detailed description of the method of eidetic variation. Cf. E. Ströker, "Husserls Evidenzprinzip. Sinn und Grenzen einer methodischen Norm der Phänomenologie als Wissenschaft," *Zeitschrift für philosophische Forschung* 32 (1978): 3–30.
45. For the following, cf. *Erfahrung und Urteil*, 31–35, 140f.; *Experience and Judgment*, 34ff., 124f. On the distinction between type and general concept (*Allgemeinbegriff*) see ibid., pp. 394–403, 365–78.
46. *Erfahrung und Urteil*, 34; *Experience and Judgment*, 37f.; *Hua* VI, 126.
47. *Erfahrung und Urteil*, 34f.; *Experience and Judgment*, 37f.

48. *Erfahrung und Urteil,* 35; *Experience and Judgment,* 38.

49. *Erfahrung und Urteil,* 33; *Experience and Judgment,* 36.

50. Cf. *Erfahrung und Urteil,* §84a.

51. *Erfahrung und Urteil,* 404f.; *Experience and Judgment,* 335.

52. This refers to the inconceivable depth of the relation of similarity, which we only approximately describe when we speak of a transformation of similarity performed by our consciousness. Husserl speaks, for example, of "the magnitude of the divergences in similarity of all the similar moments" (*Erfahrung und Urteil,* 405; *Experience and Judgment,* 336).

53. *Erfahrung und Urteil,* 405; *Experience and Judgment,* 336.

54. *Erfahrung und Urteil,* 34; *Experience and Judgment,* 37.

55. *Erfahrung und Urteil,* 137; *Experience and Judgment,*122.

56. *Erfahrung und Urteil,* 32; *Experience and Judgment,* 36.

57. *Erfahrung und Urteil,* 32; *Experience and Judgment,* 36.

58. It is well known that Husserl notices the indeterminateness of objective intention already in the *Logical Investigations.* There he writes that this indeterminateness of intention, which correlates with a "certain broadness of possible fulfillment," is itself "a determination of this intention" (*Logische Untersuchungen,* II/2, 39–40; *Logical Investigations,* 2, 211).

59. *Logische Untersuchungen,* II/2, 39–40; *Logical Investigations,* 2, 211.

60. *Erfahrung und Urteil,* 141; *Experience and Judgment,*125.

61. *Erfahrung und Urteil,* 33; *Experience and Judgment,* 36.

62. *Erfahrung und Urteil,* 141; *Experience and Judgment,* 125.

63. *Erfahrung und Urteil,* 35; *Experience and Judgment,* 38.

64. *Erfahrung und Urteil,* 140; *Experience and Judgment,* 125.

65. In a formulation that risks the conflation of type and general concept, Husserl says that the type is constituted "on the basis of the associatively awakened relation of the likeness of one object with other objects" (*Erfahrung und Urteil,* 400; *Experience and Judgment,* 332). In other words, it is constituted on the basis of a coincidence of similarity within a group of familiar objects. In a different context Husserl writes that "on the basis of associative awakening of like by like, an object no longer affects us merely for itself but in community with those akin to it" (*Erfahrung und Urteil,* 387; *Experience and Judgment,* 323).

66. *Erfahrung und Urteil,* 399; *Experience and Judgment,* 331.

67. Cf. *Erfahrung und Urteil,* 388–91; *Experience and Judgment,* 323–26.

68. Cf. *Erfahrung und Urteil,* 391; *Experience and Judgment,* 326. "We need not," Husserl writes, "thematize a dog according to its type *as* a particular of the universal 'dog'; rather, we can also be directed toward it as an individual" (*Erfahrung und Urteil,* 400; *Experience and Judgment,* 332).

69. *Erfahrung und Urteil,* 400; *Experience and Judgment,* 332.

70. *Erfahrung und Urteil,* 399; *Experience and Judgment,* 331.

71. Husserl says about a specific characteristic applied in apperception: "We anticipate this, and actual experience may or may not confirm it" (*Erfahrung und Urteil,* 399, *Experience and Judgment,* 331).

72. It seems confusing that it is possible for us to use the word "dog" for designating both the type and the general concept. We can still be directed to the individual dog of our typifying apperception—although we say "dog," and thereby use the same designator as for the concept (cf. *Erfahrung und Urteil,* 399f.; *Experience and Judgment,* 331f.). Apparently, Husserl concedes that the typifying apperception can be accompanied by a meaning-giving act, which can then come to expression. Thus, the distinction between a typifying apperception and a subsumption under a concept cannot be made on the basis of the present linguistic expression, but only by reference to the objective intention.

73. *Erfahrung und Urteil,* 400; *Experience and Judgment,* 332.

74. *Erfahrung und Urteil,* 401; *Experience and Judgment,* 333.

75. *Erfahrung und Urteil,* 401; *Experience and Judgment,* 333.

76. "Somit setzt das Erfassen der allgemeinen Gegenstände (allgemeine Wesen) das Erfassen von konkreten Wesen schon voraus, deutlicher: konkrete Wesen müssen ausgesondert sein, damit aus ihnen ein allgemeines Wesen herausgeschaut werden kann. Konkrete Wesen bedürfen nicht der 'Vergleichung,' und sie kommen zu originärer Gegebenheit durch Aussonderung, aber nicht durch Zusammenschauen von Gesondertem und Herausschauen und Herausmeinen von Allgemeinem. Konkrete Wesen sind keine Spezies" (A III 11/Bl. 15a). I would like to thank the director of the Husserl-Archive in Leuven, Prof. Dr. R. Bernet, for permission to quote from several unpublished manuscripts. On the use of the manuscript in *Experience and Judgment* see D. Lohmar, "Zu der Entstehung und den Ausgangsmaterialien von E. Husserls Werk 'Experience and Judgment,'" in *Husserl Studies* 13 (1996): 31–71. We can conclude that this manuscript was used in the last phase of cooperation on the text of the "Logical Studies" (later "Experience and Judgment") from A III 11/Bl.2. Attached to this page we find an excerpt made by Husserl from *Formal and Transcendental Logic* with the following remark: "In the '*F. u. tr. Logik*' we refer to these '*Log. Stud.*,' §84, 182f., §86, 185ff." Husserl reread the "Formal and Transcendental Logic" in March 1937, in order to prepare for an introduction to the "Logical Studies." See also the letter from Husserl to Landgrebe from 31 March 1937, *Briefwechsel,* III/4, 356–69: "I immediately threw myself into the 'Logic' again," "for the 1st time since its publication in 1929!" (Ich habe mich sofort wieder auf die Logik gestürzt, zum 1en Mal seit ihrer Publikation in 1929!) Further, see the inscription in Husserl's personal copy of *Formal and Transcendental Logic:* "For the first time, newly thought through and re-appropriated. March 1937" (Zum ersten Mal neu durchdacht und wieder mir zu eigen gemacht. März 1937) (*Logik,* 463).

77. "Erst muß Ähnlichkeit—oder Gleichheit—(das ist nicht Identität) bewußt sein, und dann kann sich darauf eine Identifikation höherer Stufe bauen: Das ens simil<itudinis>, das Identische im Ähnlichen als solchem." Z.B. das Allgemeine Farbe (A III 11/Bl. 17a).

78. Cf. A III 11/Bl. 16a.

79. *Erfahrung und Urteil,* 140; *Experience and Judgment,* 124.

80. *Erfahrung und Urteil,* 401; *Experience and Judgment,* 333.

81. Cf. *Erfahrung und Urteil,* 402; *Experience and Judgment,* 333.

82. *Erfahrung und Urteil,* 402; *Experience and Judgment,* 333.

83. Cf. *Experience and Judgment,* §§83a and b. Similarly, Husserl opposes, already in Ideas I (§74), vague, inexact morphological concepts (notched, indented, rough, . . .) and the exact ideal concepts of the natural sciences.

84. Cf. *Erfahrung und Urteil,* 398–401; *Experience and Judgment,* 331–33.

85. *Erfahrung und Urteil,* 35; *Experience and Judgment,* 38.

86. Cf. *Erfahrung und Urteil,*140f., *Experience and Judgment,* 125. Husserl there characterizes the empty pre-intention (*das leer Vorgemeinte*) as vague and general, a not fully determined frame of sense.

87. *Erfahrung und Urteil,* 399; *Experience and Judgment,* 331.

88. *Erfahrung und Urteil,* 399; *Experience and Judgment,* 331.

89. Husserl does not, in this context, discuss the issue of achievement (*Leistung*) and the problematic of self-affection, which was an essential element of Kant's explication of cognition. Husserl sees, however, that the determination of these unthematical expectations can be detected by the attempt at pre-picturing (*Vorbildlichung*). What is meant here is a voluntary "intuitive picturing in the imagination," an explication of our anticipations, "in which memories of objects already given of the same or related types play their joint role" (*Erfahrung und Urteil,* 144; *Experience and Judgment,* 127f.).

90. It is possible to draw a further connection between types and schemata of empirical

concepts. For Kant, the schema of an empirical concept is a "rule" whereby we can, by means of the imagination, imagine an unlimited multiplicity of four-legged animals (A141/B180). The schema is a method for the imaginative production of various pictorial intuitions of dogs. Similarly, "in an arbitrary creation of the imagination we can also represent other dogs to ourselves in an open multiplicity" (*Erfahrung und Urteil*, 400; *Experience and Judgment*, 332); we do this through spontaneous visualization by means of the type.

91. *Erfahrung und Urteil*, 400f.; *Experience and Judgment*, 333.

92. *Erfahrung und Urteil*, 78; *Experience and Judgment*, 75.

93. *Erfahrung und Urteil*, 137; *Experience and Judgment*, 122.

94. Nonetheless, a conscious "will" cannot be meant here, for the activity that synthesizes what is given in intuition according to a type is not guided consciously. The "will" to see what is expected through a type can sometimes manifest itself in self-affection (which is bracketed from our present investigation). In that case, we literally see what we expected (or were afraid) to see. For example, we can "see" a rope lying on the floor of a dark barn "as" a snake and run away.

95. On the forms of pre-predicative experience see my *Erfahrung und kategoriales Denken* (cf. n. 8).

96. *Erfahrung und Urteil*, 395; *Experience and Judgment*, 328f.

97. As soon as a new type is constituted, it is "ready at any time to be awakened anew by . . . association" (*Erfahrung und Urteil*, 137; *Experience and Judgment*, 122).

98. *Erfahrung und Urteil*, 400; *Experience and Judgment*, 332.

99. *Erfahrung und Urteil*, 139; *Experience and Judgment*, 123.

100. The type, which is then "narrowed down" in a certain way, also guides my regard to these characteristic particularities when I deliberately intend to retain these specific qualities.

101. Cf. *Logische Untersuchungen*, II/1, Fünfte Untersuchung, §27; *Logical Investigations*, II, Fifth Investigation, §27.

102. *Logische Untersuchungen*, II/1, 443; *Logical Investigations*, II, 138.

103. *Logische Untersuchungen*, II/1, 443; *Logical Investigations*, II, 138.

104. It is noteworthy that in this case apprehensions do not only compete with each other if they have been recently and singularly performed. On the contrary, typifying apprehensions compete as soon as they acquire a certain tendency (a "tendency of belief") in the course of continuous perception. Two typifying apprehensions fight on the ground of already acquired pre-predicative experience in a battle to be decided by the force of the tendency of belief.

105. One could push the analogy between type and schema even further by going beyond the fact that empirical concepts must be based on typifying apperception as well and by asserting that all concepts must also have a type. This position is oriented around Kant's view that all concepts need a schema in order to be potentially applied to intuitions. This claim cannot, however, be easily integrated into Husserlian phenomenology, since it presupposes the conceptual side as pre-given.

106. Cf. my contribution "Grundzüge eines Synthesis-Modells der Auffassung. Kant und Husserl über den Ordnunggrad sinnlicher Vorgegebenheiten und die Elemente einer Phänomenologie der Auffassung," *Husserl Studies* 10 (1993): 111–41.

107. Concerning the problem of the "beginning" see also A. Aguirre, *Genetische Phänomenologie und Reduktion* (The Hague: Martinus Nijhoff, 1970), §31.

108. I once had an unpleasant fish poisoning that was coincidentally linked to a certain alcoholic beverage. Due to the very deep and long-lasting nausea, the sensation of disgust was so permanently associated with the beverage that I can feel it as soon as I even think of it.

5

Developments in the Theory of Time-Consciousness

An Analysis of Protention

Lanei Rodemeyer

A LTHOUGH IT IS understood among phenomenologists that Husserl spent much less effort on analyses of the futural aspect of time than he might have, it is also understood that both protention and expectation are essential, albeit still underdeveloped, aspects of phenomenological temporality. Not only do these aspects complete the structure of the living present and temporality as a whole, but they also provide the subject with an openness toward what is new and unknown—an aspect which is necessarily integral to our intentionality and which founds our link to intersubjectivity.[1] In this essay we will focus on protention, examining the texts that span the course of Husserl's work on this topic, from his earliest to latest writings. In fact, much of our analysis will refer to texts currently being prepared for publication (Husserl's "L," or "Bernauer," manuscripts) as well as to his other unpublished works on temporality (the "C" manuscripts). These works, previously unavailable except through access to the Husserl-Archives, offer us much insight into Husserl's views on protention. Husserl may not have mentioned protention or the futural aspect of my own temporality often in his published works, but the texts we will look at here reveal both a consistency in his thinking as well as very important developments. Through our examination of these writings, we will discover and develop an understanding of the intricate relation between protention and intentionality, and we will outline the argument that protentional temporality provides a foundational link between the temporal subject and intersubjectivity.

1. Early Development of Protentional Temporality

Husserl's early works on time (1893–1917),[2] published in volume X of *Husserliana,* give very little attention to the temporal aspect of protention. In his overall studies of temporality, though, we can see that Husserl was primarily concerned with our experience of time and how it relates to our intuition of objects. Interestingly, in spite of a general neglect of the concept of protention, we find that—even in his earliest writings—Husserl's descriptions show it to be fundamental to our intentional relation to objects. In fact, these earliest works on temporality already disclose an important *futural* aspect to the relation between temporality and intentionality. In a text written as early as 1893, for example, Husserl says that time is directed forward, and that that which comes *before* an intuition (in this case, "interest") *influences* what is actualized:

> Interest is fixed on what is more vital, newer, and is directed forwards throughout.
> . . . The whole preceding development, insofar as it was followed with undivided interest, has its influence on the esthetic character, and therefore on the feeling-character, of what is actually present.[3]

Our interest in an object pulls us forward, ahead of the moment of actualization, and this interest also has an influence on the actualizing itself. Thus Husserl points out a definite relation between my momentary, actualized intuition and my future. In fact, Husserl launches in this same text into a discussion of the "striving" (*Streben*) and the "attraction" (*Reiz*) that is a necessary part of intuition.[4] Striving and attraction indicate a lack of fulfillment or satisfaction in an intuition; only when we follow this pull are we able to satisfy or fulfill the intuition. By moving into the future, in other words, I am able to fulfill my intuitions. Importantly, these notions indicate already in these early works how the "now-moment" must extend beyond itself, for if it did not, we would always be "satisfied" with what was momentarily actual and would never strive for— and thus would never have—complete, fulfilled intuitions.

It is important to point out here that "striving" requires an intending forward, an attention "beyond" what is in the now-moment; it is futural to what is now in my momentary, actualized consciousness. Furthermore, the fact that an object can draw me toward it also requires my "intending beyond" what is immediately now. Husserl deals more with the notion of "attraction" in later works, through his analyses of the concept of *Affektion* (or *Affektivität*). *Affektion*, which we will translate as affection (or affectivity), is described by Husserl as being necessarily futural, and thus we will execute a more detailed analysis of the term later. Husserl's use of such terminology will substantiate our suggestions regarding the interrelation of intentionality and protention. For now, we will return to Husserl's very early works where he discusses protention.

In another early text, written around the same time period (1893–1901), Husserl concentrates on protention more than he does in any other text from his early works. Here he insists that the futural aspect to temporality is essential to its structure: "But we are not and we cannot be entirely without apprehension directed forwards. *The temporal fringe also has a future.*"[5] Not only is time moving in a forward direction, then, but it also has a component to it that is always futural. In other words, in the sense that my temporality is "streaming," it has a direction that is futural; in the sense that it is "standing," there is always a "part" of the "form" of the living present that "stands" in the immediate future.[6] This latter aspect becomes established in Husserl's work as protention, the necessary extension of the living present into the future. Furthermore, and important for our own analysis, Husserl mentions specifically in this early text that protention is often *part of intuition:* "In the case of a given experience . . . we frequently have *intuited expectations* as well."[7] In the cases to which Husserl is referring, my protentions are almost always fulfilled, because my expectations base themselves on past experience, for example, when I am hearing a musical piece I already know. This "intuited expectation" nevertheless shows how intuitions themselves can rest in the futural aspect of my temporality. Thus Husserl establishes the interrelation of my act of intuition and a protentional temporality already in his earliest works.

Implied in this same discussion is also a distinction between protention and expectation. Although these two notions were not to be worked through carefully by Husserl until much later, in this early analysis he clearly sees protention as an extension of the now, while expectation is understood as something that is brought into the now in a way similar to recollection, that is, through reproduction. What we today understand as protention is here referred to as the "not-yet" (*Noch-nicht*); expectation, meanwhile, is called "reproductive expectation" (*reproduktive Erwartung*). The first is still a part of the "temporal fringe" of the (expanded) now, whereas the second is reproduced, not experienced as originary. Husserl explains:

> The expectation of the "not yet" connected with the "now" is fulfilled. . . . [Reproductive expectation is] not of the immediate future of the temporal field— what is immediately future in the temporal field is not the same as the more distant future, which is the object of phantasy-expectation.[8]

This "temporal field," therefore, includes what we understand as the living present as well as the "reproductions" of recollections and expectations; as "reproductions," however, neither recollection nor expectation is part of the form of the living present itself.

The actual term "protention" arises later in these (early) works and is mentioned only briefly. In a text written and corrected sometime between 1906 and 1909, Husserl explains again that protention is an extension of intuition into the future, and that it fulfills itself in the now:

> And in the same way, a continual "intention" reaches into the future: The actually present portion of the duration again and again adds a new now, and a *protention* adheres to the tone-constituting "appearances"—a protention that is fulfilled as a protention aimed at this tone just as long as the tone endures and that is annulled and changes if something new begins in its place.[9]

This description reveals both the development of Husserl's thought about protention through his work, and his consistency. From the very beginning, as we see here, protention is considered a "part" of the now, that is, of the living present, where the now is understood as a living "extension" of "momentary" temporal intuition. Even in earlier works, which we have been discussing, Husserl continually asserts that the now has a futural "fringe," that it is extended somehow into the future. Here we see how the term "protention" is brought in to emphasize the relation between intentionality and futural temporality. In fact, and even more importantly, protention itself is seen as "fulfilled," and thus as integral to the process of objective constitution.

Keep in mind that Husserl considered the notion of a mathematical "now-point" only a fiction,[10] but that after rejecting the notion of a "now-point" in his earliest works, he began to introduce the notion of a primordial impression, or *Urimpression*.[11] The latter term is also an abstraction; however, it is an abstraction of the "moment of actualization" rather than a mathematical abstraction from a "series of now-points." Interestingly, the appearance of the term *Urimpression* (and *Urempfindung*, primordial sensation) coincided with Husserl's introduction of the terms "protention" and "retention," a fact which might help us understand how the primordial impression is an abstraction of a whole "living present"—the constituting activity of protention, *Urimpression*, and retention—rather than an abstraction from a geometric time line. My intuition "now" necessarily extends "forward" into the immediate future, as well as "back" into the just-past. My experience of "now" is not at all of a point (nor of a primal impression), but instead already contains aspects of it which are futural and past, namely, protention and retention. While this explanation of the extended now and its protention clearly involves intuition, however, this interrelation is mentioned without in-depth explication. In our next section we will deal with this intricate relation in more detail, and we will compare the notion of the *Urimpression* with that of a "fulfilled protention." Thus we turn now to an explicit analysis of protention carried out by Husserl in the middle period (around 1918–28) of his work.

2. Working through the Notion of Protention

In this section we will first lay out some important aspects of Husserl's analyses, focusing primarily on how he describes protention in relation to retention and the *Urimpression*. Then we will return to a discussion of the relation of protention to intentionality, taking Husserl's brief considerations in his early works a step further. Finally, we will consider the nature of our temporal structure as protentional, and what might bring about such a structure.

The Bernauer (L) Manuscripts: A Radical Analysis of Protention

In these unpublished manuscripts, written while visiting Bernau in the summers of 1917 and 1918, Husserl begins his discussions of temporality by focusing on the relations of protention and retention, without mentioning the "now-point" or even the *Urimpression*. Having already established the "now-point" as mere fiction in his early works, he clearly no longer needs to mention it at all. Nor does Husserl use the term *Urimpression* in these manuscripts, though, focusing instead on the "fulfillment" or the "maximal point" within the temporal stream. For example, in one crucial set of "progressive" diagrams,[12] where each following diagram builds upon the one prior, he enters the horizontal line—symbolizing the stream of the urimpressional now—last. This fact would be unremarkable, were it not for the discussion that accompanies this set of diagrams and throughout the manuscript.

We should pause here for a moment and review the way Husserl used diagrams in order to elucidate his analyses of temporality. Most consistently for Husserl, a horizontal line—apparently supporting the rest of the diagram—is meant to represent our flow of perceptions in the present. It represents the ever-arriving now. In diagram 5.1, this line begins with the "experience" at "point" E_1 and continues through E. In order to represent our retentions as they "sink away," Husserl adds diagonal lines which originate at this line of presence and proceed downward, away from the horizontal line of the present.[13] For example, in diagram 5.1, we see a diagonal line originating at point E_1 and slanting downward. This represents an impression that originates perceptually at "point" E_1, and then sinks away as retention while our current perceptions continue to flow through E_2, E_3, and so on. Thus, the point E_1^2, found on the slanting line starting at E_1, represents our retention of the experience that took place at E_1 but that is retained at E_2. In the "lower half" of the diagram, then, which here represents the realm of retention, the superscripted numbers indicate the current moment in the present, whereas the subscripted numbers represent the retained moment of originary experience—in this case, a moment in the past.

In diagram 5.1 we also find vertical lines, that is, lines perpendicular to the line representing our perceptual flow in the present. These vertical lines indicate the connection we have with our retentions in the current moment. Thus they represent the extention of the living present beyond the "point" of the *Urimpression*. For example, the vertical line between the current moment at E_2 and the retained moment at E_1^2 represents the link that exists at the moment E_2 between the now-moment E_2 and the retention of the moment E_1. As we will see, these lines also represent a link with protentions in our flow of originary experience, but at this point we must return to Husserl's deliberations and follow how he integrates protention into this visual representation of inner temporality.

Husserl begins this discussion[14] by examining how protention and retention relate to one another. Specifically, he wishes to "add" protention to his analyses of the now:

> But we are missing a label for the protentions that [would take place at point E_2]. Thus we will extend the [vertical] line E_1^2–E_2 upward and in this way label the protentions which make up the missing intentionality, comprising with the lower line a unified consciousness.[15]

Thus we see the line from E_1^2 extended through the urimpressional "point" E_2 upward through a new, protentional point which we are calling E_3^2. In this way Husserl causes the area "above" the horizontal line of the present to represent the realm of protention. The "point" E_3^2 therefore indicates my protention toward what I will experience in the futural moment of E_3, a protention which

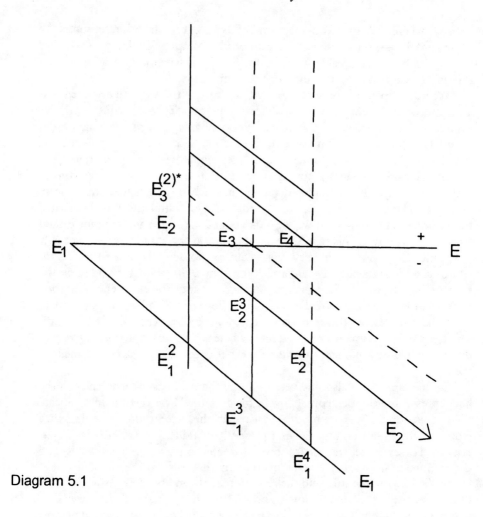

Diagram 5.1

is experienced "now" at the moment E_2. With this example, we see how the symbolization of protention parallels Husserl's symbolization of retention: sub-scripted numbers still indicate the "point" of originary experience—although now that "point" is in the future—and superscripted numbers indicate my experience "now" of that protention.

With the "addition" of protention to the "equation," as it were, Husserl comes to realize its importance. As we know, protentions are "motivated" by retentions, meaning that what I anticipate in my immediate future is based upon what has just transpired. For example, my current experience of walking down the block, which requires a constant retention of this ongoing activity (knowing where I have just been), has a direct influence on what I expect in the next immediate moments of walking as well as when I turn the corner (knowing where I am going). I protend a continuing experience of sidewalk underfoot, cars on the street, and people around me, for example. Husserl, however, also draws another conclusion: *retentions are also motivated by protentions.* This interrelation, however, is not easy to understand:

> That which came before [*die vorangegangene*] as such is retained in a new retentional consciousness and this consciousness is, on the one hand, characterized in itself as fulfillment of what was earlier, and on the other, as retention of what was earlier. But is there not a difficulty here? The earlier consciousness is protention (i.e., an intention "directed" at what comes later) and the following retention would then be retention of the earlier retention that is characterized at the same time as [its] protention. This newly arriving retention thus reproduces the earlier retention with its protentional tendency and at the same time fulfills it, but it fulfills it in such a way that going through this fulfillment is a protention of the next phase.[16]

The introduction of protention into an analysis of temporality reveals the complicated way in which the constituting temporal flow overlaps itself. According to this text, retentions are retained as both retentions of what came before (as fulfillment) and as their former protentions; each retention has a retentional and a protentional aspect. Furthermore, in the above citation the "now" itself is never mentioned, neither as an urimpressional "point" nor as the now which is constituted by this protentional-retentional activity; the protentions themselves are simply discussed as either fulfilled or unfulfilled. Each protention has a direct relationship with its own fulfillment. As a fulfilled moment passes into retention, then, it is not a retention of a momentary former now-point—that would be the "mathematical" explanation; it is a retention of a fulfilled protention, one which itself protends toward the next fulfillment. We should note, however, that this analysis continues to focus attention on the retentional aspect of the present, betraying the fact that protention is still a recent "addition" to the discussion. Nevertheless, we begin to learn more about protention even here.

We must pause to address two critical difficulties arising in our analysis so far: first, Husserl uses such vocabulary as "motivating"[17] and "projecting"[18] when discussing the relation of protention and retention, but such terms seem to address the relation of protentional and retentional *content* rather than these temporal forms. Clearly, I can say that my having been walking along the sidewalk will "motivate" what I expect in my immediate future, but if I abstract from this content, can I say the same of the relation of retention and protention as forms? It seems that we cannot easily say that one temporal form "motivates" another. We can use this terminology with reference to temporal content to help us possibly gain a better understanding of the formal relations, but not to describe them per se. We must point out here that Husserl also uses the term "modifying" in his descriptions, which seems more applicable to the relation of temporal forms. The form of protention might modify the form of retention, and vice versa, but they will not motivate or project into one another (as forms). We must assume, then, that Husserl was using descriptions of temporal content to provide examples for his analyses of temporal form. While a reference to content is indeed helpful when struggling with an analysis of the form of temporality, we must be careful—more careful than Husserl himself, perhaps— not to confuse the two in our most intricate studies.

The second difficulty is that of the *Urimpression*. We mentioned earlier how the *Urimpression* is meant to designate that "moment of actualization" which can be abstracted from the other temporal forms of the living present, namely, retention and protention. We discover here, however, that the notions of "fulfilled retention" and "fulfilled protention" provide us with the same "moment of actualization"—without insinuating any type of punctual, actualized, sensory data as does the *Urimpression*. Granted, Husserl often invokes the *Urimpression* (and the *Urempfindung*) to indicate that precise moment when a specific aspect of an experience is actualized by consciousness, but it seems that this tends to reify the abstraction. With regard to a phenomenology of temporality, the term *Urimpression* can lead us astray, giving priority to an abstract moment and to actualized, punctual data. The terms "fulfilled protention" and "fulfilled retention" describe much better both the content of my experience and the form of my temporality, which Husserl's analyses are beginning to clarify. The form of temporality, in other words, is primarily the functioning of retention and protention; that area, or zone, of actualization—I say "area" or "zone" in order to emphasize the *span* of actualization, as opposed to a *point*—is merely their fulfillment. In fact, this zone of actualization is contingent upon the form of retention-protention, and on their being fulfilled, for its existence. This is one interrelated process.

The interrelation of protention and retention can manifest itself in two essential ways so far: retentions "contain" protentions, first, in the limited sense that they "contain" protentions directed from one "moment" or "phase" to the next "moment," linking the retentions to one another, and second, in the broader sense that groups of retentions are linked to each other as events. In each way retentions are modified by protentions. Protentions and their fulfillments likewise may link serially from moment to moment or may protend toward unities interpreted as events in themselves.[19] And in both of these modes, they are modified by retention.

Given these distinctions, we can now review in detail how protention and retention overlap. We now know that what has just passed gives us a basis upon which to project into the future, with regard to my temporal content; my next moment's expectations arise out of the last moment's fulfillment. Further, retentions are retentions *of protentions;* retention is always affected by what was protended in a given manner (as well as by what continues as protention). Retention and protention, therefore, are integrated into one another such that they influence the meaning and direction of each other's content; their difference lies in how they relate to the factual fulfillment of an intention. With regard to temporal form, retentions modify protentions and protentions modify retentions. Their mutual modification, furthermore, is processed through their being fulfilled, through the shared zone of actualization. The fulfillment of an intention in the living present is thus "doubled" in the senses of retention and protention, and yet it remains one fulfillment:

> The new phase is thus not just the transformation of a retention into a retention of the next level—which in its mediated intentionality holds what was earlier in modified consciousness—and a transformation of the co-interwoven protention; instead it is also a retention of the earlier protention. . . . The new protention is new and a modification of what was earlier, which itself, however, is known through a moment of interlaced retentional consciousness.[20]

In other words, although there is clearly only one fulfillment, it functions in two very different ways: it is both the fulfillment of protention and the actualized aspect of retention. At the same time, though, this fulfillment remains one, as the zone of actualization with regard to both protention and retention. Keep in mind also that this relation can be understood both as limited to the next immediate phase and, in a broader sense, as extended to an experience as a whole.

Let us take the speaking of a sentence as an example. If I am in the middle of speaking a sentence (and you in the middle of hearing it), our retention is not merely of the last spoken syllable or last uttered sound, nor is our protention only of the next sound to be uttered. Instead, our retentions are made up of all the words I have spoken, and we protend toward the completion of my sentence or idea. A very "narrow" understanding of retention takes each retained word as linked serially to the one spoken before; a "broader" understanding shows how each "individual" retention has embedded in it all those that came before, relating the whole of the meaning to what is currently fulfilled (the word being spoken at this moment). Thus our retention is layered such that the last several words, back to the beginning of the sentence and including the contexts that might have brought about this exclamation, remain present with us as we speak and hear this sentence. Otherwise the sentence would make no sense for any of us. Likewise, the protentions we had up until this moment (which are now past), of each word leading to the next, remain embedded in these layered retentions. And the protentions experienced now, with the word being spoken at this moment, protend forward both toward the next word and toward the meaning of the whole sentence. In addition, these protentions have embedded in them the unity of retentions back through the beginning of the sentence. As speaker, I must especially have active protentions, so that I know where I have been and where I intend to take my spoken claim. Notice, also, that these protentions (and retentions) are not of gutteral sounds, but of words, showing that these temporal phases of retention and protention —and, more importantly, of their fulfillment—are not punctual but instead are complex units.

Having established the interrelation of protention and retention at a more intimate level, Husserl then takes them up as systems in themselves. He describes protentional and retentional consciousness as respectively "climbing" and "sinking" with relation to their fulfillment. He then begins to realize that this "climbing" and "sinking"—protention and retention—are what give meaning or substance to the supposedly fleeting moment of fulfillment. Without protention, there is no real fulfillment; without retention of the fulfilled protention, there is no recognition of this fulfillment. Husserl actually changes his description of his diagram in such a way that shows this thinking: "The [diagonal line representing our protention and retention] actually is not to be symbolized as a straight line with two branches [of protention and retention], rather as two lines pushing into each other [*zusammenstoßen*] with different emphases, albeit symmetrical overall."²¹ The "straight line" is the diagonal line representing the activity of the living present; its "two branches" are those of protention and retention. This first description, of a line with two branches, minimizes the importance of protention and retention, because they are described merely as two branches which are part of the line. The second description, though, replaces this image with two joined lines "pushing into each other." These two lines are those of protention and retention; they are now each a line unto themselves, representing their symmetrical but different activities, with the zone of actualization as their meeting place. In this second case, Husserl's emphasis is clearly on the activity of retention and protention, as the description itself expresses the active "pushing" of the lines and never mentions their "point" of convergence. The maximal "point" is no longer necessary. Instead, it is merely to be understood as the fulfilled zone of convergence of two different, but similar, streams.

We can take diagram 5.2 to help us visualize this description, even though this diagram is actually placed a page earlier in Husserl's manuscripts. Remember that the single horizontal line represents our flow of presentations, whereas the diagonal lines represent our protentions (above and slanting "into" the horizontal line) and our retentions (below and slanting "away" from the horizontal line). The vertical lines represent our constituted temporality at each now "point." Husserl's description actually focuses on only one diagonal line of protention and retention. The interesting thing about his description is that he ignores the horizontal line of presence entirely, changing his focus to the diagonal line. Further, he interprets the diagonal line of protention and retention as *two* lines pushing into each other. Thus it seems that the horizontal line of actualization merely arises out of the activity of protention and retention.

Husserl continues:

> So we would do better if we symbolized this through an angle, presenting the whole parallel system [of protention and retention] as two systems that create an even angle as two half-planes, whose line of intersection is the [horizontal line of actualization]. Thus we will think of the paper as bent [at this horizontal line] and [the protentional segments] pulled upward, held over the surface of the paper.²²

With this, Husserl bends the diagram in half along the horizontal line of actualization, pulling the area of protention upward, away from the flat sur-

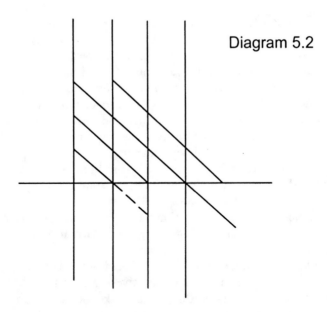

Diagram 5.2

face of the original diagram. Husserl makes an incredible move here, with two major effects. First, he changes his original visualization of temporality into two systems, protention and retention, and reduces the flow of actualized time to a crease in the paper. The zone of actualization is minimized in importance with respect to protention and retention. Second, these changes are augmented by Husserl's converting his diagram from a two-dimensional to a three-dimensional system. In other words, protention and retention are in some sense two different dimensions of the same experience. We will focus presently on the first of these moves.

These changes in the diagram and its description reflect Husserl's shift in focus to the two systems of protention and retention and away from the zone of actualization; here fulfillment functions merely as the site of convergence for both systems (although in different ways). The "moment" of the zone of actualization, for itself, practically disappears; it exists only in relation to the protentional and retentional flows. As fulfillment, of course, this zone does not disappear—it remains essential to the structure of temporality—but relative to the emphasis placed upon the "moment" of actualization in earlier writings (especially with regard to intuition), its minimized importance in this discussion is notable. Protention and retention take precedence over the actual "moment" of fulfillment. In fact, they are ontologically prior to it in such a way that the zone of fulfillment seems unable to exist except through its relation to protention and retention. Given this, we might want to ask, how can we understand this zone of actualization at all? An attempt to provide a response reveals that our understanding of fulfillment actually rests heavily upon our protention.

As Husserl describes in these manuscripts, protention is "maximized" in its fulfillment. On a more experiential level, we have also noticed that—especially in perception—we are most often focused "forward," always beyond what is actually "now" (as evidenced by our "interest" and our "striving"). And more formally, we know that protentions modify retentions even so far that protentions are integrated into our retentions and recollections. In each of these cases, the actual zone of fulfillment has very little meaning without the directedness of the flow and the expectation or openness which precedes actualization. Protention gives the zone of fulfillment both its sense and its importance. Instead of understanding protention as founded by the "now-point" or *Urimpression*— in other words, instead of understanding the "source" of temporality to be in the "instant of primordial impression"—we realize that fulfillment itself must actually be supported by the functioning of protention and retention. For example, imagine that I am looking at my desk. Without being able to protend beyond the presentation I have at this moment, this "momentary" vision would have very little meaning or coherence. I would not only be unable to perceive that the desk has more than one perspective—in fact, I would not move into other presentations because nothing would take me beyond this very moment —but I also would not be able to connect each moment's presentation with the next. Protention is the condition of possibility of my going beyond what is fulfilled in my consciousness. In fact, we can understand protention as taking us "beyond" fulfillment more specifically: it makes appresentations possible. While we know that appresentations are now, not in the future (they are embedded in a presentation), actualized consciousness alone does not allow for the possibility of being beyond this zone of actualization. Husserl comments that "This is how pre-expectation [protention] works 'apperceptively': it works cooperatively in the configuration of coexisting objects."[23] Thus it is not the futural possibility of my moving around an object that allows for my having appresentations, but a futural temporality that brings me beyond a fulfilled presence in the first place, which then begins to open me up to other perspectives that are not my own.

I find that protention's influence on intentional fulfillment becomes even more clear when we consider the notion of touch. Although it is possible to feel something without moving—for example, I can feel the impression of my chair as I sit here very still—the sensation of touch most often includes motion.[24] Usually I am running my fingers over a surface, bumping into an object, or moving about in some way when I am paying attention to how something feels (or it is moving along my skin while I remain still). This motion is in itself always one step ahead of the sensation. I must be intending motion just prior to intending the feeling in order to be moving and thus facilitating the feeling. Thus there is a double sense of immediate expectation in this activity; feeling an object (like a piece of cloth) requires both an expectation of the sensation (even as I am sensing) and the ability to be "ahead of myself" in order to move. Both of these require temporal protention. In fact, when I feel the chair pressing itself into my back and backside, there still is a sense of expectation in the experience, even though there is no apparent movement involved.

Each of these examples (looking at my desk, feeling a piece of cloth, sensing the chair) reveals that protention is not only temporally necessary for experience, but also that it is a primary source of meaning for the living present. The fact that I am always temporally ahead of the "moment" of actualization allows for my being able to intend objects, and this, in turn, is what allows for meaning to exist in my experiences. Granted, retention is also essential, but our argument here is to show that, without protention, retention would have very little to work with. Without protention, in other words, no sentences would be begun, no movement would take place, no appresentations would be apprehended, no objects would be intended as wholes—nothing meaningful would be fulfilled. Thus, although retention is required in order to maintain a sense to our experiences, this sense would not arise without protention.[25]

Protention and Intention in the Bernauer Manuscripts

Because we continually face parallels in Husserl's descriptions of protentional temporality and intending consciousness, we must return here to our consideration of the relation between protention and intention in Husserl's phenomenology. With regard to their content, both are described as building upon and interrelated with the intentions or protentions that go before and come after them. With regard to their form, intentions and protentions both extend beyond or "ahead of" their fulfillment. Protention is the openness in temporality that goes beyond its own fulfillment, an openness which then modifies retention. Intentionality is a directedness toward an object, one which includes both fulfilled and unfulfilled aspects of that object (i.e., appresentations). While it is clear to us, therefore, that intentions and protentions are not the exact same thing, we begin to see that these descriptions reveal a relationship that is more than merely "parallel." In order for us to intend objects at all, in other words, the intentional act must rely upon the temporal form of protention in order to be carried out. An intention is an act of consciousness directed toward an object; protention, meanwhile, is the temporal aspect of that same consciousness which founds the intending act. This becomes clearer in another of these unpublished manuscripts:

> The constant punctual fulfillment itself belongs to intention as intention of the arriving (*Eintreten*) of the event that is still located in the stream. In this, the intention goes constantly through the new points, holding constantly over beyond them the character of unfulfilled expectation, and the intention goes toward the fulfillments, or rather from expectation to expectation in the continuum of expectation, and by this [the intention goes toward] the always newly fulfilled expectations (fulfilled according to a phase): these are two sides of one and the same thing.[26]

Intentionality is, in itself, a pointing outward from my own consciousness toward the objects of my interest (whether or not I am specifically focused on them). As the activity of perception is necessarily temporal, then the specific act of intention, because of its function, must rest primarily in protention. Therefore, intentionality is interrelated with my protentional temporality in a very important sense. An object cannot be experienced without the involvement of both my intentionality and the protentional aspect of my temporality, without going *beyond* an immediate presentation.

We should point out here that Husserl again does not mention the *Urimpression* (or the "now-point") in the citation above. Although he does remain with the image of "punctual" fulfillment, he refers here only to *fulfillment* with relation to both intentionality and temporal expectation. In other words, the *Urimpression* is clearly being set aside in these texts, being replaced by a broader notion of actualization. The term "fulfillment"—even when described as "punctual"—indicates fulfillment of an entire object as a whole, whereas the *Urimpression* always indicates more of an actualization of sensory data (a paradox in itself). It seems that in this text as well as in those we analyzed earlier, Husserl is moving beyond the problematic notion of "data" with relation to my constituting temporality.

Husserl's discussions both of intentionality with relation to protending temporality (cited above), and of the horizons of that intentionality are in answer to his question How is intentionality, according to its structure, necessarily constituted?[27] The structure of intentionality, he says, is based upon the expectations that arise from horizons, which rest in a *protentional temporal structure*. "But the continuous appearance of new primordial presences does not just mean the appearance of these data, rather, it is also part of the essence of this process, as necessarily temporally constituting, that an intentionality that is directed forward is necessary."[28] This highlights what we pointed out earlier, that appresentations and intended objects require a protentional temporality. That which is beyond, yet part of, an experience relates to the horizons of the object. These horizons, as extensions of that which is presented, rest heavily in the protentional and retentional aspects of my temporal consciousness. Here we must also admit that Husserl is still discussing the flow of *data* with regard to my constituting temporality. We will continue to struggle with this difficulty throughout our project.

Without wishing to minimize the importance of retention, let us review the necessity of protention both to temporality and to intentionality. First, protention is an essential aspect to all fulfillment and thus, in some sense, has priority over the zone of actualization in phenomenological experience. In other words, protention provides the now phase with the framework for that which will be fulfilled, and thus retention with that which will be held in retention and memory: "The now is constituted through the form of protentional fulfillment, and the past through a retentional modification of this fulfillment."[29] The most challenging example to this claim is the situation where I am completely surprised, where suddenly the unexpected appears. Husserl addresses this situation as well in these manuscripts, primarily as an analysis of the "new." Here Husserl says that, if what I am expecting does not occur, there remains an empty protention that is not fulfilled. In the cases of specific events, I will expect the ongoing event to continue. If it does not, then I am no longer dealing with fulfilled but instead with empty protentions, which will then adjust themselves according to the new situation. Thus the very first "moment" of a completely new situation will not be apprehended as fulfilled until it is part of my retention, when the interrelation of retention and protention will once again allow me to form protentions toward the continuance of this new situation. This example shows us the basic character of protention, for protention is a constant openness to the possibility of such surprising situations. The "frame" of protention, although most often fulfilled through an interrelation with retentions where a known situation is continuing, is an openness to the ever-new, even if what is "new" is usually predictable. Only in the cases of true surprises are we suddenly aware of our capability to be surprised—a capability which is constantly possible because of the structure of protention.

Second, protention is the temporal foundation of intentionality. Without a protentional temporality, I would be unable to intend any objects as wholes, because protention is the condition for the possibility of my apprehending horizonality in objects and meanings. Here we mean horizonality in the sense of appresentations, perspectives of an object that are not directly given but that I know to be there. This horizonality also refers to meanings beyond a single object and its co-presentations, that is, apperceptions. When one aspect of an object, in other words, indicates something beyond the object's own profiles, this capability for apperception rests in a protentional temporality. Thus protention is required in order for any meaning to be constituted in the now-phase because, without protended consciousness, we would not be capable of intending an object as a whole, much less of indicating objects or meanings beyond the object of my attention. Protention is that which allows us to be ahead of, and bring meaning to, the zone of actualization.

The Formation of Protention

After having established the importance of protention to the temporal phase, and after having ascertained the functions and interrelations of protention, the next question would be how our temporal structure arises such that it has a protentional aspect. In other words, what brings protention about?[30] With this question in mind, we return to our discussion of the interrelation of protention with intentionality as some of Husserl's comments in this area provide us with some clues to the source of protention.

In these manuscripts Husserl discusses the situation of a new event, one where my expectations cannot be already delineated by my retentions (where my protentions are more or less "empty"), so that he can analyze without complication the relation of protention to an intended event. With the flow of hyletic data, Husserl says, my consciousness necessarily extends itself into a retention and a protention of that flow, turning that flow into a series of experiences or events, rather than a flow of "raw" data. Because my experiences are not merely of flowing data (then they would not be *experiences*), my temporal consciousness is necessarily one of protention and retention.

> If a piece of primordial succession [*Urfolge*] of hyletic data (and then from all other primordial experiences) has run off, then a retentional connection must create itself, but not just that—Hume already saw this—consciousness remains in its procession and anticipates what comes further, namely, a protention "directs" itself toward the continuation of the row in the same style, and that is protention regarding the course of the primordial data which function as core data, and the same goes for the course of the retentions with their adumbrations that function in them.[31]

Thus the flow of information I experience is understood as a flow (and as information) through my constituting temporality of protention and retention. Conversely, protention and retention arise in themselves through this flow.

This citation calls us to examine the "relation between" the hyletic flow and the structure of temporality. Husserl actually introduces the notion of *Urhyle* (primordial hyletic flow) in his middle and later works; here we see the beginning of that notion, in his mention of the *primordial succession of hyletic data*. We must understand this as an attempt to comprehend the source of the relation between ego and world through directly addressing primordial, that is, unconstituted, information (*Urfolge* or *Urhyle*) and constituting temporality. It would be very easy for us to classify this relation as one of content (data) and form (temporal structure), but such a classification is far too simple for this relation. Here we see a relation—not of two separate things, primordial, hyletic flow and temporal structure—but of one "dynamic structure." There is no hyletic flow "prior" to its encounter with temporal constitution. Neither is there a temporal structure that exists "in itself" without its activity of constitution, although we might speak of each of these abstractly in our analyses. Husserl says just prior to this citation that protention "arises originally" through the primordial flow, in the same way as retention.[32] Thus we can answer the question we asked above in this way: the structure of temporality exists by virtue of the hyletic flow, where their dynamic relation results in the constitution of objects.

According to this description, the hyletic flow "contains" neither objects nor "punctual data." Husserl's explanations, however, can be a bit misleading. For example, he vacillates between two descriptions of hylē: in some cases, he refers to the primordial hylē (*Urhyle*) as punctual data, and in others, the hylē (*Hyle*) is described as already somewhat objective. In our last citation he seems to lean toward the notion of "punctual data" through his use of the terms "data" and "primordial succession." As we have seen throughout our analyses, the notion of punctuality is highly problematic for a phenomenological understanding of either fulfilled objectivity or constituting temporality. Objects are fulfilled *as objects,* not as unified data-points, even though they never appear to us in their entirety at any one time. For this reason, we must understand constituting temporality as a constant, ecstatic moment which allows for our apprehension of whole objects.[33] The hylē, for its part, when taken as primordial or not, must be understood as the information through which this constitution takes place.

We turn now to the realm of constituted objects, more specifically, to the notion of affectivity. This notion reveals a direct relation between objects and my temporal consciousness, and it shows further how objectivity is related to my protentional temporality.

Protention, Affectivity, and Objectivity

Objects (after their being constituted by temporal activity) pull me to them through what is called their affectivity or affection. Affectivity is the draw that an object has upon me which causes me to turn my attention toward it or to intend it specifically. A discussion of affectivity, then, will clarify for us the function of protention with relation to perceived objects, and will reveal a direct relation between objectivity and temporality beyond the one revealed in our discussions of intentionality.

Although Husserl says that the primordial source of affection lies in the *Urimpression*—and, in fact, his discussion of affection focuses on retention and association—he importantly says that affectivity is primarily directed toward the future (rather than the past):

> In the living present, that which appears in the *Urimpression* has, *ceteris paribus,* a stronger affective tendency than that which is already in retention. For this very reason, affection has a unified tendency toward the future, with regard to the direction of its transmission; intentionality is predominantly directed toward the future.[34]

Let us focus on the description of affection with relation to the future. Husserl defines affectivity as "the attraction with regard to consciousness, the peculiar pull that a known object exercises on the ego."[35] He continues on to say that this pull relaxes itself when the ego turns toward the affective object, transforming itself into a call to learn more about the object itself, to gain knowledge of the object through closer observation.[36] The ego often originally feels the pull of an object in the case of great contrast, where a unified object stands out from its background and from other objects. While contrast is not a necessary contributor to affectivity in an object, it does often accompany an object's affective pull. An object that is not the focus of my attention cannot pull me toward it, however, unless I am able to perceive beyond what is in focus at this moment. Apperception is my ability to extend beyond my currently intended object to other objects and meanings and beyond what is now. Only if an object which has pulled me to it were at least partially constituted in the background, attracting my attention, could there have been any pull at all. Thus we discover a link between affectivity and apperception, because an object can only call me to it if my consciousness is able to extend beyond that which is in my focus now. And, because apperception must rest in a protentional temporality in order to allow for my ability to extend beyond the zone of actualization, we also find an indirect link between affectivity and protention. Therefore, affectivity requires a temporal structure that extends my consciousness beyond the immediate present and what is currently fulfilled so that an object in the periphery can attract my attention. In other words, affectivity is related to apperception, and both function through the protentional aspect of my temporality.

This relation also reminds us of the relation between protention and appresentation. Appresentation, the concept that any presentation of an object necessarily goes beyond itself to presentations of the object not currently in view—like the back side or the inside of the building across the street—clearly requires protention. As we explained earlier, protention is the condition of possibility of my going beyond the presentation at hand to other presentations or experiences. Thus the possibility of my viewing an object as having other sides, even though I am only perceiving one side at any moment, rests in a protentional temporality; my appresentations rest in protention. The transformed affectivity that draws me to learn more about an object after it has attracted my attention, then, also resides in protention; it always calls me to experience more, to move beyond what is currently presented.

As affectivity is related to my temporal structure primarily through protention, we can suggest that there might be a relation between affectivity and intentionality as well. An intention, we explained earlier, seeks to fulfill what is incomplete in its experience of an intended object. Thus we move toward or around an object so that it becomes complete. This activity, however, perfectly parallels our description of affectivity when it transmits itself to the object that has drawn us, calling us to experience the object further. Intentionality and this modified affectivity, then, describe the same situation: my being drawn to experience an object completely. Intentionality, however, describes my part in the experience—my need for completeness, for knowledge, for the satisfaction of my curiosity; affectivity, on the other hand, describes the object's play in this situation—how the object for its own part can attract my attention because it broadcasts certain features or has some special meaning. Thus these two terms, "intentionality" and "affectivity," describe two sides of the same subject-object relation. Keep in mind, though, that affectivity can also take place prior to a specific intention. Affectivity is primarily understood as a calling for my intending a certain unintended object. In fact, Husserl notes this relation: "For the object, we can also define affection as the awakening of an intention directed toward it."[37] Because both terms (intentionality and affectivity) describe my going *beyond* an immediate presentation toward the object as a whole, we can conclude that the relation of subject to object relies heavily upon a protentional temporality.[38]

In the next section, we will use several of our results in this analysis to consider protention with relation to the question of intersubjectivity. We will first expand upon our analyses of the notion of appresentation by taking up Husserl's use of the term in his *Cartesian Meditations*. Then we will turn to Husserl's unpublished manuscripts for evidence of an intersubjective structure inherent in the egoic subject.

3. Protention as Link to Intersubjective Temporality: Husserl's Later Published and Unpublished Works

The argument that the living present must necessarily be structured as it is, protention-*Urimpression*-retention, has now been well established, especially by phenomenologists such as Klaus Held and John Brough.[39] Our analyses here of fulfilled protention have caused us to suggest a similar structure, protention-[zone of actualization]-retention, which better reflects our understanding of temporal constitution with regard to certain discussions in Husserl's manuscripts.[40] In either case, protention is an essential "part" of my temporality, not to be overshadowed by an equally essential retention.

Now we turn to the relations of protention, appresentation, apperception, and intersubjectivity, but before we do so, we ought to pause for a moment and consider Husserl's use of the terms "appresentation" and "apperception" with regard to intersubjectivity in the Fifth Meditation of his *Cartesian Meditations*. Husserl attempts to explain how appresentation and apperception make possible my experience of another absolute consciousness at the transcendental level.[41] He concludes that the other person's body (*Leib*) functions as a presentation, and that the consciousness of the other subject is known to me as an appresentation. Because I can never make the consciousness of another subject a direct object of my own consciousness (unlike our experience with spatial objects, where in most cases I could move and view an appresented "other side" of an object, making it a direct presentation), I must understand the other's conscious existence through an analogy to my own consciousness. This "pairing," which is more than a mere analogy, must also take place immediately; in the same way that I know that there is another side to the building across the street, I must also know that there is another consciousness, an "alter ego," related to the body before me.

Husserl uses both terms, appresentation and apperception, in this discussion of intersubjectivity in the *Cartesian Meditations,* without making an overt distinction between the two. We turn momentarily to a later unpublished manuscript, where he indicates that appresentation relates to the immediate empathy of another subject, whereas apperception is more of a reproduction, a constitution of another subject:

> In the area of "empathy" we have, on the other hand, various differences in origin, and so in empathy itself (that of the analogical appresenting of others) and in the self-constituting apperceptions which are mediated through this empathy.[42]

The difficulty with this explanation, however, is that appresentation, which appears to be an immediate "co-presentation" of another absolute consciousness, is still described as a type of "analogy" (which would seem to be reproductive). But we can look to Husserl's use of the term "analogy" in his analyses of "association" to help us with this difficulty. There analogies refer to the "passive" association found in retention, unlike the reproductive associations which take place through recollection. My knowing a chair to be a chair, without recall of my first experience of a chair (or of learning its name), takes place through my passive association in retention. Through phenomenological analysis, I see that I know this is a chair—even though I have never experienced *this* chair—not through a direct recollection (that would not help me with this specific chair), but instead through an immediate "memory" of an analogy. A sedimentation of multiple experiences of similar objects, all chairs—maintained in retention— allows me to recognize this as a chair as well. Thus, for Husserl, although analogies may be thematized through phenomenological analysis, their functioning in conjunction with my constituting temporality is not reproductive; it is retentive. Therefore, Husserl's distinction between appresentations and apperceptions in this manuscript is consistent with his understanding of the related terms: appresentations are the immediate unthematic awareness of another subject's consciousness (through analogous association), while apperceptions are reproductive.

This distinction can be further verified through Husserl's use of the terms in the Fifth Meditation. On the one hand, Husserl himself claims that appresentation refers to a type of association, as when a child, having figured out what scissors are for, automatically knows what scissors are every time he sees them.[43] On the other hand, he says that the apperception of the other is a reproductive experience, where the body of the other awakens a specific association between my consciousness and that of the other person (reproductive association).[44] In my actual experience of other subjects, however, I do not have any original experience of another subject's consciousness by which I can create an association, nor do I derive or calculate the consciousness of another subject reproductively. I simply experience another's consciousness as a part of my experience of her body. In other words, my experience of another subject does not resonate with Husserl's *explanation* of this appresentation and apperception of another subject (i.e., through association and reproduction). Ironically, Husserl's terminology is more apt than he seems to realize: I experience the consciousness of another subject via the presence of her body as necessarily as I experience the absent back side of a building with the presence of the front. His choice of the term "appresentation" is therefore quite fitting; the appresentation of the other subject is embedded in the presentation of her body.

We should consider these distinctions between appresentation and apperception with regard to intersubjectivity further. Although we might thematically reproduce appresentations through phenomenological analysis, it is *only* through such analysis that they can be thematized; in themselves, they are immediate, unthematized experiences. Such is our experience of another subject as well. And it is for this reason that we find Husserl's choice of this term so apt. His method of attaining the other subject on the basis of my experience, carried out in the Fifth Meditation, however, better mirrors a phenomenological thematization of *apperceptions* rather than appresentations. Apperceptions move beyond one unified object to other objects or meanings by indication. One aspect of the first object will refer me to a similar aspect in a second object, and then the second object as a whole comes into view. In the same way, Husserl describes how my experience of another person's body (taken as object) refers to my own body; this in turn indicates my own consciousness, which finally refers to the assumed consciousness of the other subject. Thus Husserl's analysis is a thematization of the reproductive apperception of another subject, not of an appresentation. His analysis is quite applicable in situations where we are not sure whether we are encountering another human being (in a wax museum, for example, or in very poor lighting), but not of our common experience of other subjects. His term "appresentation" better describes our normal experiences of other subjects and is therefore much more applicable to our examination of the relation between temporality and intersubjectivity.

We turn now to consider the possibility of this relation. What would be the condition of possibility of my knowing another absolute consciousness? First of all, I must be able to extend my consciousness beyond itself, which means that I must have a consciousness that goes beyond a momentary presentation. We find this in my consciousness as living present (which includes protention). It is because of this protentional structure, furthermore, that I am capable of having appresentations. Second, my experience of the other subject cannot be simply as an ontological "Other." To put it another way, if our analysis is to remain in the realm of Husserlian phenomenology, the other subject cannot be so foreign to my consciousness that it is ungraspable.[45] There must be some similarity between myself and other subjects. Husserl suggests the similarity of our bodies, that the similar body of the other subject indicates a similar consciousness. But this is not satisfactory, because my experience of my own body, "from the inside," as it were, is essentially different from my experience of another person's body "from the outside."[46] In addition, hearing the voices or footsteps of other subjects is enough to convince me of their existence —sometimes all I need is to smell a familiar perfume. Finally, as we pointed out above, I know of the existence of another consciousness immediately, without reflection, without originary experience, without some specific prior learning experience. I must already be open to other subjects, to intersubjectivity, without any direct experience. And this openness must allow for recognition of the *consciousness* of another subject. In other words, intersubjectivity, that is, the existence of other transcendental egos, must already be an open possibility for my transcendental ego, before I encounter some individual subject's body. It must already be a part of my own consciousness—it must somehow

already be "part of me"—in order for me to be able to apprehend other individual subjects. Because we find such openness already in my temporal structure, established primarily in the living present by protention, and because this
temporal structure is *both* my "sphere of ownness" *and* my openness toward all
that is not me, then this link to intersubjectivity must rest somehow in conjunction with my temporality. In other words, there must be some kind of
intersubjective structure as part of my temporal consciousness which allows me
to apprehend other subjects the way I do. This radical notion would appear to
go beyond the scope of Husserl's own work, and yet, Husserl himself makes
claims that support these suggestions:

> The other is co-present in me. Absolute ego, as living-, streaming-, existing-,
> concrete present, has the other's present as co-present, as appresentatively mani
> festing itself as itself in me, but also manifesting the other [ego] itself as an [ego
> who] has in itself me—[me] constituted in the "co-presence" of its [the other's]
> living present.[47]

In other words, there must be an open intersubjective structure associated with
my own temporal structure that allows for my immediate appresentation of
another subject's consciousness. This intersubjective structure is actually part
of my temporal consciousness; it takes my consciousness beyond itself:

> Me and my primordial present. My primordial co-present, as first horizon: pri
> mordial world, my alien-subjectively mediated, intersubjective co-present. The
> existence of other egoic subjects with their primordial worlds—as horizonally
> co-valid for me.[48]

Intersubjectivity takes me beyond my primordial presence to my "first horizon,"
where the first horizon is the co-present other subject. Noting a correlation
between myself and my absolute present, we could suggest that the co-presence
of others might correlate with my temporal extension of protention—that
which takes me beyond my absolute present. We might even take this analogy
a step further, suggesting that my intersubjective experience founds my own
existence as a temporal living present capable of appresentations, just like protention (and retention) actually supports my zone of actualization by giving it
meaning. Psychologically, this claim is easily supported: the child learns its own
ego through the teachings of others. It is only through example, reprimand,
and guidance that I learned that I am an entity limited unto myself, neither the
center of the universe nor subsumed under the consciousness of another. But
phenomenologically we must do a more careful analysis, because of its requirement for a methodological solipsism.

  Phenomenology began with a reduction to my own temporal ego, so that
I could discover the relations between my consciousness and the meanings functioning as the "content" of its intentions. As such, intersubjectivity was bracketed with "the rest of the world." In Husserl's later considerations, however,
we find that my "sphere of ownness," my primordial consciousness, is already

"tainted" by the appresentation of other subjects. Is this a move away from phenomenology, out of the reduction? Perhaps my apprehension of other subjects can arise from my solipsistic temporal consciousness, as Husserl argues in his *Cartesian Meditations*. But his analysis relied upon reproductive consciousness and focused on an apperceptive experience of another subject, neither of which reflect our simple experience of other subjects. Our analysis here shows that the "analogy" or appresentation of another subject's consciousness is immediate, and our experience of other subjects does not coincide with Husserl's explanation. We find the other subject already there in our own subjectivity, as an open possibility that exceeds our own temporal consciousness. In other words, integrated into the temporal openness of my protention is an intersubjective openness that takes me beyond myself—not only to objects but also to other subjects. It is through our attempted reduction to my own primordial consciousness, to my "sphere of ownness," that we discover that such a reduction is never completely possible. Intersubjectivity is required for my experience, understood phenomenologically; my own consciousness always extends beyond itself to others, just as my living present always exceeds itself.

In addition, we must recognize that the *cogito* is not about *my* ego; my ego is the empirical or personal ego which has already been bracketed in phenomenology. The *cogito* is about the ego of all subjects. In this sense, the absolute ego is neither singular nor solipsistic. It is *all* egos; it is both "I" and "we." For this reason, we find in the absolute temporal ego *both* a primordial "sphere of ownness," a functioning of bringing together and unifying (temporal constitution), *and* an openness to the new and other (protention, appresentation). This openness can be understood not only as an openness to new objects and experiences but also as the open intersubjectivity that allows "me" to know other subjects immediately as other "absolute consciousnesses."

Clearly, this interpretation exceeds Husserl's own in the *Cartesian Meditations*. In his unpublished manuscripts, though, Husserl begins to intimate what we suggest, penciling the following into the margin of a manuscript:

> In all of this there dominates—as long as we have not gained primordiality—an equivocality, as everything is implied in me; the totality of consciousness is not only my "stream of consciousness," but rather it implies all other streams of consciousness, etc.[49]

And he says in another manuscript:

> The other subject is for itself just as well, but its for-itself is at the same time my for-me, in the form of my potentiality of appresentation. But it itself is appresented in me and I in it; I carry all others in me as themselves appresented and to be appresented and as carrying me myself in them in the same way.[50]

My consciousness carries the existence of other subjects in it, just as other consciousnesses carry my own existence. While this does not occur at the level of "primordiality," we also cannot understand "primordiality" to mean the solipsistic ego, because even the solipsistic ego exists at the level of a temporal consciousness that is open to the appresentations of other subjects. "Primordiality" is as abstract as the notion of the *Urimpression* or the flow of hyletic data. Thus, once we are at a level "beyond" "pure" primordiality (a level that is by definition non-egoic), we discover that my ego is not alone, but instead is already carrying the appresentations of other egos. These egos validate each other, support each other's existence; they are embedded in each other as appresentations are embedded in presentations.

Keep in mind here that these "appresentations" of other subjects cannot become presentations. It is at this point that Husserl's terminology, which was developed through analyses which used perception as their basis, is admittedly limited. Although I might be able to move my position and make an appresentation of a spatial object into a direct presentation, I will never be able to do this with my appresentations of another subject's consciousness. Nevertheless, Husserl's struggle in the *Cartesian Meditations* was not only how I can apprehend another subject as another *subject* (like me), but also how I can understand other subjects as *other* subjects (not me), that is, as not part of my own consciousness entirely.[51] His use of the term "appresentation," with the qualifier that it can never become a presentation (part of my own consciousness), solves this problem. But it also reveals that subjectivity requires intersubjectivity in order to be complete, just as a presentation only makes sense through its appresentations.

Through this link, we see an interrelated foundation in phenomenology, between the temporal subject and intersubjectivity. Of course, this interpretation goes against Husserl's claims in his early philosophy, but his later writings, as we have shown, indicate an openness to this new turn. The subject and intersubjectivity in this case would certainly not be interchangeable, just as I cannot exchange a presentation for an appresentation as my experience of each of them is intrinsically different. My ego will always be the site of my own experiences. But, just as I can move into my surroundings and often can make an appresentation into a presentation, we can also understand each individual subject as an absolute subject and at the same time as necessarily open to, and dependent upon, intersubjectivity.

If we take the subject and intersubjectivity as mutually founding each other—co-foundational—however, we cannot take them to found each other in the same way. As we mentioned, the temporal subject is still the source of my intuitions—they are not anyone else's. In fact, I cannot have any other starting point than myself. And yet, my intuitions as I experience them, that is, as having different perspectives, as appearing temporally, and as existing in a world of many consciousnesses, depend upon an intersubjective structure. In a different way, intersubjectivity supports itself on my own experience of the intersubjective world, that is, when I encounter another subject and *know* it to be another absolute consciousness. My activity in the intersubjective world, therefore, is also the validation of that world.

4. Conclusion

Our analysis has resulted in several important conclusions. First of all, we have established a fairly thorough understanding of protention, including the following points. Protention arises through the flow of information experienced, revealing for us the dynamic relation of (primordial) hylē and constituting temporality. It functions as the open framework for temporality, whose openness allows for our apprehension of new and surprising situations as well as the continuance of ongoing situations. Further, through its functioning as open framework, protention itself becomes fulfilled; this discovery caused us to call into question the necessity of the term "*Urimpression.*" Second, after grasping protention in itself, we found that there exists an essential relation between protention and intentionality, where protention is the temporal foundation of our intending consciousness, allowing for the appresentations of a presentation. We also found that there is an essential relation between protention and affectivity, which shows the "object's side" of the relation between subject and object and an indirect relation between intentionality, affectivity, and appresentation via protention. Finally, the openness of protentional temporality, its relation to appresentation, and certain indications in Husserl's later work all point to an important interrelation between intersubjectivity and my temporality, a relation which appears to contribute to the essential foundation of phenomenology.

As a final thought, let us recall Husserl's move in the Bernauer manuscripts to fold his diagram of temporality, pulling the area of protention upward, changing his representation of protentional temporality from two dimensions to three. As protention extends upward from the surface of the paper, perhaps this new symbolization unwittingly manifests the pull that takes me out of myself. Protention is affected by the draw of both objects and other subjects such that it exceeds the flat surface of the ego, connecting it with its intersubjective and objective world. Perhaps, then, through protention, we ought to understand intersubjectivity as the "third dimension" of phenomenological foundation.

Notes

I would like to thank Professors Donn Welton and Klaus Held for their detailed comments on an earlier version of this article. Also many thanks to Professors Rudolf Bernet and Dieter

Lohmar for granting me permission to publish citations from Husserl's unpublished manuscripts and for their support of my research at the Husserl-Archives.

1. Cf. Section 4 of Klaus Held's second essay in this collection (Chapter 2) for an overview of the structure of phenomenological temporality, and Section 5 of that essay for insight into the general questions that inform this article's approach to the problem of intersubjectivity in phenomenology.

2. I am constructing these "periods" of Husserl's works primarily for a better understanding of the developments in his thinking with regard to temporality and intersubjectivity. The time frames are based on the general divisions made by the editors of his work: the period he wrote his published time lectures (*Zeitbewusstsein*, 1893–1917), the time periods chosen by the editors for his intersubjectivity volumes (*Intersubjektivität I*, 1905–20; *Intersubjektivität II*, 1921–28; *Intersubjektivität III*, 1929–35), the time period of his writings on passive syntheses (*Passive Synthesis*, 1918–26), and the time periods of his unpublished L manuscripts (1917–18) and C manuscripts (1929–35). Thus the three "periods" of Husserl's work and thought, for our purposes here are early (1893–1917), middle (1918–28), and late (1929–35).

3. *Zeitbewusstsein*, 138; after *Time-Consciousness*, 142.

4. *Zeitbewusstsein*, 145–46; *Time-Consciousness*, 148–50.

5. *Zeitbewusstsein*, 167; after *Time-Consciousness*, 172. One might disagree with Brough's interpretation of "-*hof*" as "fringe" here, since *Hof* usually means a courtyard or a square or yard of sorts—even a halo. I believe Husserl wished to emphasize the *expansion* or *stretching* of the now which he discussed in many of these early texts, and which later became known as the temporal "horizon." Brough is indicating a similar problematic found in William James's work, which James presented with the term "fringe." This problem of translation and terminology, interestingly, points to the philosophical problem of the temporal horizon in general, for the difficulty in naming the "extensions" of the now-moment reveals the even more difficult problem of understanding them.

6. Cf. Klaus Held, *Lebendige Gegenwart. Die Frage nach der Seinsweise des transzendentalen Ich bei Edmund Husserl, entwickelt am Leitfaden der Zeitproblematik* (The Hague: Martinus Nijhoff, 1966).

7. *Zeitbewusstsein*, 167; after *Time-Consciousness*, 172. This relation of protention to intuition also substantiates the argument that the living present is, in a sense, pre-temporal, and that it is the active constitution of our intuitions. Cf. Klaus Held, *Lebendige Gegenwart. Die Frage nach der Seinsweise des transzendentalen Ich bei Edmund Husserl, entwickelt am Leitfaden der Zeitproblematik* (The Hague: Martinus Nijhoff, 1966), especially 63.

8. *Zeitbewusstsein*, 169; after *Time-Consciousness*, 174.

9. *Zeitbewusstsein*, 297; after *Time-Consciousness*, 308–9. Husserl also adds a footnote to this manuscript (probably having returned to it later), writing that protention is essentially different from retention because of its openness to what is coming, and to when the duration of a temporal object will end. Retention, on the other hand, is closed with regard to such possibilities, as it is "tied" to what has already been actualized. We will return to this later.

10. *Zeitbewusstsein*, 168–69; *Time-Consciousness*, 172–74.

11. See John Brough, "The Emergence of an Absolute Consciousness in Husserl's Early Writings on Time-Consciousness," in *Husserl: Expositions and Appraisals*, ed. Frederick A. Elliston and Peter McCormick (Notre Dame, Ind.: University of Notre Dame Press, 1977), 83–100, especially 93. It is highly problematic that Husserl discarded the notion of "now-point" and appears to have replaced it with an apparently similar notion, "*Urimpression*." The Urimpression, however, is meant to indicate the "moment of actualization"—a phenomenological abstraction rather than a mathematical abstraction—although the distinction is difficult to discern. In fact, as we will see here, protentions can also be actualized, and often are; as such, they call into question the need for the term "Urimpression" overall.

12. Ms. L I 15, numbers 15.7–15.9.

13. In earlier diagrams, Husserl represents retention *above* the line instead, but he realizes that the diagram would better represent "sinking away" if the diagonal lines for retention were beneath the horizontal line of the present. Cf. Husserl's note to his diagram on *Zeitbewusstsein*, 331; *Time-Consciousness*, 343.

14. In manuscript L I 15.

15. "Es fehlt aber eine Signatur für die Protentionen, die im Winkelausschnitt E E_2 E_2 liegen. Wir ziehen nun eine Verlängerung für $E_1{}^2$–E_2 nach oben und signieren damit die Protentionen, die in Bewußtseinseinheit mit denen der unteren Strecke die fehlende Intentionalität ausmachen" (Ms. L I 15, 23a).

16. "Die vorangegangene als solche wird retiniert im neuen Bewußtsein der Retention und dieses Bewußtsein ist einerseits charakterisiert in sich als Erfüllung des früheren und andererseits in sich als Retention des früheren. Aber ist hier nicht eine Schwierigkeit? Das frühere Bewußtsein ist Protention (d.i. eben auf Späteres "gerichtete" Intention) und die nachkommende Retention wäre also Retention der früheren Retention, die zugleich charakterisiert ist als Protention. Diese neu eintretende Retention reproduziert also die frühere Retention mit ihrer protentionalen Tendenz und erfüllt diese letztere zugleich, aber in einer Weise, daß durch diese Erfüllung hindurchgeht eine Protention auf die nächsten Phasen" (Ms. L I 15, 24a–b).

17. For example: "Diese Antizipation ist aber durch das Kontinuum vorangegangener Retentionen als Kontinuum motiviert" (Ms. L I 15, 24a).

18. For example: "Diese Urfolge projiziert sich in die Zukunft, in Form des protentionalen Bewußtseins, das jede Phase begleitet" (Ms. L I 15, 22a).

19. Ms. L I 15, 27a. For Husserl, here, there is also another, more abstract understanding of the event (*Ereignis*), in both a protentional and retentional sense: this is the temporal flow itself as unending, albeit divided according to its two functions. We will leave this aspect aside for this project.

20. "Die neue Phase ist also nicht nur Wandlung der Retention in eine Retention nächster Stufe, die in ihrer mittelbaren Intentionalität die frühere modifiziert bewußt hat, und eine Wandlung der mitverflochtenen Protention, sondern auch eine Retention der früheren Protention. . . . Die neue Protention ist neue und Modifikation der früheren, die aber selbst durch ein Moment eingeflochtenen retentionalen Bewußtseins bewußt ist" (Ms. L I 15, 25b).

21. "Die Ux ist eigentlich nicht zu symbolisieren als eine Gerade mit zwei Zweigen, sondern als zwei zusammenstoßende Geraden mit verschiedener Belegung, obschon im ganzen symmetrischer" (Ms. L I 15, 30a). No diagram accompanies this part of the discussion.

22. "Also hätten wir besser zu symbolisieren durch einen Winkel und das ganze Parallelensystem [darzustellen] als zwei Systeme, die als zwei Halbebenen einen ebenen Winkel bilden, deren Scheitelgerade die E-E ist. Also wir denken uns das Papier in EE geknickt und EE nach oben gezogen, über die Papierfläche gehoben" (Ms. L I 15, 30a). The text does not identify the different lines that are signified here by "EE," which obviously leads to some confusion. I believe, however, that Husserl is referring mainly to two lines: the first, that of the temporal flow (horizontal), and the second, that of protention (diagonal to and "above" the first).

23. *Passive Synthesis*, 190. Although apperception and appresentation should usually be distinguished with regard to their specific functions, here it is important merely that they share the general function of exceeding actualization.

24. One could argue here that we never are completely motionless, and thus there is always some kind of motion involved in our experience of touch. Cf. the article on "Funktionelle Entspannung" (Functional Relaxation), in *Handbuch der Salutogenese. Konzept und Praxis,* ed. Wolfram Schüffel et al. (Wiesbaden: Ullstein Medical, 1998), 227–32, especially

230, where the student discovers the rhythms of breath, digestion, heart, etc., through this form of relaxation. These are motions of our body that are continuous and necessary for our tactile experience, even when voluntary movement has ceased. In fact, these involuntary rhythms could conceivably contribute to an imperceptible movement of the skin that allows for the sensation of touch.

25. We can even take this experience of touch to another level. The position "I touch" is a form of the position "I can." In order to be in the position to express "I can," I must have a protending temporal consciousness, for without it, I would be unable to know (or express) what "I can" do. Thus protending consciousness is essential to the temporal ego.

26. "Die stetige punktuelle Erfüllung gehört doch selbst zur Intention als Intention auf Eintreten des noch im Fluß befindlichen Ereignisses. Indessen, die Intention geht stetig durch die neuen Punkte hindurch und behält stetig über sie hinaus den Charakter unerfüllter Erwartung, und die Intention geht auf die Erfüllungen bzw. von Erwartung zu Erwartung in dem Erwartungskontinuum und damit auf die immer neu erfüllten Erwartungen (erfüllt nach einer Phase): das sind zwei Seiten einer und derselben Sache" (Ms. L I 16, 5b).

27. "Wie ist diese Intentionalität ihrer Struktur nach notwendig beschaffen?" (Ms. L I 16, 5b).

28. "Das Auftreten immer neuer Urpräsenzen aber besagt nicht bloß das Auftreten dieser Daten, sondern es gehört ebenso zum Wesen des Prozesses, der notwendig zeitkonstituierender ist, daß eine vorgerichtete Intentionalität notwendig ist" (Ms. L I 16, 4a).

29. "Das Jetzt ist konstituiert durch die Form der protentionalen Erfüllung, das Vergangen durch retentionale Modifikation dieser Erfüllung" (Ms. L I 16, 9a).

30. It is important to note here that this question, which has an implication of causality to it, is meant as a phenomenological question, not as an epistemological or ontological one. Here it is a question of "motivation," to use Husserl's term.

31. "[I]st ein Stück Urfolge von hyletischen Daten (und dann von allen anderen Urerlebnissen) abgelaufen, so muß sich ein retentionaler Zusammenhang bilden, aber nicht nur das—Hume hat es schon gesehen—das Bewußtsein bleibt in seinem Zuge und antizipiert das Weitere, nämlich eine Protention 'richtet' sich auf Fortsetzung der Reihe in demselben Stile, und das ist Protention bezüglich des Verlaufs der Urdaten, die als Kerndaten fungieren, und desgleichen bezüglich des Verlaufs der Retentionen mit ihren in ihnen fungierenden Abschattungen" (Ms. L I 16, 8a).

32. "Sie ist ursprünglich erwachsen. Wir können als Urgesetz notwendiger Genesis hier den Satz in Anspruch nehmen." This directly precedes the citation quoted above (Ms. L I 16, 8a).

33. The use of the term "ecstatic" here is not meant to indicate Heideggerian ecstatic temporality directly. While there are parallels between the two, especially with reference to the "expansion" or "span" of the zone of actualization, my development of Husserlian temporality focuses on its constancy and its relation to objectivity as well as intersubjectivity. It is my understanding that the Heideggerian "authentic moment-of-vision" is meant to describe a very different aspect of our temporality.

34. *Passive Synthesis,* 156.

35. *Passive Synthesis,* 148.

36. *Passive Synthesis,* 148–49.

37. *Passive Synthesis,* 151.

38. James Mensch articulates the relation between affectivity and protention quite well, through his discussion of affection in his article "Husserl's Concept of the Future" (*Husserl Studies* 16: 41–64). Mensch shows how Husserl's notion of affection is both related to intentionality—drawing my attention outward, pulling it toward the object—and to the future. Mensch says, "This increasing draw or pull of affecting content is what yields the

protentional intentionality inherent in the retained" (48). Mensch also points out the similarity in the meanings of *intentio* and *Zug,* both of which contain an implicit tension, or stretching. In this case, the stretching and tension is directed futurally (48).

Mensch draws two conclusions from his analysis of affection. The first, "that affectivity is a necessary condition for our temporalization" (48), is an attempt to explain why my consciousness extends beyond itself into its future. It seems, however, that, if the ego must be fully formed before affectivity can occur, then my temporality must also be constituted. In fact, affectivity requires the condition of the living present in order to take place, given its reliance on each aspect, retention, Urimpression, and protention. Thus, although Mensch is correct in concluding that our temporalization requires an involvement with the world, he must be careful not to reduce this relation to one of temporality and affectivity. Mensch's second conclusion with relation to affection is that "constitution is also dependent on affection" (49). Here again, it seems that the object must be already constituted—albeit passively —in order to affect the ego. Thus it seems that Mensch wishes to apply more influence to affectivity than might be possible, given Husserl's descriptions. Nevertheless, affection is a very important notion, especially when one considers protention in Husserl's philosophy.

39. Cf. Klaus Held, *Lebendige Gegenwart. Die Frage nach der Seinsweise des transzendentalen Ich bei Edmund Husserl, entwickelt am Leitfaden der Zeitproblematik* (The Hague: Martinus Nijhoff, 1966), and John Brough, "The Emergence of an Absolute Consciousness in Husserl's Early Writings on Time-Consciousness."

40. Cf. also Klaus Held, *Lebendige Gegenwart,* 30, where he says that there is "no core phase without a surrounding field of presence, and no such field without a source-point of presentation that is itself accompanying it." Note that this dependent core phase is itself a phase and not a point. In addition, see Rudolf Bernet, "Die ungegenwärtige Gegenwart. Anwesenheit und Abwesenheit in Husserls Analyse des Zeitbewußtseins," in *Zeit und Zeitlichkeit bei Husserl und Heidegger, Phänomenologische Forschungen,* vol. 14 (Freiburg/Munich: Karl Alber Verlag, 1983), 16–57, especially 45.

41. The following is a summary primarily of §§50–52 of the *Cartesianische Meditationen* (138–45), although of issue is actually the entire Fifth Meditation (121–77).

42. "Im Gebiet der 'Einfühlung' haben wir wiederum mancherlei Unterschied der Ursprünglichkeit, so in der Einfühlung selbst (dem analogisierenden Appräsentieren von Anderen) und in den mittels dieser Einfühlung sich konstituierenden Apperzeptionen" (Ms. C 3 V, 64a).

43. *Cartesianische Meditationen,* 141; *Cartesian Meditations,* 111. We take this to be the type of association we just described—association by analogy.

44. *Cartesianische Meditationen,* 147; *Cartesian Meditations,* 117–18.

45. This claim, of course, goes against Levinas's position when he discusses phenomenology and our apprehension of other subjects. Cf. especially Emmanuel Levinas's *Time and the Other,* trans. R. A. Cohen (Pittsburgh: Duquesne University Press, 1987).

46. Cf. Gail Soffer's insightful article "The Other as Alter Ego: A Genetic Approach," *Husserl Studies* 15 (1999): 151–66, where she argues that the appresentation and empathy of the other subject cannot rely upon associative analogy alone. Instead, it is a combination of certain qualities that are already part of the human infant at birth and a lengthy learning process that takes place from birth well into childhood. Thus the solipsistic individual could not conceive the notion "if I were there" without a presupposition of intersubjectivity.

47. "Der Andere ist in mir mitgegenwärtig. Ich absolut, als lebendig strömend seiende konkrete Gegenwart, hat seine Gegenwart als Mitgegenwart, als appräsentativ sich als er selbst bekundend in mir, aber auch ihn selbst bekundend als mich in Selbstbekundung habend in ihm, in seiner lebendigen Gegenwart konstituiert in der Weise der Mitgegenwart" (Ms. C 3 III, 44b).

48. "Ich und meine primordiale Gegenwart. Meine primordiale Mitgegenwart, als erster Horizont: primordiale Welt, meine fremdsubjektiv-vermittelte, intersubjektive Mitgegenwart. Das Dasein anderer Ichsubjekte mit ihren primordialen Welten—als mir mitgeltenden in Seinsgewißheit oder in Seinsmodalitäten, horizonthaft" (Ms. C 16 VII, 5–6).

49. "In all dem herrscht, solange die Primordialität nicht gewonnen ist, Zweideutigkeit; denn in mir ist doch alles impliziert; Totalität des Bewußtseins ist nicht nur mein 'Bewußt-seinsstrom,' sondern impliziert aller Anderen Bewußtseinsströme etc." (Ms. C 16 VI, 79b).

50. "Der Andere ist für sich ebenso, aber sein Für-sich ist zugleich mein Für-mich, in Form meiner Potentialität der Appräsentation. Aber er selbst ist appräsentiert in mir und ich in ihm, ich trage alle Anderen in mir als selbst appräsentierte und zu appräsentierende und als mich selbst ebenso in sich tragend" (Ms. C 3 III, 44b).

51. *Cartesianische Meditationen,* 139; *Cartesian Meditations,* 109.

PART III

Self-consciousness, Transcendental Subjectivity, and the Question of the Unconscious

6

Inner Time-Consciousness and Pre-reflective Self-awareness

Dan Zahavi

IF ONE LOOKS at the current discussion of self-awareness there seems to be a general agreement that whatever valuable philosophical contributions Husserl might have made, his account of self-awareness is not among them. This prevalent appraisal is often based on the claim that Husserl was too occupied with the problem of *intentionality* to ever pay real attention to the issue of self-awareness. Due to his interest in intentionality Husserl took object-consciousness as the paradigm of every kind of awareness and therefore settled with a model of self-awareness based upon the subject-object dichotomy, with its entailed difference between the intending and the intended. As a consequence, Husserl never discovered the existence of pre-reflective self-awareness, but remained stuck in the traditional, but highly problematic, reflection model of self-awareness.

To a certain extent this is an old criticism that can be traced back to Heidegger. In Heidegger's lecture course *Prolegomena zur Geschichte des Zeitbegriffs* from 1925, Heidegger writes that Husserl operated with a too narrow concept of Being. Because of his exclusive interest in intentionality, Husserl identified the Being of consciousness with the Being of objects and consequently failed to uncover the unique mode of Being characterizing intentional subjectivity itself. Heidegger consequently states that a more radical phenomenology is called for—a phenomenology that has to return to the original givenness of subjectivity, and not merely consider it, as Husserl did, insofar as it is a (potential) *object* of reflection.[1]

More recently, Tugendhat has formulated a related criticism. Tugendhat claims that Husserl understood self-awareness as a kind of internal perception, that is, as a subject-object relation between two different experiences (a perceiving and a perceived), and as he then adds, Husserl never succeeded in explaining why such a relation should result in self-awareness.[2] Similar views can be found in Henrich, Frank, and Gloy, who all argue that Husserl's analysis of self-awareness never managed to escape the reflection-theoretical paradigm.[3] As Manfred Frank puts it: "In any case, Husserl does not know any other concept of self-awareness than the reflective one."[4] Frank even claims that Husserl not only failed to provide a convincing analysis of self-awareness, but that he basically did not even understand the very problem.[5]

A common feature of these critical interpretations is their narrow textual basis. By and large they restrict themselves to Husserl's position in two of his published works, namely, *Logische Untersuchungen* (1900–1901) and *Ideen zu einer reinen Phänomenologie und phänomenologischen Philosophie I* (1913). Occasionally, they also draw on material from *Zur Phänomenologie des inneren Zeitbewusstseins* (1893–1917), but they very rarely consider any further material, neither from any of the posthumously published volumes of *Husserliana* nor for that matter from any of the still unpublished research manuscripts found in the Husserl-Archives.

If there is anything that contemporary Husserl scholarship has demonstrated, however, it is that it is virtually impossible to acquire an adequate insight into Husserl's philosophy if one restricts oneself to the writings that were published during his lifetime. This is not only the case when it comes to topics such as the problem of intersubjectivity, the role of the body, or the structure of temporality, but also when it concerns the question of self-awareness.

Drawing on posthumously published material, I will in the following show that the standard interpretation must be rejected. The notion of pre-reflective self-awareness is not only to be found in Husserl, he also subjects it to a highly illuminating analysis. It is true that one rarely finds analyses dedicated exclusively to the problem of self-awareness. But this is by no means because the topic is absent, but rather because Husserl's reflections on this problem are usually integrated into his analysis of a number of related issues, such as the nature of intentionality, spatiality, embodiment, temporality, attention, intersubjectivity, etc. This fact makes any attempt at a systematic account both challenging and rewarding. Rewarding because Husserl's phenomenological analysis of self-awareness is far more detailed, concrete, and substantial than the more formal considerations to be found in the writings of, for instance, Frank or Henrich. Challenging because although there is a profound and complex theory of self-awareness to be found in Husserl's writings, it is a theory that will first have to be pieced together; simply to isolate the relevant elements and avoid getting lost in the adjacent discussions will demand effort. Since space will not allow me to outline the full scope of Husserl's theory, I will in the following content myself with arguing for the claim that Husserl does in fact operate with the notion of a pre-reflective self-awareness.

Before I start, however, a few words about the reflection theory might be appropriate. Why is it at all necessary to find an alternative to the view that self-awareness is the result of consciousness directing its "gaze" at itself, taking itself as an object, and thus becoming aware of itself?[6] If one takes a look at the writings of Henrich, Cramer, Pothast, Frank, Gloy, et al., one will find an entire arsenal of arguments (including different versions of what is basically the same argument) showing the deficiencies of the reflection model. The criticism is particularly directed against the claim that there is no self-awareness prior to reflection, and that self-awareness comes about only in the moment consciousness objectifies itself. Let me present their central argument.

The reflection model of self-awareness operates with a duality of moments. Whether it comes about by one experience taking another experience as its object, or one experience taking itself as an object, we are dealing with a kind of self-division and have to *distinguish* the reflecting from the reflected. Of course, the aim of reflection is then to overcome or negate this difference and to posit both moments as identical. Otherwise, we would not have a case of *self*-awareness. This strategy is, however, confronted with fundamental problems. The reflection theory claims that in order for a perception to become self-aware it must await its objectivation by a subsequent act of reflection. In order to speak of *self*-awareness, however, it is not sufficient that the experience in question be reflexively thematized and made into an object. It must be grasped as being *identical* with the thematizing experience. In order to be a case of *self*-awareness, it is not sufficient that A is conscious of B: A must be conscious of B as being identical with A. In other words, to count as a case of self-awareness the perception must be grasped as being identical with the act of reflection (and since a *numerical identity* is excluded in advance, the identity in question must be that of belonging to the same subject or being part of the same stream of consciousness). But how can the act of reflection (which lacks self-awareness) be in a position to realize that the perception belongs to the same subjectivity as itself? If the reflecting experience is to encounter something as itself, if it is to recognize or identify something different as itself, it needs a prior acquaintance with itself. Consequently, the act of reflection must either await a further act of reflection in order to become self-aware, in which case we are confronted with a vicious infinite regress, *or* it must be admitted that it is itself already in a state of self-awareness *prior to reflection*. The latter, of course, would involve us in a circular explanation, presupposing that which was meant to be explained, and implicitly rejecting the thesis of the reflection model of self-awareness, that is, that all self-awareness is brought about by reflection.[7]

The general lesson to learn from this argument is that one should avoid theories that describe self-awareness as a kind of relation—be it a relation between different experiences, or between the experience and itself—since every relation, especially the subject-object relation, presupposes a *distinction* between two (or more) relata, and this is exactly what generates the problem.

I

What does Husserl have to say about self-awareness? Let me start by showing that he, in a manner not unlike Sartre, took self-awareness to be an essential feature of subjectivity and that he considered reflection to be a founded and non-basic form of self-awareness.

According to Husserl, to be a subject is to exist for-itself, that is, to be

self-aware. Thus, rather than being something that only occurs during exceptional circumstances, namely, whenever we pay attention to our conscious life,
self-awareness is a feature characterizing subjectivity as such, no matter what
worldly entities it might otherwise be conscious of and occupied with:[8]

> To be a subject is to be in the mode of being aware of oneself.[9]

> *An absolute existent* is existent in the form of an intentional life—which, no mat-
> ter what else it may be intrinsically conscious of, is, at the same time, conscious-
> ness of itself. Precisely for that reason (as we can see when we consider more
> profoundly) it has at all times an essential ability to *reflect* on itself, on all its
> structures that stand out for it—an essential ability to make itself thematic and
> produce judgments, and evidences, relating to itself.[10]

> For this is not merely a continuously streaming lived-experiencing [*Erleben*],
> rather when it streams there is always simultaneously consciousness of this stream-
> ing. This consciousness is self-perceiving. Only exceptionally is it a thematic no-
> ticing performed by the I. To that exception belongs the reflection, possible at
> any time. This perception, which makes all experiencing conscious, is the so-
> called internal consciousness or internal perception.[11]

It is important not to misunderstand Husserl. When he claims that subjectivity is as such self-aware, he is not advocating a strong Cartesian thesis concerning total and infallible self-transparency; rather he is simply calling attention to the intimate link between experiential phenomena and first-person
givenness, in much the same way as Nagel and Searle have later done.[12] Thus,
when Husserl speaks of a pervasive self-awareness he is concerned with the question of how consciousness experiences itself, how it is given to itself, how it
manifests itself. In Husserl's view, the subjective or first-person givenness of an
experience is not simply a quality added to the experience, a mere varnish as it
were. On the contrary, it constitutes the very mode of being of the experience.
In contrast to physical objects, which can exist regardless of whether or not
they *de facto* appear for a subject, experiences are essentially characterized by
their subjective givenness, by the fact that there is a subjective "feel" to them.[13]
To undergo an experience necessarily means that there is something "it is like"
for the subject to have that experience.[14] But insofar as there is something "it
is like" for the subject to have the experience, there must be some awareness of
the experience itself along with its inherent "quality" of *mineness;* in short,
there must be some minimal form of self-awareness. As Flanagan puts it: "all
subjective experience is self-conscious in the weak sense that there is something
it is like for the subject to have that experience. This involves a sense that the
experience is the subject's experience, that it happens to her, occurs in her
stream."[15] Self-awareness is consequently not something that only comes about
the moment one scrutinizes one's experience attentively (not to speak of it being something that only comes about the moment one recognizes one's own
mirror image, or refers to oneself using the first-person pronoun, or is in possession of identifying knowledge of one's own life story). Rather, it is legitimate

to speak of self-awareness the moment I am no longer simply conscious of a foreign object, but of my experience of the object as well, for in this case my subjectivity reveals itself to me. If the experience is given in a first-person mode of presentation to me, it is (at least tacitly) given as *my* experience, and it can therefore count as a case of self-consciousness. On this account, the only type of experience which would lack self-awareness would be an experience I was not conscious of, that is, an "unconscious experience."

Granted that I am aware of my experience even when intentionally directed at objects in the world, the central question, of course, is *how* this self-awareness comes about. Is it the result of a reflection? Husserl's answer is no. For Husserl, the act of reflection, say, an explicit consciousness of an occurrent perception of a Swiss Army knife, is *founded* in a twofold sense. It does not present us with a self-enclosed subjectivity, but with a self-transcending subjectivity directed at an object, and it consequently presupposes the preceding act of object-intentionality.[16] Moreover, as an explicit self-awareness, it also relies upon a prior tacit self-awareness. To utilize a terminological distinction between perceiving (*Wahrnehmen*) and experiencing (*Erleben*) dating back to the *Logical Investigations:* prior to reflection one perceives the intentional object, but one experiences (*erlebt*) the intentional act. Although I am not intentionally directed at the act (this only happens in the subsequent reflection, where the act is thematized), it is not unconscious but conscious,[17] that is self-given. In Husserl's words:

> The term lived-experience [*Erlebnis*] expresses just this [quality of] being experiential [*Erlebtsein*], that is having conscious awareness in internal consciousness, which at any time makes it pregiven to the I.[18]

> [E]very experience is "consciousness," and consciousness is consciousness *of*. . . . But every experience is *itself experienced* [*erlebt*], and *to that extent* also "conscious" [*bewußt*].[19]

> Every act is consciousness of something, but there is also consciousness of every act. Every act is "sensed," is immanently "perceived" (internal consciousness), although naturally not posited, meant (to perceive here does not mean to grasp something and to be turned towards it in an act of meaning). . . . To be sure, this seems to lead back to an infinite regress. For is not the internal consciousness, the perceiving of the act (of judging, of perceiving something external, of rejoicing, and so forth), again an act and therefore itself something internally perceived, and so on? On the contrary, we must say: Every "experience" in the strict sense is internally perceived. But the internal perceiving is not an "experience" in the same sense. It is not itself again internally perceived.[20]

In a regular intentional act, I am directed at and preoccupied with my intentional object. Whenever I am intentionally directed at objects I am also self-aware. But when I am directed at and occupied with objects I am not thematically conscious of myself. And when I do thematize myself in a reflection, the very act of thematization remains unthematic.[21] When subjectivity functions it is self-aware, but it is not thematically conscious of itself, and it therefore lives in *anonymity*.[22]

> Thus we always have the separation between the I and *cogito* as functioning but not grasped (functioning subjectivity), and the possibly thematized, direct or self-grasped I and its *cogito*, or more simply, it is necessary to distinguish between the functioning subjectivity and the objective subjectivity (the objectified, thematically experienced, presented, thought, predicated subjectivity), and whenever I take myself or something else as an object, I am always necessarily unthematically cogiven as a functioning I, accessible to myself through reflection, which, on its part, is a new unthematic activity of the functioning I.[23]

In a moment I will return to Husserl's use of the term "perception" when it comes to the basic form of self-awareness, but it should be quite obvious that he has seen the aporetic implications of the reflection theory: The claim that self-awareness only comes about when the act is apprehended by a further act ultimately leads to an infinite regress.[24]

As far as the interpretation of Henrich, Gloy, Tugendhat, and Frank is concerned, it must be acknowledged that Husserl occasionally writes that we do not *perceive* our own subjectivity prior to reflection, but live in a state of self-oblivion and self-forfeiture (*Selbstverlorenheit*). But when he then adds that we only *know* of our acts reflectively, that is, that we only gain *knowledge* of our conscious life through reflection,[25] it becomes clear that he is using the term "perception" to denote a thematic examination. Husserl does not deny the existence of a tacit self-awareness. But he does deny that this self-awareness can provide us with more than awareness. It cannot give us *conceptual knowledge* of subjectivity. As Husserl says:

> The actual life and lived-experiencing is of course always conscious, but it is not therefore always thematically experienced and known. For that a new pulse of actual life is necessary, a so-called reflective or immanently directed experience.[26]

It is, however, also possible to unearth passages where Husserl does in fact describe the tacit self-awareness as a type of *internal perception*,[27] but a closer examination of these texts does not substantiate the claim that Husserl is trying to reduce self-awareness to a type of object-intentionality. Husserl's terminology is taken from his classical investigation of the hierarchy of foundation existing between different types of acts. In contrast to various kinds of presentifying (*vergegenwärtigende*) acts, such as recollection, fantasy, or empathy, perception is characterized as bringing its object to an originary kind of presentation. That which appears in perception is given *leibhaftig*, and it is exactly this feature which Husserl focuses upon in his discussion of basic self-awareness. This is brought to light in a passage from *Erste Philosophie II*, where Husserl writes that the life of the subject is a life in the form of original self-awareness. He then equates this self-awareness with an *innermost* perception, but adds that it is a perception, not in the sense of being an active self-apprehension, but in the sense of being an *originary* self-appearance.[28] In two of the passages quoted above, passages from, respectively, *Analysen zur passiven Synthesis* and *Vorlesungen zur Phänomenologie des inneren Zeitbewusstseins*, Husserl speaks alternately of the tacit self-awareness as an internal perception and as an internal consciousness (*inneres Bewußtsein*—one feels the influence from Brentano).[29] As will gradually become clear, Husserl ultimately opts for the latter expression, and much misunderstanding might have been avoided if he had always distinguished as clearly between the two as he does in *Ideen II,* where he equates "internal perception" with reflection, and "internal consciousness" with a nonthematic kind of self-awareness that precedes reflection.[30]

According to Husserl, our acts are tacitly self-aware, but they are also accessible for reflection. They can be reflected upon and thereby brought to our attention.[31] An examination of the particular intentional structure of this process can substantiate the thesis concerning the founded status of reflection. Reflective self-awareness is often taken to be a thematic, articulated, and intensified self-awareness, and it is normally initiated in order to bring the primary intentional act into focus. However, in order to explain the occurrence of reflection it is necessary that that which is to be disclosed and thematized is (unthematically) present. Otherwise there would be nothing to motivate and call forth the act of reflection. As Husserl points out, it is in the nature of reflection to grasp something, which was already given prior to the grasping. Reflection is characterized by disclosing, and not by producing its theme:

> When I say "I," I grasp myself in a simple reflection. But this self-experience [*Selbsterfahrung*] is like every experience [*Erfahrung*], and in particular every perception, a mere directing myself towards something that was already there for me, that was already conscious, but not thematically experienced, not noticed.[32]

> Whenever I reflect, I find myself "in relation" to something, as affected or active. That which I am related to is experientially conscious—it is already there for me as a "lived-experience" in order for me to be able to relate myself to it.[33]

In short, reflection is not an act *sui generis,* it does not appear out of nowhere, but presupposes, like all intentional activity, a *motivation.* According to Husserl, to be motivated is to be *affected* by something, and then to respond to it.[34] That which motivates reflection is exactly, with a term I will later return to, a prior *self-affection.* I can thematize myself, because I am already passively self-aware; I can grasp myself, because I am already affected by myself.[35]

When I start reflecting, that which motivates the reflection and which is then grasped has already been going on for a while. The reflected experience did not commence the moment I started paying attention to it, and it is not only given as still existing, but also and mainly as having already been. It is the *same* act, which is now given reflectively, and it is given to me as enduring in time, that is, as a temporal act.[36] When reflection sets in, it initially grasps something that has just elapsed, namely, the motivating phase of the act reflected upon. The reason why this phase can still be thematized by the subsequent reflection is that it does not disappear, but is retained in the *retention*, wherefore Husserl can claim that retention is a condition of possibility for reflection. It is due to the retention that consciousness can be made into an object.[37] Or to rephrase, reflection can only take place if a *temporal horizon* has been established.

II

So far I have argued that Husserl takes self-awareness to be a pervasive feature of consciousness, and that he considers reflection in the sense of an explicit and thematic type of self-awareness to be a founded and non-basic form of self-awareness. Is this sufficient to demonstrate the existence of a pre-reflective type of self-awareness for Husserl? The answer is yes as long as pre-reflective self-awareness is merely understood as a type of self-awareness that precedes and is more basic than reflective self-awareness. However, the answer is no if pre-reflective self-awareness is understood as a type of self-awareness that emphatically lacks any kind of dyadic structure. To put it differently, in order to escape the problems facing the reflection-theoretical model, it is not sufficient simply to acknowledge the existence of a tacit and unthematic type of self-awareness. One also has to avoid interpreting this tacit and pervasive self-awareness in a manner analogous to the way in which reflection is understood; that is, it will not do to argue that tacit self-awareness comes about as the result of some mediated, dyadic, and relational process of self-objectification. But so far, it has not been shown that Husserl avoids this trap. And until that is done, it cannot be concluded that he in fact did surpass the reflection-theoretical model and discovered the existence of a truly pre-reflective type of self-awareness.

I have just mentioned that Husserl took reflection to depend upon *temporality*. In fact, it is exactly in his theory of *inner time-consciousness* that one finds his most elaborate account of the structure of pre-reflective self-awareness. So let me turn to that theory, and thereby to a nest of problems, which have often and rightly been characterized as being among the most important and difficult ones in the whole of phenomenology.[38]

In *Ideen I* Husserl confined himself to an analysis of the relation between the constituted objects and the constituting consciousness.[39] He accounted for the way in which the givenness of objects are conditioned by subjectivity, but apart from stressing that experiences are not given in the same (perspectival) way as objects, he did not pursue the question concerning the givenness of subjectivity itself any further. However, such a silence was *phenomenologically* unacceptable. Any analysis of the conditioned appearance of objects would necessarily lack a foundation as long as the givenness of the subjective condition were itself left in the dark.[40] Husserl was well aware of this, and he explicitly admits that he, in *Ideen I*, left out the most important problems, namely, those pertaining to inner time-consciousness. Only an analysis of time-consciousness will disclose the truly absolute, he adds.[41] The reason why Husserl speaks of the absolute, and more generally attributes such immense importance to his analysis of temporality, considering it to constitute the bedrock of phenomenology, is exactly because it is not a mere investigation of the temporal givenness of objects. It is not just a clarification of how it is possible to be conscious of objects with temporal extensions—that is, objects such as melodies, which cannot appear all at once, but only unfold themselves over time—rather, it is also an account of the *temporal self-givenness* of consciousness itself.

If we briefly consider Husserl's account of how we are able to intend temporally extended objects, we come across his crucial distinction between the *primal impression,* the *retention* and the *protention.* Husserl's well-known thesis is that a perception of a temporal object (as well as the perception of succession and change) would be impossible if consciousness merely provided us with the givenness of the pure now-phase of the object, and if the stream of consciousness were a series of unconnected points of experiencing, like a string of pearls. In fact, Husserl does have a name for our consciousness of the narrow now-phase of the object. He calls this consciousness the *primal impression.* But as he then argues, this alone cannot provide us with consciousness of anything with a temporal duration, and it is in fact only the abstract core-component of the full structure of experiencing. The primal impression is embedded in a two-fold temporal horizon. On the one hand, it is accompanied by a *retention* which provides us with consciousness of the phase of the object which has just been, that is, which allows us to be aware of the phase as it sinks into the past, and, on the other hand, by a *protention* which in a more or less indeterminate fashion anticipates the phase of the object yet to come:[42]

> In this way, it becomes evident that concrete perception as original consciousness (original givenness) of a temporally extended object is structured internally as itself a streaming system of momentary perceptions (so-called primal impressions). But each such momentary perception is the nuclear phase of a continuity, a continuity of momentary gradated retentions on the one side, and a horizon of what is coming on the other side: a horizon of "protention," which is disclosed to be characterized as a constantly gradated coming.[43]

However, as already mentioned, it is not sufficient to analyze the way in which we are able to be conscious of temporal objects; we also need to understand how we are able to be aware of the very acts that intend these temporal objects. Our perceptual objects are temporal, but what about our very perceptions of these objects? Are they also subjugated to the strict laws of temporal constitution? Are they also temporal unities, which arise, endure, and perish? Husserl often speaks of the acts themselves as being constituted in the structure: primal impression–retention–protention. They are only given, only self-aware, within this framework.[44] But how is this self-awareness to be understood? And how do we avoid an infinite regress? If the duration and unity of a tonal sequence is constituted by consciousness, and if our consciousness of the tonal sequence is itself given with duration and unity, are we then not forced to posit yet another consciousness to account for the givenness of this duration and unity, and so forth *ad infinitum*?[45]

Unfortunately, I do not think that Husserl ever managed to achieve complete clarity on this issue. Both his published and unpublished analyses remain characterized by ambiguities, and it is ultimately possible to find textual evidence in support of several different interpretations. Needless to say, this is not a very satisfying situation, but in the following I have opted for the interpretation that provides us with the most adequate account of self-awareness.[46]

On one dominant interpretation, Husserl is said to argue in the following way: just as we must distinguish between the constituted dimension in which transcendent objects exist and the constituting dimension that permits them to appear, we must distinguish between the constituted dimension in which the acts exist and the constituting dimension that permits them to appear. The acts are themselves temporal objects existing in *subjective time,* but they are constituted by a deeper dimension of subjectivity: by the *absolute flow* of inner time-consciousness.[47] Although it is possible to unearth some passages in support of this interpretation, I think it must ultimately be rejected, not only for systematic reasons—it presents us with an unattractive and very problematic account of self-awareness—but also because there are many other passages that speak against it. To say that the acts are originally given as *objects* for an internal consciousness, to interpret their primal givenness as an object-manifestation, leads us right back into a version of the reflection theory. This account does not explain self-awareness, it merely defers the problem. Obviously one is forced to ask whether inner time-consciousness is itself in possession of self-awareness or not. If it is denied that this consciousness is itself self-aware, the regress is indeed halted, but as already mentioned, this account cannot explain why the relation between inner time-consciousness and the act should result in *self-*awareness. If the answer is yes, one must ask how the self-awareness of inner time-consciousness is established. Two possibilities seem open. One, it comes about in the same way in which the act is brought to givenness. In this case we are confronted with an infinite regress. Or, the second possibility, inner time-consciousness is in possession of an implicit or intrinsic self-manifestation. But if it is acknowledged that such a type of self-awareness exists, one might reasonably ask why it should be reserved for the deepest level of subjectivity, and not already be a feature of the act itself. Furthermore, to claim that the absolute flow of inner time-consciousness is itself self-aware, and to claim that this is something apart from and beyond the givenness of the acts, is to operate with an unnecessary multiplication of self-awareness. Nevertheless, this is exactly the position that Husserl has been assumed to hold. According to one dominant interpretation, Husserl considers the acts to be *full-blown internal objects* that are immediately given as such, even prior to reflection. Apart from this, however, the flow is also given to itself. Thus, if we examine a reflection on a perception of a Swiss Army knife, the following should be the case: (1) the Swiss Army knife is given as a transcendent object, (2) the act of reflection is pre-reflectively given as an internal object, (3) the act of perception is reflectively given as an internal object, and finally (4) the flow for which all of these objects are given also reveals itself in a fundamental *shining*. Reflection should consequently present us with a threefold self-awareness with one transcendent object and two internal objects.[48] That seems excessive. Not only is the distinction between (2) and (4) hard to fathom, but the characterization of (2) also seems misleading. Even if one takes pre-reflective self-awareness to be a "marginal form of consciousness" and consequently distinguishes the pre-reflectively given internal object from the reflectively given internal object by emphasizing that the first is merely a marginal object,[49] this will not solve the problem. In fact, Husserl himself explicitly rejects this suggestion:

> *One should not mistake the consciousness of the objective background [gegenständliche Hintergrund] and consciousness understood in the sense of experiential being [Erlebtseins].* Lived-experiences as such do have their own being, but they are not objects of apperception (in this case we would end in an infinite regress). The background however is given to us objectively, it is constituted through a complex of apperceptive lived-experiences. We do not pay attention to these objects . . . , but they are still given to us in a quite different manner than the mere lived-experiences themselves, say the objectifying apperceptions and acts. (We could also say that experiential being is not mere-unnoticed-being, or unconscious-being in the sense of the unnoticed-being of the objective background.) The attentional consciousness of the background and consciousness in the sense of mere experiential givenness must be completely distinguished.[50]

It is definitely necessary to distinguish between thematic and marginal modes of consciousness. One must dismiss any narrow conception of consciousness that equates it with attention and claims that we are only conscious of that which we pay attention to. But although consciousness is not given thematically prior to reflection, this does not justify the claim that pre-reflective self-awareness is a marginal form of consciousness, that is, that our pre-reflective experiences remain in the background as potential themes in the same way as, say, the hum of the refrigerator. Pre-reflective self-awareness is not a kind of marginal, inattentive, object-consciousness, and prior to reflection, consciousness is not given to itself as a marginal object. The entire analogy is misleading, since it remains stuck in the subject-object model.[51]

I would like to propose a different interpretation, an interpretation that ultimately permits one to link Husserl's analysis of inner time-consciousness to his differentiations between functioning and thematized subjectivity, and pre-reflective and reflective self-awareness, respectively.

One of the problems confronting Husserl's analysis was how to avoid an infinite regress. However, one should not conceive of the relation between inner time-consciousness and the intentional act as if it were a relation between two radically different dimensions in subjectivity. When Husserl claims that the intentional act is constituted in inner time-consciousness, he is not saying that the act is brought to givenness by some other part of subjectivity. Inner time-consciousness *is* the pre-reflective self-awareness of the act, and to say that the act is constituted in inner time-consciousness simply means that it is brought to awareness thanks to itself. It is called *inner* time-consciousness because it belongs *intrinsically* to the *innermost* structure of the act itself. To phrase it differently, Husserl's description of the structure of inner time-consciousness (primal impression–retention–protention) is exactly an analysis of the structure of the pre-reflective self-manifestation of our acts and experiences. Thus, Husserl's position is relatively unequivocal. The intentional act is conscious of something different from itself, namely, the intentional object. The act is intentional exactly because it permits hetero-manifestation. But the act also manifests itself. The object is given through the act, and if there were no awareness of the act, the object would not appear. Thus, apart from being intentional, the act is also characterized by its "internal consciousness," or "*Urbewußtsein*," or "impressional consciousness," to mention three different terms for one and the same.[52] This internal consciousness is not a particular intentional act, but a pervasive dimension of self-manifestation, and it is exactly this which precedes and founds reflective self-awareness.[53] In short, Husserl would claim that to have an experience, for example, a perception of a flowering apple tree, is to be aware of the experience. But this self-awareness is not itself a separate experience in need of yet another awareness. The self-awareness of the experience is an internal, non-reflective, irrelational feature of the experience itself, and thus the regress is stopped.[54]

Husserl is typically taken to distinguish three different layers or levels of temporality: The objective time of the appearing objects, the subjective, immanent, or pre-empirical time of the acts and experiences, and finally the absolute pre-phenomenal flow of inner time-constituting consciousness.[55] Where does the interpretation I am offering stand in regard to this tripartition? It accepts the tripartition but argues that the second level is the least fundamental. At first, we only have level one and level three, that is, the level of constituting subjectivity and the level of constituted objects. At first there is no level two, there is no layer of subjective time where the experiences are given sequentially as temporal objects. This level is only constituted the moment we engage in reflection and recollection. Prior to reflection there is no awareness of internal objects, and there is no distinction between the lived self-manifestation of the experiences and the flow of inner time-consciousness. Inner time-consciousness simply is the name of the pre-reflective self-awareness of our experiences.

As mentioned above, I do not only think that there are systematic reasons for favoring this interpretation. There is also a large amount of textual evidence in support of it. In §37 of *Zur Phänomenologie des inneren Zeitbewusstseins,* for instance, Husserl writes that our perceptual act is not in immanent time, is not a constituted temporal unity, but a moment of or a wave in the self-temporalizing, flowing experiencing itself.[56] Later in the same volume he writes:

Therefore *sensation*—if by "sensation" we understand *consciousness* (not the immanent enduring red, tone, and so forth, hence not that which is sensed)—and likewise *retention, recollection, perception,* etc. are *non-temporal;* that is to say, *nothing in immanent time.*[57]

But whereas Husserl claims that our acts (be they perceptions, recollections, anticipations, imaginations, judgments, etc.), *qua* absolute constituting consciousness, reveal themselves, but not as immanently given temporal objects, he also quite explicitly writes that the very same acts appear in subjective time with duration and temporal location *qua objects of reflection.*[58] As it is formulated in, respectively, the C 12 and the C 16 manuscripts:

> But my thematic experience of I and consciousness is by itself the founding of a continuous validity—the founding of a lasting being, the being of the immanent.[59]

> Do we not have to say: of course, the stream is objectified by the "apperceiving" I. But the sheer streaming is indeed objectified only as it is [reflectively] observed, etc., and through the possibility of the "again and again."[60]

Originally, the intentional acts are moments of the self-temporalizing streaming and, therefore, *not* temporally constituted distinct and enduring objects. It is only the moment we start to thematize these acts, be it in a reflection or recollection, that they are constituted in subjective, sequential time.[61] Prior to reflection, there is no awareness of internal objects, just as there is no distinction between the givenness of the act and the self-manifestation of the flow. As for the acts objectified by reflection, these cannot be separated from the flow either, since they are nothing but the flow's own *reflective* self-manifestation. That is, the absolute flow of experiencing and the constituted stream of reflectively thematized acts are not two separate flows, but simply two different manifestations of one and the same. As Husserl writes: "We say, I am who I am in my living. And this living is a lived-experiencing [*Erleben*], and its reflectively accentuated single moments can be called 'lived-experiences' [*Erlebnisse*], insofar as something or other is experienced in these moments."[62] Through inner time-consciousness one is aware not only of the stream of consciousness (pre-reflective self-awareness), but also of the acts as demarcated temporal objects in subjective time (reflective self-awareness), and of the transcendent objects in objective time (intentional consciousness).

So far I have been arguing that there are *not* two different types of pre-reflective self-awareness at play: the constituted marginal object-givenness of our acts, and the self-manifestation of the absolute flow. The absolute flow of experiencing simply is the pre-reflective self-manifestation of our experiences. However, to make this point is not to deny that there are good reasons for insisting upon the *difference* between our singular and transitory acts and the abiding dimension of experiencing, between *die Erlebnisse* and *das Erleben.*[63]

In fact, there seems to be an excellent reason for not simply identifying the experience and the experiencing, the intentional act and the pre-reflective self-givenness of the act. Let us compare three different intentional acts: a visual perception of a bird, a hearing of a melody, and the smelling of a rose. These three different acts obviously have different intentional structures. The self-givenness of the three acts, however, does not have a different structure in each case. It is one and the same basic structure. But if that is the case, we need to distinguish the act and its self-givenness. Whereas we live through a number of different experiences, our self-awareness remains as an unchanging dimension. It stands—to use a striking image by James—permanent, like the rainbow on the waterfall, with its own quality unchanged by the events that stream through it.[64] In other words, it is highly appropriate to distinguish the strict singularity of the *lebendige Gegenwart* from the plurality of changing experiences.[65] But, of course, this should not be misunderstood. Distinguishability is not the same as separability. We are not dealing with a pure or empty field of self-manifestation upon which the concrete experiences subsequently make their entry. The absolute flow has no self-manifestation of its own, but *is* the very self-manifestation of the experiences.

Hopefully, these remarks should make it clear that the interpretation I am offering does not deny the distinction between the flow and the act; it simply rejects a misleading account of their relationship.

III

I have repeatedly mentioned that Husserl's most profound investigation of self-awareness can be found in his analysis of inner time-consciousness. Although Husserl denies that our experiences are pre-reflectively given as temporal objects, he does claim that self-awareness has a temporal infrastructure, and that pre-reflective self-awareness is a type of manifestation that is intrinsically caught up in the ecstatic-centered structure of primal impression–retention–protention. One consequently finds an elaboration of his theory of self-awareness in his renowned analysis of the double intentionality of the retention, its so-called *Quer-* and *Längsintentionalität* (transverse and longitudinal intentionality). If $P(t)$ is the primal impression of a tone, then $P(t)$ is retained in a retention $Rp(t)$ when a new primal impression appears. As the notation makes clear, however, it is not only the conscious tone which is retained, but also the primal impression. Each retention is not only retaining the preceding tone, but also the preceding primal impression. That is, the actual phase of the flow is retaining not only the tone, which has just been, but also the elapsing phase of the flow.[66] In short, the retentional modification does not only permit us to experience an enduring temporal object, it does not merely enable the constitution of the identity of the object in a manifold of temporal phases, it also provides us with temporal self-awareness.[67] Whereas the flow's constitution of the duration of its object is called its *Querintentionalität*, the flow's awareness of its own streaming unity is called its *Längsintentionalität,*[68] and, although the latter carries the name intentionality, it would be a decisive misunderstanding of Husserl's theory if one were to identify it with a type of object-intentionality.[69] Husserl's account of the *Längsintentionalität* does not succumb to the lure of the reflection theory, but is in fact an analysis of the pre-reflective self-manifestation of consciousness. It is because consciousness is characterized by this self-manifestation that it is possible to escape the infinite regress of the reflection theory:

> The flow of the consciousness that constitutes immanent time not only *exists* but is so remarkably and yet intelligibly fashioned that a self-appearance of the flow necessarily exists in it, and therefore the flow itself must necessarily be apprehensible in the flowing. The self-appearance of the flow does not require a second flow; on the contrary, it constitutes itself as a phenomenon in itself.[70]

This central passage from *Zur Phänomenologie des inneren Zeitbewusstseins,* however, has not been overlooked by Husserl's critics. It has generally been met with two distinct arguments.

Cramer has argued that Husserl's notion of self-appearance is vulnerable to the same criticism that has been directed against the reflection theory. If one claims that the stream of consciousness is characterized by self-appearance, one must ask what it is that appears when the stream appears to itself. According to Cramer, the only answer possible is that the stream appears to itself as a self-appearing stream. But he takes this account to be both redundant and circular.[71]

The pertinence of this criticism is, however, questionable. First of all, Cramer erroneously identifies Husserl's notion of self-appearance with a kind of "quasi perception," thereby overlooking its non-objectifying and non-relational character. Secondly, and more importantly, Cramer seems to expect something of a theory of self-awareness which it, *qua* explication of a phenomenon *sui generis,* will forever be prevented from providing, namely, a decomposition of the phenomenon into more simple elements without self-awareness. To put it differently, the impossibility of providing a non-circular definition of self-awareness is hardly a problem for an account that explicitly acknowledges the irreducible and fundamental status of self-awareness. It is only a problem for an account that seeks to explain self-awareness by reducing it to something more basic. In this sense, it might be more correct to say that it is Cramer's criticism rather than Husserl's theory that is indebted to the reflection theory.

The second argument can be found in Frank (and with different emphasis in both Henry and Derrida). If the self-appearance of the stream of consciousness is to be accounted for by means of the notion of *Längsintentionalität* and if this is a kind of retentional modification, then there will only be self-awareness of the just-past phase of the stream, since the initial phase of consciousness will only become conscious when it is retained. There consequently seems to be a blind spot in the core of subjectivity: Initially, consciousness is unconscious, and it only comes to presence *nachträglich* through the retentional modification. But how does this agree with our conviction that we are in fact aware of our experiences the moment they occur? And how can we at all be aware of something *as* past, unless we are also aware of something present against which we can contrast it? If self-presence is only constituted in the difference between retention and primal impression, there will be nothing left to explain this difference, or more correctly, there will be nothing left to explain our experience of this difference. It will be a merely postulated difference, with no experiential basis. Thus, self-awareness will ultimately become a product of an unconscious difference.[72] But to make this claim is basically to face all the problems of the reflection theory once again.

Husserl himself was well aware of these difficulties. He anticipated the line of thought, and although he occasionally seriously considered it,[73] he ultimately and quite explicitly rejected it:

> What about the beginning-phase of an experience that is in the process of becoming constituted? Does it also come to be given only on the basis of retention, and would it be "unconscious" if no retention were to follow it? We must say in response to this question: The beginning-phase can become an object only *after* it has elapsed in the indicated way, by means of retention and reflection (or reproduction). But if it were intended *only* by retention, then what confers on it the label "now" would remain incomprehensible. At most, it could be distinguished negatively from its modifications as that one phase that does not make us retentionally conscious of any preceding phase; but the beginning-phase is by all means characterized in consciousness in quite positive fashion. It is just nonsense to talk about an "unconscious" content that would only subsequently become conscious. Consciousness is necessarily *consciousness* in each of its phases. Just as the retentional phase is conscious of the preceding phase without making it into an object, so too the primal datum is already intended—specifically, in the original form of the "now"—without its being something objective.[74]

Thus, Husserl's analysis is not meant to imply that consciousness only becomes aware of itself through the retention. On the contrary, Husserl explicitly insists that the *retentional* modification presupposes an *impressional* (primary, original, and immediate) self-manifestation, not only because consciousness is as such self-given, but also because a retention of an unconscious content is impossible.[75] The retention retains that which has just appeared, and if nothing appears, there is nothing to retain.[76] Thus, retention presupposes self-awareness. It is this self-awareness which is retentionally modified when P(t) is transformed into Rp(t): The tone is not only given as having-just-been, but as having-just-been *experienced*.[77]

Is it possible to specify the nature of this impressional self-manifestation, this absolute experiencing, any further? The terminology used, and the fact that we are confronted with an unthematic, implicit, immediate, and passive occurrence, which is by no means initiated, regulated, or controlled by the ego, suggest that we are dealing with a given state of pure passivity, with a form of *self-affection*. This interpretation is confirmed by Husserl, for instance, in the manuscript C 10 (1931), where he speaks of self-affection as an essential, pervasive, and necessary feature of the functioning ego, and in the manuscript C 16 (1931–33), where he adds that I am ceaselessly (*unaufhörlich*) affected by myself.[78] We are here confronted with a type of non-relational self-manifestation that lacks the ordinary dyadic structure of appearance.[79] There is no distinction between subject and object, or between the dative and genitive of appearing. On the contrary, it is a kind of self-manifestation, a fundamental *shining*, without which it would be meaningless to speak of the dative of appearance. Nothing can be present *to me* unless I am *self*-aware.[80]

This clarification allows for a final remark about the relationship between the *impressional* self-manifestation (internal consciousness) and the *Längsintentionalität*. We are not dealing with two independent and separate types of pre-reflective self-awareness, but with two different descriptions of the same basic phenomenon. As already mentioned, Husserl uses the term *Längsintentionalität* to designate the flowing self-manifestation of consciousness, but this self-givenness does not merely concern the elapsing phases, but takes its point of departure in an immediate impressional self-manifestation. Conversely, this impressional self-manifestation stretches to include the retentionally given. As Husserl writes: "In this respect we take the impressional consciousness to stretch as far as the still living retention."[81]

To summarize: Taken in isolation the primal impression is not unconscious, and to suggest that is to succumb to a variant of the reflection theory. But when this is said, it should be immediately added that the primal impression taken in isolation is a theoretical limit-case. It is in fact never given alone, but is always already furnished with a temporal density, always already accompanied by a horizon of protentional and retentional absencing. Thus Husserl would claim that the full structure of pre-reflective self-awareness is primal impression–retention–protention.[82] Pre-reflective self-awareness has an internal differentiation and articulation—and Husserl insists that only this fact can explain the possibility of reflection and recollection—but it is not a gradual, delayed, or mediated process of self-unfolding; rather, consciousness is "immediately" given as an ecstatic unity. One has to avoid the idea of an instantaneous non-temporal self-awareness, but one must also stay clear of the notion of a completely fractured time-consciousness, which makes both consciousness of the present, and of the unity of the stream unintelligible.[83]

IV

This brief account of Husserl's theory of self-awareness leaves a number of aspects untouched: What is the connection between time-consciousness and kinaesthesis, and between intentionality and self-awareness? What is the connection between our pre-reflective self-awareness and our lived body, and between selfhood and alterity? What is the more precise difference between the temporality of, respectively, reflective and pre-reflective self-manifestation? How should one exactly understand the notion of self-affection? Are there forms of self-awareness which are intersubjectively mediated? And what is the relation between transcendental reflection *qua* thematization of subjectivity and natural reflection *qua* mundanization of subjectivity?[84] All of these topics are treated by Husserl, however, and, in contrast to a widespread assumption, it is simply not true that he was so taken up by his "discovery" of object-intentionality that he never escaped the reflection model, but always operated with a model of self-manifestation based upon the subject-object dichotomy, and never managed to raise the more fundamental problems concerning the Being of consciousness. In fact, as the above interpretation should have demonstrated, the topic of self-awareness was by no means of mere incidental interest to Husserl. On the contrary, he considered its elucidation to be even more fundamental to phenomenology than the analysis of intentionality. Not only did his own reflective methodology make such extensive use of reflection that an examination of reflective self-awareness was called for, but Husserl also very well knew that his analysis of intentionality would lack a proper foundation as long as the problem concerning the self-manifestation of consciousness remained unaccounted for. That is, without an elucidation of the unique givenness of subjectivity, it would be impossible to account convincingly for the appearance of objects, and ultimately phenomenology would be incapable of realizing its own proper task, to provide a clarification of the condition of possibility for manifestation.

Notes

This study was supported by the Danish National Research Foundation.

   1. Martin Heidegger, *Prolegomena zur Geschichte des Zeitbegriffs*, GA 20 (Frankfurt am Main: Vittorio Klostermann, 1979), 143, 152.
   2. Ernst Tugendhat, *Selbstbewußtsein und Selbstbestimmung* (Frankfurt am Main: Suhrkamp, 1979), 15, 17, 53.
   3. Dieter Henrich, "Fichtes ursprüngliche Einsicht," in *Subjektivität und Metaphysik. Festschrift für Wolfgang Cramer,* ed. Dieter Henrich and Hans Wagner (Frankfurt am Main: Klostermann, 1966), 231; Karen Gloy, *Bewusstseinstheorien. Zur Problematik und Problemgeschichte des Bewusstseins und Selbstbewusstseins* (Freiburg: Alber, 1998), 203.
   4. Manfred Frank, *Was ist Neostrukturalismus?* (Frankfurt am Main: Suhrkamp, 1984), 300; *Zeitbewußtsein* (Pfullingen: Neske, 1990), 53-57.
   5. Manfred Frank, *Die Unhintergehbarkeit von Individualität* (Frankfurt am Main: Suhrkamp, 1986), 45. In contrast, one might point out that already Sartre acknowledged that

Husserl had described the pre-reflective being of consciousness (cf. Jean-Paul Sartre, "Conscience de soi et conaissance de soi," *Bulletin de la Société Française de Philosophie* XLII [1948], 88).

6. It is not difficult to find contemporary defenders of some version of this theory. For a presentation and criticism cf. Dan Zahavi and Josef Parnas, "Phenomenal Consciousness and Self-awareness: A Phenomenological Critique of Representational Theory," *Journal of Consciousness Studies* 5 (1998): 687–705.

7. Let me mention one additional and more classical argument: According to the reflection theory, self-awareness comes about the moment an act of reflection reflects upon an experience, say, a perception of a die, and takes this experience as its object. However, given this view, it is obvious that there is something crucial the act of reflection will forever miss, namely, itself *qua* subject of experience. Even though a second-order reflection might be able to capture the first-order reflection, this will not change the fact, since there will still be something that eludes its grasp, namely, itself *qua* subjective pole, and so forth *ad infinitum*. One implication of this view is that self-awareness in the strict sense (understood as an awareness of oneself as subject) is impossible.

8. One can find numerous statements to this effect. See, for instance, *Cartesianische Meditationen*, 81; *Cartesian Meditations*, 43; *Ideen II*, 318; *Ideas II*, 330–31; *Erste Philosophie II*, 189, 412, 450; *Intersubjektivität I*, 252, 462; *Intersubjektivität II*, 151, 292, 353, 380; Ms. C 16 81b.

9. *Intersubjektivität II*, 151; cf. *Intersubjektivität I*, 462; *Erste Philosophie II*, 412.

10. *Logik (Hua)*, 279–80; modified *Logic*, 273.

11. *Passive Synthesis*, 320.

12. Cf. John R. Searle, *The Rediscovery of the Mind* (Cambridge, Mass.: MIT Press, 1992), 172; David Woodruf Smith, *The Circle of Acquaintance* (Dordrecht: Kluwer, 1989), 95; David J. Chalmers, *The Conscious Mind: In Search of a Fundamental Theory* (New York: Oxford University Press, 1996), 4; Galen Strawson, *Mental Reality* (Cambridge, Mass.: MIT Press, 1994), 71.

13. Thomas Nagel, *The View from Nowhere* (Oxford: Oxford University Press, 1986), 15–16; Frank Jackson, "Epiphenomenal Qualia," *Philosophical Quarterly* 32 (1982): 127–36; William James, *The Principles of Psychology I–II* (London: Macmillan, 1890/1918), I: 478.

14. Thomas Nagel, "What Is It Like to Be a Bat?" *Philosophical Review* 83 (1974): 436; Searle, *The Rediscovery of the Mind*, 131–32.

15. Owen Flanagan, *Consciousness Reconsidered* (Cambridge, Mass.: MIT Press, 1992), 194.

16. *Intersubjektivität III*, 78; *Erste Philosophie II*, 157.

17. *Ideen I (Hua)*, 162, 168, 251, 349; *Ideas I*, 174, 180, 261, 360; *Phänomenologische Psychologie*, 29; *Phenomenological Psychology*, 19–20; *Zeitbewusstsein*, 291; *Time-Consciousness*, 301.

18. *Intersubjektivität II*, 45.

19. *Zeitbewusstsein*, 291; modified *Time-Consciousness*, 301.

20. *Zeitbewusstsein*, 126–27; modified *Time-Consciousness*, 130.

21. However, one should not forget that the act of reflection is itself a pre-reflectively self-given act. The reflected act must already be self-aware, since it is the fact of its being already mine, already being given in the first-person mode of presentation that allows me to reflect upon it. And the act of reflection must also already be pre-reflectively self-aware, since it is this that permits it to recognize the reflected act as belonging to the same subjectivity as it*self*.

22. Thus it is worth emphasizing that anonymity and self-givenness are by no means incompatible notions. Cf. Dan Zahavi, "Anonymity and First-Personal Givenness: An At-

tempt at Reconciliation," in *Subjektivität-Verantwortung-Wahrheit. Neue Aspekte der Husserlschen Phänomenologie*, ed. David Carr and Christian Lotz (Frankfurt am Main: Peter Lang, 2002), 61–72.

23. *Intersubjektivität II*, 431; cf. *Intersubjektivität II*, 29; *Krisis (Ergänzung)*, 183–84; Ms. C 2 3a.

24. *Ideen I (Hua)*, 550; *Zeitbewusstsein*, 119; *Time-Consciousness*, 123.

25. *Erste Philosophie II*, 88; *Phänomenologische Psychologie*, 306–7.

26. *Aufsätze II*, 89.

27. *Erste Philosophie II*, 471; *Zeitbewusstsein*, 126; *Time-Consciousness*, 129.

28. *Erste Philosophie II*, 188; cf. *Ideen I (Hua)*, 549.

29. Cf. Franz Brentano, *Psychologie vom empirischen Standpunkt* I (Hamburg: Felix Meiner, 1874/1973), chaps. II–III.

30. *Ideen II*, 118; *Ideas II*, 125.

31. *Ideen II*, 248; *Ideas II*, 259–60.

32. *Intersubjektivität III*, 492–93.

33. Ms. C 10 13a. I am grateful to the Director of the Husserl-Archives in Leuven, Prof. Rudolf Bernet, for permitting me to consult and quote from Husserl's unpublished manuscripts.

34. *Ideen II*, 217; *Ideas II*, 228–29.

35. *Krisis*, 111; *Crisis*, 109; *Intersubjektivität III*, 78, 120.

36. *Ideen I (Hua)*, 95, 162–64; *Ideas I*, 98–99, 174–77.

37. *Zeitbewusstsein*, 119; *Time-Consciousness*, 123.

38. *Zeitbewusstsein*, 276, 334; *Time-Consciousness*, 286, 346.

39. Normally the term "constitution" has been used to designate the process of bringing to appearance. More specifically, something (an object) is said to be *constituted* if it is brought to appearance by something else, that is, if it owes its manifestation to something different from itself, whereas something (transcendental subjectivity) is said to be *constituting* if it is itself the condition for manifestation. To speak in this way obviously raises a question concerning whether or not that which constitutes does itself appear or not. Traditionally one has then had the choice between two formulations, both of which were ambiguous. Either one could say that transcendental subjectivity is itself unconstituted, or one could say that it is self-constituting. The first formulation might suggest that transcendental subjectivity does not at all manifest itself, the second that it manifests itself in the same way as objects do.

40. Of course, it could be argued along Kantian lines that the transcendental condition is not itself given, is not itself a phenomenon. But since such a conclusion would exclude the possibility of a phenomenological investigation of transcendental subjectivity, it would not be an option for a phenomenologist.

41. *Ideen I (Hua)*, 182; *Ideas I*, 193–94.

42. Ms. L I 15 37b.

43. *Phänomenologische Psychologie*, 202; modified *Phenomenological Psychology*, 154.

44. *Passive Synthesis*, 233, 293; *Ideen II*, 102; *Ideas II*, 108; *Erfahrung und Urteil*, 205; *Experience and Judgement*, 175–76.

45. *Zeitbewusstsein*, 80; *Time-Consciousness*, 84.

46. For a more extensive account, cf. Dan Zahavi, *Self-awareness and Alterity: A Phenomenological Investigation* (Evanston, Ill.: Northwestern University Press, 1999).

47. Cf. J. B. Brough, "The Emergence of an Absolute Consciousness in Husserl's Early Writings on Time-Consciousness," *Man and World* 5 (1972), 308–9; R. Sokolowski, *Husserlian Meditations* (Evanston, Ill.: Northwestern University Press, 1974), 156–57.

48. Sokolowski, *Husserlian Meditations*, 154, 156–57; Brough, "Absolute Consciousness," 318. Let me stress that I am obviously not accusing either Sokolowski or Brough of having

overlooked the existence of the notion of pre-reflective self-awareness in Husserl, that is, of having made the same mistake as Frank, Tugendhat, and Henrich. To a certain extent, but only to a certain extent, the difference between my interpretation and Brough's and Sokolowski's interpretation might simply be a question of different accentuation and terminology.

49. Brough, "Absolute Consciousness," 304, 316.

50. *Einleitung in die Logik,* 252.

51. It is interesting to notice that Gurwitsch in his noematically oriented analysis apparently commits this error and consequently claims.that the self-awareness which accompanies every act of consciousness is a marginal datum (Aron Gurwitsch, *Marginal Consciousness* [Athens: Ohio University Press, 1985], 4). Cf. Aron Gurwitsch, *Das Bewußtseinsfeld* (Berlin: de Gruyter, 1974), 339–40.

52. *Ideen II,* 118–19; *Ideas II,* 125–26; *Zeitbewusstsein,* 83, 89–90, 119, 126–27; *Time-Consciousness,* 88, 93–95, 129–31; *Phantasie,* 321; cf. Ms. L I 15 35a–36b.

53. *Logik,* 279–80; *Logic,* 317–18; *Ideen II,* 118; *Ideas II,* 125.

54. When criticizing the standard interpretation, I am not denying that consciousness can appear to itself as an internal temporal object, I am only denying that it does so already pre-reflectively. For a more detailed discussion of how our acts are *reflectively* constituted as enduring objects in subjective time cf. Zahavi, *Self-awareness and Alterity.*

55. *Zeitbewusstsein,* 73, 76, 358.

56. *Zeitbewusstsein,* 75–76; cf. *Krisis (Ergänzung),* 194.

57. *Zeitbewusstsein,* 333–34; cf. *Zeitbewusstsein,* 371–72.

58. *Zeitbewusstsein,* 112, 285, 293; *Intersubjektivität II,* 29.

59. "Aber meine thematische Erfahrung vom Ich und Bewußtsein ist in ihrer Art selbst Stiftung einer Fortgeltung—eines bleibenden Seins, des Seins des Immanenten" (Ms. C 12 3b).

60. "Müssen wir nicht sagen, natürlich ist es das 'apperzipierende' Ich, durch das der Strom gegenständlich wird. Aber das bloße Strömen wird eben erst durch das Betrachten etc. gegenständlich und durch die Vermöglichkeiten des 'immer wieder'" (Ms. C 16 59a).

61. For passages that might corroborate this interpretation, see *Ideen II,* 104; *Zeitbewusstsein,* 36, 51, 112; Ms. A V 5 4b–5a; Ms. C 10 17a; Ms. C 16 59a; Ms. C 12 3b; Ms. L I 19 3aMb; and Ms. L I 19 10a.

62. "Wir sagen, ich bin, der ich bin in meinem Leben. Und dieses Leben ist Erleben, seine reflektiv als einzelne abzuhebenden Bestandstücke heißen rechtmäßig 'Erlebnisse,' sofern in ihnen irgendetwas erlebt ist" (Ms. C 3 26a).

63. *Phantasie,* 326; cf. *Intersubjektivität II,* 46; Ms. L I 1 3a.

64. James, *Principles of Psychology,* I: 630.

65. Erich Klawonn, "Kritisk Undersøgelse af Kritikken," in *Kritisk Belysning af Jeg'ets Ontologi,* ed. David Favrholdt (Odense: Odense Universitetsforlag, 1994), 143; Brough, "Absolute Consciousness," 316.

66. Brough, "Absolute Consciousness," 319.

67. Husserl alternately speaks of absolute time-constituting consciousness as an unchangeable form of presence (as a *nunc stans*), and as an absolute flux (*Ding und Raum,* 65; cf. *Zeitbewusstsein,* 74, 113; *Time-Consciousness,* 78, 118). Regardless of which description one chooses—and ultimately both are attempts to capture the unique givenness of this dimension—it should be obvious why one must not only avoid speaking of the absolute flow as if it were a temporal object, but also avoid interpreting the flow as a sequence of temporally distinct acts, phases, or elements. "This streaming living Presence is not what we elsewhere have designated transcendental-phenomenologically as stream of consciousness or a stream of lived-experience. It cannot be depicted as a 'stream' in the sense of a spe-

cial temporal (or even spatio-temporal) whole that has a continuous-successive individual being consisting in the unity of a temporal extension (individuated by this temporal form in its distinguishable stretches and phases). The streaming living Presence is 'continuous' streaming-being, and yet it is not a separated-being, not a spatio-temporal (world-spatial) being, not an 'immanent'-temporal extended being; not a separation [*Außereinander*] that implies a succession [*Nacheinander*], a succession in the sense of a punctual-separation taking place in time properly so called." (Diese strömend lebendige Gegenwart ist nicht das, was wir sonst auch schon transzendental-phänomenologisch als Bewußtseinsstrom oder Erlebnisstrom bezeichneten. Es ist überhaupt kein "Strom" gemäß dem Bild, als ein eigentlich zeitliches (oder gar zeiträumliches) Ganzes, das in der Einheit einer zeitlichen Extension ein kontinuierlich-sukzessives individuelles Dasein hat (in seinen unterscheidbaren Strecken und Phasen durch diese Zeitformen individuiert). Die strömend lebendige Gegenwart ist "kontinuierliches" Strömendsein und doch nicht in einem Auseinander-Sein, nicht in raumzeitlicher (welträum-licher), nicht in "immanent"-zeitlicher Extension Sein; also in keinem Außereinander, das Nacheinander heißt—Nacheinander in dem Sinne eines Stellen-Außereinander in einer eigent-lich so zu nennenden Zeit) (Ms. C 3 4a). For further distinctions between "das Strömen" and "der Strom," cf. Ms. B III 9 8a, Ms. C 15 3b, Ms. C 17 63b). Inner time-consciousness cannot be temporal in the empirical sense of the word; it cannot be reduced to a succession of mental states. Not only would such a succession not enable us to become conscious of succession, it would also call for yet another consciousness, which would be conscious of this succession, etc., and we would be unable to avoid an infinite regress. As Husserl writes, it makes no sense to say of the time-constituting phenomena that they are present and that they have endured, that they succeed each other, or are co-present, etc. They are, in short, neither "present," "past," nor "future" in the way empirical objects are (*Zeitbewusstsein*, 75, 333, 375–76; *Time-Consciousness*, 79, 345, 386–87). Inner time-consciousness is a field of expe-riencing, a dimension of manifestation, which contains all three temporal dimensions. The structure of this field of experiencing—primal impression–retention–protention—is not tem-porally extended. The retentions and protentions are not past or future in regard to the primal impression, nor are they simultaneous, as long as "simultaneity" is used in its ordinary sense. They are "together" or "co-actual" with it. Ultimately, the structure of constituting time-consciousness cannot be adequately grasped using temporal concepts derived from that which it constitutes. Thus, in a certain way inner time-consciousness is atemporal (*Zeitbewusstsein*, 112), but only in the sense that it is not intra-temporal. Time-constituting consciousness is not *in* time, but it is not merely a consciousness *of* time, it is itself a form of temporality (cf. Iso Kern, *Idee und Methode der Philosophie* [Berlin: de Gruyter, 1975], 40–41; Rudolf Bernet, *La vie du sujet* [Paris: PUF, 1994], 197; Maurice Merleau-Ponty, *Phénoménologie de la percep-tion* [Paris: Éditions Gallimard, 1945], 483; Martin Heidegger, *Kant und das Problem der Metaphysik* [Frankfurt am Main: Vittorio Klostermann, 1991], 192). Temporality constitutes the infrastructure of consciousness. Consciousness is inherently temporal, and it is as temporal that it is pre-reflectively aware of itself. Thus, although the field of experiencing has neither a temporal location nor extension, and although it does not last and never becomes past, it is not a static supra-temporal principle, but a living pulse (*Lebenspuls*) with a certain temporal density and articulation, and, variable width: it might stretch (*Zeitbewusstsein*, 78, 112, 371, 376; *Time-Consciousness*, 82, 116–17, 382, 387; *Passive Synthesis*, 392; *Intersubjektivität III*, 28; Ms. C 2 11a; Ms. C 7 14a; cf. Mary Jeanne Larrabee, "Inside Time-Consciousness: Diagram-ming the Flux," *Husserl Studies* 10 [1994], 196; Klaus Held, *Lebendige Gegenwart* [The Hague: Martinus Nijhoff, 1966], 116–17). In fact, the metaphor of *stretching* might be appropriate not only as a characterization of the temporal ecstasis, but also as a description of the *Längsin-tentionalität*, since it avoids the potentially misleading and objectifying talk of the flow as a sequence or succession of changing impressions, slices, or phases. For an interesting related observation, cf. §72 in Heidegger's *Sein und Zeit*.

68. *Zeitbewusstsein* 80–81, 379; *Time-Consciousness*, 84–86, 390. At one point Husserl speaks of the *Längs-* and *Querintentionalität* as the noetic and noematic-ontical temporalization (Ms. B III 9 23a). He also calls them, respectively, the inner and outer retention (*Zeitbewusstsein*, 118; *Time-Consciousness*, 122).

69. An error Gloy seems to commit (*Bewusstseinstheorien*, 319); cf. *Zeitbewusstsein*, 333; *Time-Consciousness*, 345.

70. *Zeitbewusstsein*, 83; after *Time-Consciousness*, 88.

71. Konrad Cramer, "'Erlebnis.' Thesen zu Hegels Theorie des Selbstbewußtseins mit Rücksicht auf die Aporien eines Grundbegriffs nachhegelscher Philosophie," in *Stuttgarter Hegel-Tage 1970*, ed. Hans-Georg Gadamer, *Hegel Studien*, Beiheft 11 (1974), 587.

72. Frank, *Was ist Neostrukturalismus?*, 307, 314, 321–22, 335.

73. Cf. *Zeitbewusstsein*, 83; *Time-Consciousness*, 89. As Bernet has often pointed out, Husserl's description of the relation between primal impression and retention is by no means unequivocal. It contains both a confirmation and an overcoming of the metaphysics of presence (Rudolf Bernet, "Die ungegenwärtige Gegenwart. Anwesenheit und Abwesenheit in Husserls Analyse des Zeitbewußtseins," *Phänomenologische Forschung* 14 [1983]: 18). On the one hand, the retention is interpreted as a derived modification of the primal impression. But on the other hand, Husserl also states that no consciousness is possible which does not entail retentional and protentional horizons, that no now is possible without retentions (*Passive Synthesis*, 337–38), and that the primal impression is only what it is when it is retained (Ms. L I 15 4a; cf. Ms. L I 16 12a; Ms. L I 15 22a; *Passive Synthesis*, 315). Husserl was clearly wrestling with these issues, and it is undeniable (and perhaps also unavoidable) that he occasionally opted for some highly problematic accounts. Let me mention a few further examples. In *Ideen II* Husserl characterized the retention as an objectifying immanent perception (*Ideen II*, 14; *Ideas II*, 16), and in the manuscript L I 15 22a he claimed that the *Längsintentionalität* is characterized by its *indirect* nature.

74. *Zeitbewusstsein*, 119; after *Time-Consciousness*, 123.

75. *Zeitbewusstsein*, 119; *Time-Consciousness*, 123.

76. *Zeitbewusstsein*, 110–11, 119; *Time-Consciousness*, 114–15; 123; *Passive Synthesis*, 337.

77. *Zeitbewusstsein*, 117; *Time-Consciousness*, 121–22.

78. Ms. C 10 3b; Ms. C 10 5a; Ms. C 10 7a; Ms. C 10 9b–10a; Ms. C 16 82a; cf. Ms. C 16 78a; Ms. A V 5 8a; Ms. C 5 6a; *Intersubjektivität III*, 78.

79. It could be objected that the very term "self-affection" is singularly unsuited as a designation for a non-relational type of manifestation. Does it not, after all, entail a structural difference between something that affects, and something that is affected? (Cf. Jacques Derrida, *La voix et le phénomène* [Paris: PUF, 1967], 92; *De la grammatologie* [Paris: Les Éditions de Minuit 1967], 235.) In reply, it could be argued that Husserl is not the only phenomenologist to conceive of self-awareness in terms of self-affection. One finds related reflections in Merleau-Ponty, *Phénoménologie de la perception*, 469, 487; Heidegger, *Kant und das Problem der Metaphysik*, 189–90; and Michel Henry, *L'essence de la manifestation* (Paris: PUF, 1963), 288–92, 301. Particularly Henry has been anxious to stress the non-dyadic nature of self-affection (cf. Dan Zahavi, "Michel Henry and the Phenomenology of the Invisible," *Continental Philosophy Review* 32, no. 3 [1999]). As he points out, self-affection should not be understood in the same way as we would normally understand (outer) affection, namely, as a process involving a difference between an organ or faculty of sensing and a sensed object. On the contrary, it is to be taken as an immanent occurrence that involves no difference, distance, or mediation. To put it differently, when speaking of self-affection one should simply

bear in mind that we are dealing with a non-relational type of manifestation, and that the choice of the term is mainly motivated by its ability to capture a whole range of the defining features of pre-reflective self-awareness, including its immediate, implicit, non-objectifying, and passive nature.

80. Sokolowski, *Husserlian Meditations,* 166; James G. Hart, "Intentionality, Phenomenality, and Light," in *Self-awareness, Temporality, and Alterity,* ed. Dan Zahavi (Dordrecht: Kluwer, 1998).

81. *Passive Synthesis,* 138.

82. *Passive Synthesis,* 317, 378; Ms. C 3 8b; Ms. C 3 76a.

83. Frank, *Zeitbewußtsein,* 62–63.

84. For further analyses of Husserl's theory of self-awareness, cf. Zahavi, "Husserl's Phenomenology of the Body," *Études Phénoménologiques* 19 (1994); "Self-awareness and Affection," in *Alterity and Facticity: New Perspectives on Husserl,* ed. Natalie Depraz and Dan Zahavi (Dordrecht: Kluwer, 1998); "The Fracture in Self-awareness," in *Self-awareness, Temporality, and Alterity,* ed. Dan Zahavi (Dordrecht: Kluwer, 1998); Zahavi, "The Three Concepts of Consciousness in *Logische Untersuchungen,*" *Husserl Studies* 18 (2002). For a full-scale presentation and discussion of the theories of self-awareness found in some recent analytical philosophy of mind, in the Heidelberg School, and in phenomenology, cf. Zahavi, *Self-awareness and Alterity.*

7

Transcendental and Empirical Subjectivity
The Self in the Transcendental Tradition

David Carr

IN THE FOLLOWING pages I want to attempt some reflections on the concept of the transcendental subject and on the distinction between that and the empirical subject. In doing so I want to range beyond Husserl and consider these concepts in the larger context of the idea of transcendental philosophy and what I choose to call the transcendental tradition. I admit that I have a somewhat idiosyncratic notion of what that tradition is, and part of my overall concern is working out that idea. It is inaugurated by Kant, of course, and it includes Husserl. But it does not include Fichte, for reasons I will briefly explain; whereas it does include some post-Husserlian thinkers who would probably not want to see themselves included. In any case the distinction between transcendental and empirical subjectivity is at the heart of this tradition, and by getting clear on that distinction we can understand a lot about transcendental philosophy.

Let me describe briefly the key features of transcendental philosophy as I understand it, before getting on to the two sorts of subjectivity. Contrary to the widely accepted interpretation of Heidegger, transcendental philosophy is not a metaphysical doctrine or theory, but a critique of metaphysics, of science, and of the experience that underlies them. A critique is not a theory but a *research program* or method, a way of looking at and interrogating experience so as to bring to the surface its deepest-lying, uncritically accepted assumptions. Introducing his major work and justifying its title, Kant writes: "this inquiry . . . should be entitled not a doctrine but only a transcendental critique."[1] Husserl also describes phenomenology as a critique of knowledge,[2] and speaks of it as "nothing more than a consequentially executed self-explication," a "*sense-explication* achieved *by actual work*."[3]

Transcendental philosophy is widely seen, again under the enormous influence of Heidegger's interpretation, as a variation of the metaphysics of the subject. That is, the subject is taken as the modern version of the classical notion of substance, and the world is reduced to representations belonging to this subject as predicates belong to substance. But this is simply to interpret Kant and Husserl as idealists, overlooking the fact that their work is sharply critical of just such a metaphysics. Kant's attacks on rational psychology, which identifies the subject with substance, and on all forms of subjective idealism, are well known. Husserl introduces the concept of intentionality as part of his attack on psychologism, that is, on the attempt to reduce the object of thought to the mind, and intentionality remains the central concept of his thought and the key to his method. Like Kant, he sharply condemns subjective idealism and rebukes those who interpret his thought as merely a form of idealism.

The picture is complicated, of course, and my reading of transcendental philosophy made more difficult, by the fact that both Kant and Husserl refer to their position as *transcendental idealism*. But if we recall that the term *transcendental* is properly applied to *critique* and *phenomenology*, then we can understand transcendental idealism not as a metaphysical theory, perhaps some intermediate position between idealism and realism, but as a methodological concept. Both thinkers could be said to be concerned with the objects of experience, but from a particular point of view, namely, not straightforwardly or directly, that is, not as they are in themselves, but as they appear. Speaking of Kant, Henry Allison writes that

> the distinction between appearances and things in themselves refers primarily to two distinct ways in which things (empirical objects) can be "considered": either in relation to the subjective conditions of sensibility (space and time), and thus as they "appear," or independently of these conditions, and thus as they are "in themselves."[4]

Paul Ricoeur, describing Husserl's procedure, speaks of a "methodological rather than a doctrinal idealism."[5] In other words, Husserl proposes that we consider the world exclusively as phenomenon, purely as sense for us. This is very different from asserting that it *is* nothing but phenomenon, nothing but sense. For Husserl this proposal is formulated in the idea of the phenomenological *epoche* and reduction. For both thinkers, then, one and the same world can be looked at in two different ways. They propose to look at it from the perspective of how it is experienced.

The reason I do not include Fichte in the transcendental tradition, so conceived, is that he is not content with this perspectivism. Fichte claims to be doing nothing but rethinking Kant. He comes close to the Kantian spirit in the first introduction to the *Wissenschaftslehre* (1797) when he speaks of "idealism" and "dogmatism" as two opposed "systems," neither of which can refute the other. "What sort of philosophy one chooses," he writes of these two alternatives, "depends, therefore, on what sort of man one is."[6] This much-quoted sentence expresses well the Kantian idea of the antinomy of pure theoretical reason and the primacy of the practical, where no theoretical resolution to the paradox is possible. But Fichte disregards his own precepts, going on to argue copiously for the truth of idealism as a "system," and making the primacy of the practical into a theoretical claim about the subject.

As for Kant and Husserl, just as they propose two ways of considering one and the same world, so the distinction between the transcendental and the empirical subject is similarly a distinction between two ways of considering one and the same self. The subject can be considered either "straightforwardly," as an object in the world, or from the perspective of the experience-world relation. To explore the experience-world relation is to assume a subject of experience (the "I think") whose whole function is to stand in a meaning-bestowing or (to use Husserl's term) "constituting" relation to the world. Here the primary distinction is between meaning-bestowal and meaning bestowed, or constituting and constituted. The "I" in this relation is not the "I" of personal identity that distinguishes me from other persons, but the "I" of subjectivity which distinguishes me from everything else, the world as a whole. Rejecting idealism, Husserl affirms the *transcendence* of the world, which means that "neither the world nor any worldly Object is a piece of my Ego, to be found in my conscious life as a really inherent part of it, as a complex of data of sensation or a complex of acts."[7] By the same token, the "I" is not "a piece of the world" either, but a condition of its very possibility—its possibility not as existing, of course, but as meaning.

But there is an obvious sense in which the "I" *is* part of the world. Reflecting in the natural way, I take myself to be a person among persons, even a thing among things, an object for both myself and others, alongside the other objects in the world. As Husserl makes clear, especially in *Ideas II*, it is not as if intentionality is excluded when the subject is considered in this way: I as person am one who thinks, perceives, and acts, and who in doing so relates to a natural and social world of meanings and complexes of meaning. But at the same time I am related in other, nonintentional ways to the world. As body I am in space and relate to other bodies in objective space. The events of my life, both bodily and mental, are in objective time and as such relate temporally to other worldly events. And above all these events in my life belong to the *causal* order of the world and stand in relations of causal dependence and regularity to the things and events in my surroundings.

Here the self is simply one item among others in the world, different in many respects from other things but like them in being a grammatical or metaphysical subject (in the sense of substance) with its predicates or properties. It is thus quite "natural" (as in Husserl's natural attitude) that philosophers should have had recourse to the notion of substance in treating the self. But this had led them to include it in a general metaphysics of substance that has raised more problems than it has solved. Kant and Husserl both address themselves to these problems, and it is here that their *critique* of the metaphysics of substance comes into play. If experiences, thoughts, ideas are conceived as properties of the self, how do they relate to the objects and the world they are about? The answer is usually a confused mixture of causality and resemblance, which come together in the problematic notion of representation. Posing the question in this way sets up a barrier between self and world that cannot be bridged, and the result is either a skepticism that gives up on knowledge altogether, or an idealism that reduces the rest of the world to the ideas we have of it. The first denies the openness to the world that is constitutive of our being as subjects; the second denies the transcendence of the world which is an ineradicable feature of its sense.

The distinction between transcendental and empirical subject, in both Kant and Husserl, is introduced as a response to this situation. It expresses their view that both aspects of subjectivity—being subject for the world and being an object in the world[8]—must be recognized, that neither can be effaced in favor of the other. The problem is that their distinction has been misunderstood, for example, by Heidegger, as just another metaphysical doctrine. In particular, it has been taken as following the idealist rather than the skeptical alternative, with the transcendental subject playing the role of ultimate substance, while the world, including the empirical ego, is reduced to a mere representation. This is to construe the distinction as if it were between the real and the merely phenomenal subject, as if there really were two distinct egos with entirely different features and metaphysical status. But in fact both philosophers are clearly speaking about one and the same subject and suggesting that different contexts require radically differing descriptions of that same subject. Neither believes that one of the two descriptions can simply be eliminated in favor of the other, or that one is of something real and the other of something merely apparent.

There are various ways of characterizing these different descriptions. All of them have something to do with the type of relations which obtain between the subject and the world of objects—keeping in mind, of course, that intentionality is not a "relation" in the strict sense of the term. Husserl speaks of subject for the world versus object in the world. We can describe the relations between subject and world as purely intentional relations as opposed to (objective) spatial, temporal, and causal relations. We can appeal to the distinction between belonging to the world of objects and being a condition of the possibility of the meaningful world of objects. Perhaps the broadest terms for these relations would be the *transcendental* relation and the *part-whole* relation. "Transcendental" here is used in both the Kantian and Husserlian senses, which are not quite identical. Kant usually uses the term to refer to something that functions as the condition of the possibility of experience. Husserl uses it to indicate the relation of subjectivity to the transcendence of the world. As for the part-whole relation, the whole in question can be a spatial and temporal whole as well as a causal whole, that is, a causal order.

Husserl's distinction between "subject for" and "object in" might suggest another way of distinguishing transcendental and empirical subjects. One might appeal to the concepts of subjectivity and objectivity themselves, or even the grammatical distinction between the "I" and the "me." That is, we might say that the empirical subject emerges when the reflective gaze is turned upon it; not only does it become an object of the gaze, but in doing so it takes on the primary features of objectivity in general: that of being "out there" in the world, among other objects, and of course among other persons as well. Here it might be said that I become an object for myself just as I am for other people, or even that I am aware of myself in just the way others are aware of me. To reflect in this way is to take the point of view of another on myself, or alternatively to see myself as if I were another.

The transcendental subject, by contrast, might be considered the subject that can never become object. Husserl speaks of it as "indeclinable,"[9] meaning that it can never become a "you" or a "he" or a "she," much less a "him" or "her." As Kant puts it, "any judgment upon [the transcendental 'I'] has already made use of its representation."[10] Similarly,

> the subject of the categories cannot by thinking the categories acquire a concept of itself as an object of the categories. For in order to think them, its pure self-consciousness, which is what was to be explained, must itself be presupposed.[11]

The transcendental subject is as elusive as it is necessary, in other words, since if we try to make it an object it must be an object *for* the subject, and it is this latter subject we are after. Trying to grasp it is like trying to jump over your own shadow, or trying to see your eyes seeing. It is this sort of consideration that led Kant to the view that the transcendental I cannot be known, since no intuition of it can be given.

Yet the transcendental subject obviously *is* an object, at least in the sense that we can speak meaningfully about it, describe its characteristics, and distinguish it from the empirical subject. Here Kant faces the same reproach that is often made of his concept of the thing-in-itself: he claims we cannot know them, yet says we know that they exist. Here too Kant seems to limit knowing to the empirical knowledge based on sense intuition; we arrive at the thing-in-itself, and apparently at the transcendental subject as well, not from any intuition but as the conclusion of an *argument* about the conditions of the possibility of experience. In the case of things-in-themselves we may know nothing but that they exist; but in the case of the transcendental subject, by contrast, we have the whole complex Kantian account of its functions as evidence that we are hardly in the dark about it. Why not call this knowledge?

Husserl frequently addresses this question to Kant. He describes Kant's account of transcendental subjectivity as "mythical constructions"[12] which result from the fact that Kant did not recognize or admit the possibility of a "transcendental reflection" with its own, legitimate form of intuition. He believes that Kant took all reflection to be based on inner sense, and thus empirical, and hence merely psychological and unworthy of transcendental philosophy. Husserl thinks that if Kant had only advanced to the stage of conceiving the phenomenological reduction, he would have recognized that reflection can take itself out of the realm of the empirical and psychological, and become transcendental. And with the transcendental-phenomenological attitude comes a genuinely transcendental experience and intuition. Thus for Husserl it is in no way correct to assert that the pure Ego is a subject that can never become an Object, as long as we do not limit the concept of Object at the very outset and in particular do not limit it to "natural Objects, to mundane real Objects."[13]

However, Husserl must admit that the manner in which the transcendental subject becomes an object is unique, so different from the givenness of any other object that Kant might well be justified in claiming that it would be wrong to compare it to experience at all or to describe it as a form of intuition. Because the "I" of transcendental subjectivity is not *in* the world, it does not situate itself in relation to other objects, nor can it be said to obey the rules applicable to objects, at least not in the way that worldly objects do. This, of course, is what Kant means by saying it is not an object of (i.e., is not "subject to") the categories. But even if we complain, with Husserl, that Kant's categorical scheme is too narrow, too restrictive in its notion of what kinds of objects there are, clearly there is a sense in which Husserl has the same problem. For him the givenness of any object is always a function of the regional essence or ontology to which it belongs, and these ontological regions belong to the world as a whole. When Husserl "discovers" transcendental consciousness through the reduction, he describes it, in *Ideas I,* as a "new region of being." But there are great difficulties with this formulation: transcendental consciousness is properly characterized neither as merely one region alongside the others (because it *intentionally* takes them all in), nor as the region of all regions (because it does not "ontologically" or "really" contain them at all). It is considerations of this sort that doubtless led Husserl to stop speaking of consciousness as a "new region of being."

There is, of course, another sense in which the transcendental subject, when it becomes an "object," is not comparable to any other object. It is directly accessible, namely, to itself alone. It emerges when I reflect on myself in a certain way, distinguishing myself and my intentional, meaning-bestowing consciousness from the meaningful world as a whole. It is, as we might say, a reflection *on* the first-person point of view, *from* the first-person point of view, a point of view I share, by definition, with no one else. The empirical subject, by contrast, is myself as experienced by others as well as myself, the public "me." Here I view myself as if I were another. Of course, what Husserl calls "natural reflection," and what Kant calls empirical self-consciousness, is also reflection or self-awareness; and it is only *as if* I were another looking at myself. I still have a direct access to my thoughts, experiences, and intentions that others do not have. But because I take myself to be *in* the world, not merely intentionally but also really and causally related to my surroundings, there is much about me that is important to my being and my behavior which is not directly available to my self-consciousness. For example, my physiological and neurological make-up, my hidden psychological states and dispositions, my character and temperament are all aspects of me that I am aware of, or can become aware of, in myself. They all figure in the view of myself that I have in natural reflection. But I do not come to know them any *differently* from the way others come to know them in me; and in these respects others may certainly know me better than I know myself.

It seems to follow that the transcendental subject is not exactly a subject that can never become object; but the manner in which it becomes an object, and its status *as* an object of reflection have still not been adequately clarified. Such a description is needed by our own exposition, which seeks to bring together the insights of Kant and Husserl, partly because these points are unclear in the works of the philosophers themselves. The problems encountered in this regard should at least confirm our claim that Kant and Husserl are not simply making metaphysical assertions about the existence of a substantial transcendental subject and reducing the rest of the world to its representations. At most they are both convinced that the subject must be described differently from different points of view.

But the question is: what are these points of view, and how do they help us understand the concept of the subject in the transcendental tradition? In particular, what is the point of view from which the transcendental subject comes into view? What Kant calls empirical self-consciousness, and what Husserl calls natural reflection, is readily understood, even though much can be said about it. It is just the ordinary self-directed gaze that takes place in everyday life, and that can under some circumstances serve as the basis for certain kinds of self-knowledge. But why do both philosophers insist that there is *another* form of self-consciousness? Can we describe that form of reflection in a way that takes in both Kant's and Husserl's pronouncements? And most important of all, what does this form of reflection tell us about the status of the transcendental subject?

Husserl distinguishes between natural and transcendental reflection, and the latter is possible only through the phenomenological *epoché*.[14] It is only when our naive, straightforward belief in the existence of the transcendent world is bracketed, so that its meaning-structure as constituted comes into view, that the role of consciousness and the subject as meaning-*constituting* can be appreciated. Only then can the intentional relation to the world be fully understood in all its ramifications. Husserl indeed believes that transcendental subjectivity can be given intuitively, but like any other form of intuition this one presupposes a general framework, corresponding to a particular "attitude" (*Einstellung*).

This explains the much-quoted footnote on this topic in the second (1913) edition of the *Logical Investigations*. In the first edition (1901), Husserl had declared that, search as he might, he was "quite unable to find" what the Kantians called the "pure ego." But then in the 1913 footnote we are told that subsequent researches had turned it up after all.[15] If we did not know the context we might imagine Husserl as a David Hume, searching diligently among his experiences, looking for one called EGO, coming up empty-handed, then looking harder and harder until he finally found it. What really happened, of course, is that in 1901 Husserl had no fully worked-out phenomenological method, and in 1913 he had worked it out in explicit detail. It was not a question of looking harder but of looking differently, of having a new *way* of looking, which was precisely the method.

What this indicates is that it is the phenomenological attitude itself, as distinguished from all forms of the natural attitude, which makes the intuition of the transcendental subject possible. The phenomenological attitude is circumscribed by a set of theoretical goals and expressed in a philosophical method for reaching those goals. As the contrast with the "naturalness" of the natural attitude suggests, and as Husserl admits in several places,[16] the phenomenological attitude goes against the grain of our normal way of looking at things: it is "unnatural" and even "artificial." These considerations suggest that there is something contrived about transcendental subjectivity, that it has the a status of something introduced only in order to serve certain methodological purposes.

Is there anything corresponding to this in Kant? How does the transcendental subject come into view, and on what presuppositions, if any, does it depend? It is, of course, in the context of the "transcendental deduction of the pure concepts of the understanding" that the distinction between empirical and transcendental self-consciousness is first made. Kant's purpose is to show how the categories work to make experience, and finally empirical knowledge, possible. It is all part of the larger project of transcendental philosophy, or rather critique, as an inquiry into the conditions of the possibility of experience and into the question whether metaphysics is possible.

Kant's project, like Husserl's, is an elaborate program of reflection which differentiates itself from science, mathematics, and traditional philosophy. As his famous comparison with Copernicus's revolution in astronomy shows,[17] Kant, like Husserl, thought of his project as running counter to our normal way of thinking. Above all the *question* was new, and again it can be contrasted with Hume's question. Instead of looking for everything in experience, we should ask after the conditions of the possibility of experience. Of course, the "I think" will not turn up in experience, he tells Hume, because it belongs to those conditions of experience. In fact, it is chief among them. Thus only by pursuing a philosophical project with a particular set of questions are we brought to the point of recognizing the transcendental subject and its role in experience.

These considerations suggest another approach to the transcendental-empirical distinction. In both philosophers transcendental subjectivity emerges thanks to a deliberate theoretical move away from our "natural" way of seeing ourselves. We might be led by these considerations to think of the transcendental subject as a kind of theoretical fiction, something *posited* in the context of a theory by the theoretician in order to account for certain things that need an account, but something which has no function or meaning outside the context of the theory. As such it could be compared to certain concepts in classical physics (the inertial motion of Newton's first law), social science (the average consumer), or the law ("legal fictions" like the corporation treated as a person). In a certain way it makes no sense to ask whether such things exist, or whether they can be known: after all, we (or somebody, sometime) just made them up! What is more, everyone who uses these concepts knows that they are fictitious: no one supposes that an inertial motion ever occurs, or goes in search of the average consumer, or asks what a corporation eats for breakfast. While these concepts are useful and meaningful within the context of their respective domains, no one would impute any ontological status to their referents.

The idea of fiction puts us in mind of Hume's use of this concept in connection with the self.[18] We know that Kant opposed Hume's fictionalism. Husserl opposed it, too.[19] Nevertheless, the idea of the transcendental self as fiction (transcendental fiction?) needs to be explored. We have seen that the transcendental subject is elusive and difficult to characterize, hardly an object for us at all in any ordinary sense. All that really emerges from the discussions of Kant and Husserl is a certain *description* of an intentional, spontaneous activity of synthesis or constitution. We have argued that this description is at odds with another description which emerges from our ordinary reflection on ourselves, that of the so-called empirical self. The empirical self is quite "natural," while the transcendental subject seems to be suggested to us by some very complex philosophical considerations and seems to make little sense outside a certain methodological framework. Furthermore, the empirical subject has its place firmly in the world, whereas there is literally no place *in* the world for the transcendental subject as conceived by Kant and Husserl.

Could we not conclude, then, that in the end the transcendental subject is *nothing but* a description—a description, that is, that applies to *nothing* at all? Why not say, in other words, that there *are* just empirical subjects, ordinary people, some of whom, because of certain very complicated historical-philosophical considerations, have devised this odd, somewhat self-aggrandizing way of describing themselves?

This conception of the subject might seem to accord very well with the non-metaphysical character of transcendental philosophy, on which we have insisted. Affirmation of existence, after all, and the deeper-lying "ontological commitment" belong to metaphysics, of which transcendental philosophy is the perpetual critique. To say that something exists is always the cue for the critical philosopher, the phenomenologist, to ask questions like: *How* does it exist? What is the meaning of its existence? What are the conditions of the possibility of its having the meaning it does? On our interpretation, transcendental philosophy is not in the business of affirming or denying the existence of anything. Would it not be something like the betrayal of the critical spirit, and its ontological neutrality, to claim that the transcendental subject exists?

This may be so, but what must be understood is that it would equally betray the critical neutrality to declare it a fiction. The concept of fiction is anything but ontologically neutral. To call something a fiction is to say clearly that it does not exist, and in so doing to contrast it with what does exist. This is in effect what Hume was doing when he declared the self a fiction. In the larger context of his religious skepticism, his fictionalism may be seen as an attempt to dispense with the immortal soul as a serious contender for philosophical attention.

In somewhat the same spirit, the contemporary materialist Daniel Dennett seizes on the notion of fiction as a way of dealing with the self as an element of "folk psychology." Whereas Hume begins with the empiricist principle that everything must be traced back to experience, and then reports that he is unable to find the self among his experiences, Dennett begins with the materialist principle that what exists must be "an atom or subatomic particle or . . . other physical item in the world."[20] He then reports, not surprisingly, that the brain contains no such item that we could identify with the self. In a move which initially appears less dismissive of the notion of the self than is Hume, Dennett finds a place for it by proposing that the brain, like a computer, could generate biographical stories. The central character these stories are about would be the self. But stories don't have to be about anything real, as we know from novels. The self can be considered a fictional character, just as Sherlock Holmes is a fictional character! In this way Dennett has not only denied the existence of the self by declaring it fictitious, he has also explained this fiction by accounting for its origins, by tracing it to something real, the brain.

The flaw in Dennett's account lies in the notion that brains, conceived as computers, could generate *stories*. Of course, it is quite conceivable that computers could generate printouts that could be read and interpreted as stories, just as participants in a party game, to use another of his examples, can supply random bits of information that can be hilariously combined into stories.[21] But they have to be so combined by *someone*, just as the printout has to be read and interpreted by *someone*, in order to become a story. But who is this *someone*? It is someone with the capacity to read stories and imagine fictional situations. Like a deconstructionist eagerly announcing the death of the author, Dennett finds a way to dispense with the writers and tellers of stories. But he cannot dispense with the reader-hearer-interpreters who make them stories. And these are the very meaning-bestowing conscious selves he is trying to explain away. Without them the "stories" are nothing but dried ink marks, or sounding tongues and vocal chords.

Dennett's fictionalism is a valiant attempt at reductionism: instead of reducing the self to a bit of matter, he thinks he has reduced it right out of existence by making it a figment of the imagination. But he seems not to notice that this presupposes the imagination itself, which we might say is consciousness in its most sophisticated form, that is, its intentional or meaning-bestowing relation not only to the existing world, but also to the non-existent, the fictional. When we speak of fiction, we must ask: fiction for whom? Answer: for an existing, meaning-bestowing subject. But could not that subject be fictional as well? Of course, but again: for whom? *For* a meaning-bestowing subject. Thus we come back to the transcendental self as the always presupposed (i.e., *a priori*) subject of any awareness, even of itself as an object, even if it tries to "fictionalize" itself.

We must conclude from these considerations that the transcendental subject cannot be dismissed as a mere fiction. In any case, both Kant and Husserl describe transcendental self-consciousness as a consciousness of my own existence. Kant speaks of it as the "consciousness that I am,"[22] and Husserl describes it as consciousness of the "ego sum."[23] Of course, transcendental reflection has to be more than mere consciousness of existence, since it includes a particular description of the existing subject—namely, *as* the intentional rather than the merely substantial subject. Still, the emphasis on existence in both the Kantian and Husserlian accounts means that in this form of self-awareness I take myself to *exist* as an intentional subject, rather than, say, merely entertaining the possibility that I *might* exist in this way, or considering myself such even though I know I am not so. This latter would be a genuinely fictive consciousness: *imagining* or *pretending* that I am something, knowing all the while that I am not. This is clearly not what Kant and Husserl have in mind.

It is also not quite correct to say that the transcendental subject has a place only in the framework of Kant's and Husserl's elaborate theories. On the contrary, both give us the sense, precisely in their theories of the subject, that they are "discovering" rather than merely "inventing" something. As Husserl says, "as an Ego in the natural attitude, I am likewise and at all times a transcendental Ego, but . . . I know about this only by executing phenomenological reduction."[24] Are they not telling us something important about human existence, rather then merely spinning out the consequences of a very abstract method?

Also counting against the view of the transcendental subject as theoretical fiction is the strong suggestion in both authors that the theoretical conception arises out of a pre-theoretical context. For Husserl, indeed, *all* theoretical concepts have their origin in the pre-given life-world. This is a view found not only in the *Crisis* but also in the much earlier *Ideas II*.[25] If this is so, there must be some reflective experience of the transcendental subject prior to the explicit introduction of the *epoché*, some pre-theoretical self-awareness on which the phenomenologist can draw as a source of the theoretically refined concept. The self-awareness of intentional experience is described in those sections of *Ideas I* and *II* in which he speaks of the intentional act or cogito as an object of potential and actual reflection. *"The essence of the pure Ego . . . includes the possibility of an originary self-grasp, a 'self-perception.'"*[26] Statements like this are meant as descriptions of ordinary conscious life, not of the practices of the phenomenologist. Apparently there is some sense in which this kind of self-awareness takes place, at least potentially, prior to the explicit distinction between natural and transcendental reflection, or exists even at the heart of natural reflection itself.

The situation is similar in Kant. He introduces the transcendental subject in the context of his theory of the unity of apperception or self-consciousness. It is this unity of apperception which is revealed as the supreme principle of the understanding in the context of the transcendental deduction. But transcendental apperception itself is not something that occurs only in the philosopher who is engaged in the project of transcendental deduction. "It must be possible for the 'I think' to accompany all my representations,"[27] says Kant. This mode of self-consciousness belongs, then, at least potentially, to experience, not merely to philosophical analysis. While not itself an experience, at least in Kant's sense, transcendental self-consciousness can "accompany," and must at least potentially accompany, all experience. It is experience itself, and not the transcendental critique of experience, which requires that I be conscious of myself as transcendental subject.

It appears, then, that the subject as transcendental or intentional is something that we have some acquaintance with in everyday, pre-theoretical life, and that the form of reflection in which it is given is not merely a philosophical contrivance. When we begin to think about it in this way, however, the paradoxical character of such reflection becomes all the more obvious.

This paradox is evident in Kant. He is engaged in a transcendental analysis of experience or empirical knowledge, in which the natural world becomes accessible to us as an object of scientific cognition. Nature is the realm of events which are governed by relations of strict causality, and in empirical self-consciousness I even take myself to be part of it. But the very experience that gives me access to this realm, and indeed imposes the requirement of strict causality upon it, *also* requires that I take myself to be spontaneous and intentional, that is, that I take myself to be exempt from the causal requirement and thus not to belong to nature after all.

For Kant this duality is, of course, extremely important, since it opens the door to freedom and thus serves as the bridge to the full-fledged notion of practical reason in the Second Critique. The description of the two forms of self-awareness is clearest in Kant's discussion of the Third Antinomy:

> Man is one of the appearances of the sensible world, and in so far one of the natural causes the causality of which must stand under empirical laws. . . . Man, however, who knows all the rest of nature solely through the senses, knows himself also through pure apperception. . . . He is thus to himself, on the one hand phenomenon, and on the other hand . . . a purely intelligible object.[28]

As such an intelligible object, Kant goes on to say, I stand not under laws of nature but under the *ought* of obligation, which in turn requires that I be a free moral agent. It must be pointed out that this passage confirms our claim that pure apperception is anything but empty for Kant, since he presents it here as ascribing definite characteristics—spontaneity as freedom from natural causality—to myself. It is also noteworthy that, in this passage, Kant seems to contradict his claim that pure apperception is not a form of self-knowledge. But he is far from suggesting that pure apperception gives me a view of myself that is somehow "truer" than that provided by empirical self-consciousness. Indeed, the two forms of self-"knowledge," radically different though they are, seem here to be on equal footing.

In Husserl a similar paradox is obvious: If there is something like a pre-phenomenological awareness of the transcendental subject, then the attitude of transcendental reflection would not be in effect. Still immersed in the natural attitude, with all that it implies about the world and myself as a part of it, I would also somehow be conscious of something—of myself as transcendental subject—which is not worldly at all. In other words, within the natural attitude there would lurk a form of consciousness which would break with the natural attitude without embarking on the full-fledged suspension which constitutes the phenomenological reduction.

Both thinkers, then, seem to postulate a pre-theoretical awareness in which I take myself to be "exempt" or "absent" from the general conditions of world-liness in which I exist. What sort of awareness would this be?

One philosopher who addresses this question explicitly is Jean-Paul Sartre. In his early essay *The Transcendence of the Ego*,[29] Sartre takes up the problem raised in a much-quoted 1933 article by Eugen Fink, Husserl's last assistant.[30] In Husserl, the transcendental subject seems "artificial" because it can be understood only from the point of view of a method which seems unmotivated in the natural attitude. By asserting that there are no motives within the natural attitude for effecting the phenomenological *epochē*, Fink is in effect claiming that there is no experience prior to the reduction which would give us access to the transcendental subject. The natural standpoint is perfectly coherent as it stands; there are no "cracks" or difficulties which would lead us to question it, much less to suspend it wholesale in the manner recommended by Husserl. Once the *epochē* is performed, and the role of intentionality is fully grasped, transcendental subjectivity can be understood. But the *epochē* itself seems like an *acte gratuit*. Husserl describes it as an act of our "perfect freedom"; that is, he stresses that we are free to do it. But do we have any reason for doing it?

Sartre agrees with Fink that there are no reasons, no *rational* motives for the *epochē*. As Husserl presents it, he says, it appears to be a "miracle."[31] Yet on Sartre's view it is not completely arbitrary. Indeed, it is "imposed on us" from time to time in the form of *anxiety* or anguish (*angoisse*). This is the phenomenon Sartre elsewhere calls *nausea*, that emptiness in the pit of the stomach which signals the awareness of the sheer contingency of things in general. He is suggesting that the suspension of the natural attitude first comes to us as an *affective* break in its hold on us. In the natural attitude we unquestioningly take the world to exist and take ourselves to be part of it. Anxiety transforms the world into a *phenomenon* whose ontological status is suspended, and whose meaning-constituted character comes to the fore; as such its meaning is revealed as depending on *me*, or rather on my meaning-bestowing consciousness, not as a thing in the world (for the world is no longer taken for granted), but purely as subject for the world. This vertiginous form of self-awareness, which is not reflection in any ordinary sense at all, is nevertheless the self-awareness of intentional consciousness itself, not as the attribute of a worldly object (i.e., the empirical ego) but as a meaning- and self-constituting process.

Thus Husserl's full-fledged phenomenological method, according to Sartre, is the explicit articulation and working-out of a pre-philosophical, even pre-rational, form of awareness. On this view

> the *epochē* is no longer a miracle, an intellectual method, an erudite procedure: it is an anxiety which is imposed on us and which we cannot avoid: it is both a pure event of transcendental origin and an ever possible accident in our daily life.[32]

As anxiety it is more than just a *self*-awareness: like the phenomenological reduction itself it encompasses self and world, as they appear in the natural attitude, and transforms the status of both. Another way of putting it is that in this anxiety the "arbitrary" or "gratuitous" character of the *natural* attitude is revealed. Husserl implies this when he claims it is within our "perfect freedom" to suspend the natural attitude. If from *within* the natural attitude the *epochē* appears arbitrary, gratuitous, or contrived, and the natural attitude itself quite necessary (this is what "natural" means here), anxiety can suddenly reverse those values. This idea of the transcendental *epochē* as a reversal or upheaval, an up-ending of our ordinary way of looking at things, accords well with Kant's and Husserl's claims that they are effecting nothing less than a "revolution" in philosophy. But it has its origin in ordinary—or rather extraordinary, but pre-philosophical—experience.

For Sartre, anxiety is more than just an affective intimation of the phenomenological reduction. It is at the same time the consciousness of my radical freedom or spontaneity, a freedom impossible to attribute to the empirical ego which is part of the world. Like Kant, he sees us as alternating between conflicting views of ourselves: on the one hand as worldly and determined, on the other hand as transcendental and free. As is well known, the Sartrean approach to ethics is in many ways Kantian: he sees human action not as subjected to rules imposed from without, but as following norms that consciousness imposes on itself.

The point of Sartre's short essay was to attack what he thought was a fundamental defect in Husserl's phenomenology, its concept of the transcendental ego. Sartre claims that in speaking of such an ego Husserl was betraying his own best insights, since the phenomenological description of consciousness reveals and requires no such entity. In effect he accuses Husserl of falling prey to a metaphysical prejudice, the view that consciousness needs to be anchored to some underlying substance which holds it together and unifies it. Husserl himself had shown, in his lectures on time-consciousness, according to Sartre, that consciousness unifies itself from within and needs no external, unifying principle. The only valid phenomenological concept of the ego is that of the empirical ego, which is "outside, *in the world*,"[33] that is, transcendent, not transcendental. Hence Sartre's title, which also, however, suggests that phenomenology should transcend, or "get beyond," the (transcendental) ego. There is an ego *for* consciousness; *in* or *behind* or *beneath* consciousness, however, "there is no I" (il n'y a pas de *Je*).[34]

But on our interpretation of Husserl, Sartre's position is in fact entirely consistent with the basic outlines of phenomenology and of transcendental philosophy generally. The same sort of argument, for a "non-egological conception of consciousness," was made by Aron Gurwitsch, a loyal though not uncritical follower of Husserl's.[35] Sartre may have misread, perhaps even deliberately for his own rhetorical purposes, some of Husserl's statements about the ego. In any case his focus in this critique seems to be certain formulations in *Ideas I*, and Sartre argues against Husserl by pointing out that the substantial ego was found neither in Husserl's earlier work (the lectures *On the Consciousness of Internal Time*) nor in his later work (the *Cartesian Meditations*).[36] The term "transcendental ego" can be taken as an expression for just that transcendental unity of consciousness which Sartre admits is essential to it without being in any way substantial. It is this non-egological conception of consciousness, of course, which leads directly to the "phenomenological ontology" presented in Sartre's *Being and Nothingness*. Anguish, as the consciousness of freedom, is at the same time the "apprehension of nothingness."[37] Consciousness, the "for-itself,"

> must be its own nothingness. The being of consciousness qua consciousness is to exist *at a distance from itself* as a presence to itself, and this empty distance which being carries within itself is Nothingness.[38]

Thus Sartre goes beyond asserting merely that "There is no I." His version of the paradox of subjectivity is that the "being of consciousness" is nothingness —*le Néant*.

Historically, we have just traced the improbable transition from the somewhat dry and intellectual rationalism of Husserl to the literary and supposedly irrationalist philosophy of existentialism. The mediating figure in this development is, of course, none other than the early Heidegger, to whom Sartre appeals in introducing anguish as the "apprehension of nothingness." In *Being and Time* and *What Is Metaphysics?* anxiety (*Angst*) is presented as the most fundamental of all dispositions (*Grundbefindlichkeit*). Unlike fear, anxiety has no particular object or situation it seeks to avoid. We know what we fear. Asked what we are anxious about, by contrast, we might say, "nothing in particular." While anxiety has no object, it nevertheless reveals something; what it reveals is *das Nichts*.[39]

What this means for Heidegger is that in anxiety we no longer are at home in the very place where we are always at home: the world. The world becomes, we could say, meaningless, and yet in so doing reveals its meaning to us. Its meaning, of course, is its meaning *for us;* what is revealed is thus not just the world but our being in it. Thus, *"that in the face of which one has anxiety [das Wovor der Angst] is Being-in-the-world as such."*[40] Anxiety reveals, then, in an affective way, exactly what Heidegger's "existential analytic of Dasein" seeks to expose philosophically. To put it in Sartre's Husserlian terms, which of course Heidegger would not use, *Angst* is the pre-figuration, from within the natural attitude, of the phenomenological *epochē*. As we have seen, like Sartre, Heidegger is opposed to the idea of the self as substance: the self is not a thing. It is partly in order to avoid the substance view that he chooses the term *Dasein*, rejecting any terminology involving the "I" or even consciousness. But there is no doubt that *Dasein* plays the role transcendental consciousness does for Husserl and Sartre: it is meaning-bestowing and world-constituting.

On this reading of Heidegger and Sartre, they turn out to be much closer to Husserl's (and Kant's) original insights than they made themselves out to be, for all their terminological revisionism and their explicit or implicit criticisms of their predecessors. They belong, in this sense, to the transcendental tradition. At the same time, their talk of "nothingness," as revealed in a kind of pre-theoretical, affective self-awareness, suggests that there is a genuine (transcendental) insight behind the claim of Hume and Dennett that there is something *fictional* about the self. As part of a strategy for carrying out an empiricist or physicalist reduction, the notion of fiction will not work, as we have seen. But as an expression of the insight that the self is *not a thing*, indeed *no-thing at all,* and above all is not part of the *world* of things, or indeed part of the world at all, the idea of fiction can be part of a transcendental conception. Hume is making a point against Descartes, and Dennett, like many analytic philosophers, has not progressed much beyond Hume in this regard. The point is a valid one as far as it goes: if the self is not a physical thing, on which everyone agrees, it does not help to make of it a non-physical thing, whatever that would be. The real point is that transcendental subject is not any kind of thing—it is more like an "absence," or "exemption," as we have called it. But in its paradoxical role as inescapable condition of the possibility of experience, it cannot be denied or argued away.

With reference to the distinction between transcendental and empirical subjectivity, we must conclude, it seems to me, by accepting what Husserl calls the paradox of subjectivity: that we are both subjects for the world and objects in the world. The transcendental tradition introduces us to this radical opposition and provides us with no means for getting beyond it. It gives us two descriptions of the self which are equally necessary and essentially incompatible. According to my account, neither of these forms of self-consciousness takes precedence over the other. From the perspective of each, the other appears somehow bizarre, unreal. From that of the natural attitude, the transcendental subject seems artificial, contrived, a mere fiction. From that of the transcendental attitude, the world as a whole, and my empirical self within it, looms as "phenomenon," its reality placed in suspension. When this happens we feel what the existentialists try to capture by speaking of nausea, vertigo, or anxiety. We feel, rather than understand, the two radically incompatible senses of self.

Most philosophers are temperamentally and occupationally incapable of accepting such a paradox and will do anything to find its resolution, even when there is none to be found. Idealism reduces the world and the empirical subject to representations. Realism, more prevalent in our day, tries hard to make transcendental subjectivity go away. Metaphysics, in either form, seeks unity, closure, the one over the many. Transcendental philosophy, by contrast, is not metaphysics but rather the perpetual critique and unending examination of metaphysics and the experience which underlies it.

Notes

1. A12/B26. In citations from Kant I use the standard Academy pagination found in German editions and translations. Translations are from *Immanuel Kant's Critique of Pure Reason*, trans. Norman Kemp Smith (London: Macmillan, 1963).

2. *Idee der Phänomenologie*, 3.

3. *Cartesianische Meditationen*, 119; after *Cartesian Meditations*, 86.

4. Henry Allison, *Kant's Transcendental Idealism* (New Haven, Conn.: Yale University Press, 1983), 8.

5. Paul Ricoeur, *Husserl* (Evanston, Ill.: Northwestern University Press, 1967), 36.

6. J. G. Fichte, *The Science of Knowledge*, ed. and trans. P. Heath and J. Lachs (Cambridge: Cambridge University Press, 1988), 16.

7. *Cartesianische Meditationen*, 65; after *Cartesian Meditations*, 26.

8. See *Krisis*, 182; *Crisis*, 178.

9. *Krisis*, 188; after *Crisis*, 185.

10. A346/B404.

11. B422.

12. *Krisis*, 116; after *Crisis*, 114.

13. *Ideen II*, 101; after *Ideas II*, 107.

14. *Cartesianische Meditationen*, 72; after *Cartesian Meditations*, 33.

15. *Logische Untersuchungen*, II/1, 361; after *Logical Investigations*, 549.

16. *Logische Untersuchungen*, II/1, 9; *Ideen II*, 180.

17. Bxvi f.

18. David Hume, *A Treatise of Human Nature*, ed. L. A. Selby-Bigge (Oxford: Clarendon Press, 1965), 254.

19. *Krisis*, 88ff.

20. Daniel Dennett, "Why Everyone Is a Novelist," *Times Literary Supplement*, September 1988, 17.

21. See Dennett, *Consciousness Explained* (Boston: Little, Brown, 1991), 10.

22. B157.

23. *Cartesianische Meditationen*, 61; *Cartesian Meditations*, 22.

24. *Cartesianische Meditationen*, 75; after *Cartesian Meditations*, 37.

25. See *Ideen II*, 90; *Ideas II*, 96.

26. *Ideen II*, 101; after *Ideas II*, 107; see also *Ideen* II 73.

27. B131.

28. A546f./B574f.

29. Trans. F. Williams and R. Kirkpatrick (New York: Hill and Wang, 1993).

30. "Die phänomenologische Philosophie E. Husserls in der gegenwärtigen Kritik," in Fink, *Studien zur Phänomenologie, 1930–1939* (The Hague: M. Nijhoff, 1966), 110ff.

31. Sartre, *Transcendence of the Ego: An Existentialist Theory of Consciousness* (New York: Noonday Press, 1957), 102.

32. Ibid., 103.

33. Ibid., 31.

34. Ibid., 48.

35. "A Non-egological Conception of Consciousness," in Aron Gurwitsch, *Studies in Phenomenology and Psychology* (Evanston, Ill.: Northwestern University Press, 1966).

36. *Transcendence of the Ego*, 38–39.

37. J.-P. Sartre, *Being and Nothingness*, trans. Hazel E. Barnes (New York: Philosophical Library, 1956), 29.

38. Ibid., 78.

39. M. Heidegger, *Was ist Metaphysik?* (Frankfurt am Main: Vittorio Klostermann, 1977), 32–33.

40. M. Heidegger, *Sein und Zeit* (Tübingen: Max Niemeyer Verlag, 1957), 186.

8

Unconscious Consciousness in Husserl and Freud

Rudolf Bernet

Translated by Christopher Jupp and Paul Crowe

F REUD'S UNDERSTANDING OF the Unconscious is rooted in the clinical-empirical observation of phenomena such as dreams, slips of the tongue, and other neurotic symptoms, regressive-infantile types of behavior in adults, delusions in schizophrenia, etc. Based on this there are in Freud's work also "metapsychological" observations that strive for a theoretical determination of the essence of the Unconscious in its relation to consciousness. These observations find their most pregnant expression in the theories of repression and the "drive-representative" (*Triebrepräsentanz*).

Many philosophers have experienced Freud's theory of the Unconscious as a provocation and have discussed it with constantly growing interest. They have pointed out that Freud's concept of the Unconscious has a rich philosophical prehistory (Kant, Schelling, Schopenhauer, von Hartmann, Nietzsche) and that it requires a philosophical postscript because of its fragmentary character and obvious theoretical deficiencies. Some among them were of the opinion that the historical investigation of its philosophical precursors already presented a clarification of the Freudian concept of the Unconscious; others, in their debate with Freud, have availed themselves of philosophical viewpoints that are hardly accommodating to the originality of Freud's thinking. These philosophical efforts often awaken the justified suspicion that they make judgments about the existence or nonexistence of the Unconscious without having taken into consideration the rich material of Freud's clinical descriptions.

Freud himself contributed very little toward a fruitful debate between philosophy and psychoanalysis. On the basis of his limited knowledge of philosophy and, in particular, his very narrow concept of consciousness, Freud maintained that philosophy as philosophy of consciousness would necessarily lack an appropriate understanding of the Unconscious, and he expected nothing more from it than a reduction of the Unconscious to consciousness, that is to say, a sterile denial of the existence of the Unconscious.[1] It is therefore quite understandable that Freud and his pupils and successors gave little attention to philosophical considerations concerning the Unconscious. Lacan's attempt at a transcendental-philosophical grounding of psychoanalysis is in this respect a unique exception, but it is also burdened by a lack of reflection on consciousness *and* especially on its bodily, affective, emotional, and temporal constitution.

By contrast, the extensive works of the phenomenologically inspired psychoanalysts (Binswanger, Boss) and psychoanalytically interested phenomenologists (Scheler, Sartre, Merleau-Ponty, Ricoeur, M. Henry, Derrida) have impressively demonstrated the possibility of a fruitful conversation between philosophy and psychoanalysis. However, some of them cannot be spared the objection that they criticized Freud's discovery of the unconscious too quickly and reasoned it away. In addition, in their critical appropriation of Freud many of these thinkers have let themselves be influenced one-sidedly by Heidegger, and this has led to the regrettable neglect of the genuine Freudian question of the status of the Unconscious "in" consciousness. They have translated Freud's "mechanical" economy of drive[2] into the language of the *analytic of Dasein* and thereby evaded the philosophical question of the essence of drive and the possibility of its "representation" ("*Repräsentation*") in intentional representations (*Vorstellungen*). More seriously still, they have hardly taken notice of Freud's own attempts at a phenomenological clarification of the Unconscious, that is to say, his descriptions of the way in which unconscious representations appear in consciousness without negating their origin in the Unconscious. They thereby invite the justified objection that they have developed a phenomenological psychoanalysis which hasn't given sufficient attention to the phenomenon of the Unconscious and the Unconscious as a phenomenon.

By contrast, Freud repeatedly returned in his work to the question of the appearing of the Unconscious. However, his accounts have a purely descriptive character and so cannot satisfy the transcendental-philosophical demands of a phenomenology of consciousness. For Freud, it goes without saying that the Unconscious necessarily requires consciousness in order to appear, even though in appearing it also brings to appearance its difference from consciousness. Concretely, this means that the Unconscious manifests itself through *gaps* within the coherent connections of consciousness: in illogical trains of thought, in forgetting, in the fantastic formations of phantasies and manifest dream contents, in phobias and other neurotic symptoms.[3] Inexplicable conscious states of feeling such as *Angst* also occupied Freud intensely.[4]

Taking its point of departure from this Freudian determination of the connection between the conscious and the Unconscious, a transcendental phenomenology of consciousness is confronted with the task of showing how it is possible that consciousness can bring to present appearance something unconscious, that is, something foreign or absent to consciousness, without thereby incorporating it into or subordinating it to the conscious present. In the following I would like to sketch how Husserl's theory of the intuitive presentifications (*anschauliche Vergegenwärtigungen*) and of phantasy in particular can in fact achieve this apparently impossible task. However, I will merely intimate the specifically transcendental-phenomenological character of this solution by referring to the grounding of Husserl's theory of phantasy in inner time-consciousness as a form of life that is at once impressional and originally reproductive.

It is by no means thereby claimed, however, that Freud's concept of the Unconscious in its full empirical-descriptive scope is derivable from Husserl's concept of imaginative presentification. Instead, using Husserl's analysis of phantasy-consciousness, an attempt will be made to show how a present consciousness can comport itself toward a non-present, and hence peculiarly foreign, consciousness belonging to the same (intentional) stream of consciousness. Reproductive inner time-consciousness demonstrates that consciousness possesses the originary ability to distance itself from the immediate perception of its own life, instead of immediately and completely coinciding with it. What results from this is not only a range of new insights into the essence of the difference between consciousness and the Unconscious, but also the possibility of a conscious and symbolic presentation of instinctually driven (*triebmässig*) life itself. At the same time, this phenomenological founding of Freud's concept of the Unconscious in the theory of an originally reproductive consciousness leads to a partial critique of Freud's metapsychological determination of the Unconscious as a *simple*, internally unperceived representational consciousness. The Unconscious is not simply an amputated, unperceived consciousness or a simple representational consciousness entangled in illogical primary processes, but is instead *another (self-) consciousness*. As Freud himself remarked, the riddle of the Unconscious is in fact the riddle of consciousness itself.

1. Husserl's Analysis of the Consciousness of the Absent

At first sight it looks as if Husserl and Freud shared not only the same conception of consciousness but also of the Unconscious. If one considers the fact that they were both students of Brentano's and came into contact with the same authors and psychological theories during their studies, then such an agreement is less astonishing. As is well known, in his *Psychology from an Empirical Standpoint,* Brentano defined consciousness as a unitary connection of intentional representations that are accompanied by a pre-reflective internal consciousness. Consequently, his extensive discussion of the concept of the Unconscious is primarily concerned with the question of whether there can be an intentional consciousness which lacks such an accompanying internal consciousness and whether the supposition that there is such an unconscious consciousness can avoid the danger of an infinite regress in the performance (*Vollzug*) of self-consciousness.[5]

Throughout their lives, Freud and Husserl always held on to this Brentanian definition of the Unconscious as an internally unperceived consciousness. But neither thought it was sufficient. Freud searched for the instinctually driven roots of consciousness and the way in which the libidinal energy of drive combines itself with primitive memory traces and cathects representations which, under certain conditions, can push their way from the Unconscious into the preconscious and into perceptual consciousness. Husserl undertook a de-

tailed investigation of the different forms of intentional acts of consciousness
and repeatedly occupied himself with the clarification of Brentano's conception
of inner consciousness. In working on both of these areas of research he surpasses by far the insights of Brentano and Freud even if, usually without realizing it, he regularly crossed their paths. Thus, it is necessary to seek the Husserlian contribution to the problem of the Unconscious in the spheres both of
intentional acts and of inner consciousness. In Husserl, the Unconscious as the
presence of the non-present is first of all a matter of the particular type of
act-intentionality called presentification (*Vergegenwärtigung*)[6] which characterizes the acts of phantasy, memory, and empathy. It can be shown that the possibility of these acts of presentification is ultimately grounded in the temporal
structure of inner consciousness and that a correct phenomenological understanding of the Unconscious is first of all opened up through the analysis of
this inner consciousness. Then, of course, the essence of the Unconscious can
no longer be understood on the basis of the mere absence of inner perceptual
consciousness. Instead, its appearance, and thereby its phenomenologically determined essence, results from the possibility of another form of inner (time-)
consciousness, namely, the reproductive form. Husserl himself did not develop
this new phenomenological understanding of the Unconscious any further, although he prepared for us all the means for doing so.

It was never difficult for Husserl to think the possibility of the presentification of something non-present because he always understood consciousness as
the subjective achievement of intentional apperception and appresentation and
never as the mere presence of sense data. In his early work in the *Philosophy of
Arithmetic* and the *Logical Investigations,* presentifications were still understood
as inauthentic, that is, non-intuitive forms of *thought.* According to this theory,
that which withdraws from intuitive or authentic thought is presentified by
means of a sign functioning as a surrogate or by an image that represents by
similarity. It is not surprising therefore that initially, and up to and including
the 1904–5 lecture on the *Main Issues in the Phenomenology and Theory of
Knowledge,*[7] Husserl conceived of the acts of sensuous presentification, like
memory and phantasy, as types of pictorial consciousness (*Bildbewusstsein*). He
could base this view on an already extensive exploration of perceptive pictorial
consciousness, one with which he continued to occupy himself later, especially
in connection with the analysis of aesthetic pictorial consciousness. Thus, phantasy and memory were forms of pictorial consciousness in which an inner pictorial image (called by Sartre the "*image mentale*") takes the place of a physical
perceptual picture. A past occurrence or an unreal phantasy-world would therefore come to appearance in a present depiction without thereby forfeiting its
absence from this present.

Imagination and Pictorial Consciousness

It cannot be our task here to present in detail either Husserl's analysis of
perceptual and imaginative pictorial consciousness or its constant development

and elaboration. For us, in the present context, the only important question is why it was that after 1904–5 Husserl repeatedly doubted the determination of phantasy and memory as variants of pictorial consciousness and from 1909 onwards definitely rejected this conception. There are two reasons for this that quickly reveal themselves as the same issue:

1. The failure of the "apprehension of a content of apprehension" schema, derived from the analysis of perception, in the clarification of the acts of intuitive presentification.[8]

2. The analysis of the temporal character of inner consciousness and its impressional and reproductive form.[9]

Perceptive pictorial consciousness implies a double perception, that is, a perception of the physical "picture-thing" (*Bild-Ding*) and of the "pictorial object" (*Bild-Objekt*) in which the absent "pictorial subject" (*Bild-sujet*) is depicted and thereby achieves intuitive presence.[10] The pictorial object does not belong to the same physical space as the picture-thing; there is a "conflict" (*Widerstreit*) between the two, as a consequence of which, the appearance of the pictorial object is counted as an "apparent perception" (*Scheinwahrnehmung*). Translated into the terminology of Husserl's early analysis of perception, this means that in pictorial consciousness there are two apprehensions, one based on the other, the first of which is supported by sensations and brings the pictorial image to appearance while the other animates mere "phantasms" and thereby explains the givenness of the pictorial subject depicted in the pictorial object. In the appearance of the pictorial object as an apparent perception the pictorial subject is "presentified" in its absence, for here too a "conflict" arises, indicating that the pictorial object and the pictorial subject do not belong to the same reality.

This conflict between the pictorial object and the pictorial subject has, however, a different character to the conflict between the pictorial object and the picture-thing. The pictorial object is perceived, but, in contrast to the picture-thing, it has to be degraded to an apparent object (*Scheinobjekt*) if it is to function as a depiction of the pictorial subject. On the other hand, the conflict between the pictorial object and the pictorial subject does not lead to a "nullification" (*Nichtigung*) because from the start it is clear that the pictorial image and the depicted cannot belong to the same reality. As long as pictorial consciousness is explicitly performed as pictorial consciousness no one believes that the depicted pictorial subject is bodily present and is perceived as real in the picture. Hence, pictorial consciousness as well as phantasy presuppose that the ego can live in two different worlds (a real and an unreal one), which necessitates that the possibility of this "splitting of the ego" (*Ichspaltung*) be incorporated into the concept of the human subject.

Husserl devoted a great deal of attention to the precise analysis of the different forms of these conflicts, and we will see below that the investigations that deal with them can serve as a fruitful starting point for a phenomenological determination of what Freud called "repression" (*Verdrängung*). For Freud, too, repression is explicitly connected to a "splitting of the ego." For Freud, the division between reality and phantasy is the result of a process of repression, and wherever this process of repression is lacking (as in schizophrenia), the distinction between hallucination and perception also dissolves. Freud's conception of repression and of a hypothetical "original repression" in particular suggest in addition to this that not only phantasy but also reality itself is constituted on the basis of an experience of conflict (or experience of a difference). We will also encounter this idea in Husserl in his reflections on the "modificational"-relation that obtains between presentation (*Gegenwärtigung*) and presentification (*Vergegenwärtigung*).

Husserl's application of the description of perceptive pictorial consciousness to the analysis of *phantasy* implies that the latter, as an "inner" or "*imaginative*" *pictorial* consciousness, likewise consists in a double apprehension. In this case, however, because the phantasy-image is not a physical pictorial image and cannot therefore be perceived, there are no sensations here, only phantasms. These phantasms are apprehended in two different ways, that is, both in relation to the pictorial image and in relation to that which is depicted in it. Without the physical picture-thing in the imaginary pictorial consciousness of phantasy, one of the forms of conflict disappears, and with it goes a clear index of the division between perception and phantasy. Accordingly, Husserl expends a great deal of effort in fending off the risk of confounding phantasy with apparent perception (i.e., neutralized perception). But because he could not ground the distinction between sensations and phantasms in a convincing manner, Husserl was left with no alternative but to make phantasy-consciousness, *qua* consciousness of a *phantasy*, dependent on the experience of a contrast with simultaneously occurring perceptual events. The lived experience of phantasy would therefore be a lived experience that, in contrast to actual perception, is a diminished or deficient quasi-perception with a diminished intensity and duration as well as a horizonal intentionality of only limited scope.[11]

The greatest difficulty with this analysis of phantasy as an imaginary pictorial consciousness lies not in the distinction between phantasy and perception but in its inability to clarify the essence of phantasy as the presentification of a non-present object (an inability nevertheless connected to the former distinction). Husserl talks of a presentifying apprehension of present phantasms, but how a present apprehension of present contents of apprehension should succeed, without the mediation of a physical pictorial image, in bringing to present appearance a non-present object in its non-presence remains inexplicable and borders on a miracle.

Husserl formulated this objection himself for the first time in connection with his old theory of retention and concluded that the present consciousness of something past cannot contain something of this past as a real (*reell*) content of consciousness without thereby forfeiting its character of pastness.[12] It is therefore certainly no coincidence that his new analysis of phantasial presentification is no longer oriented toward the analysis of the *perception* of a pictorial image (*Bild*) but toward the *remembering* (*Wiedererinnerung*) of a past present.

We will return to this soon. In any case, it is already certain that what is reproduced cannot really (*reell*) inhabit the presentifying consciousness and that the present apprehension of a present content cannot reach out beyond the present to enter the realm of the intuitive presentifications. This insight into the functional inadequacy of the schema "apprehension of a content of apprehension" for the explanation of the intuitive presentifications is phenomenologically supported by a new theory of the temporality of inner consciousness from which the new theory of presentification will emerge.

Remembering and Reproductive Inner Consciousness

The inner, implicit consciousness of the performance of an intentional lived experience that Brentano called an "inner representation" (*innere Vorstellung*) —and not "observation"[13]—is renamed "absolute" (time-) consciousness by Husserl from 1906–07 onwards.[14] This new terminology draws attention to the fact that from then on Husserl attributes to inner (time-) consciousness a transcendental-constitutive function with respect to intentional acts and the noematic correlates of acts and also, in particular, to their temporality. This absolute time-consciousness is a flow of continually new "originary-impressions" (*Urimpressionen*), which are united with each other in a weave of retentional and protentional intentionality. In this way, every originary-impression is "inseparable" from retentions and protentions which relate themselves, in a process of "intentional nesting" of each in the other (*intentionale Verschachtelung*), both to those originary-impressions of the same living flow of consciousness which have already been absorbed and to those which are still coming. In every phase of this inner time-consciousness a temporally enduring act is consciously known (*bewusst*), and in the gathering continuation of these phases the temporal forms of the simultaneity, succession, and duration of the whole intentional life of a subject's acts constitute themselves.

The more precise phenomenological analysis of this absolute time-consciousness and its temporalization of intentional acts through a "retentional vertical intentionality" (*Querintentionalität*) is not as important in the present context as a reflection on the fact that it is also a matter of that unique form of self-consciousness called "retentional horizontal intentionality" (*Längsintentionalität*). According to Husserl, inner time-consciousness is an originarily *impressional* and at the same time *intentional* self-consciousness due to the retentions and protentions that belong together with the originary-impressions. Hence, it is a matter of an impressional-intentional, pre-reflective, and non-objective self-consciousness, that is to say, an impressional self-affection of one's own conscious life which, according to Husserl, is combined with a "unique," namely, likewise impressional, form of intentionality.[15] If one calls this self-affection of subjective life "drive" or "instinctual drive" (*Trieb*), then this inner time-consciousness clearly merits the name which Husserl actually uses: "drive-intentionality" or "intentionality of instinctual drive" (*Triebintentionalität*). As an inner experience of intentional life this is both instinctual drive and representation (*Repräsentation*) of drive in one.

It has already been indicated that the theory of drives forms the core of Freud's theory of the Unconscious and that Freud's accounts of the "representation" of drive in the Unconscious and (pre-) conscious intentional "representations" pose the philosophically interested reader with the greatest riddle. As Schopenhauer and Nietzsche did before him, Freud leads us with his theory of the representation of drive to the question of how drive actually begins to "think." If the Unconscious and the conscious are both interpreted as a realm of "representations" (*Vorstellungen*) which "represent" (*repräsentieren*) drives, then Freud cannot avoid characterizing the Unconscious and the conscious as two distinct forms of representational "thinking" which nevertheless feed off the same drive-structure. These unconscious and conscious processes in which instinctual drive "cathects" (*besetzt*) unconscious and conscious representations in order to achieve its aim of the "discharge" (*Abfuhr*) of tension are called "primary" and "secondary processes."

A phenomenological contribution to the foundation of the Freudian concept of the Unconscious would, at the very least, have to prove that such a double form of representation of drive (*Triebrepräsentation*) by representations (*Vorstellungen*) is possible. If Freud's theory of the representation of drive in unconscious and (pre-) conscious intentional representations is re-thought from the point of view of Husserl's analysis of the self-affection of intentional lived experiences in inner, instinctually driven consciousness, then there would also have to be a double form of inner consciousness. Thus the phenomenological clarification of the Freudian Unconscious can be successful only if the *impressional* inner consciousness of intentional lived experiences, which has already been sketched, is not the only possible form of an instinctually driven relation to intentional representations. We will soon see that remembering and phantasy, as reproductive presentifications of intentional lived experiences, in fact imply such a second form of inner consciousness. This *reproductive* form of inner consciousness involved in acts of presentification could make a decisive contribution to the phenomenological clarification of the possibility of the Unconscious.

Husserl first achieved the breakthrough to his new theory of phantasy as a *non-positing*, intuitive-reproductive presentification after working out his new theory of remembering as a *positing*, intuitive-reproductive presentification. His early analysis of remembering as an immanent pictorial consciousness collapsed under the same arguments that we mentioned above in the context of the critique of the old analysis of phantasy as pictorial consciousness. In remembering, an object presently appears and yet as belonging to the past. An inner time-consciousness that posits the past in relation to the present without this temporal distance being leveled off or merged "telescopically" is therefore constitutive of memory. Instead of the doubling of objects (as in pictorial consciousness), the present appearance of a past object requires a doubling of consciousness itself. As a consciousness of consciousness, remembering resembles reflection, and Husserl expended much effort in the precise determination of the distinction between these two types of acts. These efforts not only improved the analysis of memory, they also contained the core of a new theory of reflection according to which reflection is not an inner perception but an objectifying presentification of a lived experience that has already "flowed away."

In remembering, by contrast with reflection, intentional interest is directed toward a past object and not an earlier perception. Nevertheless, an earlier perception is intentionally implied by a memorially presentified past object. Expressed in Husserl's terminology: the presentification of a past object implies the reproduction of the original experience of that object. I experience the memorial appearance of an object as a reproductive modification of an earlier perceptual consciousness in which the object was self-given in its bodily presence. The inner consciousness of a memory is therefore not an impressional consciousness of a perception but a reproductive consciousness which bears within itself the earlier perception in the manner of an intentional implication (and not as a real [*reel*] component). What I experientially live through in remembering is neither simply a past perception nor a present memory but a present memory *as* a reproduction of an earlier perception. Consequently, the object appears as presentified, that is, it gives itself ("originarily") and not as an image, all the while maintaining its temporal distance from the present. Husserl says that it "hovers" before me (*mir vorschwebt*) without my being really able to grasp it bodily.

Husserl combined this new theory of remembering with many extensive specialized investigations which we cannot go into here. Only the comprehensive discussions of the doxic modalities in the performance of remembering and in their relation to what is remembered will be mentioned. These clearly demonstrate that presentification (*Vergegenwärtigung*) as the reproductive modification of presentation (*Gegenwärtigung*) can combine itself with the modifications of position-takings (*Stellungnahmen*) but should not be reduced to them. This insight will be especially important when phantasy is described as being a *non-positing* form of reproductive presentification and therefore gives the impression of being distinguished from the corresponding perception merely through its neutralized position-taking (*Stellungnahme*).

A second object of Husserl's attention, always attended by renewed doubts, concerns the relation between reproduction and inner consciousness. Husserl vacillates between determining reproduction as an achievement of inner (time-) consciousness and as a phenomenon belonging to the sphere of the intentional acts of consciousness.[16] In the case of remembering, the question is whether it is an intentional act that is impressionally conscious in inner consciousness and that relates itself to an earlier perceptual act, or whether it is a question of an intentional act that is not impressionally but reproductively conscious as the modification of another act. If, as in the first view, the remembering is understood as a present intentional act that relates itself to an earlier (perceptual) act, then the earlier act appears as that which is objectively meant in the memory, and the remembering threatens to transform itself into a reflection. According to the second view, the earlier act is neither intentionally meant nor somehow presently given but merely intentionally implied in the presentified givenness of the past *object*. The intentional act of remembering directed toward the (past) appearances of the object is not experienced impressionally in inner consciousness but reproductively. As reproductive consciousness, inner consciousness is thus the consciousness of a modificational connection between two acts and not the consciousness of an act that directs itself toward another act. This second view is for Husserl, despite its greater plausibility, not without its problems. For it entails that there is an inner consciousness that is both present, that is to say, impressional, as well as reproductive, whereas otherwise Husserl consistently regarded impression and reproduction as opposites. As an inner consciousness of an earlier act it is a matter of a reproductive and not an impressional consciousness of this act, although, according to Husserl's general theory, as a present inner consciousness it must nevertheless have the form of an impressional consciousness.

A solution to this difficulty cannot be attempted here, for this would demand extensive consideration of the basic questions of Husserl's analysis of time-consciousness and the forms of ego-participation operative in it. We will encounter again, in a sharpened form, this difficulty concerning the understanding of the presentifying reproduction and its modified performance of a nonpresent presentation, this time in the context of Husserl's new determination of phantasy. According to this new theory phantasy is a reproductive consciousness of a presentation, that is to say, a reproductive modification that produces the modified in such a way that it modifies it. In this instance, it appears to be much more difficult to avoid the onset of a genuinely reproductive inner consciousness.

Phantasy and Reproductive Inner Consciousness

Husserl's new theory of phantasy is oriented by memory and no longer by pictorial consciousness or apparent perception. Phantasy as intuitive, reproductive presentification is best compared with a neutralized remembering which would not be related to a past perception of an object but to one that is both present and absent. Some years before, Husserl occasionally assumed that the phantasial, neutral hovering of an object is also implied in memory itself. This led him to the supposition that every memory is founded in a phantasy.[17] Hence a memory would be a phantasy in which the phantasized object is at the same time incorporated into the past and thereby posited as a past object. Before we move on to the characterization of the difference between phantasy and memory as two different types of reproductive modification, reference must be made to the fact that Husserl by no means puts into question the similarity between these two acts. A comparable emphasis on the kinship between phantasy and memory can also be found in Freud, in particular in the context of his analysis of screen-memory and the experience of *déjà vu*, in which phantasies and memories are mixed in such a way that they cannot be disentangled because of their structural similarity.[18] Phantasy and memory both seem to have the same special ability to lend themselves to a conscious representation of unconscious desires. It is thus evident once again that reproductive consciousness is characterized by a wholly unique affinity with the Unconscious and its presentifying appearance in consciousness.

For Husserl, the similarity between phantasy and memory lies above all in their distanced relation to an object that is merely presentified and thus not bodily present. In the case of memory, this distance is derived from the fact that its object belongs within the original context of an *earlier* act of perception. The presentification of a past object is the achievement of a reproduction that one could call a present repetition of an earlier act. In the case of phantasy the distanced relation to an object of the phantasy world comes to expression above all through the fact that one does not believe in the reality of this object, that is to say, one forestalls or neutralizes positing it as a real being. This absence of belief no longer results from the conflict between the perceptual world and the phantasy-world, for there can be no talk of a conflict as long as the phantasized does not extend into the perceptual world and gives itself out to be a supposed perception. Knowledge of the phantasy *qua* phantasy obviously belongs to the performance of phantasy itself. Phantasy knows itself as phantasy because it is an inner reproductive consciousness of a (quasi-) perception.

But what does this mean, and what does talk of "*reproduction*" mean in the case of phantasy? In phantasy, unlike memory, there is no *past* perception that is presently reproduced. Instead, a *present* perception is experienced as non-present or experienced as belonging to a life of phantasy because it is innerly performed in the mode of "as-if" or "quasi performance." Nevertheless, this phantasial reproduction of a non-present perception has in common with a memorial reproduction the fact that it gives itself as the modification of an original present perception. However, this "*modification*" used in the context of memory and phantasy does not have exactly the same meaning. Memory is the modification of an earlier perception which it bears within itself as reality in the manner of an intentional implication. Phantasy, by contrast, is the modification of a perception that is implied as a possible and not an actual act. In its phenomenological genesis memory presupposes a real experience of a remembered object while phantasy is only related to the mere possibility of a real experience of its object, a possibility that it freely creates.

Phantasy, as intuitive presentification, is therefore a productive form of reproduction. It is a modification that implies something unmodified which need not exist prior to or independently of this modification. It is a modified form of perception which indicates the possibility of a perception without presupposing its factual givenness. Hence, the reproductive modification that makes up the essence of phantasy does not explain how the presentifying phantasy is derivable from a present perception, but rather the other way around. In other words, this reproductive modification explains how phantasy implies the possibility of a perception.

However, it is not thereby contended that every perception presupposes an actual phantasy as the condition of its possibility. Just as phantasy is not derivable from a perception, so perception is not derivable from a phantasy. Nevertheless, it can be said both that the essence of a real perception is co-determined by the possibility of its phantasial modification and also that it belongs to the essence of a real phantasy that it implies by the possibility of an unmodified perception of its object. That is to say, an object can never be simultaneously both really perceived and really phantasized, even though it is nonetheless true that real perception implies the possibility of phantasy and that real phantasy implies the possibility of perception. Thus, phantasy and perception can never be reduced the one to the other, although they are still necessarily related to each other in the form of a relationship of modification. Husserl would certainly emphasize, in addition, that for perception phantasy signifies a negative possibility which is to be excluded and that perception is contained in phantasy as a positive possibility which is to be striven for. One can therefore claim that phantasy is the repressed of memory and that perception is the repressed of phantasy, even though for Husserl the "repression" would not in both cases have exactly the same meaning.

The reproductive consciousness operative in phantasy is also characterized by the possibility of a *distanced* and *symbolic* self-consciousness. This possibility is absent in the impressional inner consciousness operative in perception. Accordingly, perceptual consciousness, in which the subject immediately gives itself over to its drive to see, appears to be a type of loss of self (*Selbstverlust*) or, more precisely, a loss of the *distanced* self-representation (*Selbstdarstellung*) of drive. Regarded from this point of view, phantasy enjoys a privilege over perception, and there are therefore good grounds to doubt Husserl's prioritizing of perception over phantasy. Dreaming is a typical example of a symbolic self-representation of drive that is made possible by phantasy, but, of course, language is also one. If immediate, impressional inner consciousness were the only form of self-awareness, then it would be impossible to understand how man could become a speaking subject, which, in speaking—even before beginning to speak about itself—always already represents itself symbolically. Of course, it is not thereby claimed that dreaming and speaking are nothing other than a kind of phantasizing. But the possibility of language, and of the linguistic expression of perception in particular, appears to be inextricably interwoven with the possibility of phantasizing.

2. Freud's Concept of the Unconscious

This concept of a reproductive inner consciousness of intentional acts of consciousness, derived from Husserl's analysis of phantasy, opens up wholly new perspectives on Freud's concept of the Unconscious and its relationship to consciousness. According to Freud, the Unconscious expresses itself in intentional representations (*Vorstellungen*), "wishes," with which the subject cannot readily identify itself because they are *alien* to it. The *Unconscious's mode of appearance* corresponds exactly to the mode of appearing of phantasized lived experiences, that is, intentional acts that are imaginatively reproduced by inner consciousness. In contrast to perceptions, phantasized lived experiences do not really belong to the ego, although they also do not belong to any really alien ego. They do not order themselves into the ego's infinite nexus of experience but remain alien to it, although not as alien as the experiences of another subject. Thus, Freud's "*descriptive*" concept of the Unconscious corresponds exactly to Husserl's determination of the appearance of the presentified: in both cases it is a matter of something alien that belongs to the self but which the self cannot immediately lay claim to as a real presence.

The Unconscious and Its Modes of Appearance

This rapprochement between Freud's concept of the Unconscious and Husserl's analysis of phantasy, and the reproductive inner consciousness operative in it, also has the consequence that the conscious *expressions* of the Unconscious made possible through phantasy appear as a form of liberation from an immediate, impressional relation to self. As is well known, Freud subsequently refers to the fact that unconscious representations typically express themselves consciously in the form of phantasies and dreams. The creative freedom of reproductive inner consciousness remarked upon in the presentation of Husserl's analysis of phantasy should not therefore be understood as a liberation from instinctual drive but rather as opening up the possibility of its free, conscious presentation in the form of phantasies. The freedom issuing from the reproductive inner consciousness does not free one from instinctual drive but from the other form of inner consciousness, the impressional form of instinctually driven inner consciousness. Husserl's distinction between a reproductive and an impressional form of inner consciousness is therefore still situated within instinctually driven consciousness itself.

What is distinctive about impressional consciousness is that it lacks any distance between instinctual drive and intentional representations so that the subject is immediately and irremediably affected by its own representations. Because of this, impressional inner consciousness typically externalizes itself in the form of *Angst:* the affective reaction of the subject to the experience of its defenseless thrownness amid its own life. Reproductive inner consciousness, on the other hand, frees the subject from this anxious experience of itself; it makes possible a self-distanciation and symbolic self-representation and protects the subject from a traumatic affection by and through its own instinctual drives. *Angst,* as an experience of impressional inner consciousness, also has to be understood as a sign of a loss of both reproductive inner consciousness and the possibility of a symbolic representation of instinctual drive that it implies. By contrast, in phantasy-representations and dreams, instinctual drives or unconscious wishes can be freely lived out because these representations are not taken to be real and are only "quasi" experienced, that is, only performed "as if" they were real. Reproductive inner consciousness in a phantasy or a dream allows a distanced intercourse with an instinctual drive without which both the drive itself and the possibility of *Angst,* as the expression of immediate self-affection by the instinctual drive, would in the end be incomprehensible.

However, one will want to object that impressional inner consciousness is typically accompanied not by *Angst* but by the performance of a perception directed toward the real world. Husserl never speaks about *Angst;* instead, without further ado, he identifies impressional inner consciousness with the performative-consciousness of a presentational act. Nevertheless, the insight that our abandonment to the perception of the real world signifies at the same time a type of self-loss, and as such implies a form of the "Unconscious," was by no means foreign to him.[19] In the majority of instances this loss of a symbolic self-representation does not lead to *Angst* because it is compensated for by the achievement, and enrichment of, a relationship to the world. Heidegger has convincingly shown that *Angst* arises only if the relationship to the familiar world is put into question.[20]

Husserl's analysis of impressional inner consciousness allows us to better understand the possibility of such a reversal from contentment in the world to anxiety in the face of one's own life: in the abandonment to the world the ego is exposed to a doubly impressional immediate affection—from "inside" through its perceptual activity, and from the "outside" through the attraction exercised by objects in the world. If the world, as the harmonious and constantly confirmed horizon of experience, is put into question, then the subject is thrown back upon itself to the immediate experience of its empty and sense-less perceiving; *Angst* is the expression of this immediate and inescapable self-enclosure of one's own life. It is a fact familiar to all of us, which is also confirmed through research into schizophrenia, that the *Angst* originating from the loss of the world is compensated for through phantasies and delusions.[21] Accordingly, *Angst,* as the expression of an impressional inner consciousness, is the consequence of a double loss, the loss of the world as the possibility of a happy forgottenness of self as well as the loss of phantasy as the possibility of a distanced relation to self and symbolic self-representation.

We can therefore conclude that there are significant correspondences between Freud's "descriptive" concept of the Unconscious and Husserl's eidetic determination of phantasy as an act of intuitive presentification. Accordingly, the alien mode of appearance as well as the symbolic expression of the Freudian *Unconscious* can be understood as modes of a distinctive presentifying (*Phantasy-*) *consciousness.* The analysis of the modificational connection that joins phantasy to perception has also brought to light the fact that the symbolic representation of the Unconscious in dreams or language signifies a liberation from a purely impressional inner consciousness. The impressional consciousness tied to the performance of perception signifies a second concept of the Unconscious. This is above all characterized by the fact that it lacks the possibility of a symbolic self-representation. Nevertheless, this does not mean that it has no form of conscious expression. The Unconscious in the sense of impressional inner consciousness externalizes itself in the form of an affective representation and in the feeling of *Angst* in particular. Thus, nothing unconscious remains without appearance in consciousness; instead, there is a double—both representational and affective—form of conscious representation of the Unconscious. But it proved necessary to combine this (Freudian) description of a double form of representation of the Unconscious with the hypothesis of a double form of the Unconscious. Husserl's analysis of a twofold form of inner consciousness, that is, an impressional and a reproductive relation to intentional conscious lived experiences, makes it possible to cash out phenomenologically this hypothesis of a double concept of the Unconscious.

Husserl's determination of the connection between phantasy and perception can also serve as the point of departure for a phenomenological investigation of Freud's "*dynamic*" concept of the Unconscious. Both Freud's determination of psychic life as an unstable equilibrium in the field of tension between antagonistic forces and the resulting necessity of "*repression*" receive new illumination from Husserl's analysis of the "conflict" between perception and phantasy.[22] According to Husserl, perception and phantasy are necessarily related to each other in the manner of an "intentional implication" while each excludes the other from existing contemporaneously. Phantasy "represses" or "covers" (*verdeckt*) perception, and the perception of the real world reacts allergically to every uncontrolled mixing with phantasy. One can therefore justifiably state that pure perception implies a repression of phantasy. For Husserl and Freud the process of repression is a process of separation. Moreover, for Husserl this separation is necessary because phantasy and perception constantly threaten to contaminate each other just as much as for Freud the Unconscious and the conscious threaten to contaminate each other. In both Husserl and Freud repression is a process of the purification of consciousness and as such is an achievement of consciousness.

If the Unconscious is equated with the repressed and if perception represses phantasy just as phantasy represses perception, then this confirms once more that the Unconscious can have the form of both the reproductive inner consciousness operative in phantasy as well as the impressional inner consciousness operative in perception. Phantasy represses impressional inner consciousness as well as the *Angst* bound up with it, and perception represses reproductive inner consciousness and the appearing to oneself as alien that is in turn bound up with it. Considered from the point of view of the dynamic concept of the Unconscious, that is to say, repression, the Unconscious proves to be a relative or dialectical concept. The Unconscious, in the sense of reproductive inner consciousness, implies the onset of perception as the conscious, and the

Unconscious, in the sense of impressional inner consciousness, implies the onset of phantasy as the conscious. Nothing is unconscious in itself; instead, every-thing unconscious is unconscious in relation to something conscious. What the content of the Unconscious signifies in each case is determined by the form of what it posits as conscious.

Instinctual Drive and Its Representations

However, it is well known that for Freud the core of his metapsychological observations is formed by the "*economic*" concept of the Unconscious and not by the "descriptive" or "dynamic" concept. Conscious and unconscious repre-sentations are neither distinguishable by their content nor primarily through their own forms of intentionality but by the way in which they *represent in-stinctual drives*. Freud is of the opinion that, in the first place, instinctual drives necessarily cathect unconscious representations which can then eventually pene-trate through into consciousness. Thus, all conscious representations have their origin in unconscious representations, and hence "consciousness" for Freud is an epiphenomenon of the Unconscious, albeit an admittedly mysterious one.

Hence, psychic life has its origin in the tension-loaded and primary somatic energy of instinctual drive which attaches itself to intentional (unconscious and [pre-] conscious) psychic representations, using them as a means to discharge any unpleasurable tension. This "abreaction" of tension occurs in "uncon-scious" representations under the form of a "*primary process*" in which instinc-tual drive cathects different representations without regard for logical coherence or spatio-temporal order and connects them together in a nonrealistic manner by means of "displacements" (*Verschiebungen*) and "condensations" (*Verdi-chtungen*). In the primary process a merely hallucinatory representation of the object suffices to satisfy instinctual drive. Dreams are the best examples of a primary process of this kind in which an unconscious wish fulfills itself through hallucinated images without bowing to the constraints of reality. The "con-scious" perception of reality is likewise still directed by the demands of inner instinctual drive even when they demand the total abandonment of one's self to the attractions of the external world. Actually perceived objects thereby also make themselves suitable for the satisfaction of instinctual drive, a satisfaction that has the form of a "*secondary process.*"[23] This conscious secondary process is steered by a "reality principle," which, however, does not have to block the path of drive-satisfaction and thus can wholly put itself in the service of the "pleasure principle." In contrast, a scientific-objective perception of reality de-mands the price of a subjective renunciation of instinctual drive or, in other words, a sublimation of the drive's aim.

In addition, this "economic" determination of psychic life as both the rep-resentative of instinctual drive and the satisfaction of drive (in the form of either an unconscious primary process or a [pre-] conscious secondary process) can be given a new determination and foundation from within the confines of the Husserlian determination of consciousness. How instinctual drive comes to representation (*Vorstellung*) and how precisely one is to conceive its cathexis of the representation is a great riddle in Freud. In contrast, Husserl's inner consciousness concerns from the very start both drive and its representation in one. It is at the same time an anonymous self-affection of subjective life (drive) and a sensing of egoic intentional experiences (representation). Inner consciousness is both the driving motor of intentional representations as well as the unthematic awareness of their performance. Thus this relationship of reciprocal dependency and inseparable interweaving between drives and representation indicates not only how instinctual drive comes to be represented but also that there can be no drive without representation.

Freud's distinction between primary and secondary processes can also be newly interpreted from within the framework of Husserl's analysis of consciousness and once again with reference to the double form of inner consciousness. It is on account of its inner consciousness that the subject has the possibility of behaving toward its own intentional acts in both the manner of a distanced, reproductive self-relation as well as in the manner of an immediate, impressional self-affection. Freud's conception of a *primary process* operative in dreaming corresponds to Husserl's conception of the reproductive inner consciousness operative in phantasy. Husserl is obviously not blind to the fact that phantasy has a poetic freedom that elevates it above the constraints of logic and reality. Thus it is not surprising that in Husserl's description of phantasy and memory the consideration of "displacement" and "condensation," which for Freud are characteristic of the primary process, is by no means absent.[24]

Freud's determination of the *secondary process* can also be rethought from within Husserl's analysis of the impressional inner consciousness operative in perception. The reality principle that directs perception implies the possible non-pleasure of an immediate affection by real objects as well as the possible pain occasioned by their loss. Even though its pleasure premium is dependent on reality and is therefore constantly at risk, perceptual consciousness does not necessarily have to be unpleasurable. Nevertheless, perceptual consciousness always faces the threat of a loss of reality and thus also, in the background, the threat of the total non-pleasure of unmediated, traumatic affection by the burden of one's own life, a non-pleasure bound up with the feeling of *Angst*. For Husserl, perception, as a secondary process, also implies a repression of the primary process of phantasy together with its accompanying possibilities of developing pleasurable representations and of a distanced staging of one's own life.

Against the background of the difference between reproductive and impressional inner consciousness, the phenomenological determination of the primary and secondary processes has an important advantage over Freud's, in that it makes the interweaving and reversibility between both processes more clearly visible. Thus the relation between the primary and secondary processes (Freud's economic determination of the distinction between the Unconscious and the [pre-] conscious) is not a relation of one-sided derivability but of equi-primordiality and of irreducible difference. Pure primary or pure secondary processes are abstract limit-concepts for a subjective life in which perception negatively implies (repressed) phantasy as much as phantasy implies (repressed) perception. It is on account of its inner consciousness that the subject constantly has the possibility of comporting itself toward its own intentional representations both in the manner of a distanced, reproductive self-relation as well as in the manner of an immediate, impressional self-affection. However, both these modes of comportment cannot be simultaneously adopted by consciousness, and so each is accompanied by its own form of the Unconscious.

One consequence of the extensive correspondence between Freud's determination of the primary and secondary processes and Husserl's determination of the connection between phantasy and perception is that there is finally no reason to identify the Unconscious exclusively with the primary process. The Unconscious need not necessarily or in every instance be the phantasizing which, with its alien self-appearing of subjective life, is repressed in the perceptual process and its relation to reality. If the subject lives in the primary process operative in phantasy, then in this form of life the secondary process operative in perception is repressed and unconscious. In dreams, the Unconscious is not so much the wish that fulfills itself according to the lawfulness of the primary process as it is the waking life directed toward reality. Dreams repress waking life which nevertheless in turn presents itself, though absently and unconsciously, as an inhibited possibility.

Finally, one should not conceal the fact that our understanding of the primary and secondary processes does some violence to Freud's theory of *instinctual drives*. Because we connect the primary process with the reproductive inner consciousness we also attribute to it the possibility of a distanced self-presentation of instinctual drive. Freud does relate the primary process to dreams too, but he emphasizes at the same time that, in dreams, instinctual drive achieves an immediate, undistanced satisfaction through a hallucinated object. It is also true that the secondary process is understood by us as an immediate and sometimes traumatic instinctually driven self-affection, while Freud emphasizes the distance that is imposed by the satisfaction of instinctual drive via the detour through a real object. However, this opposition between our observations and those of Freud does not imply a contradiction because immediate self-affection by no means excludes the possibility that this impressional self-affection operates at the same time as the awareness of an intentional representation directed toward reality. Similarly, reproductive inner consciousness operative in phantasy can, at the same time, be both a distanced self-presentation of instinctual drive as well as an immediate relation to a hallucinatory object of pleasure liberated from the constraints of reality. However, the opposition to Freud is not thereby completely abolished. This is because for a phenomenology of presentational and presentifying consciousness, the Freudian concept of an instinctually driven relation to real and hallucinatory objects is only approachable in consciousness through the determination of instinctual drive as immediate or distanced self-awareness. Here it must remain an open question whether this also means that in fact no purely economically determined instinctual drive can exist.

In summary, it has been established that the Freudian Unconscious is a concept with many meanings which are connected to quite different phenomenological findings: the Unconscious is a *phenomenon* that does not allow itself to be integrated into the harmonious course of conscious experience; it is the *self-forgetting* abandonment to perceived reality; it is the *repressed* phantasy or perception; it is the distanced *self-representation* of instinctual drive, for example, in dreaming or in language; it is the pleasure of *liberation from the constraints of reality;* it is the *primary process* that satisfies itself with a hallucinated object of pleasure. In both Freud and Husserl the unitary ground of these different phenomena of the Unconscious must be sought in instinctual drive. Whereas Freud is satisfied with claiming that instinctual drive is located at the threshold between the somatic and the psychic, Husserl's analysis of inner consciousness offers the possibility of understanding instinctual drive as the self-affection of the subjective stream of life. In addition, the reproductive inner consciousness operative in phantasy allows for an understanding of the distanced and possibly symbolic self-representation of instinctual drive. In contrast, the impressional inner consciousness of the performance of an act of perception is bound up with an instinctually driven life (*triebhaften Leben*) that is immediately experienced under the form of affects and, in limit cases, expresses itself in the feeling of *Angst*. Thus neither instinctual drive nor the various phenomena of the Unconscious can be understood independently of consciousness and especially of inner consciousness.

Thus a phenomenological understanding of the phenomena of the Unconscious analyzed by Freud implies a critique of every attempt to determine the Unconscious in total independence from consciousness or as its hidden origin. Hence the "*topographical*" concept of the Unconscious, rejected by Freud himself, is untenable: the Unconscious is not simply a psychic process that operates in a different location to consciousness, nor could it exist fully separated from consciousness. The (Brentanian) concept of the Unconscious as an intentional consciousness that is no longer accompanied by an inner consciousness must also be rejected. We have seen that inner consciousness is by no means a reflective self-consciousness but an awareness of the accomplishment of an intentional act of perception or phantasy. It is a self-affection of consciousness that has an instinctually driven character, and as such it is the common ground of all the phenomena of the Unconscious. Finally, Freud's economic determination of the Unconscious as a primary process appeared questionable to us unless it is combined with the phenomenologically understood process of repression.

Nevertheless, a phenomenological determination of the Unconscious in its relation to a concealed, impressional, or reproductive inner consciousness es-

sentially implies less a critique of Freud's account than a reflection on its presuppositions. In the end, our phenomenological considerations were nothing
but a meditation on Freud's own determination of the Unconscious as an alien
form of *psychic life* that explodes the traditional concept of consciousness.
Freud's consistently held emphasis on the psychic character of the Unconscious
forces the philosopher interested in the Unconscious into a new determination
of consciousness and not to a premature rejection of every philosophy of consciousness. A new determination of consciousness on the lines of Freud's concept of the Unconscious must make comprehensible how consciousness can appear to itself as something alien and how it behaves toward the Unconscious
in such a way that it can neither exclude it nor immediately and completely
appropriate it. The phenomenological determination of phantasy as a process
in which something alien or non-present presently appears as such and in
which one's own self achieves a distanced and alienated self-awareness and self-
representation proved to be a fruitful point of departure for the still incomplete
fulfillment of this task.

Notes

An earlier, German version of this text was published as "Husserls Begriff des Phantasie-
bewusstseins als Fundierung von Freuds Begriff des Unbewussten," in *Grundlinien der Ver-
nunftkritik,* ed. C. Jamme (Frankfurt am Main: Suhrkamp, 1997), 277–306.

  1. Cf. P.-L. Assoun, *Freud, la Philosophie et les Philosophes* (Paris: Presses Universitaires
de France, 1976), esp. 9–44.

  2. "*Trieb*" is translatable as "drive," "instinct," "instinctual drive," etc. While Husserl
commentators have so far generally used "drive" to render Husserl's "*Trieb*," the standard
edition of Freud in English generally translates Freud's use of the noun in the singular by
pluralizing it to "instincts" (as in the title of Freud's essay "Trieb und Triebschicksale" rendered as "Instincts and Their Vicissitudes"). The latter practice, while implicitly acknowledg-
ing that for Freud drive is differentiable, fails to capture the connotations of anonymous,
impersonal, and indeterminate *force* implied by both Freud's use of the singular term and the
obviously intimate connection for Freud between unconscious "drive" and the theory of the
impersonal Id ("*Es*"). In the following, irrespective of whether the context is the discussion of
Freud or Husserl, the term "*Trieb*" and "*der Trieb*" has been rendered, depending on context, mostly as "instinctual drive," sometimes by "drive," and only occasionally as "drives."
"*Triebmässig*" has been translated throughout as "instinctually driven" (translator's note).

  3. Cf. S. Freud, *A Note on the Unconscious in Psychoanalysis* (1913), Standard Edition
of Collected Works (C.W.), ed. J. Strachey, 12: 255–66, and especially *The Unconscious* (1915),
C.W., 14: 166ff.

  4. Cf. S. Freud, *On the Grounds for Detaching a Particular Syndrome from Neurasthenia
under the Description "Anxiety Neurosis"* (1895), C.W., 3: 90–115; *Introductory Lectures on Psychoanalysis* (Lect. XXV) (1917), C.W., 16: 392–408; *Inhibitions, Symptoms, Anxiety* (1924),

C.W., 20: esp. 87–156; *New Introductory Lectures on Psychoanalysis* (Lect. XXXII), C.W., 22: esp. 81–95.

5. F. Brentano, *Psychology from an Empirical Standpoint*, ed. O. Kraus, English edition ed. L. McAlister, trans. A. Rancurello, D. Terrel, and L. McAlister (London: Routledge, 1973), book 2, chap. 2, §§2–13.

6. The standard translation of Husserl's "*Vergegenwärtigung*" is presentification, though "presentation," "representation," and "re-presentation" are also sometimes used (translator's note).

7. As well as considering phantasy and pictorial consciousness this important lecture also deals with the themes of perception, attention, and time. The part concerned with the analysis of phantasy and pictorial consciousness is published in full in *Phantasie*, 1–108.

8. Texts from 1909 onwards, in *Phantasie*, esp. no. 8 (265–69).

9. Texts from 1911–12, in *Phantasie*, esp. no. 14 (301–12), Beilage XXXV (320–28), no. 15 (329–422).

10. *Phantasie*, 18ff.

11. *Phantasie*, 58ff.

12. Cf. R. Bernet, "Einleitung," in E. Husserl, *Texte zur Phänomenologie des inneren Zeitbewusstseins (1893–1917)* (Hamburg: Meiner, 1985), XLVff.

13. *Psychology from an Empirical Standpoint*, 128.

14. Cf. R. Bernet, "Einleitung," XXXIIIff.

15. Cf. R. Bernet, *La vie du sujet* (Paris: Presses Universitaires de France, 1994), 321ff.

16. Cf. esp. *Phantasie*, no. 9, 272; no. 14, 301–12; Beilage XXXV, 320–28; no. 15, 330ff. (and notes) and also 339ff.

17. Cf. *Phantasie*, no. 3, 212–17; no. 5, 229–23; no. 11, 286–88.

18. Cf. R. Bernet, "Imagination et fantasme," in J. Florence et al., *Psychanalyse. L'homme et ses destins* (Paris: Peeters, Louvain, 1993), pp. 191–206.

19. Cf. *Phantasie*, no. 20: 574.

20. M. Heidegger, *Being and Time*, trans. J. Macquarrie and E. Robinson (Oxford: Blackwell, 1962), §40.

21. Cf. R. Bernet, "Délire et réalité dans la psychose," *Etudes phénoménologiques*, no. 15 (Bruxelles: Ousia, 1992): 25–54.

22. For Freud's concept of repression cf. esp. *Repression* (1915), C.W., 14: 141–58, and *The Unconscious* (1915), C.W., 14: 159–215. Husserl also speaks occasionally of "repression": cf., e.g., *Phantasie*, no. 20: 580f.

23. On Freud's theory of the primary and secondary process cf. especially *The Interpretation of Dreams* (1900), C.W., 5: 588–610, and *The Unconscious* (1915), C.W., 14: 186–89.

24. Cf. *Passive Synthesis*, 192ff.

PART IV

Intersubjectivity and the Question of the World

9

World as Horizon

Donn Welton

THERE ARE A number of ways in which one can place Husserl in contrast to what I would call the standard interpretation,[1] but the one that is perhaps the most surprising is the claim that Husserl's most enduring and promising insight is not his characterization of subjectivity in terms of a theory of intentionality—as groundbreaking and radical as that is—but his characterization of the world. It is this notion that keeps Husserl and the Heidegger of *Being and Time,* contrary to their own acute feelings of difference, within the same field of discourse.[2] And it is this notion, once suitably modified, that comes to displace that of subjectivity in the work of Derrida and Foucault.

Of course, this first contrapositioning of subjectivity and world is simply false, that is, already transcended by the phenomenological concept of world. The world, as we will suggest, is a nexus of significance. Insofar as world is a nexus of significance, "subjectivity is unfolded and deployed in it."[3] Our thesis must be formulated differently. Kant had already shown the founding function of transcendental subjectivity; Husserl's most enduring discovery was how a transcendental characterization of subjectivity and a transcendental characterization of world mediate each other.

At the same time there is little agreement as to just how "world" is to be understood, firstly, in the context of Husserl's elaboration of a contrast between static and genetic phenomenology, and, secondly, in the context of a pragmatic semantics (of the type that we find in Brandom and Habermas, for example). This essay will keep the first on the margins of its concerns in order to provide not so much a critique but rather the foundation of a critique of the second. My wager, which I can introduce for consideration only by turning directly to the way that the notion of world functions in a phenomenological semantics, is that pragmatic semantics works with an implicit reduction of world, one that undercuts its horizonal character. The analysis of world that I would like to offer is not so much an exposition of Husserl's concept as my own elaboration and appropriation of it.[4]

The phenomenological problem of the world finds its origins in the fact that each scientific attempt to conceptualize the world rests upon an attitude that is capable only of apprehending the world as some sort of natural complex. This attitude, according to Husserl, is called the natural attitude. In the natural attitude, the world as world withdraws. In every scientific discussion the world is silent.

The sciences do not apprehend the world falsely but objectivistically, that is, they are capable of apprehending the world only as something having the character of an object. What confirms this apprehension is just that the world does appear in this way. But what makes possible the world appearing in this way is not itself an appearance. The worldliness of the world can never be manifest as something having the character of an object and, therefore, never as the field of an "objective" investigation.

Philosophy can also be held captive in the natural attitude. In this case, the world that so appears becomes itself a semblance (*Schein*). One of the first, yet uncontrived misunderstandings of world was to treat it as something like a natural environment or a socio-historical reality or the totality or whole of all such worlds. But the second book of Husserl's *Ideas*[5] already alerts us to the mistake: natural environments, psychophysical domains, and social or cultural milieus are to be treated as "regional ontologies" and, as such, are situated within the world.

If one avoids this first mistake, one falls easily into a second: the world is the totality of all regional worlds. But the first book of *Ideas*[6] contradicts this interpretation: the concept of totality is purely formal. As such this concept of the world is not transcendental but rather stands in need of transcendental underpinnings, as Heidegger understood better than any of his contemporaries. Husserl's later transformation of his initial notion of world into that of life-world strengthened his struggle against the positivist misinterpretation of the concept of the world.

In an effort to capture this difference between an objectivistic and a transcendental concept of the world, Husserl and then Heidegger characterized the world as *horizon* and horizon as a nexus of *significance* that situates not only our multiple discourses about different regions but also the regions themselves.

But what does this mean? What do we mean by nexus of significance? Does it have an internal structure? How are our more structured accounts of various regions and the various regions themselves related to our everyday talk about matters at hand? And what might first open up the world as world experientially? Expressed differently, how can one break through the natural attitude?

I will attempt to answer these questions in three steps.

Dissonance and Disintegration

As we stand just months after the collapse of the World Trade Center, let me get at the notion of world by recalling the experiences that many of us went through as that event unfolded. I begin with a statement uttered six days after September 11 by one of the firefighters from Indiana who came to help:

> Thousands of people got up and went to work.
> Now they are no more.
> And we can smell the death.

Nothing matches these three short sentences in capturing the sense in which the events were so utterly overwhelming. As they began to gradually unfold, what we first experienced was really a sense of *dissonance*. When a friend hears on the radio as he was driving into work that the first tower had been hit, he responds, "Well, that was really stupid," and shakes his head in disbelief at a commercial pilot who would be so dumb as to fly his plane into the tower. For him the news produces irritation, perhaps sadness, but the event still keeps most of its coherence and thus its distance. This tenuous resolution, however, flew apart in the face of ongoing events, which by this point were being broadcast over television, not just in the States but internationally as well. The second tower erupts in flames as we watch a second plane being driven directly into the building. It begins to burn, people are seen clinging to the sides of the tower, a woman waves a handkerchief out of a window countless stories above the pavement, and then the second tower collapses, sending people frantically running through the streets in sheer terror.

Dissonance is always organized teleologically by unity, by the anticipation of a coming resolution. The content of one momentary phase is connected to that of the next in what Husserl in one of his lecture manuscripts calls "cohesive" or "integral togetherness" (*Zusammengehörigkeit*).[7] An event may be different from what we have experienced before, but it takes place within a stable and familiar world and eventually becomes integrated. But as the events of September 11 unfold, dissonance devolves into *disintegration*. For most, the images of the second plane being deliberately driven into the second tower mark the moment when the meaning of the event suddenly and violently shifts and ceases to cohere. With the collapse of the second tower the world itself literally flies part.

But how are we to understand what we mean by world here?

Fields and Context

Let us take another segment, from one who saw the collapse of the two towers as he, overwhelmed by sorrow, is being interviewed by the BBC:

> There are people jumping out of windows.
> I saw 13 or 14 people jumping.

These two sentences function as *claims* in which a horrible state of affairs is presented to us. I call them claims for the simple reason that they are proposed not just as descriptions but descriptions that are true; that is, they are descriptions that purport to present facts that actually took place. They are not offered as segments of an imaginative story or of a poem or of a prayer. Neither is this a case of using descriptions to coordinate our efforts to build a log cabin, nor, perhaps, a case of chatting as we pass away the evening after such labors. Rather, a different interest is in play, one controlled by the obligation to tell the truth, to offer a direct account both of the events taking place and of what the speaker himself observed.

We have spoken of claims presenting facts, but how are we to account for this? This question arises because claims do not just open facts to view, do not just enable us to encounter facts. They also present things from a certain perspective by offering a certain "take" on or interpretation of the matter at hand. They carry a conceptual organization of their own that contributes to the way things are uncovered. How are we to understand this?

A somewhat standard answer to this question, as we might find in Frege or Strawson, would introduce a distinction between meaning and reference and then analyze the different ways that logical subjects and logical predicates function in propositions. Once the sentence is cast in the canonical form of *S is p,* the meaning of the predicate-term in particular becomes construed as a concept that either sorts or characterizes the object(s) denoted by the logical subject. But notice that there is already a process of reflection and clarification in play here that contributes to our construing predicates as concepts and concepts as ideal entities. Because of this process the meaning of the predicate-term of a claim is framed as a *concept* whose content—which includes the markers that an object would have to possess to fall under its scope—is determined by a relationship of *logical entailment* to yet other concepts and claims. Concepts, in turn, are situated in *disciplinary* and eventually *scientific fields* with various frames of entailment controlling the concepts and claims forming such fields. To say that objects are presented from a certain conceptual perspective by claims simply means, then, that they, being set apart or picked out by the logical subject, are either sorted or characterized by these predicates and thereby integrated into *contestable* fields. This is the discourse of textbooks. A type of critical reflection is already in play. At this level of reflection, what makes such concepts "objective" and "rigorous," as Husserl once labeled them, is the fact that they are rule governed. While field dependent, they are context independent in the sense that they are not "occasional" or "inexact" terms. And this is precisely what rigorous discourse strives for.

What generally goes unnoticed in this type of analysis, however, is that claims are not primitive or irreducible ways of speaking from which all others are derived. They are themselves the result of specific transformations of a much broader group of declarative sentences that also function descriptively. There are countless situations in which we exchange sentences having the form *S is p* that are not concerned with issues of correctly representing facts but rather with directing, controlling, enhancing, discouraging, curtailing, implementing, and facilitating our working together. This is the language that carries our practical involvement in situations. Like "gandy" workers on the railroad, we "sing" as we shift and realign the track. Like farm women, we "sing" as we harvest the rice. In these situations, our descriptions themselves function much more like tools that allow us to work with others in tilling the soil, building a house, or maintaining the railroad than like mirrors that reflect the world. They present rather than represent. They "unfold" rather than "enfold."

Notice that the speaker is now reporting sometime after the fact. The claim still presents the fact, but now it is a fact that by being past is absent. Placing the modal difference between absent and present on the side of what is presented spares us the mistake of saying that since the referent is now absent the string must refer to an ideal content or meaning that is itself present and somehow stands as proxy for or projects what is absent. We have two components: the description and the fact (absent or present). Only in the case of claims can we speak of three components, namely, the well-formed sentence being used by the speaker as a claim, the propositional content that forms the meaning of the sentence, and the referent or the fact (present or absent) which it presents.[8]

To better understand the difference between descriptions and claims, however, is to understand how the latter are derived from the former. Generally, it is when we *interrupt* the otherwise seamless flow of descriptions facilitating our involvement in situations and *reflect* upon what is being proposed by the speaker that we can isolate a description as a claim. This sometimes explicit, sometimes implicit distancing and reflection is operative in any report that is taken as a proposition. There might be any number of reasons for doing this. Perhaps the state of affairs presented in the speaker's description is at odds with what we experienced or what we know to be the case. Our normal believing, accepting attitude is replaced by questioning. Perhaps the description is offered in response to a journalist, as in our example, who is already asking about what we in fact saw, who is already asking us to give her or him reports that tell the truth. Perhaps the description itself is so alarming, also in our example, that we are immediately overwhelmed and cannot believe or go along with what we are hearing. Or perhaps the sentence is simply muddled. In each of these cases the description becomes reframed as a claim, as a proposition being offered by the speaker, which we then can interrogate in terms of its meaning and then its reference. The difference between conceptual content and reference, and then the manifestation of the propositional content as "ideal," is itself spawned pragmatically in response to questions or issues that arise from efforts to engage the world truthfully.

We must always keep in mind that descriptions are segments of speech, utterances offered in dialogue. Claims are derived from our reflection upon descriptions, and only then can claims be characterized as having a certain propositional content being proposed by the speaker. It is this content that can be dismantled and diagnosed.

At this point in the analysis, however, we must move with great caution. From what we have just said, we can legitimately conclude that a claim, which we have identified through reflection and analysis, is actually a description being used as a claim. To analyze the way claims refer is to articulate the way speakers can use descriptions to refer truthfully. But it would be a fatal philosophical error to assume that the rules governing propositional content also set the conditions for our *using* the description to begin with and, then, the conditions for descriptions in general to have a connection to the world.[9] This would be a classic philosophical error: one takes the *post hoc* as *propter hoc*. It would be to assume that the rules regulating the game of football were also constitutive of the linguistic competence and the discussions of the players.

But this only leads us to the nasty question of how to characterize a notion of meaning that is appropriate to descriptions.

Many times the approach we take determines the outcome. Given our tentative distinction between descriptions and claims, we should begin not with the semantic question of representation, of the relationship between propositional content and facts, but with speech-acts as integrated into everyday actions, and then look for the way in which those actions engage our surrounding world. Taking a clue from Heidegger,[10] let me call this involvement (*Bewandnis*) and let us view its articulation in speech as designed not to represent facts to a thinker from a distance but to get a grip on or unfold those things with which we are engaged. Perhaps we can say here that the *Zeigen* of involved speech is always a kind of *Greifen,* not *Begreifen.* At this level, speech is what facilitates and even enhances our involvement. To trace the meaning of words and sentences here is to engage in a linguistic study of the patterns of their use as we, for example, clear a site, dig a foundation, assemble building materials, and then frame and enclose the shell of what will be our new dwelling.

These patterns of usage can be gleaned by a study of various paradigmatic and syntagmatic relations that signs have to other possible terms that might be substituted in the string.

- Paradigmatic relations are defined by what could be substituted for a term under a particular syntactic marker: *window* stands in this relation to such terms as *skylight, glass, door,* etc.
- Syntagmatic relations are the lateral relations that a given term has to others in different grammatical slots: in our example *windows* stands in this relation to *people* and *jump* as well as to other terms that could function paradigmatically for them.

Whatever identity the meaning of a term has is internally connected to differences with other terms across these two axes. But these are not nodes in a formal system but terms in use, and so these patterns are understood functionally as possible schemes of differentiation. Accordingly, the tie of one sign to another is one of *differential implication,* not logical entailment.[11] The patterns of use reflect patterns of engaged intentions or "takings" exchanged by those at work. Before we have disciplinary fields we have mappings of difference that facilitate our movement through a space of action. Descriptions "articulate" our field of action and thus provide us with our bearings. And they also force matters to stand out: everyday predicates make differential "cuts" in matters or open up the "folds" of things gathered together in a type of understanding that Heidegger calls *Umsicht,* circumspection.[12] Even as a description, the BBC report puts us in a bind, for it creates a tension at the level of how we act. To take something as a window is to take it as something through which we do not jump. To take something as a tall building is to take it as something out of which we do not leap.

To be sure, there is an easy and natural transition from differential schemata to concepts, from patterns of implication to patterns of logical entailment. The *differences* that descriptions make can become *distinctions* that we employ and then argue for in claims. And this is precisely where the notion of rule finds its proper place: by specifying a basic or essential content to the concept, they give us the conditions under which an object falls under that concept, and then, at another level of analysis, the conditions under which a claim can be true.

Summarizing this section, we can say that we have discovered, behind our claims organized by an interest in (re)presenting disciplinary fields, descriptions motivated by an interest in engaging and acting upon the world. The horizon, not only situating but making possible meaningful descriptions, is what I want to call *context*. Context is borne by speech that is practically oriented. It consists of *differential schemata*, indicated by the contrasting use of terms, that are the meaning of descriptions. They account for the way in which we approach the environment in which we are engaged.

Context and Background

We have just suggested that we can get at the notion of context by treating patterns of how signs are used in descriptions as indications of how we cognitively approach or grasp an environment with which we are involved. Context, however, does not stand alone. In addition to our speaking about this environment, we are also engaged with it bodily. There are not only acts of speaking but also actions in which we take what is spoken about to hand and use it practically. Actions can "constitute" the determinations of things apart from speech: placing a rock in front of an open door "unfolds" its significance as a door stop; the action of taking the round stick in hand and using it to hit a ball is what determines it as a bat. And even circumspective perception (*Umsicht*), it seems, employs schemata of discrimination that are not yet schemata of differentiation. Let us follow both Husserl and Heidegger and call this kind of significance *sense* (*Sinn*), and let us at the outset not confuse it with *meaning* (*Bedeutung*), which was the focus of our analysis of propositions and descriptions. We are on familiar territory here and so can be even briefer.

The senses of things, I am suggesting, arise in the course of our bodily interaction with them. While this interaction is often, perhaps usually, directed by speech, as we just described, it does not require this, nor is the significance and determinacy of things ready-to-hand itself produced by the way they are taken in descriptions. Rather than looking to differential schemata, which we have linked to our speaking about the world, there is another level of organization that is in play, one suggested by the actions of the body and the way perception itself is organized. Space allows me to suggest only two facets of this fascinating and complex level of constitution:

1. The interplay of profiles and then of profiles and the object as a whole is organized in such a way that in perception the object as a whole exceeds whatever profile or set of profiles mediates its presence as it is itself simultaneously given in and through them. Profiles point to yet other profiles not because they are signs that undergo some kind of conceptual interpretation, but because of a very different relationship, that of *indication*. As one profile indicates another, the concatenation of profiles indicates the object as a whole. What accounts for this organization is the fact that the object has a sense, and this sense is what requires us to treat profiles not as givens that are somehow manifest on the stage of a passive mind but internally linked to one engaging the object that appears. The inclusion of the perceiver, naturally forgotten, is required by the very interplay of profile and object.

2. Profiles, however, are also *perspectives*. This means that the one engaging the object is an embodied perceiver. Because the perceiver has a body, the perceptual field exercises "affective" powers upon the perceiver, on one hand, and is "effectively" engaged by the perceiver, on the other. As exercising affective powers over the perceiver, the perceived object calls forth certain "aesthetic" syntheses or what Husserl would have called "passive syntheses," that account for the temporal, spatial, and material determinacy of perceptual objects.[13] Merleau-Ponty spoke of this level of affective, perceptual organization in terms of the interplay of figure and ground and the *Gestalten* that regulate that interplay. At the same time, the perceiver takes up a bodily position that enables the perception of the object by a series of accommodations and movements relative to the object. Even the stationary eye, Husserl says at one point, is a mode of the "I can." As the locus of movement, the perceiver is *Leib*, lived-body, the body understood not as object but a repertoire of possible bodily action. The lived-body consists of motor programs, flexible and corrigible, that account for the way the body engages environments and then for the way it manipulates, uses, and sometimes abuses the things it takes to hand. Once established, these programs become habits. We can call them *body schemata*.

The stable interplay of styles of perceptual assimilation and discrimination, on the one hand, and schemata of bodily movement and accommodations, on the other, account for the way that there is a constant habitual world in and against which our particular actions take place. I want to call this world *background*.

Perhaps now we have at least a rough outline of a theory of the world that does not confuse it with environments or disciplinary fields. The background forms a horizon of senses internally connected to possible schemata of action; their interplay accounts for the "hands on" or practical significance things have for us. Context forms a horizon of meaning, of possible ways of differentially describing the matters of the world with which we are engaged. To cast this in terms of their interconnections, disciplinary fields are always situated in a context, and contexts are always arrayed within a background. The world, phenomenologically characterized as horizon, consists of context and background.

With this we return to our starting point: it was not a particular fact or a string of facts within the world, but the world itself, the very context and background of our everyday life, that came unraveled on September 11:

> Thousands of people got up and went to work.
> Now they are no more.
> And we can smell the death.

Notes

This paper is a highly revised version of the first part of Donn Welton, "Violence and Meaning," in *Fenomenologia Hoje II: Significado e Linguagem*, ed. Ricardo Timm de Souza and Nythamar Fernandes de Oliveira, *Coleçao Filosofia* 149 (2002), 497–517.

1. See Donn Welton, *The Other Husserl: The Horizons of Transcendental Phenomenology* (Bloomington: Indiana University Press, 2001), 393–404, for a characterization of the standard interpretation.

2. See Welton, *The Other Husserl*, chaps. 13 and 14.

3. Klaus Held, "Horizont und Gewohnheit. Husserl's Wissenschaft der Lebenwelt," in *Krise der Wissenschaften—Wissenschaft der Krisis? Wiener Tagungen zur Phänomenologie,* ed. Helmuth Vetter (Frankfurt am Main: Peter Lang, 1998), 11.

4. See the last three chapters of Welton, *The Other Husserl*, for a fuller account.

5. Edmund Husserl, *Ideen zu einer reinen Phänomenologie und phänomenologischen Philosophie*, vol. 2: *Phänomenologische Untersuchungen zur Konstitution*, ed. Marly Biemel, *Husserliana*, vol. 4 (The Hague: Martinus Nijhoff, 1952); *Ideas Pertaining to a Pure Phenomenology and to a Phenomenological Philosophy*, book 2: *Studies in the Phenomenology of Constitution*, trans. Richard Rojcewicz and Andre Schuwer, *Collected Works*, vol. 3 (Dortrecht: Kluwer, 1989). It was written around 1912 but not published until 1952.

6. *Ideen zu einer reinen Phänomenologie und phänomenologischen Philosophie*. Buch 1: *Allgemeine Einführung in die reine Phänomenologie, Jahrbuch für Philosophie und phänomenologische Forschung,* Band 2 (Halle a.d.S.: Niemeyer, 1913), erste Teil; *Ideas Pertaining to a Pure Phenomenology and to a Phenomenological Philosophy.* Book 1: *General Introduction to a Pure Phenomenology*, trans. F. Kersten, *Collected Works*, vol. 2 (The Hague: Martinus Nijhoff, 1983), part one.

7. Edmund Husserl, *Analysen zur passiven Synthesis (1918–1926)*, ed. Margot Fleischer, *Husserliana*, vol. 11 (Hague: Nijhoff, 1966), 165; *Analyses Concerning Passive and Active Synthesis: Lectures on Transcendental Logic*, trans. Anthony Steinbock, *Collected Works*, vol. 9 (Dordrecht: Kluwer, 2001), 213.

8. It is, of course, tempting to simply make the last two one, to identify the two by

saying that facts just are claims that are true, and then, as we find in Brandom's recent account, to introduce an account of truth that looks to how claims are assessed and accepted by the community into the body of what it already takes as acceptable claims. In short, we dispense with the problem of the relationship between meaning and reference by getting rid of the notion of reference. See Robert Brandom, *Making It Explicit: Reasoning, Representing and Discursive Commitment* (Cambridge, Mass.: Harvard University Press, 1994). But this account makes the mistake of assuming that claims are primitives implicit in all uses of descriptions and fails to understand the sense in which they are derived from transformations of yet other uses of descriptions, as I will show shortly. In short, it takes implicit claims as context and fails to understand the production of claims as requiring a transformation of context.

9. The entire edifice of Brandom's account depends upon our understanding all descriptions as implicit claims, which means that the meaning of all descriptions is defined by the various rules that specify truth conditions. But perhaps the reverse is the case: perhaps claims are implicit descriptions, and perhaps the meaning of claims is not the condition of our using descriptions meaningfully but is a transformation of whatever meaning might belong to descriptions in order to be able to construe them as claims. If this is the case, if descriptions are not reducible to implicit claims, then Brandom's account suffers from the fallacy of treating what is *post hoc* as *propter hoc*, of treating the rules governing claims, which arise from transformations of descriptions into claims, as rules making possible the use of descriptions to begin with. The fatal mistake, if this is correct, would be to assume that the analysis of the meaning that derives from reflecting upon a claim (which is a description used as a proposition) would give us the conditions of using the sentence as a description in the first place.

10. Martin Heidegger, *Sein und Zeit* (Tübingen: Niemeyer [1927] 1967), §18; *Being and Time,* trans. J. Macquarrie and E. Robinson (New York: Harper and Row, 1962), §18.

11. Logical entailment works according to rules that delimit content by regulating material combinations, while differential implication is a function of operational or functional relationships between meanings. According to the first we cannot say that cats fly because they are essentially a species that is quadrupedal, while according to the second cats could be said to fly if we used that term of them more than walk and if that is how we in fact operationally differentiate them from, say, dogs.

12. *Sein und Zeit,* §15; *Being and Time,* §15. The semantic import of these terms cannot be defined by rules for three very simple reasons: (a) they are inherently indexical or what Husserl called "occasional" in the sense that they depend upon concrete situations of utterance and differential implication to determine their meaning; (b) they lack fixed borders and thus cannot be captured by an algorithm; (c) talk here is integrated into involvement, which itself does not consist of actors following rules.

13. These studies are undertaken in his *Analysen zur passiven Synthesis; Analyses Concerning Passive and Active Syntheses.*

10

Husserl's Intersubjective Transformation of Transcendental Philosophy

Dan Zahavi

> If one interprets transcendental subjectivity as an isolated ego
> and in the spirit of the Kantian tradition ignores the whole task of
> establishing a transcendental community of subjects, then every chance
> of reaching a transcendental self- and world-knowledge is lost.
>
> —Husserl (1935)[1]

A DOMINANT TRAIT in the philosophy of our century has been the critique of the philosophy of subjectivity. Among transcendental philosophers this critique has been taken into consideration most conspicuously by K.-O. Apel, who explicitly calls for an intersubjective transformation of transcendental philosophy. Not the single, isolated, self-aware ego, but language community, that is, intersubjectivity, has to be regarded as the reality-constituting principle.

It is possible to find a similar interest in and treatment of intersubjectivity in Husserl. From the winter of 1910/11 and until his death, he worked thoroughly with different aspects of the problem of intersubjectivity and left behind an almost inestimable amount of analyses that from a purely quantitative point of view by far exceeds the treatment given this topic by any of the later phenomenologists.[2]

This study is based on research undertaken at the Husserl-Archives in Louvain. I am grateful to Prof. S. IJsseling for permission to consult and quote from Husserl's unpublished manuscripts. In the following, I will try to provide a systematic outline of Husserl's investigations, and at the same time argue that Husserl, whose position has often been regarded as solipsistic, was actually occupied with the elaboration of a transcendental theory of intersubjectivity.[3]

I

The easiest way to introduce Husserl's analysis of intersubjectivity is through his concept of the *life-world*, since Husserl claims that it is intersubjective through and through. This is not merely to be understood as an accentuation of the fact that I, in my being in the world, am constantly confronted with intersubjective meaning, understood as meaning-formations (such as social institutions, cultural products, etc.), which have their origin in community and tradition, and which therefore refer me to my fellowmen and ancestors. Husserl also advocates the more fundamental view, that already my perceptual experience is an experience of intersubjectively accessible being, that is, being which does not exist for me only, but for everybody.[4] I *experience* objects, events, and actions as public, not as private,[5] and consequently Husserl claims that an ontological analysis, insofar as it unveils the being-sense (*Seinssinn*) of the world as intersubjectively valid, leads to a disclosure of the transcendental relevance of foreign subjectivity and thus to an examination of transcendental intersubjectivity;[6] and as he ultimately formulates it: Transcendental intersubjectivity is the absolute ground of being (*Seinsboden*) from which the meaning and validity of everything objectively existing originate.[7]

Thus, Husserl characterizes the intersubjective-transcendental sociality as the source of all real truth and being,[8] and occasionally he even describes his own project as a *sociological* transcendental philosophy[9] and writes that the development of phenomenology necessarily implies the step from an egological to a transcendental-sociological phenomenology.[10] In other words, a radical implementation of the transcendental reduction leads with necessity to a disclosure of transcendental intersubjectivity.[11]

Given this background, it is fairly easy to establish why Husserl occupied himself so intensively with the issue of intersubjectivity. He was convinced that it contained the key to a philosophical comprehension of reality, and since Husserl considered this problem, or more exactly, an account of the *constitution* of objective reality and transcendence, as one of the most important concerns of transcendental phenomenology,[12] it should be obvious what kind of systematic importance his analyses of intersubjectivity possess, and how much is actually at stake. If transcendental phenomenology for some principal reasons was prevented from accounting for intersubjectivity (eventually due to its alleged methodical solipsism or subjective idealism), the consequence would not merely be its inability to carry out an ambitious and detailed investigation, but its failure as a fundamental philosophical project.

Husserl's phenomenological investigation of intersubjectivity is an analysis of the *transcendental,* that is, constitutive function of intersubjectivity, and the aim of his reflections is exactly the formulation of a theory of transcendental intersubjectivity and not a detailed examination of the concrete sociality or the specific I-Thou relation. Thus, Husserl's interest is directed toward *transcendental* intersubjectivity, and not toward *mundane* intersubjectivity, which, for instance, A. Schütz has analyzed in detail. This must be stressed, since most of the critical estimations of Husserl's phenomenology of intersubjectivity have so far focused on exactly those aspects. Thus, it has been customary to discuss either whether Husserl's concept of empathy implies a direct or an indirect experience of the Other, and whether this account is phenomenologically sound, or whether Husserl's (idealistic) model of constitution could at all establish a symmetrical relation between the I and the Other—a discussion which was often quite inadequate, since one did not at the same time analyze the actual meaning of constitution, but simply presupposed a (faulty) interpretation of it.[13]

It would be wrong to claim that these problems are completely irrelevant, especially since Husserl's concept of intersubjectivity is in fact a concept of *inter*-subjectivity, that is, of the relation between subjects, and consequently implies an examination of empathy: how can I experience another subject? According to the phenomenological approach intersubjectivity cannot be examined adequately from a third person's view, but must be analyzed in its manifestation in the life of the individual subject. As Husserl writes in *Krisis:* intersubjectivity can only be treated as a transcendental problem through a radical "mich-selbst-befragen."[14] Only my experience of and relation to another subject, and those of my experiences which presuppose the Other, really merit the name "intersubjective."

The reason why it is still problematic to do what has most often been done is that one confuses the way to and the aim of Husserl's analysis of transcendental intersubjectivity. Furthermore, it will be shown that Husserl's theory of intersubjectivity is more complex than normally assumed. He operates with several *kinds* of intersubjectivity and is for that reason able to guard himself against the type of critique which by questioning his account of the bodily mediated intersubjectivity assumed that the entire foundation of his analysis would break down.[15]

The purpose of this article is not to deliver, once again, an analysis of the often discussed problems, but to demonstrate that Husserl's phenomenology implies an intersubjective transformation of transcendental philosophy and to present some of the more radical (and less well known) consequences of this transformation. For that reason I will not go into a more detailed account of Husserl's analysis of the complex structure of the concrete bodily mediated experience of the Other, but simply assume that it exists one way or the other, and instead go directly to what I take to be the core in Husserl's reflections on intersubjectivity.[16]

It is well known that Husserl claimed that the objectivity and transcendence of the world is constituted intersubjectively and that a clarification of this constitution consequently demands an analysis of transcendental intersubjectivity, and more concretely an examination of my experience of another subject. Why is it, however, that a subject can only constitute objectivity after having experienced an Other? Why is the Other a necessary condition of possibility for my experience of an objective world; why is my experience of objects changed radically the moment I experience foreign subjectivity? Husserl's thesis is that my experience of objective validity is made possible by my experience of the transcendence (and inaccessibility) of foreign subjectivity, and that this transcendence, which Husserl designates as the first real alterity and as the source of all kinds of real transcendence, endows the world with objective validity:[17]

> Here we have the only transcendence which is really worth its name, and anything else that is also called transcendent, as the objective world, depends upon the transcendence of foreign subjectivity.[18]

> The transcendence in which the world [is] constituted consists of the following: It is constituted through the Others and the generatively constituted co-subjectivity.[19]

> All Objectivity, in this sense, is related back constitutionally to what does not belong to the Ego proper, to the other-than-my-Ego's-own in the form, "someone else"—that is to say: the non-Ego in the form, "another Ego."[20]

Why is foreign subjectivity so central a condition of possibility for the constitution of transcendent objects? Why are objects only able to appear as transcendent through the Other? The explanation is that the objects cannot be reduced to being merely my intentional correlates if they can be experienced by Others. The intersubjective experienceability of the object guarantees its real transcendence,[21] and my experience (constitution) of it is consequently mediated by my experience of its givenness for another transcendent subject, that is, by my experience of a foreign world-directed subject. (It is exactly for that reason that the Other's transcendence is so vital. If the Other were only an intentional modification or an eidetic variation of myself, the fact that he experienced the same as me would be just as conclusive as if one found the same report in several copies of the same newspaper.) Only insofar as I experience that Others experience the same objects as myself do I really experience these objects as objective and real. Only then do the objects appear with a validity that makes them into more than mere intentional objects. Now they are real (that is, objective, that is, intersubjectively valid) intentional objects.[22]

Even if one is willing to concede that there is a connection between intersubjectivity and reality—which can be stated negatively in the following way: That which in principle is incapable of being experienced by Others cannot be ascribed transcendence and objectivity—there is, however, an unsolved problem. Under normal circumstances I still experience that which I accidentally experience alone (for instance, the IBM computer that I am writing on now) as transcendent, objective, and real, although I am not simultaneously experiencing that it is being experienced by Others. And this is even implicitly admitted by Husserl, who writes that, even if I knew with absolute certainty that a universal plague had destroyed all life but my own, my worldly experience would still be dependent upon co-functioning transcendental intersubjectivity.[23] The problem can be solved, however, if one differentiates between our first primal experience of Others, which once and for all makes the constitution of objectivity, reality, and transcendence possible, and thus *permanently* transforms our categories of experience, and all subsequent experiences of Others. This does not mean that all these subsequent experiences are insignificant, but their contribution is of a different nature. They no longer make the constitution of the categories *objectivity* and *transcendence* possible, they *fulfill* them. To phrase it differently: although my solitary experience of the IBM computer is an experience of it as real and objective, these components of validity are at first only given *signitively*. Only the moment I experience that Others are also experiencing it is the validity-claim of my experience fulfilled intuitively, that is, in evidence.

As I have indicated, it is important that my experience of another subject is an experience of another experiencing subject, and Husserl even claims that the validity of the other subject's experience is accepted along with my experience of that subject.[24] This can be illustrated by reference to Husserl's analysis of the body, since Husserl claims that the experience of another as incarnated subject is the first step toward the constitution of an objective (intersubjectively valid) shared world.[25] The reason he gives is that my experience of something as the body of another must be accompanied by another's experience of the *same* as her own body.[26] In the experience of the body of another, one is confronted with a congruity between one's own experience and the Other's experience—a congruity which according to Husserl is the foundation of every subsequent experience of intersubjective objects, that is, objects which are also experienced (experienceable) by Others.[27]

Husserl continues his analyses by describing a special kind of experience of the Other, namely, those situations where I experience the Other as experiencing myself. This kind of "original reciprocal co-existence" where I take over the Other's objectifying apprehension of myself, that is, where my self-apprehension is mediated by the Other, and where I experience myself as alien, is of decisive importance for the constitution of an objective world. When I realize that I can be an *alter ego* for the Other just as he can be it for me, a marked change in my own constitutive significance takes place. The absolute difference between self and Other disappears. The Other conceives of me as an Other, just as I conceive of him as a self.[28] I realize that I am only one among many, that my perspective on the world is only one among several, wherefore my privileged status in relation to the objects of experience is suspended to a certain degree. Whether I or an Other is the subject of experience makes no difference for the validity of that experience.[29] As Waldenfels formulates it: the experience of the Other implies an alienation of one's own experience.[30]

Husserl claims that my experiences are changed when I experience that Others experience the same as I, and when I experience that I myself am experienced by Others. From then on, my object of experience cannot any longer be reduced to its mere being-for-me. Through the Other, it has been constituted with a subject-transcendent validity. No longer do I experience it as being dependent upon me and my factual existence. Quite to the contrary, as an intersubjective object it is endowed with an autonomy of being that transcends my finite existence.[31]

To summarize: Husserl claims that the sense and the categories *transcen-*

dence, objectivity, and *reality* are constituted intersubjectively. These categories can only be constituted by a subject that has experienced other subjects. Husserl also stresses, however, that the same is the case for the categories *immanence, subjectivity,* and *appearance.* His line of thought is the following: when I realize that my object of experience can also be experienced by Others, I also realize that there is a difference between the thing in itself and its being for me. The same object can appear for different subjects,[32] and when I realize this, I understand that what I earlier took to be the object itself is in reality merely an appearance of something objectively (that is, intersubjectively) existing.[33] Thus, it only makes sense to speak of and designate something as a mere appearance, as merely subjective, when I have experienced other subjects and thus acquired the concept of intersubjective validity.[34]

The structures that have been emphasized so far (my experience of the world-directed transcendent foreign subject, and my experience of the Other's experience of myself) take up a decisive place in Husserl's account of the transcendental-constitutive function of intersubjectivity. It would be a mistake, however, to assume that Husserl understands intersubjectivity as something which is exclusively attached to concrete bodily mediated interaction. If this had been the case, it would have been easy to criticize him, by pointing to the fact that exactly this kind of experience seems to be both contingent and fallible —which Husserl himself occasionally admits[35]—and exactly for that reason, not the best foundation for a transcendental philosophy.[36] Husserl, however, does not operate with only one kind of transcendental intersubjectivity, which has been the common assumption, but with three different kinds. Apart from the kind which has already been described, he not only claims that the being of the subject as an experiencing and constituting subject implies a reference to other subjects, already prior to its concrete experience of them, that is, *a priori;* he also claims that one should ascribe a constitutive function to the anonymous community which manifests itself in our inherited linguistic normality (in our tradition).

To account in detail for the two last kinds of intersubjectivity would by far exceed the limits of this article, but let me briefly outline Husserl's leading ideas.[37] Concerning the first and most fundamental kind of intersubjectivity, Husserl writes that the analysis of the transcendental ego ultimately leads to a disclosure of its *apodictic* intersubjective structure.[38] Each and every one of my experiences does not imply a reference only to myself as experiencing subject, but also to the Others as co-subjects:[39]

> My experience as mundane experience (that is, already each of my perceptions) does not only entail Others as mundane objects, but also and constantly in existential co-validity as co-subjects, as co-constituting, and both are inseparably intertwined.[40]

In order to understand this chain of reasoning, it is necessary to take a look at Husserl's theory of perception.

Husserl claims that our perceptual experience of objects to a certain degree is an experience of an adumbration of the object, but that it is nevertheless true to say that we are intending and perceiving the object itself, which in its transcendence always possesses a plurality of (simultaneous) adumbrations. If one analyzes this horizon of simultaneous coexisting adumbrations, it is revealed that they cannot be actualized by a single subject, since it at any given time is restricted to a single perspective. Since, however, the ontological structure of the object implies a simultaneous plurality of adumbrations, Husserl is forced to refer to a plurality of possible subjects, who are to be understood as the noetic correlate of the object's noematic plurality of coexisting aspects. Provided that the subject as subject is directed toward objects, provided that every experience of objects is characterized by the horizonal appearance of the object, where a certain aspect is present and the others are absent, and provided that this horizonal intentionality, this interplay between presence and absence, can only be accounted for phenomenologically through a reference to a plurality of possible subjects, the consequence is that I in my being as subject am referred to Others, regardless of whether I experience them concretely or not, regardless of whether they actually exist or not. My intentionality is *a priori* dependent upon something, which Husserl calls "open intersubjectivity." Thus, in *Zur Phänomenologie der Intersubjektivität II* he writes:

> Thus everything objective that stands before me in experience and primarily in perception has an apperceptive horizon of possible experience, own and foreign. Ontologically speaking, every appearance that I have is from the very beginning a part of an open endless, but not explicitly realized totality of possible appearances of the same, and the subjectivity belonging to this appearance is open intersubjectivity.[41]

If these considerations are combined with Husserl's account of the actual, *horizonal*, experience of another bodily subject, it is obvious that the *a priori* reference to the open intersubjectivity is already presupposed. Prior to my concrete encounter with the Other, intersubjectivity is already present as co-subjectivity, for which reason Husserl's analysis of perceptual intentionality can be said to demonstrate the untenability of a solipsistic position. Perhaps Husserl was referring to this when he in the manuscript C 17 wrote: "When empathy occurs, is the community, the intersubjectivity there already in advance, and is empathy merely a disclosing performance?"[42] This is a question which he answers positively shortly thereafter.

So far we have been dealing with two types of intersubjectivity, and it is important to emphasize that the concrete experience of the Other, although it presupposes the intersubjectivity at work in horizonal intentionality, is still transcendental, that is, constitutive. Thus, the concrete experience of the bodily Other is not a mere intra-mundane episode, since it is only here that I can experience the true alterity and transcendence of the Other, only here that I can take over his objectifying apprehension of myself, and according to Husserl, precisely these experiences are conditions of possibility for the constitution of objectivity.

Husserl, however, also operates with a third type of transcendental inter-subjectivity, which is different in kind from the previous two, although it pre-supposes both.[43] Thus, as I will show in more detail below, Husserl also claims that certain types of self- and world-apprehension are only made possible by a linguistically sedimented and traditionally handed-down *normality*. Thus, nor-mality *qua* anonymous community possesses constitutive implications.

II

So far it has been amply demonstrated that Husserl took intersubjectiv-ity very seriously. Thus, when he claims that the subject can only be world-experiencing insofar as it is a member of a community,[44] that the ego is only what it is as a *socius*, that is, as a member of a sociality,[45] and that a radical *self*-reflection necessarily leads to the discovery of absolute intersubjectivity,[46] the general line of thought has been indicated. In its being as experiencing and constituting, the subject is dependent upon intersubjectivity. That this is not only the case for the empirical, mundane subject has already been shown and can be further confirmed by numerous passages in Husserl's work. In *Erste Philosophie II*, for instance, he writes that transcendental subjectivity in its full universality is exactly *inter*-subjectivity,[47] and in a research manuscript from 1927, which has been published in *Zur Phänomenologie der Intersubjektivität I*, Husserl writes that the absolute reveals itself as the intersubjective relation be-tween subjects.[48] Thus, Husserl's recurrent point is that a sufficiently radical carrying out of the transcendental reduction leads not only to subjectivity, but also to intersubjectivity,[49] and it is no coincidence that in periods in which he made reference to Leibniz he called his own theory a *transcendental monad-ology*.[50]

It is obvious that Husserl believed the notion of a plurality of transcenden-tal subjects to be coherent, that is, *possible*. Ultimately, he would even strengthen this assertion and claim that it is *necessary*, insofar as "subjectivity is what it is—an ego functioning constitutively—only within intersubjectivity."[51] The claim that subjectivity only becomes fully constitutive, that is, fully transcen-dental, through its relation with Others is in striking contrast with any tradi-tional Kantian understanding of transcendental subjectivity. Curiously enough, it is exactly this traditional understanding which A. Schütz tacitly accepts in his well-known critique of Husserl's theory of intersubjectivity. Thus Schütz writes:

> it must be earnestly asked whether the transcendental Ego in Husserl's concept is not essentially what Latin grammarians call a "singulare tantum," that is, a term incapable of being put into the plural. Even more, it is in no way established whether the existence of Others is a problem of the transcendental sphere at all,

i.e. whether the problem of intersubjectivity does exist between transcendental egos . . . ; or whether intersubjectivity and therefore sociality does not rather belong exclusively to the mundane sphere of our life-world.[52]

Husserl, however, takes issue with this position in a manuscript now published in the supplementary volume to *Krisis*, where he explicitly states that the possibility of a transcendental elucidation of subjectivity and world is lost if one follows the Kantian tradition in interpreting transcendental subjectivity as an isolated ego and thereby ignores the problem of transcendental intersubjectivity.[53]

This remark could easily have been ascribed to K.-O. Apel. It is, however, of utmost importance to notice that Husserl in contrast to the philosophers of language does not conceive of his own phenomenology of intersubjectivity as a break with (a correctly understood) philosophy of subjectivity. It is, moreover, characteristic that it is possible to find reflections concerning the fundamental significance of intersubjectivity in his manuscripts side by side with remarks concerning the importance of the transcendental ego, and even statements saying that the transcendental primal ego (*Ur-Ich*) cannot be pluralized.[54]

To say the very least, this seems to imply an inconsistency in the very core of Husserl's reflections. Two dominant "solutions" have consisted in claiming either that Husserl changed his mind within a few years, and alternately attributed priority to the ego (in *Cartesianische Meditationen*) and to intersubjectivity (in *Krisis*), or, alternatively, that Husserl never abandoned his egological point of departure, for which reason his treatment of intersubjectivity remained superficial and without any real fundamentality. Both of these interpretations are, however, encumbered with some obvious problems. In the first because it is possible to find the alleged alternatives within both *Cartesianische Meditationen* and *Krisis*. In both works Husserl speaks about the fundamental importance of both ego and intersubjectivity. The second because it is confronted with a large number of passages (some already quoted) where Husserl seems quite unambiguously to ascribe a fundamental and decisive function to intersubjectivity.

A closer reading reveals that this is only a seeming inconsistency. It disappears the moment it is realized that Husserl's emphasis on the singularity of the primal ego does not clash in any way with his intersubjective transformation of the transcendental philosophical project. Quite to the contrary. Once more the exceptional in Husserl's phenomenology of intersubjectivity has to be stressed. The transcendental intersubjectivity is not an objectively existing structure in the world which can be described and analyzed from a third-person view, but a relation between subjects, where the ego itself participates. To phrase it differently: transcendental intersubjectivity can be disclosed only through a radical explication of the ego's structures of experience. This does not only indicate the intersubjective structure of the ego, but also the egological attachment of intersubjectivity.[55] Husserl's accentuation of the fundamental importance of the ego must be seen as an accentuation of the fact that inter-subjectivity, my relation to an Other, always passes through my own subjec-tivity. Only from this point of view are intersubjectivity and the plurality of constitutive centers phenomenologically accessible.

The remaining problem is to explain how Husserl can keep on designating the transcendental primal ego as singular and unique. An examination of the manuscript B I 14, however, can solve the problem. Husserl writes that "I" does not admit of any plural as long as the word is used in its original sense. Others can experience themselves as I, but I can only experience myself as I. Besides myself there is no other I, about which I can say, "this is me." Precisely for that reason it is impossible to speak about *an* I, as long as "I" really means I. I is absolutely singular and individual.[56] When Husserl mentions the absolute sin-gularity of the ego, and denies that it can be put into plural, he is obviously referring to the unique egocentric givenness of my own consciousness. I am only self-aware of myself and can never ever be self-aware of anybody else. This singularity is of a kind which admits of Others: "The singular I—the transcen-dental. In its singularity it posits 'other' singular transcendental egos—as 'oth-ers,' who then in turn as singular posit Others."[57]

This is offered merely as a demonstration of the consistency of Husserl's position. When he speaks about the absolute priority of the ego, this does not contradict his reflections concerning transcendental intersubjectivity as the ab-solute field of being. Transcendental intersubjectivity is the transcendental foundation, but as Husserl says, it possesses a necessary I-centering.[58] Intersub-jectivity can unfold itself only in the relation between singular subjects, and it is for this reason that Husserl writes that the disclosure of transcendental sub-jectivity effectuated by the reduction is ambiguous, since it leads to subjectivity as well as to intersubjectivity.[59]

Now, it would have been appropriate to provide a more detailed investiga-tion of the role played by intersubjectivity on the most fundamental level, namely, when it concerns the self-temporalization of the subject. On the one hand, it is important to emphasize the significance of intersubjectivity when it comes to the subject's self-constitution. But, on the other hand, it is also im-portant to insist on the fact that each single subject has to possess a certain amount of ontological autonomy—since a complete elimination of this would make the very concept of intersubjectivity impossible. If the difference between the subjects were negated, there would not be any plurality and consequently no intersubjectivity.[60] Thus, if one wants to preserve intersubjectivity, and keep the plurality of individual and transcendent subjects, it is necessary to reject the proposal that they have their ground of being in a prior unity.[61] However, a detailed analysis of Husserl's complex account of the ego's many structural moments (including a differentiation between those which are intersubjectively constituted and those which must be presupposed *sui generis* in order for the notion of intersubjectivity to be coherent) would lead too far. Let me only mention that Husserl's position apparently is that the very temporal flow of consciousness, which merely constitutes the most basic level of subjectivity, is a process which does not depend upon the relation to the Other.[62] At the same time, however, he would probably claim that the relation to the Other can be traced back to and is made possible by the ecstatic self-alteration taking place in this process of temporalization.[63]

I will turn instead toward some aspects of Husserl's thinking which can illustrate the radical implications that his treatment of transcendental intersubjectivity had for his own understanding and elaboration of phenomenology.

If one accepts Husserl's conviction that reality is intersubjectively valid and that my reality-positing acts are dependent upon my experience of Others, one is bound to take not only the consensus but also the *dissent* of the world-experiencing subjects seriously. Husserl's extended analyses of this problem eventually made him enter fields that have traditionally been reserved for psychopathology, sociology, anthropology, and ethnology. Whereas a strict Kantian transcendental philosophy would have considered such empirical and mundane domains as without any transcendental relevance, due to his interest in transcendental intersubjectivity, Husserl was forced to consider these from a transcendental point of view.[64] Thus, I believe that Husserl's late thinking is characterized by a decisive expansion of the transcendental sphere, an expansion which was brought about by his interest in intersubjectivity and which ultimately forced him to consider the transcendental significance of generativity, tradition, historicity, and normality.[65]

Let me focus on the problem of *normality,* with which Husserl has dealt intensively in different contexts and which he considers a constitutional core-concept. Basically, Husserl claims that our experiences are guided by anticipations of normality. We apprehend, experience, and constitute in accordance with the normal and typical structures, models, and patterns which our earlier experiences have sedimented in our mind.[66] If that which we experience happens to clash with our earlier experiences—if it is different—we have an experience of *anormality,* which subsequently leads to a modification and specification of our anticipations.[67] Originally Husserl examined this process in connection with his analysis of the *passive synthesis,* but it is not only at work in the solitary subject. As Husserl says, I have been together with people as long as I remember, and my anticipations are therefore structured in accordance with the intersubjectively handed-down forms of apperception.[68] Normality is also *conventionality,* which in its being transcends the individual.[69] Thus, already in *Ideen II* Husserl pointed to the fact that, next to the tendencies originating from other persons, there also exist indeterminate general demands made by custom and tradition: "One" judges thus, "one" holds the fork in such and such a way, etc.[70] What is normal I learn from Others (and first and foremost from my closest relatives, that is, by the people by whom I am brought up, and who educate me),[71] and I am thereby involved in a common tradition, which through a chain of generations stretches back into a dim past.

As I have just mentioned, one consequence of Husserl's treatment of intersubjectivity is that he also has to take the *disagreement* between world-experiencing subjects seriously. If my constitution of objectivity is dependent upon my assurance that Others experience or can experience the same as I, it is a problem if they claim to be experiencing something different—although the fact that we can agree upon there being a disagreement already indicates a common ground.[72] It is, however, in this context that Husserl emphasizes that only the (dis)agreement between the *normal* members of the community are of relevance. When it is said that real being has to be experienceable by everybody, we are dealing with a certain averageness and idealization.[73] "Everybody" is the person who belongs to a normality of subjects, and who is exactly normal in and through the community.[74] Only with her do we fight about the truth and falsity, being and non-being of our common life-world. Only the normal is apprehended as being co-constitutive,[75] whereas my disagreement with an anormal is (at first) considered inconsequential.[76]

It is here necessary to differentiate between at least two fundamental types of normality. First of all, we speak of normality when we are dealing with a mature, healthy, and rational person. Here the anormal will be the infant, the blind, or the schizophrenic. Secondly, we speak of normality when it concerns our own *homeworld*, whereas anormality is attributed the foreigner, which, however, if certain conditions are fulfilled can be apprehended as a member of a *foreign normality*.

It is precisely in this context that the disagreement gains a vital constitutive significance. According to Husserl, the experience of discrepancy between normal subjects (including the experience of a plurality of normalities, each of which has its own notion of what counts as true) does not merely lead to a more complex world-comprehension insofar as we, if we are able to synthesize the standpoints, can gain a *richer insight*. The disagreement can also *motivate* the constitution of *scientific* objectivity, insofar as we aim toward reaching a truth which will be valid for us all.[77] Thus, eventually it becomes necessary to differentiate between (1) "normal" objectivity, which is correlated with a limited intersubjectivity (a community of normal subjects), and (2) "rigorous" objectivity, which is correlated with the unlimited totality of all subjects.[78] When a community of color-blind subjects jointly examine a painting, they are dealing with an intersubjectively constituted object. When people with normal vision examine the "same" painting, they are also dealing with an intersubjectively constituted object. The apprehension of both groups can, however, be mediated by a geometrical description, which due to its more formal (and empty) validity possesses a higher degree of objectivity.[79]

In connection with the last and highest level of constitution—the constitution of theoretical scientific objectivity—Husserl touches on the significance of *writing*. It is not merely the case that meaning only acquires full objectivity the moment it as written down is detached from its indexical connection to person, time, and place. As written down, meaning can be handed down to later generations and thus be incorporated into the body of knowledge, which generations of scientists are working on, and as Husserl remarks in *Ursprung der Geometrie*, comprehensive and complex theories, which are developed through centuries, would not be possible if it were not for the documenting, conservating function of writing.[80]

We can establish that Husserl believed a correlation to exist between different levels of normality and different levels of objectivity.[81] Even absolute objective being and truth is correlated with a subject-dependent normality: the normality of rational subjects.[82]

Husserl's treatment of normality as transcendental philosophical category throws light on some of the more far-reaching consequences of his phenomenology of intersubjectivity. For instance, the dimension of historicity in Husserl's thinking has become visible. My own homeworldly normality is instituted through tradition and generativity and is therefore historical. Normality is a tradition-bound set of norms. Thus, Husserl designates the normal life as generative and claims that any normal person is historical as a member of a historical community.[83] Moreover, the very constitution of objectivity and of a common objective world is a historical process.[84] Far from being already constituted,[85] the meaning-formations "objectivity" and "reality" have status as intersubjective presumptions, which can be realized only in an infinite process of socialization and horizon-fusion. To phrase it differently—and here Husserl is speaking, not Apel or Habermas—absolute truth (real being) is a token of an idealization; we are dealing with a regulative ideal, with a correlate to the ideal consensus of an open intersubjective community, which can be approximated in a process of permanent correction, although it can never be reached, since every factually realized consensus is in principle open for further corrections.[86] Consequently, Husserl can write that there is no stagnant world, since it is only given for us in its relativity of normality and anormality.[87] The being of the world is only apparently immobile, in reality it is a construction of normality, which in principle can collapse.[88]

That Husserl tried to add a historical dimension to transcendental philosophy can also be illustrated in a different way. In a passage quoted earlier, Husserl writes that the transcendence of the world is constituted through the Others and through the generatively constituted co-subjectivity.[89] Exactly this concept of *generative intersubjectivity*[90] indicates that Husserl did no longer regard the birth and death of the subject as mere contingent facts, but as transcendental conditions of possibility for the constitution of the world.[91] As he says in *Krisis:* the incorporation into a historical generative context belongs just as inseparably to the ego, as its very temporal structure.[92]

> What I generate from out of myself (primally instituting) is mine. But I am a "child of the times"; I am a member of a we-community in the broadest sense—a community that has its tradition and that for its part is connected in a novel manner with the generative subjects, the closest and the most distant ancestors. And these have "influenced" me: I am what I am as an heir.[93]

In other words, Husserl considered the subject's embeddedness in a living tradition to have constitutive implications, and as I mentioned in the first part, it is consequently possible to speak of an anonymous normality as a third kind of transcendental intersubjectivity. It is not merely the case that I live in a world, which as a correlate of normality is permeated by references to Others, and which Others have already furnished with meaning, or that I understand the world (and myself) through a traditional, handed-down, linguistic convention-ality. The very category "historical reality" implies a type of transcendence which can be constituted only insofar as I take over traditional meaning, which has its origin outside of me, in a historical past.

Is it on this background possible to conclude that Husserl in the last phase of his thinking substituted the transcendental ego as the phenomenological point of departure for the historical community of the life-world? No, of course not. Although the transcendental intersubjectivity is the transcendental foun-dation, it is vital not to forget Husserl's phenomenological approach. There is no community without ego-centering, and consequently no generative inter-subjectivity without a transcendental primal ego, where the intersubjectivity can unfold itself.[94] As Husserl has emphasized several times, the "we" stretches *from me onwards* to the simultaneous past and future Others;[95] the historically primary is our present.[96] In other words: the transcendental analysis of the his-torical past, of the previous generations, and more generally the transcendental phenomenological treatment of meaning, which transcends the finiteness of the subject, must always take its point of departure from the first-person per-spective.

There is probably no one who would claim that Husserl has managed to synthesize historicity and transcendentality in a definite and systematic way. This is, nevertheless, what he attempted to do in his last analyses, and this has to be appreciated when it comes to an evaluation of the scope and comprehen-siveness of his thinking. Whether it is a fruitful approach that has to be devel-oped or a final aporetical draft can be discussed. That Husserl did not advocate a classical Cartesian-Kantian subject-philosophy, and that he was not a solipsist but, on the contrary, treated intersubjectivity as a transcendental philosophical notion of utmost importance, should, however, have been demonstrated.[97]

Notes

Apart from some minor changes this piece is a reprint of an article originally published in *The Journal of the British Society for Phenomenology* 27, no. 3 (1996): 228–45.

    1. *Krisis* (*Ergänzung*), 120.

    2. On several occasions, Husserl has called attention to the lecture course *Grund-probleme der Phänomenologie* from 1910/11 (now in *Intersubjektivität I*, 111–94), as the place where intersubjectivity was assigned a decisive role for the first time (*Logik [Hua]*, 250, *Ideen*

III, 150, *Intersubjektivität I*, 245, *Erste Philosophie II*, 433, *Intersubjektivität II*, 307). Although his reflections in *Ideen I* (from 1913) appear strictly egological, Husserl was already at that time aware of the significance of intersubjectivity, and he later wrote that he originally had planned that his presentations in *Ideen I* were to be complemented by the reflections on intersubjectivity to be found in *Ideen II*. However, these reflections were published only posthumously (*Ideen III*, 150).

3. Cf. K.-O. Apel, *Transformation der Philosophie I–II* (Frankfurt am Main: Suhrkamp, 1973), I: 60, II: 315; J. Habermas, *Der philosophische Diskurs der Moderne* (Frankfurt am Main: Suhrkamp, 1985), 178.

4. *Phänomenologische Psychologie*, 431; *Intersubjektivität II*, 289, 390; *Logik (Hua)*, 243; *Krisis*, 469.

5. *Cartesianische Meditationen*, 123; *Intersubjektivität III*, 5.

6. *Intersubjektivität III*, 110.

7. *Phänomenologische Psychologie*, 344.

8. *Cartesianische Meditationen*, 35, 182; *Erste Philosophie II*, 449; *Phänomenologische Psychologie*, 295, 474.

9. *Phänomenologische Psychologie*, 539.

10. This formulation, which is from Husserl's London lectures in 1922, can be found in K. Schuhmann, *Husserls Staatsphilosophie* (Freiburg: Karl Alber, 1988), 56.

11. *Cartesianische Meditationen*, 69; *Phänomenologische Psychologie*, 245–46; *Erste Philosophie II*, 129.

12. *Erste Philosophie II*, 465.

13. Cf. H. Zeltner, "Das Ich und die Anderen. Husserls Beitrag zur Grundlegung der Sozialphilosophie," *Zeitschrift für philosophische Forschung* 13 (1959): 309–10; M. Theunissen, *Der Andere* (Berlin: Walter de Gruyter, 1977), §§19–28; A. Schütz, "Das Problem der transzendentalen Intersubjektivität bei Husserl," *Philosophische Rundschau* 5 (1957), 107; P. Ricoeur, "Phenomenology and Hermeneutics," in Thompson, ed., *Hermeneutics and the Human Sciences* (Cambridge: Cambridge University Press, 1981), 124–25; U. Rohr-Dietschi, *Zur Genese des Selbstbewußtseins* (Berlin: Walter de Gruyter, 1974), 144–50. I will not go into an analysis of Husserl's concept of constitution in this article, but simply refer to my presentation in D. Zahavi, *Intentionalität und Konstitution—Eine Einführung in Husserls Logische Untersuchungen* (Copenhagen: Museum Tusculanum Press, 1992), and to the detailed analysis of the constitution of the Other in D. Zahavi, *Husserl und die transzendentale Intersubjektivität —Eine Antwort auf die sprachpragmatische Kritik* (Dordrecht: Kluwer, 1996).

14. *Krisis*, 206. This approach can also be found in Sartre, who in *L'être et le néant* (Paris: Tel Gallimard, 1976) writes that the disclosure of our being-for-the-other takes place through a radicalized cogito-reflection (cf., e.g., 265, 289, 314, 319, 329).

15. Cf. A. Schütz, "Das Problem der transzendentalen Intersubjektivität bei Husserl," *Philosophische Rundschau* 5 (1957): 81–107.

16. However, I do find Husserl's account in the Fifth Cartesian Meditation less aporetic than normally assumed. In this I lean on I. Yamaguchi, *Passive Synthesis und Intersubjektivität bei Edmund Husserl* (The Hague: Martinus Nijhoff, 1982); R. Boehm, "Zur Phänomenologie der Gemeinschaft. Edmund Husserls Grundgedanken" in *Phänomenologie, Rechtsphilosophie, Jurisprudenz*, ed. T. Würtenberger (Frankfurt am Main: Vittorio Klostermann, 1969), 1–26, and N. Depraz, *Transcendance et incarnation* (Paris: Vrin, 1995).

17. *Intersubjektivität II*, 277; *Intersubjektivität III*, 560; *Cartesianische Meditationen*, 173.

18. *Erste Philosophie II*, 495.

19. "Die Transzendénz, in der die Welt konstituiert <ist>, besteht darin, daß sie sich mittels der Anderen und der generativ konstituierten Mitsubjektivität konstituiert" (Ms. C 17 32a).

20. *Logik (Hua)*, 248; modified *Logic*, 241.

21. Whereas the guaranty in every single case is fallible—what I took to be a valid experience of another could turn out to be a hallucination—this is not the case when it comes to the fundamental connection between intersubjective experienceability and transcendence. Such an experienceability is, of course, not to be interpreted as a mere epistemic criterion for the assumption of a mind-independent reality, since this would be a relapse into the objectivism that was suspended by the effectuation of the epochē.

22. For an account of the relationship between respectively the mere intentional and the real and intentional object see D. Zahavi, "Constitution and Ontology: Some Remarks on Husserl's Ontological Position in the *Logical Investigations*," *Husserl Studies* 9 (1992): 111–24.

23. *Cartesianische Meditationen*, 125; *Intersubjektivität III*, 6; *Krisis*, 81.

24. *Intersubjektivität II*, 388. That every experience of an Other implies the validity of the Other's experience should not be misunderstood. Of course, Husserl is claiming neither that it is no longer possible to speak of disagreement or dissent (but only that all disagreement presupposes a common world), nor that our experience of an Other is always accompanied by a thematic representation of the Other's object of experience (which K. Arp claims in "Intentionality and the Public World: Hussserl's Treatment of Objectivity in the Cartesian Meditations," *Husserl Studies* 7 [1991]: 91). Husserl's claim is merely that the *validity* of the Other's experience is implicitly accepted when we experience her, and that this furnishes our own object of experience with the validity, that it can also be experienced by another subject, that it is a common intersubjective object and consequently transcendent. This can take place without any explicit representation of the content of the Other's experience (*Krisis*, 308; *Intersubjektivität I*, 469).

25. *Intersubjektivität II*, 110; *Intersubjektivität III*, 18, 572.

26. *Intersubjektivität I*, 252; *Intersubjektivität II*, 485.

27. For a more detailed account of Husserl's phenomenology of the body see D. Zahavi, "Husserl's Phenomenology of the Body," *Études Phénoménologiques* 19 (1994): 63–84.

28. *Intersubjektivität I*, 243–44.

29. *Logik (Hua)*, 245; *Intersubjektivität III*, 645; *Cartesianische Meditationen*, 157.

30. B. Waldenfels, "Erfahrung des Fremden in Husserls Phänomenologie," *Phänomenologische Forschungen* 22 (1989): 56.

31. *Intersubjektivität III*, 218; *Erste Philosophie II*, 495; *Intersubjektivität I*, 242. This finiteness is according to Husserl hidden until the co-being (*Mitsein*) of the Other is taken into account (Ms. C 17 32a). Death only gains a meaning for me through the Others (*Intersubjektivität III*, 452).

32. *Intersubjektivität I*, 9.

33. *Krisis*, 167; *Ideen II*, 82.

34. *Phänomenologische Psychologie*, 453; *Intersubjektivität I*, 382; *Intersubjektivität I*, 388–89, 420–21.

35. *Intersubjektivität II*, 474–75.

36. A similar kind of argumentation can be found in D. Carr, "The 'Fifth Meditation' and Husserl's Cartesianism," *Philosophy and Phenomenological Research* 34 (1973): 14–35. Carr claims that Husserl's incorporation of transcendental intersubjectivity led to a radical revision of his earlier concept of philosophy, insofar as the *nos cogitamus* does not possess the same kind of infallible apodictic certainty as the *ego cogito* (32–35). However, this is a truth with modifications, which will be obvious in a moment.

37. For a more extensive discussion, see D. Zahavi, *Husserl und die transzendentale Intersubjektivität—Eine Antwort auf die sprachpragmatische Kritik* (1996), and D. Zahavi,

"Horizontal Intentionality and Transcendental Intersubjectivity," *Tijdschrift voor Filosofie* 59, no. 2 (1997): 304–21.

38. *Intersubjektivität III*, 192. This interpretation can be supported by Dorion Cairns's account of a conversation with Husserl, June 4, 1932; cf. D. Cairns, *Conversations with Husserl and Fink* (The Hague: Martinus Nijhoff, 1976), 82–83.

39. *Krisis*, 468.

40. "Meine Erfahrung als Welterfahrung (also jede meiner Wahrnehmungen schon) schließt nicht nur Andere als Weltobjekte ein sondern beständig in seinsmäßiger Mitgeltung als Mitsubjekte, als Mitkonstituierende, und beides ist untrennbar verflochten" (Ms. C 17 36a).

41. *Intersubjektivität II*, 289. Cf. *Phänomenologische Psychologie*, 394, and *Intersubjektivität III*, 497.

42. "Wenn Einfühlung eintritt—ist etwa auch schon die Gemeinschaft, die Intersubjektivität da und Einfühlung dann bloß enthüllendes Leisten?" (Ms. C 17 84b).

43. It must be emphasized that the relation between the three kinds of intersubjectivity is a relationship of founding. That something is founded on something else implies, according to Husserl's definition in the Third Logical Investigation, neither that it can be deduced from it nor that it can be reduced to it, but merely that it cannot exist without the existence of its foundation (*Logische Untersuchungen II [Hua]*, 281–82). In other words: the three types are hierarchically structured, but different and irreducible kinds of transcendental intersubjectivity, each with its own special constitutive function and performance.

44. *Cartesianische Meditationen*, 166.

45. *Intersubjektivität III*, 193.

46. *Krisis*, 275, 472.

47. *Erste Philosophie II*, 480.

48. *Intersubjektivität I*, 480.

49. *Phänomenologische Psychologie*, 344.

50. *Erste Philosophie II*, 190. For a more detailed account of Hussserl's use of Leibniz, see R. Cristin, "Phänomenologie und Monadologie. Husserl und Leibniz," *Studia Leibnitiana* XXII, no. 2 (1990): 163–74.

51. *Krisis*, 175; after *Crisis*, 172.

52. A. Schütz, *Collected Papers I* (The Hague: Martinus Nijhoff, 1962), 167.

53. *Krisis (Ergänzung)*, 120.

54. *Krisis*, 188.

55. E. Marbach (*Das Problem des Ich in der Phänomenologie Husserls* [The Hague: Martinus Nijhoff, 1974], chap. 5) argues that it was exactly Husserl's insight into the necessity of construing a transcendental theory of intersubjectivity which made him abandon the nonegological theory of consciousness that he had advocated in *Logische Untersuchungen*. As long as there was no ego as principle of unity, there were merely experiences, and it was consequently impossible to differentiate between one's own and the Other's experiences. In a related way, A. Gurwitsch has claimed that his own non-egological theory of consciousness made the problem of transcendental intersubjectivity superfluous. If there is no transcendental ego, but merely an empirical, then the relation between ego and Other must be an empirical-mundane problem (A. Schütz and A. Gurwitsch, *Briefwechsel 1939–1959* [Munich: Wilhelm Fink Verlag, 1985], p. 369).

56. Ms. B I 14 138a.

57. "Das einzige Ich—das transzendentale. In seiner Einzigkeit setzt es 'andere' einzige transzendentale Ich—als 'andere,' die selbst wieder in Einzigkeit Andere setzen" (Ms. B I 14 138b). Cf. *Intersubjektivität II*, 212. Of course, Husserl would deny that this first-personal

singularity—which refutes a number of "substantial" misinterpretations of his position—is merely a contingent linguistic fact. Quite to the contrary, we are dealing with a transcendental necessity, which is ultimately connected with the problem of individuation. "I am" is for the ego that thinks it, the intentional ground. It is, as Husserl says, the primal fact that I as a philosopher must never overlook (*Logik [Hua]*, 243–44, *Intersubjektivität II*, 307, *Krisis [Ergänzung]*, 165).

58. *Intersubjektivität III*, 426.

59. *Intersubjektivität III*, 73–75.

60. *Intersubjektivität III*, 335, 339.

61. A position which E. Fink mistakenly has advocated in a number of his otherwise very knowledgeable articles. Cf., for instance, E. Fink, *Nähe und Distanz* (Munich: Karl Alber, 1976), 223; and Fink's remarks to the English version of Schütz's article, "Das Problem der transzendentalen Intersubjektivität bei Husserl," in A. Schütz, *Collected Papers III* (The Hague: Martinus Nijhoff, 1975), 86. See also D. Zahavi, "The Self-pluralisation of the Primal Life: A Problem in Fink's Husserl-Interpretation," *Recherches husserliennes* 2 (1994): 3–18.

62. *Intersubjektivität II*, 170–75.

63. *Intersubjektivität III*, 589, 634, 642; *Krisis*, 189. Just like Heidegger (cf. *Die Grundprobleme der Phänomenologie* [Frankfurt am Main: Vittorio Klostermann, 1989], 360, 377, 426) and Merleau-Ponty (cf. *Phénoménologie de la perception* [Paris: Éditions Gallimard, 1945], 428).

64. *Intersubjektivität III*, 391.

65. As Merleau-Ponty remarks apropos Husserl's idea concerning the intersubjective structure of transcendental subjectivity: "Now if the transcendental is intersubjectivity, how can the borders of the transcendental and the empirical help becoming indistinct? For along with the other person, all the other person sees of me—all my facticity—is reintegrated into subjectivity, or at least posited as an indispensable element of its definition. Thus the transcendental descends into history. Or as we might put it, the historical is no longer an external relation between two or more absolutely autonomous subjects but has an interior and is an inherent aspect of their very definition. They no longer know themselves to be subjects simply in relation to their individual selves, but in relation to one another as well" (Merleau-Ponty, *Signes* [Paris: Éditions Gallimard, 1960], 134). It is actually possible to find numerous similarities between Husserl and Merleau-Ponty, and it is worth noticing, that Merleau-Ponty, who already before World War II gained access to Husserl's unpublished manuscripts (cf. H. L. Van Breda, "Maurice Merleau-Ponty et les Archives-Husserl à Louvain," *Revue de métaphysique et de morale* 67 [1962]: 410–30), often interpreted Husserl in a way which was not in accordance with the prevailing view—for instance, when he claimed that Husserl took the problem of historicity more seriously than Heidegger (Merleau-Ponty, *Merleau-Ponty à la Sorbonne* [Paris: Cynara, 1988], 421–22).

66. *Passive Synthesis*, 186.

67. *Intersubjektivität III*, 438, cf. Ms. D 13 234b.

68. Cf. *Intersubjektivität II*, 117, 125; *Intersubjektivität III*, 136.

69. *Intersubjektivität III*, 611. Cf. G. Brand, "Die Normalität des und der Anderen und die Anomalität einer Erfahrungsgemeinschaft bei Edmund Husserl," in *Alfred Schütz und die Idee des Alltags in den Sozialwissenschaften* (Stuttgart: Enke, 1978), 118.

70. *Ideen II*, 269.

71. *Intersubjektivität III*, 428–29, 569, 602–4.

72. *Intersubjektivität III*, 47.

73. *Intersubjektivität III*, 141, 231, 629.

74. *Intersubjektivität III*, 142.

75. *Intersubjektivität III*, 162, 166; *Phänomenologische Psychologie*, 497.

76. To give a concrete example: our constitution of colors is not impeded by the fact that there are blind people, who are unable to perceive them (*Cartesianische Meditationen,* 154; *Intersubjektivität III,* 48). For a more extended treatment of this problem see, for instance, *Zur Phänomenologie der Intersubjektivität I,* text 14: "Solipsistische und intersubjektive Normalität und Konstitution von Objektivität"; *Zur Phänomenologie der Intersubjektivität III,* text 10: "Die Welt der Normalen und das Problem der Beteiligung der Anomalen an der Weltkonstitution"; and text 11: "Apodiktische Struktur der transzendentalen Subjektivität. Problem der transzendentalen Konstitution der Welt von der Normalität aus."

77. *Krisis,* 324.

78. *Intersubjektivität II,* 111.

79. Although the mathematical characterization of the object, which is valid for all rational subjects, is the most objective, Husserl emphasizes that this kind of description is completely irrelevant in our daily practical life. There we are not occupied with scientific objects, but with tools and values, with pictures, statues, gardens, houses, tables, etc. (*Ideen II,* 27). Furthermore our practical interest is led by practical concerns. That which is sufficient in our daily life counts as the *thing in itself* (*Passive Synthesis,* 23).

80. *Krisis,* 369–74; *Logik (Hua),* 38, 349. In connection with his reflections on the constitutive function of language, Husserl also touches on its seductive power (*Krisis,* 372). Instead of living and acting responsibly according to evidence, we can be, and most often are, seduced by the assumptions and structures of comprehension and apperception which are imbedded in language (cf. *Ideen II,* 269). Husserl's analysis has much in common with Heidegger's analysis of idle talk (*Gerede*) in *Sein und Zeit* (Tübingen: Max Niemeyer, 1986), §35.

81. *Intersubjektivität III,* 155.

82. *Intersubjektivität III,* 35–36.

83. *Intersubjektivität III,* 138–39, 431. For an extensive discussion of this aspect, see A. Steinbock, *Home and Beyond: Generative Phenomenology after Husserl* (Evanston, Ill.: Northwestern University Press, 1995).

84. *Intersubjektivität III,* 421.

85. *Intersubjektivität III,* 220.

86. *Erste Philosophie II,* 52; *Ideen I,* 331; *Krisis,* 282; *Cartesianische Meditationen,* 138; *Intersubjektivität III,* 33. This does not imply, however, that there are no apodictic truths whatsoever, but only that that which can be corrected is always open for further corrections.

87. *Intersubjektivität III,* 212, 381; *Krisis,* 270, Ms. C 17 31a.

88. *Intersubjektivität III,* 214.

89. Ms. C 17 32a.

90. *Intersubjektivität III,* 199.

91. *Intersubjektivität III,* 171.

92. *Krisis,* 256.

93. *Intersubjektivität II,* 223.

94. *Intersubjektivität III,* 426.

95. *Intersubjektivität III,* 61, 139, 142, 499.

96. *Krisis,* 382.

97. Thus, S. Strasser was right when he wrote that the publication of Husserl's manuscripts on intersubjectivity has uncovered surprising material, which has shown that all current views about the content of Husserl's philosophy were inadequate (S. Strasser, "Grundgedanken der Sozialontologie Edmund Husserls," *Zeitschrift für philosophische Forschung* 29 [1975]: 33).

PART V

Phenomenological Method

11

The Systematicity of Husserl's Transcendental Philosophy

From Static to Genetic Method

Donn Welton

> In its main line I am coming to a—system.[1]
> —Husserl to Bell, 1920

IT SEEMS STRANGE to use the notions of "system" and "systematicity" in relation to Husserl's transcendental philosophy as a whole. Did he not think of his phenomenology as standing in opposition to the great systems of thought coming to us from German Idealism? Did he not reject system building as speculative and antithetical to the spirit of "rigorous science" that should pervade genuine philosophy? Did he not view systems of philosophy, like those of Fichte, Schelling, Hegel, and even Kant, as "mythical" fabrications, without foundations in experience? In contrast to them, did he not champion a philosophical procedure that returns to the concrete texture of experience, with its open and inescapable "horizonal" character, and describes the various structures of the different regions of existence? In short, did not Husserl's phenomenology displace system with method?

With this in view, we are surprised to find Husserl preoccupied with the question of system in the very late teens into the twenties. Originally Husserl projected three volumes to his *Ideas Pertaining to a Pure Phenomenology and Phenomenological Philosophy.* The first was published in 1913, but the second remained in manuscript form, and the third progressed no further than sketches.[2] The war, the loss of one son, the serious wounding of another (twice), and the difficult times afterwards would have contributed to long delays in bringing this project to completion, but they cannot account for his decision to set it aside all together. Rather, he grew increasingly unhappy with his first formulation of transcendental phenomenology, and, thus, it was his desire to press further in his understanding of the phenomenological method that was decisive.

In 1921 he began preparing what he called a "large systematic work," a project which superseded his original plan to finish the publication of the three volumes of *Ideas*. At the end of November 1921 he wrote Roman Ingarden: "For several months now I am working through my much too large mass of manuscripts and am planning a large systematic work, which, building up from below, could serve as [the] foundational work of phenomenology."[3] I begin this paper by tracing three projects that Husserl worked on intensely between 1920 and 1923 in an effort to construct what he now calls systematic phenomenology.

In another letter to Ingarden the very next month, Husserl reassured him that he would not "overthrow" *Ideas I*, even though a number of its points were not well developed and all of its principal matters needed to be "purified." "Indeed, I have come so much further," he says.[4] In this context, Husserl mentioned his current courses over four semesters, but specifically he had in view his lectures on transcendental logic, first given in the Winter Semester of 1920–21. These lectures, which were expanded and given again in the Summer Semester of 1923 and the Winter Semester of 1925–26,[5] have been printed in part as *Analysen zur passiven Synthesis,* the text from which I draw at several points in my analysis. Husserl worked on them intensely. Their importance became clear to others as well. Pfänder, writing from Munich in March of 1921, knew of them,[6] and one of Pfänder's students, Phillip Schwarz, decided to begin his further studies in Freiburg early in order to hear them.[7] The material found in these lectures is part of Husserl's larger project to expand the scope of his previous phenomenology and to develop a system. While planning and drafting these lectures, he wrote Bell in September of 1920: "I want to draft the Logic [lectures] in an entirely new spirit, as the most universal formal doctrine of the principles of the whole of philosophy. In its main line I am coming to a—system."[8] The lectures, he also told Ingarden in December of 1920, were "the fruit of labor over many years."[9] It seems that his belief in the importance of these lectures for his system only increased when they were repeated in the Winter Semester of 1925–26, for he wrote Mahnke during that semester that they handle "the basic fundamentals of a systematic phenomenology of world-constitution."[10]

The invitation to give the London lectures in the summer of 1922 delayed his progress on the Logic because the first half of 1922 was spent largely on their preparation. As is true of his lectures given abroad—here in London and later in Paris—Husserl attempted to introduce those unfamiliar with his thought to the heart of his theory in direct fashion. The London lectures were largely a new account of his Cartesian way. Husserl then offered a lecture course, "Introduction to Philosophy,"[11] during the following Winter Semester of 1922–23 and decided to use the London lectures as his springboard. In a letter to Bell in December of 1922, he referred to these lectures in connection with his effort to construct a systematic method. The lectures themselves, however, are preoccupied with the first step in that larger project, that is, with the issue of a proper "beginning" or point of access to a systematic method:

> It is for me the most difficult course and actually I am working, for over a year, on the systematic course of thought that I am now bringing to lecture form—it is the same that was lectured in London in compressed form. It has become clearer time and again for me—precisely from being bound to teaching and from the many attempts (under different titles) at lectures directed towards an introduction into phenomenology—that here is where one of the largest tasks of a system of philosophy lies: the question [*Aufgabe*] of the proper beginning, the guided ascent of the knower from the step of natural conceptual naiveté to the step of the beginning of "absolutely justified science," that of "philosophy."[12]

His 1922–23 lecture course "Introduction to Philosophy" blended materials from the London lectures but then expanded on their basic concepts in an effort to think through the starting point of phenomenology. The letter continues:

> The production of the correct motivation, laying bare the necessity of "beginning" with the ego cogito, to give it the sense of the phenomenological reduction, moving from transcendental consciousness and ego to the eidetic analysis of the transcendental sphere, and, thereby, to expand the ego, the pure I to the "I-all," taking up empathy, and so on—I am breaking my head over this, which is not for comfortable people.[13]

The first project, the Logic lectures, was largely concerned with an analysis of what he called "passive synthesis" and was an account of perception and the various modalities of experience that bring one to reflective judgment. The second project, his lecture course "Introduction to Philosophy," was preoccupied with the question of the starting point of a transcendental analysis. But there is a third project from this period that is equally important. During the fall of 1922 and the winter of 1923, the same period when he was giving his "Introduction to Philosophy," he composed the first three of what are known as the *Kaizo* articles.[14] In contrast to the Logic lectures, this was a study of "active synthesis" extended beyond acts of judgment to the movements of intellectual culture as a whole. The *Kaizo* articles were the first published works in which he sketched his own theory of history, a project to which he returned in the later manuscripts and the *Crisis*.

What unifies these three projects is the fact that with the turn to a systematic philosophy Husserl developed a distinction within his transcendental phenomenology between "static" and "genetic" method. Contrary to most interpretations, I want to show that this difference is not an afterthought but was already in play, though not developed, in his first formulation of transcendental phenomenology in *Ideas I*. And I want to suggest not only that it is coherent but that it is essential to understanding both the scope and the depth of Husserl's work as a whole. But first we must complete this introductory sketch.

This effort to find a proper route into his systematic phenomenology, to find an appropriate point of access, led to frustration. "Introduction to Philosophy" builds upon but adjusts the Cartesian approach of the London lectures, thereby complicating its execution. He returned to the Logic lectures, expanded them, and gave them again in the Summer Semester of 1923. But they were more of an application of genetic method to the sphere of passive synthesis than a discussion of method proper. The next semester, the Winter Semester of 1923–24, Husserl began to explore in systematic fashion alternative routes to the reduction in his lecture course "First Philosophy."[15] His concerns with a proper beginning to transcendental analysis deflected Husserl from his original design of constructing a systematic phenomenology, though he clearly had most of the basic ideas in place by the end of 1924. At the same time, the idea of not just a single but different points of access to phenomenological analysis was encouraged by his further reflections on genetic method. It took him another five or six years to return to the system as a whole.[16]

It is tempting to continuing tracing this history. But I intend this only as a preface to the question of systematicity in Husserl's transcendental method, and thus in what follows I will refer to his own historical development only as it fits into the systematic difference between static and genetic phenomenology.[17]

1. The Transcendental Turn and the Idea of a Transcendental Method in *Ideas I*[18]

> The transcendental "absolute," which we have open to view through the reductions, is, in truth, not the final [level], which is something that constitutes itself in a certain profound and completely peculiar sense of its own and has its ultimate source in what is finally and truly absolute.
>
> Fortunately, we can leave out of consideration the enigma of time-consciousness in our preliminary analyses without endangering their rigor.
>
> —Husserl (1913)[19]

To capture Husserl's first formulation of transcendental method and, thereby, his first account of what he came to call "static method," we need to turn briefly to *Ideas I*.

The story of Husserl's shift from a descriptive psychological method in the *Logical Investigations* (1900–1901) to a transcendental phenomenological method in *Ideas I* (1913) is well known and need not occupy us here. As we look at *Ideas I* itself, we discover that Husserl had been sobered by his reading of Kant and was concerned to settle any lingering suspicion that he was still in the grip of psychologism. At the same time, he rejected the method of "reconstruction" employed by a neo-Kantian like Natorp[20] and searched for a method that does not employ hypothetical constructions. His study of Descartes between the *Investigations* and *Ideas I* suggested the "principle of all principles." Husserl thought of it as his "*absolute beginning* called upon to serve as a foundation, a *principium* in the genuine sense of the word."[21] In contrast to what we will see in Fichte, it is basically an epistemological principle and is used to establish his notion of evidence. Thus it reads: "every originary presentive intuition is a legitimizing source of cognition."[22] Whatever one might say about the covert metaphysical commitments implicit here, Husserl viewed this not as a substantive but as a methodological starting point. This principle was then unfolded in terms of an internal difference between the immanent and transcendent mode of givenness and a corresponding contrast between "adequate" and "inadequate" evidence. When Husserl, looking over his shoulder at Descartes, applied this principle to the "natural world," these criteria led him to distinguish between the "merely phenomenal being of what is transcendent" and the "absolute being of the immanent."[23] The latter, as we know, is the dimension in which "absolute consciousness" or "transcendental subjectivity" comes to givenness and is thematized. The world, in turn, becomes relative to "pure" subjectivity and is understood as that which appears to or in consciousness. What Husserl did at this point is crucial to the course of our deliberations. He did not treat transcendental subjectivity as a being from which the rest of being can be deduced or, by the power of the dialectic, can be elicited. He steadfastly resists introducing a metaphysical characterization of absolute consciousness from which one could spin out the world. Rather, the method that secures the ground of all ontic regions in subjectivity also provides each with its basic form of analysis: since the as-structure of appearances is understood in terms of the one to or for whom objects and complexes are manifest, all analysis is "correlational." In accounting for the determinacy of phenomena, the relevant type of sense structure (noema) is placed in relation to the type of act (noesis) in and through which objects or complexes are intended and apprehended. This is Husserl's well-known theory of intentionality. Consciousness was thereby given a transcendental characterization: it is a universal *a priori* structure, bipolar in nature, basic to all phenomena. Transcendental subjectivity was not a principle from which one could make speculative deductions but a correlational noetic-noematic structure undergirding the various ontic regions. The "absolute" provides an account of the *constitution* of phenomena, of their presentational structure, not their *creation* or their *construction*.

One could say that in place of a system Husserl introduced the idea of a method in *Ideas I*. Husserl spoke of it as the reduction. Its application not only frees up subjectivity as a sphere of analysis, but also insures that the reflection upon that field does not exercise its own transformative effects upon what is given. The reduction secures the idea that phenomenology is a *descriptive* and not an explanatory or reconstructive enterprise. Since the reduction is also an "eidetic reduction," its descriptions are always structural. Its application uncovers not the fact but the essence of subjectivity, or, to put it more accurately, the essence or the "possibility" of the fact of subjectivity. Reflecting back on his first formulations, he said "the reduction does not, first of all, simply lead to the *actual* stream of consciousness (and its ego-pole), but, as I put it in 1910, each experienced thing . . . is an index for an infinite manifold of *possible* experience."[24]

What analytic, deconstructive, and critical theory interpretations of Husserl share is the idea that what I just described gives us the core and exhausts the scope of Husserl's method. Since his Cartesian notion of evidence is problematic and since it unknowingly imported certain metaphysical categories with it, the method is flawed, and the results of its application must be rejected.

What they fail to realize is that *Ideas I* provided only a first approximation. Husserl later characterizes the working method of *Ideas I* as "static" analysis. At the very least, this means that it is a method that gives us general *structural* descriptions of the various domains of being in correlation to types of mental acts in and through which those domains "show" the general determinations that they have. From the perspective of his later work, we can say that the transcendental phenomenology of *Ideas I* was limited to the immediately intuitable, essential structures of transcendental subjectivity.[25] But in *Ideas I* Husserl also gives us the most important reason why his analyses there cannot be more than an introduction: he expressly eliminated the question of time from his account: "Fortunately, we can leave out of consideration the enigma of time-consciousness in our preliminary analyses [of the transcendental absolute] without endangering their rigor."[26] The transcendental analysis of subjectivity, as a result, studied its *being*, not its *becoming*. This also means that Husserl's first method lacked strategies of transformative and historical interpretation. Yet these considerations were not eliminated, were not excluded on principle, but only set aside for the time being. The suspension of any temporal analysis, itself understood as essential to phenomenology in its full scope, marks the place into which genetic analysis moves.

What complicates our account is that Husserl characterized the transcendental domain in quasi-metaphysical terms as "a systematically self-enclosed infinity of essential properties" and as an "absolute being" in the sense of being "a primal category" or a "primal region" in which all other regions are rooted.[27] The treatment of intentionality as a grounding "realm of being" was spawned by his Cartesian formulation of the reduction in *Ideas I*, itself fostered by his theory of "Cartesian evidence."[28] They combined to create an ontological divide between the being of the world and the being of subjectivity. As a result the ground of the various regions of the world is secured apart from a *regressive* analysis that would move back from their structures to their origins. Instead, we are limited to an account that gives us an irreducible, necessary, and universal structure apprehended "all at once" in a transcendental reflection, without a clear understanding of how it is internally connected to the regional ontologies we are attempting to clarify. Husserl is expressly critical of the way in which his first formulations of static analysis are dominated by what he later calls the "Cartesian way." The extensive discussions of the various ways into phenomenological analysis in the 1920s had the effect not only of enhancing his conception of transcendental method but also, as I will now suggest, of framing a static analysis outside the strictures of the Cartesian way.

2. The Scope of Constitutive Phenomenology[29]

For I am working not on a mere phenomenology of time[30]—one that allows itself to be separated purely for itself—but on the colossal problem of individuation, of the constitution of individual (thus "factual") being in general, and that according to its essentially basic formations. Thus it is now a matter of a . . . radical phenomenology.

—Husserl to Ingarden (1918)[31]

In 1921 Husserl devoted some eight handwritten pages to an analysis that he entitled "Static and Genetic Phenomenological Methods."[32] This text is important not only because of its clarity but also because of its hesitations, its turns, and its reversals. We do not find this text completely coherent, but it is one of those rare passages where Husserl attempted to define his own operative terms at a time when he was reframing the systematic scope of his phenomenological method.

Like sparks leaping from metal on a rapidly moving stone, the key concepts in Husserl's analysis fly quickly from his pen. In a note he distinguishes between not two but *three* different kinds or levels of phenomenological analysis:

Phenomenology:
Universal phenomenology of the general structures of consciousness
Constitutive phenomenology
Phenomenology of genesis.[33]

Husserl then immediately contrasts a "descriptive" or "static" phenomenology to an "explanatory phenomenology" (*beschreibende* vs. *erklärende Phänomenologie*).[34] How are we to understand these terms? In particular why do we find a discipline called constitutive phenomenology inserted between a phenomenology of the general structures of consciousness and genetic phenomenology?

At first Husserl thinks of "constitutive phenomenology" as belonging to static or descriptive phenomenology. "With these descriptions, the constitutive ones, there is no questioning after an explanatory genesis."[35] And we know that there is an even broader use of the notion of constitutive phenomenology as a synonym for his phenomenological method as a whole, as in a letter to Boyce Gibson in 1932: "I am of absolute certainty that constitutive phenomenology and it alone has future."[36] But in a few pages constitutive analysis seems much more like a bridge between static and genetic accounts. At the beginning constitutive phenomenology treats the "interconnections" of those items first introduced whole cloth in a static account. But, later, there is

another "constitutive" phenomenology, that of the genesis, [which] follows the history, the necessary history of this objectification and, thereby, the history of the object itself.[37]

With this, the border between static or descriptive and genetic or explanatory phenomenology seems to fade, for Husserl thinks that constitutive analysis somehow belongs to both.

So far we have but a string of names. We do not understand their import, nor do we see how these new reflections upon method are related to Husserl's first comprehensive introduction to transcendental phenomenology in *Ideas I*.

We find a phrase from our 1921 text that interprets the whole of *Ideas I* for Husserl; static analysis is a "universal phenomenology of the general structures of consciousness."[38] He adds that it is a

> phenomenology of the possibly essential forms in pure consciousness, however they have come about, and their teleological order in the domain of possible reason under the titles "object" and "sense."[39]

The program of tracing the general structures of consciousness is a "first ordering" of phenomenology; it schematizes the structure of intentionality in terms of the three interdependent moments of the ego-cogito-cogitatum.[40] Sometimes Husserl calls this "analytic phenomenology." I want to call this first ordering "categorial phenomenology." The key to categorial phenomenology is that it is built upon, as it restricts itself to, the relationship between the as- and for-structures, to the relationship between things appearing *as* something and the one *to* whom or *for* whom they appear. By classifying or categorizing the essential forms of cognition, it supplies a typology of intentionality.

In *Ideas I* transcendental phenomenology was taken to be constitutive phenomenology. But with the development of a genetic phenomenology, Husserl came to treat constitutive analysis as a further extension or deepening of the first "universal phenomenology of the general structures of consciousness." The notion of horizon, uncovered in *Ideas I,* is applied to transcendental consciousness itself.[41] Constitutive phenomenology must penetrate to the underlying modalizations and transformations that give rise to manifest structures. In this way constitutive analysis uncovers a depth to "the sphere of being" first opened by the transcendental reduction and described by categorial analysis.

We could say, then, that constitutive phenomenology isolates the deep structures of different types or levels of experience. The *correlation* between achievement and sense—first discovered in a reflection upon the transcendent object given in and through its appearances—is framed as a *constitutive* condition of that object in its difference from others, and then expanded through an account of the various "levels" or "layers," nested in a given categorial type, that *motivate* "the achievement of transcendence."[42] Constitutive phenomenology provides an account of regions by recourse to the way they are "built up." It accounts not only for structure but also for "origins."

Husserl's "systematic phenomenology"[43] works with several contrasting features of categorial and constitutive analysis. The *topic* of the former is a typology or classification of the different "essential shapes"[44] of noetic-noematic correlations, while the second provides a description of the "modal modifications" that "encompass all categories of apperception," both passive and active.[45] The *starting point* for categorial analysis is the "division of apperceptions according to regions of objects," that is, regional ontologies.[46] Constitutional analysis proper simply builds upon the results of such a classification. Constitutive phenomenology, then, does not give us yet "another" region besides the ones opened by categorial analysis but rather describes structures, belonging to the order of sense or meaning, which allow them to become determinate fields. Gathering these two together, Husserl asked: "Is not static phenomenology precisely the phenomenology of guiding threads, the phenomenology of the constitution of leading types of objectivities?"[47] The clearest contrast can be seen in the *scheme* of analysis. Working with the difference between profile and object, categorial analysis uses the distinction between intention and fulfillment to frame its descriptions. "I follow the correlation: unity of the appearing object and multiplicity of the appearances uniting in such a way that they are noetically harmonious."[48] In contrast to such horizontal studies, a vertical analysis provides us with a "typology of the interconnections in consciousness of a particular developmental level,"[49] as well as a description of the "modalizations" transforming one level into another. While the focus in categorial phenomenology is on the identity and difference of eidetic structures of a given field, the concern in constitutive phenomenology is to trace the implicit "origin" of those structures. For example, it examines the transformations by which everyday speech becomes rigorous propositional discourse, or the levels of experience implicit in what we might call epistemic perception.

The contrast between categorial and constitutive analysis is essential to understanding the nature of phenomenological descriptions. In contrast to a horizontal axis along which we may situate various regions, a vertical axis is opened, transforming the grounding structure of intentionality into a transcendental *field*. In adding depth, it enables us to understand how the regions explicated by regional ontologies are *derived*.[50] The difference between surface and depth establishes an *internal* connection between regional and transcendental fields. This is the first sense in which we can speak of phenomenology as a system.

The richness of Husserl's constitutive analyses results from viewing a phenomenon and its attending act(s) in terms of the modalizations to which they are connected. In that the theory of modalization is used to examine the relationship between various act-object correlations latent or implicit in a manifest structure, it begins to provide account of horizonal background. Beginning with an object of experience, we move regressively, from the aesthetic qualities to the spatial configurations to the temporal deployment of the correlation. In this way temporality is discovered as a condition and yet analyzed *structurally*. In breaking with the usual way this is understood, I am suggesting that the difference between static and genetic analysis cannot be construed simply as a contrast between synchronic and diachronic analysis. What we are speaking of as static or synchronic analysis also has a diachronic side to it since a constitutive account generally requires comparisons of features at T_1, T_2, ... T_n. We allow temporal "form" to factor into the description of the given. These, however, are structural comparisons that do not raise the question of development and of the *transformation* of T_1 into T_2 into T_n. They are not yet an "internal" diachronic account. But what does this mean?

Although his theory of time leads into some of Husserl's most profound studies and, as we will suggest, provides the key to his genetic account, its analysis makes its first entry at the level of constitutive analysis. Here we can only attend to a provisional answer to our immediate question. We find a certain development in Husserl's understanding of the nature of temporality not just between 1905 and about 1910, as studied in Brough's and Bernet's excellent accounts,[51] but also between that period and the early 1920s. As Husserl reflected upon his first studies of temporalization, he suggested that they treated time only according to its form, and viewed its transformations only as modalizations. As a result, we have arrived at, but not entered, a genetic account:

> With these descriptions, the constitutive ones, there is no question of an explanatory genesis. Nor is there one if we move from original impressions (perceptions) —as a generally typical or generic characterization applicable to all apperceptions —to a constitutive characterization, to descriptions of all the modal transformations in retentions, recollections, expectations, etc., and thereby follow a principle systematically ordering the apperceptions, one that [vertically] cuts across the sorting of the apperceptions according to the most general genera of objects.[52]

To view time as a "generic" or "typical" feature or as a "modal transformation" of apperceptions is really to treat time as no different than other modal "forms." But "the span of living retention" belonging to the "living present," Husserl realized, is not itself a modalization, nor is it, by itself, capable of being modalized.[53] However, the special tie between the nonmodal phases of temporality or premodalized objects of experience and temporality itself is not clear at first in his account.

We find other hints that Husserl grew increasingly concerned with his initial analysis of time. In particular the account of the present was too abstract, as though it were a form that could be severed from its content. Thus he says, "mere form is obviously an abstraction, and thus the intentional analysis of time and its achievement is, from the outset, an abstractive one." As a consequence, the first theory of time does not give us "the necessary synthetic structures of the streaming present and the unified stream of the present somehow affecting what is specific to content."[54] Husserl exclaimed, "and so the entire theory of time-consciousness is a conceptual idealization."[55] In short, we do not yet have a theory that articulates the "concrete present" in its essential "streaming,"[56] nor have we accounted for the sense in which time is *internal* to the "difference of content."[57] In view of these self-critical remarks, it seems plausible to suggest that while time was understood as the most basic level of constitution, the account of time-consciousness itself was initially a piece of *constitutive* phenomenology. As such its results work well for the type of analysis we just sketched but need to be deepened for a genetic account. In any case, time is in play for constitutive analysis, and this accounts for the reason that constitutive analysis is the hinge between a static and a genetic account.

But what, then, is genetic analysis? We will approach this question both historically (Section 3) and systematically (Section 4).

3. Transposing Genetic Analysis into a Transcendental Register

> For more than a decade I have already overcome
> the stage of static Platonism and have framed the idea of
> transcendental genesis as the main theme of phenomenology.
> —Husserl to Natorp (1918)[58]

We find the term "genetic" as early as the first edition of the *Logical Investigations* (1900–1901), where it is used in a entirely negative fashion as roughly equivalent to the type of analysis that we find in Locke and thus as part of a psychologistic theory of knowledge. In section 7 of the Fifth Investigation, a section so poorly written that he dropped it altogether from the second edition (1913), Husserl is struggling to understand the scope of psychology as a natural scientific discipline. He speaks of it as dealing with the "soul." The term "soul" is "what designates the field of empirical psychology, which is a doctrine of 'psychic' lived experiences or 'contents of consciousness.'"[59] He then supplies a mixed characterization of psychology as having two levels:[60]

> Psychology's task—descriptively—is to study the ego-experiences (or conscious contents) in their essential species and forms of combination, in order to explore —genetically—their origin and perishing, and the causal patterns and laws of their formation and transformation. For psychology, conscious contents are contents of an ego, and so its task is to explore the real essence of the [empirical] ego . . . , to explore the interweaving of psychic elements in the ego and their subsequent development and degeneration.[61]

By contrast, the proper subject matter of phenomenology, as he warned his readers in the foreword (1913) to the second edition of his *Investigations,* is not "lived experiences or classes of lived experiences of empirical persons" but the structure of "pure" experience.[62] The consequence of this difference for our considerations is clear: since genetic analysis always belonged to a natural causal description of the development of human cognition in the *Investigations,* it too is banished from his transcendental phenomenology. At best, it belongs to a part of the regional discipline of psychology. Giving Husserl's division of natural psychology a descriptive and a genetic side, one can see why his characterization of the method of phenomenology in the first edition of the *Investi-*

gations as a "descriptive psychology" created such massive confusion and was dropped by the time of *Ideas I.*

Genetic Analysis and Psychology in Natorp

We get an important clue as to source of this notion of genetic analysis from the next section of the Fifth Investigation (first edition). Section 8, in an effort to argue that phenomenology does not need an egological conception of consciousness, an idea Husserl retracted in *Ideas I,*[63] cites and criticizes Paul Natorp's *Einleitung in die Psychologie nach kritischer Methode,* a book published in 1888.[64] Apart from the question of an egological conception, Natorp speaks in that work of the place and validity of a genetic analysis. For Natorp the question of whether objective space and objective time is an "acquisition of experience," whether it is related to "representational space" or "representational time," both "originary and immediate," is a "genetic insight."[65] In section 13 of his book Natorp then raises the question of whether psychology is only a descriptive discipline or whether it also offers explanation (*Erklärung*). If we, like Kant, assume that science proper always requires mathematical grounding, then psychology could never be one since it lacks both experiments and any application of mathematics. Accordingly, it would be a "merely descriptive science."[66] Natorp objects that psychology does employ causal explanations and thus is not merely descriptive. This leads to this account, quoted at length, as it will bear a striking resemblance to what we will find in Husserl shortly:

> In fact, psychology itself has been unable to choose to restrict itself to mere description. It strives to go forward "genetically," tracing psychic products back to their simplest factors when possible, following the "development" of psychological life from germ-like beginnings, from given structures as elementary as possible, and it does this not only in individual lives but also in the life of the people and, finally, of humanity.[67]

Natorp, however, views psychology strictly as a natural science and incapable of thematizing consciousness in its immediacy or what Husserl would call its pure self-givenness. This is because any psychic event that is immediate would be something subjectively given before all determinations. As soon as we reflect on it and describe it, however, it becomes what it is not, for reflection and description are themselves constitutive of the determinacy of the psychic event. Natorp views reflective experience as a process of objectifying the appearance and thus as a "scientific achievement."[68] To get at the event in its immediacy we must resort to reconstruction. Descriptive and genetic analyses are legitimate parts of psychology, but left to themselves they will not capture consciousness as it is first given to us. This alignment of descriptive and genetic analysis is echoed in Husserl, who also thinks of psychology, including its genetic component, as a natural science.

Husserl's view that the natural science of psychology has both a descriptive and a genetic side is also found in lectures from 1906–7.[69] Husserl's critique there is a significant refinement over the *Investigations*, for he strongly distinguishes epistemological clarification (*erkenntnistheoretische Aufklärung*) from both "descriptive psychology" and "genetic" psychological accounts of origins or development. Genetic accounts relate "intellective function" to "a manifold of biological functions."[70] There is only one place that might point to the idea of genetic analysis that we will find in Husserl's later work. After speaking about how psychology must describe the various types of psychic events, Husserl pauses to think about conceptual formations:

> To the extent that these are events that have a logical function or that gain a logical function, we, in a way that goes beyond description, have to lay out [*darlegen*] and clarify genetically how they came to this function.[71]

In context Husserl argues that psychobiological origins can clarify neither the "logical dignity" of notions essential to epistemology nor "the dignity of knowledge"[72] as a whole. Genetic analysis belongs to psychology as a "natural science,"[73] not "epistemology." The consequence of this difference for our considerations is clear: since genetic analysis always belonged to a psychological description of the development of human cognition in the *Investigations* and in his 1906–7 lectures, *Einleitung in die Logik und Erkenntnistheorie*, it too is banished from his transcendental phenomenology to a part of the regional discipline of psychology.

Given all this, we are stunned when we find Husserl writing to Natorp in 1918 that "for more than a decade I have already overcome the stage of static Platonism and have framed the idea of transcendental genesis as the main theme of phenomenology."[74] What could this possibly mean? Even if we grant that the time span might be exaggerated, why did Husserl make this turn to genetic analysis and even call it the "main theme" of the transcendental phenomenology he is developing? And what would such an analysis look like?

I want to suggest that Natorp's influence may be at work here as well. In 1912 Natorp published his *Allgemeine Psychologie*.[75] In *Ideas I* Husserl pauses to say that he has not yet read nor considered this most recent work of Natorp, which Husserl must have seen just as his own book was going to press.[76] By the time he wrote the foreword to the second edition of the *Investigations* (1913), however, it seems that he was familiar with its content.[77]

Picking up themes we found in his *Einleitung in die Psychologie*, Natorp disputes the claim by his contemporaries that because psychology is not a strict science of laws (*Gesetzeswissenschaft*), psychology must be a merely descriptive science and not an explanatory one.[78] "Fact and principle, description and explanation belong together," he says.[79] Still, description only has a "preparatory function."[80] In psychology, description is primarily "analysis" and "abstraction," for it "lifts individual moments out of the totality of the nexus of lived experience."[81] It thereby sets the direction that explanation must subsequently follow.

Natorp, however, was worried about how we can do psychology in a way that avoids objectivation, that is, avoids turning the subject into what it is not. Psychology seeks the "subjective of consciousness" on this side of all "objectivation" and the "indeterminate" on this side of the "determinate."[82] But how are we to thematize consciousness while avoiding objectivation?

While consciousness is immediate, we do not grasp and observe subjective consciousness immediately in the course of our everyday experience. We have to reflect. Echoing what we found in his earlier work, the intervention of reflection means that the immediate is no longer the immediate. Anticipating a problem that Husserl's reduction was designed to prevent, reflection exercises functions of its own upon what it experiences. It analyzes, dissects, and decomposes.[83] To "restore" what is immediately experienced, we would have to neutralize, in some way, the work of analysis. This means that for Natorp psychology is always a "reconstruction."[84] In particular, analysis always carries an abstraction with it. The goal of the reconstruction, however, is to go beyond that and restore the connections found in the original complex. Natorp hopes to do this by suggesting that three different levels to the analysis are necessary to comprehend consciousness in its unity and originality. Here is where we find a surprising parallel to Husserl's account in the 1921 manuscript "Static and Genetic Phenomenological Method":

1. The first province of psychology is a general description of the different types of consciousness. He spoke of this as a phenomenology of consciousness and even claimed that it "approximately corresponds to what Husserl refers to with that name."[85] It consists of a "sheer description of the formations of consciousness according to their types."[86]
2. The second area traces the step-like succession of the unities of consciousness. This analysis is largely concerned with referring the contents of "lived experience" to the "living ego"[87] and ordering different types of mental phenomena (sensations, interconnected presentations, and the unity of thought) to the activities of consciousness.
3. The third domain of psychology, however, is what Natorp calls genetic analysis, which we now need to investigate further.

Natorp suggests that the first two levels "correspond to the predominant objectivating direction of psychology up to now; it was and ever wants to be research into the laws [of psychology]."[88] This new third discipline, however, does not stress the immutable laws of recurring types of mental acts but rather "the change, the development and the genetic construction" of psychological life.[89] This does not mean that we abandon the general standpoint or attitude that gave us laws. But now we are concerned to discover "laws of becoming, of development" and not "laws of a being uniformly maintained and at rest, which, indeed, does not exist in the entire area of psychological life."[90] Since "all development takes place in differentiation,"[91] however, the account of development depends upon the "differentiations" of each type of life found in the first two levels of analysis.

When Natorp raises the question of how we are to understand "development" in terms of time, we find new ideas that take him beyond his simple identification of genetic analysis with natural, causal explanations. Following Kant here, Natorp employed a strictly transcendental interpretation of "origin," "production," and "spontaneity." As a consequence, he argued for "a purely logical genesis that in itself contains nothing of the order of objectivated time."[92] In fact, the thorough separation of the transcendental from the psychological standpoint meant that for Kant the order of time "springs" out of the "logical, in themselves timeless relations of pure thought."[93] From a transcendental standpoint, time is itself constituted. This point allowed Natorp to argue that while we cannot think of consciousness as being in time from a transcendental perspective, we can think of time as being in consciousness.[94] Husserl, he thinks, would agree.[95] Time is not basic to consciousness, but consciousness is basic to time. This has important implications for Natorp's method. Consciousness must be presented in terms of the expansion and differentiation of its content and range, not its "temporal course."[96] The effect of this is to derive time from consciousness, not consciousness from temporality. His descriptions introduced a very different notion of genetic analysis from what we find in empirical psychology:

> The whole temporal disposition of lived experiences finds it place under this "development" of consciousness, not temporal in itself. The construction of consciousness in psychology should certainly be genetic, but this genesis, as in logic and mathematics, must be considered, purely according to its content, primarily as a development of relations into relations under relations, and so on, not as temporal development—though it might follow. As in the case of all sortings [*Sonderungen*] in consciousness, so also temporal sorting is to be thought of as an abstraction, which is precisely what in the final, strictly concrete treatment of the life of consciousness, must be rescinded [*aufgehoben*].[97]

Unlike Husserl, Natorp's genetic analysis roots temporal development in a consciousness not temporal "in itself." Natorp seems blind to the whole idea of "internal time-consciousness," so central to Husserl's own account. Husserl will integrate time much more fully into his genetic analysis and his genetic analysis into transcendental analysis proper.[98] But like Husserl, Natorp's notion of genetic is not a piece of causal history. And like Husserl, genetic analysis depends upon two subdisciplines, both of which are descriptive. As Husserl will put it, genetic analysis requires static analysis as its *Leitfaden*.

With the origins of time accounted for, Natorp's psychology viewed the psyche not as temporal but in terms of temporality (provided that we understand that this involves an abstraction). Natorp, however, was convinced that this does not diminish its importance for an account of psychological life. "Thereby time retains its full meaning for the explication of the psychical. It is also the presupposition for a pure presentation of its interconnections."[99] In fact, Natorp directly chided Husserl [100] for having much too static a picture of conscious life. In words that were almost prophetic of Husserl's development, he wrote that Husserl has only arrived at

> Platonism, and, at that, the Platonism in [Plato's] first phrase, that of the essence at rest. But as Plato himself moved beyond this to the deeper insight of the "kinesis" of ideas, of knowledge as the "limit of the unlimited" and, therewith, as eternal process, so Lipps and Husserl must also bring back their fixed world of essences into the flow of movement if they want to end with a true psychology. Only this, the "genetic" insight, provides final clarity about the basic relationship of the subjective and the objective, and does justice to the whole scope of the pressing problems condensed in this basic correlation. [101]

From Husserl's perspective after the transcendental turn, Natorp's analysis could be viewed only as an unwelcome mixture of psychological and transcendental analysis. While the three levels of Natorp's analysis are roughly parallel to the three levels of phenomenology for Husserl, and while the accusation of Platonism must have stung, Husserl would certainly not introduce a genetic account that consists of causal explanations. Nor did he want to think of his difference between a description of the various formations of consciousness and genetic analysis as belonging to psychology. This would be to confuse a natural science with transcendental analysis. But how, then, is Husserl to incorporate genetic analysis into his transcendental theory? Where can Husserl turn for assistance for his new view? Does he find a forerunner in the history of philosophy that might provide guidance here?

Genetic Method and Transcendental Philosophy in Fichte

I suspect that some help might be coming from an unlikely source, from the philosophy of Johann Fichte. Husserl's private and public pronouncements on Fichte would certainly lead us to believe otherwise. In a typical diatribe against the lack of clarity and the utter nonsense (*Widersinnigkeiten*) of the theories of knowledge in modern philosophy, Fichte is listed in bad company along with those who are "blind to the absolute," whose "nonsense remains concealed through a kind of mythology, and whose real strength, at best, rests in intuitions lacking, in their theoretical presentations, strict conceptual articulation." [102] Some ten years later in the *Crisis,* the assessment is much the same, but Husserl's comments also give us an important clue. Fichte, in particular his several versions of his *Wissenschaftslehre,* along with Hegel, is singled out as one whose thought was animated by the "will to science [*Wissenschaft*]." Husserl comments:

> These philosophers were in no way mere conceptual poets. They did not at all lack the serious will to bring forth philosophy as a science that provides ultimate grounds, however much one may wish to change the meaning of ultimate grounding. (One thinks, for example, of the emphatic statements of Fichte in the drafts to his theory of science, or those of Hegel in the "Preface" of his *Phenomenology of Spirit.*) [103]

But this only leads to a puzzle:

> How did it come to pass that they remained bound to their style of mythical conceptual constructions and of an interpretation of the world [shrouded] in dark metaphysical anticipations, and could not penetrate to a scientifically rigorous conceptuality and method? [104]

This argument against Fichte is long-standing, for we find it in a letter to the American Hocking some thirty years earlier:

> Fichte also misconstrued the essential problem of a critique of knowledge and landed, as a consequence, in his . . . mythical ego-metaphysics. [105]

These comments, combined with the complete absence of any analysis of Fichte in Husserl's published works, make it all the more puzzling why I am invoking Fichte in a discussion of Husserl's method. But as is generally the case with Husserl, the plot is much thicker.

We now know—thanks to the collections of essays and lectures edited by Tom Nenon and Hans Rainer Sepp—that Husserl gave a series of three public lectures in 1917, repeated twice in 1918, entitled "Fichte's Ideal of Humanity," in connection with a course for those involved with the war effort. [106] These lectures were written and delivered at a time when Husserl, unhappy with *Ideas I*, was rethinking "the problem of individuation," as he put it to Ingarden, [107] and shortly before he began to draft texts on the difference between static and genetic analysis. They are revealing because they show that Husserl knew not only Fichte's theory of culture and ethics but also his transcendental philosophy and his theory of science in great detail. In reading these lectures one is genuinely surprised at how sympathetically he handles Fichte. Generally, Husserl tends to see historical figures through a twofold interpretative scheme: (a) most thinkers suffer from mythical or poetic thinking and lack rigor; and (b) whatever scattered good insights we do find have all been completed and given systematic rigor in his transcendental phenomenology. Locke, Hume, and even Kant, with whom he is sympathetic, are handled with iron gloves. But with Fichte we are suddenly in a different register. Husserl is comparatively patient, and he spends time doing exact, systematic exposition of Fichte's thought. Fichte, it seems, commands his respect. This is also reflected in a letter to his student Adolf Grimme from this time. Grimme had sent him his own printed lecture on Fichte, which Husserl read. [108] In contrast to Scheler, who earns the caustic remark that "he is a genius, a genius of reproductivity and secondary originality," Husserl says that Fichte has "genuineness" (*Echtheit*). [109]

Fichte is a wonderfully complex thinker, and I can only select one line of thought essential to our account, hoping that you have enough of his theory in hand to fill in the gaps. Fichte was in search of a single principle that could serve as foundational not only for an account of how things are known but also how they come to be. This principle was the ego, but the difficulty is that it, like the basic axiom of any system of all truths, is itself not knowable as itself true. His solution to this problem, as is well known, was to treat it not as a theoretical subject, as in Kant, but pure *Thun,* pure deed or doing. [110] The ego is creative action itself. As soon as the ego is characterized in terms of pure action, Fichte recovered at the level of practical intelligence what we could not get with theoretical intelligence: because the ego is not treated as a mental event but as an achievement, the ego is deployed in what it accomplishes and thereby capable of being directly apprehended. One grasps oneself "as performing the act whereby the self arises" in an *intellectual intuition,* [111] he added. He spoke of intellectual intuition as "the immediate consciousness that I act [*handle*] and what I enact; it is that whereby I know something because I do it." [112] Once he has the ego as active, creative action, he can then unfold, in a series of propositions or a deduction, the way in which the ego, in limiting its own activity, "posits" a difference between ego and non-ego. By modifying Kant's theory of productive imagination Fichte characterizes the sensations, drives, and feelings of the ego as structured in such a way that it requires the non-ego, reality, to exist. This provides him with an operative contrast between what we normally mean by subject and object. With an internal connection between ego and non-ego in hand, Fichte can derive the rest of existence.

According to Fichte, the science of knowledge is both transcendental and deductively organized. Its goal is to derive from the free and fully self-regulating action of the intellect—its "one and only rationally determined and genuinely explanatory assumption" [113]—the entire system of "the necessary mode of its own operation and, with it concurrently, the objective presentations created thereby." [114] In this way "the whole compass of our presentations comes gradually into being before the eyes of the reader." [115] Fichte thought that philosophy begins with this basic principle and moves systematically and by necessity from one presentation to another. The result is that the entirety of experience—the system of necessary presentations—"emerges" as the final result. [116] What is striking is that Fichte calls this entire analysis a *genetic* understanding of experience. This calls for a few additional remarks.

In general Fichte claimed that the genius of idealism, in contrast to "dogmatism," is that the idealist can "clarify the intellect genetically." [117] By this he meant that genetic analysis accounts for the "origins" of our various experiences by seeing how they are connected to the absolute ego. In the course of discussing how an intuition of an object or, more broadly, the not-I gives rise to a "real" intuition of the I, Fichte clarified this by stating that "beginning with this specific state, we can obtain an understanding of the genesis of the intuitions and feelings we have here been discussing." [118] Genetic insight allows us to see how one element in the analysis is derived from or is grounded in another. "So understood, transcendental philosophy, and thus the entire *Wissenschaftslehre,* is a quest for a 'genetic understanding' of human experience in its entirety," [119] he claimed. Interestingly, he also believed that he could give us a "a genetic understanding of the origin of time." [120] Because Fichte recognized that his system is not itself an element of the system, that is, not one of the regions of knowledge but outside of what qualifies as knowledge,[121] his philosophy is in a broad sense descriptive: "The *Wissenschaftslehre* itself does not generate any new cognition. It merely observes the human mind in its original generation of all cognition."[122]

What we find, then, is Fichte characterizing his system of transcendental philosophy, which he thought of as rigorous and as science, as a "genetic understanding" of human experience in its entirety. Husserl, of course, will emphatically reject Fichte's "mythical ego-metaphysics" and the derivation of the existence of the various regions of human experience from the existence of the ego. But the characterization of philosophy as both transcendental and genetic and Fichte's strict separation of philosophy and psychology would be attractive to him. As he put it in a letter written in 1908: "The separation of psychology and logical considerations is the heritage of Kant, Fichte, and all those who have coupled on to these great thinkers."[123]

Of course, there are other similarities, but each also contains important differences that would have to be taken into account. In Fichte's case the *order* of his genetic analysis began with self-consciousness and moved to those things that are derived from it. While this is generally not recognized, Fichte has a procedure of inferring (though never proving) the *existence* of a transcendental foundation for experience from differences within experience itself.[124] It is comparable to Husserl's notion of the *reduction*, which also moves from differences within experience between inner and outer perception. The *ego* for both is primary but treated differently. Because Fichte characterized the ego as productive activity itself—as though Kant's productive imagination were a principle of action and not just syntheses contributing to cognition—the ego becomes the creative source from which all things flow. He says:

> We have to specify how, from the consciousness of ourselves, in accordance with the laws of our consciousness, there flows all the consciousness that, from the ordinary viewpoint, we consider to be [a consciousness of] something outside of us.[125]

Husserl's Cartesian way also began with the ego and understood this as a "sphere of immanence." He, too, was unhappy with Kant's strictly formal characterization of the ego as transcendental unity of apperception. But his theory of the ego was positioned somewhere between Kant and Fichte. It is a "pole" of experience unifying cognitive acts, as in Kant, but its acts are understood as "achievements" (*Leistungen*), as forms of activity. Like Fichte, the ego is also given in "intellectual intuition." But unlike Fichte, what is given is not itself a substantive entity from which the rest of existence can be derived. For Husserl, transcendental subjectivity accounts not for the *existence* of the world but for the *presence* of the world, not for the *being* of the world but for the *constitution* of the world. Since Husserl treated transcendental subjectivity not as a substantive being-for-itself but as the fundamental structure of cognition, he was never tempted to perform deductions from it. And once he moved beyond his Car-

tesian way, his dependence upon intellectual intuition was modified by his notion of eidetic variation. In place of deduction we have adduction. To be more
accurate, genetic analysis in Fichte was understood as a piece of *construction:*

> We receive insight in that we construe *genetically.* If we had not done that, we
> would not have received it for it lies solely in the genesis—in the seeing. Evidence
> is precisely the absolute insight that is shown in the construction. [126]

By contrast we can say that genetic analysis for Husserl was a process of *Abbau,*
of *de-construction.* This means that genetic method for Fichte is designed to
illuminate the organic unity of reason and being, whereas for Husserl the
method is designed to track interconnected webs of significance, temporally
developed and deployed, without an *a priori* assumption that all of them fit
into a single system of thought, or that they all can be deduced from a basic
principle. For Husserl, transcendental subjectivity functions not as a principle
from which the multiple modes of experience can be deduced, but as nexus of
constitution, having a correlative structure, that illuminates the structures of
various regions in their diversity and resemblance.

4. Genetic Method and Systematic Phenomenology [127]

> To trace [the order of] constitution is not to trace the [order of] genesis, which
> is, precisely, the genesis of constitution, itself actuated as genesis in a monad.
>
> —Husserl (1921) [128]

In the first section of this paper I suggested that static analysis *per se* could
be distinguished from those features spawned by Husserl's Cartesian way into
that method. The next section attempted to make good on this claim by looking at Husserl's elaboration of the idea of constitutive phenomenology during
the early 1920s. Let me put this in a way that Husserl did not. His elaboration
of constitutive phenomenology at that time introduced a shift away from characterizing the absolute ground as "the stream of experience" toward treating
it as transcendental subjectivity. As a consequence, I suggested, the transcendental should be viewed not as an immanent *sphere* but as a transcendental *field,*
cocoordinated by horizontal and vertical axes, along which constitutive descriptions move. [129] Because that subjectivity which is marked as "mine" [130] can be
understood only as one in relation to others in this field, this shift makes possible, I believe, Husserl's argument in his later analysis that transcendental subjectivity is intersubjectivity. Notice, however, that these two axes cover both
surface and depth of the phenomenological field. They seem exhaustive. What
else would be required? This claim is further substantiated by the surprising
fact that our constitutive analysis already invoked the notions of retention and
protention, recollection and expectation. According to Husserl's theory, the
analysis of temporality brings us to the most basic "form," the deepest "abso-

lute" [131] beyond which there is nothing further to explore. What would be left for genetic analysis?

There is a second problem. The claim that Husserl has a systematic phenomenology must face a serious challenge: to account for the radical diversity and heterogeneity of that which is covered by the term "genetic phenomenology." Husserl applied this label to areas so different from one another that we are perplexed as to how they could ever be placed under a single category and why he even attempted to do so. In the early 1920s, Husserl wrote that genetic analysis gives an account of "the ethical form of life as an a priori and essential formation of possible human life," and even "the idea of true humanity and its method of giving shape to itself." [132] But it also deals with "the constitutive physiological processes and the way in which they condition the unity of a physical world with a counterpoised lived body." [133] Genetic phenomenology somehow bridges two extremes. On the one hand, there are the macrocosmic analyses of ethical and cultural contributions to our present understanding and experience of the world—including the entire history of scientific and philosophical thought, as we find in the *Kaizo* articles Husserl wrote between 1922 and 1924, [134] and then again in the *Crisis*. On the other hand, he offers detailed microcosmic accounts of precultural, structural components of our most rudimentary perceptions and the way in which they yield a shared experience of nature. We might well wonder whether genetic analysis simply designates all the issues left out of consideration, for either contingent or principled reasons, by static phenomenology. While consistently standing in opposition to static theory, genetic analysis itself may lack any systemic tie between its diverse topics. If Husserl was merely sweeping together the remainders left by static phenomenology, it would be futile to seek a unifying principle to such studies and, as a consequence, to argue that Husserl actually has a systematic phenomenology.

Three Abstractions

In Husserl's theory, a structural phenomenology of the various domains of experience gives us a *Leitfaden* to deeper analyses. This first carries us from a categorial to a full constitutive account, as we saw above. But constitutive analysis itself becomes the hinge upon which yet deeper studies turn. Genetic analysis moves beyond Husserl's static analysis by *rescinding* three "abstractions" that made his first structural characterization of intentionality possible. First, recall that the "pure ego" is initially described as a "pole" of unity definable only in terms of the acts and actions that it serves to relate. It is clear from his lectures on epistemology in 1906–7 that "persons and their characters, their dispositional properties," were excluded from "Cartesian evidence" precisely because "habitual condition, disposition, and character" cannot be grasped within the sphere of "inner experience." He comments: "The only thing permitted to be definitive here is a description dwelling in the sphere of actual phenomena in the strict sense, *nota bene,* of phenomena in the strict sense of the Cartesian *cogitatio.*" [135] In his later work, however, Husserl recasts the pure ego as an "abstract" structure of the "concrete ego," which has yet other transcendental features. Borrowing from Leibniz, Husserl calls this ego the "monad." It is not "an empty pole of identity" but a "fixed and abiding personal ego." [136] It possesses general capabilities or capacities, whose exercise leads to the acquisition of dispositional tendencies to experience things one way rather than another, to the acquisition of "habitualities." [137] In addition, it is always understood as internally connected to others, and it shares a history with them. As a result, the notion of the subject is expanded into that of the person in community.

Second, the world, which *Ideas I* reduced and drew into the sphere of "immanence" as a counter-pole, as "something identical" posited by consciousness, [138] is reframed as a concrete horizon that has undergone a process of sedimentation in which past achievements have been deposited into its being. In short, the static notion of intentional consciousness is now elaborated as intentional *life;* the first notion of world is recast as *life-world.*

Third, Husserl reintegrates the analysis of time-consciousness into his account of transcendental subjectivity. Even though *Ideas I* understood phenomenological time as "the unitary form of all lived-experiences," [139] it excluded any consideration of it from its scope. This changes partially in his constitutive analysis, when time is treated in connection with the modalities underlying various surface domains, and completely in his genetic analysis. As he puts it in 1922, "Time, seen from within, is the form of intentional genesis." [140]

Genetic Analysis and the Concept of Horizon

As a result of rescinding these abstractions, genetic analysis *expands* the parameters of the structure of intentionality opened by static analysis. In contrast to Husserl's first characterization, the concrete ego itself is understood as essentially relational, as immersed in intersubjectivity and situated in community. In addition, the world is now elaborated both as equiprimordial with intersubjectivity and as a historically generated life-world. The effect of this reframing and expansion was to internally connect the *being* of the field of intentionality with its *becoming,* thereby transforming Husserl's notion of horizon. We need to elaborate.

Because the horizon is not itself an appearance, because it does not belong to "the sphere of sheer phenomena" that can be "open to view [*erschauen*] in inner consciousness with Cartesian evidence," [141] Husserl's Cartesian way cannot thematize it in principle. [142] Even when we separate it from the strictures of Husserl's Cartesian program, static analysis deals with the structural features of phenomena and thus gives us only a "formal" characterization of horizon. As such it is treated only as an implicit or implicated set of act-meaning correlations connected to the manifest intentional act that is actual in that moment. The question of temporality is not raised. This first provisional account is deepened when we turn to genetic analysis.

The distinct subject matter of genetic analysis is so difficult to understand because, in the final analysis, it does not describe yet another layer in the constitution of things but, I would suggest, is the deepest transcendental account of *the constitution of the horizon itself.* In turning to the horizon itself and understanding it as temporal, genetic analysis studies the dynamic and developing interplay of background and context against and within which experience is deployed. [143] Thus genetic analysis deals not with the distinct temporal character attending various modalizations of different types of experiences, for this is handled in constitutive analysis, but with the becoming of the horizon itself. In the final analysis, it accounts for the historicity of intentional life.

The first place this comes to expression in Husserl's published works is *Formal and Transcendental Logic:*

> Static analysis is guided by the unity of the intended object. Thus it starts from the unclear modes of givenness and, following what is indicated by them as intentional modification, strives toward what is clear. Genetic intentional analysis [by contrast] is directed toward *the entire concrete interconnection* in which each consciousness and its intentional object as such actually stand. Then immediately there come into question the other intentional indications that belong to the *situation,* in which, for example, the one exercising the activity of judging stands. And this entails the question of the immanent unity of the temporality of life that has its "history" therein, in such a way that every single conscious experience occurring temporally has its own "history," that is, its temporal genesis. [144]

The account of "situations" is an account of the whole concrete "nexus" or "interconnection" (*Zusammenhang*) in which our acts "stand." Genetic analysis, taking its clue from those vertical syntheses attending different kinds of act/object correlations, as in a constitutive account, deals with that which is no act, no synthesis, with that which contextualizes consciousness. Recovering an entire dimension deliberately excluded at the very outset of his account of meaning and intentionality, Husserl says that the analysis of "indication" (*Anzeige*) in the *Logical Investigations* "already forms there the nucleus of genetic phenomenology." [145] Indication, you will recall, is what wedded the account of meaning to the "occasion" and to context. [146] Husserl suspends it in an effort to get at the pure expressive function of signs and the ideality of their meaning. Indication, however, is what genetic analysis recovers. Ultimately, genetic analysis accounts for the invisible nexus of significance without which things would have no place, no situated intelligibility, no concrete presence, and without which our actions and acts would have no direction, no orientation, no concrete effects. But this is also a dynamic account: our acts and actions reshape and reorganize the horizon in which they are situated. Not only are

our acts and actions "sedimented" into the world, but the horizon itself undergoes elaboration and modification over time as a result of these achievements.
This is why he dared to call this analysis "explanatory" and why his account is
so difficult to understand. At first it looks as if he is uncovering aspects of acts
and objects not available to his first model of descriptive analysis. In fact, it is an
account of the *interconnections* of acts and objects and meanings not manifest
in any particular act or any set of acts studied vertically. As such genetic analysis
treats the horizon as a *temporal nexus of indications* or *referential implications*,
a *Verweisungzusammenhang*.

Horizontal, Vertical, and Lateral Analyses

Before discussing the particular genetic studies Husserl undertook, I need
to pause to place this opening characterization of genetic analysis in relation
to categorial and constitutive analysis.

The task of categorial phenomenology is to give us an account of the general structures of consciousness that are foundational to various regional ontologies. In attempting to characterize this, I spoke of categorial analysis as a
piece of *horizontal* (not horizonal) analysis; here the theory of intentionality
provides us with a scheme of description that accounts for the content of each
region and then the differences between them. Constitutive analysis opens the
deep structure implicit in categorial descriptions and expressly deals with various structural modalizations or transformations that give rise to different types
of intentional acts. It provides a *vertical* account. The depth first discovered
through a constitutive account, however, can be described in terms of not only
structural but also *temporal* transformations. Husserl is keen to distinguish
them. As he puts it in a manuscript from 1921, "to trace [the order of] constitution is not to trace the [order of] genesis, which is, precisely, the genesis of
constitution, itself actuated as genesis in a monad." [147] If constitutive analysis
deals with vertical transformations according to schemes of implicated and im-
plicator, of conditioned and condition, genetic analysis treats *lateral* transformation, that is, the spatial and temporal schemes that account for development.
Genetic phenomenology deepens the account of the *world* by adding to a constitutive account an analysis of the role of background and context in the configuration of regions of experience. It deepens the account of our *being in* the
world by schematizing the *temporal* interplay of experience and discourse constitutive of transformations within a region or between regions. Genetic analysis studies the dynamic interplay of experience and discourse as deployed over
time and as part of a process, historical in nature, that accounts for the *concrete*
configuration of various domains of experience.

In general we can say, then, that genetic analysis treats transformative structures as temporal. What is distinct about genetic analysis is that it accounts for
various *lateral* relationships between different *vertical* lines of constitution
found in the transcendental field. These lateral relations define the diachronic

interplay of language, experience, and appearances in terms of background and context, an interplay that is at work in the deep structure of those regions covered by categorial phenomenology.

Horizon as Context and Background

During the period we are considering, Husserl's own genetic studies concentrated on the temporal constitution of perception and then on the movement from perception to discourse. Later he takes up the transition from everyday talk to rigorous speech, what he generally calls judgments, understood as rational discourse. The account of perception and its modalizations is found in his Logic lectures beginning in 1920, which were themselves construed as an introduction or preface to his account of scientific discourse, developed mainly in *Formal and Transcendental Logic*. The application of genetic analysis to culture, first found in the *Kaizo* articles written in 1922–23, is really an extension of the theory of rational discourse. In that experience and discourse are themselves conditions for the formations of all the phenomena distributed throughout various regional ontologies, they form the proper subject matter of his transcendental account. This insight allows us to expand on our notion of horizon. Treating perception genetically provides us with a theory of *background*. Studying discourse genetically supplies us with a theory of *context*. The analysis of the interplay of background and context gives us a theory of the *horizon*. These studies are vast, and we cannot do them justice here. I will touch on only a few elements essential to a genetic analysis of horizons.

Active and Passive Synthesis

The acts of experience in and through which objects, fields, and even the self are presented are all characterized as syntheses by Husserl. Static analysis describes them in terms of their form and then examines the rules regulating different noetic-noematic correlations. By contrast, genetic analysis understands syntheses not just in terms of form, but also as productive achievements, not just in terms of their being but also their becoming. Husserl is unusually clear on this score:

> The stream of consciousness is a stream of a standing genesis, not a mere after-one-another but rather an out-of-one-another. It is a becoming according to laws of necessary succession in which concrete apperceptions of different types grow out of primal apperceptions or out of apperceptive intentions of a primitive kind—underneath them all, the apperceptions which allow the universal apperception of a world to come about. [148]

Husserl dealt mainly with two forms of genesis, which he distinguishes as active and passive. Active genesis refers to the conscious or deliberate production of different *ideal* complexes of understanding or *real* cultural complexes from preconstituted elements or objects. Complexes of understanding may range from something like simple inferences to advanced scientific theories. Real cultural complexes may run from a shepherd's song to Beethoven's Ninth Symphony, from a child's sketch to a composition by Paul Klee.

As integral to his transcendental account, in contrast to his regional ontologies, however, Husserl's dealt with the transformations of meaning that allow us to effect a change from "occasional," everyday talk to something like propositional discourse. He suggested that all truth statements indicate "earlier" types of speech and then experiences from which they arise. Judgments have a "genesis of meaning." They point back, level by level, to modal transformations from which they are derived. They refer back to nested or implied meanings in any one of those levels; to a context not directly expressed in their content, yet constitutive of the meaning in play; and, finally, to the origination of their semantic elements from experience.

To do justice to the subject, there is one complication to which we need to attend. When Husserl speaks of a genetic account of "active synthesis" and when he has in view the active syntheses attending different types of judgments, he will use the term "genetic" to speak about "constitutive presuppositions." [149] This is not surprising given the fact that he has the constitution of ideal or "trans-temporal" complexes in view. What the term genetic adds to a straightforward vertical analysis of modalization is a larger account of the "relation between passive and active modalization" and of what he calls "motivation." ("Motivation" is the term that replaces in his transcendental account his and Natorp's concept of causality, a notion that belongs to a "genetic" psychological account.) [150] At an even deeper level, genetic analysis provides a temporal characterization of the ideal nature of the content of judgments. "They are constituted in immanent time in a process of becoming." As a result "a temporal form" [151] belongs to the ideal constructs of understanding:

> The timelessness of objectivities of understanding, their being "everywhere and nowhere," proves to be a distinguishable form of temporality. . . . A trans-temporal unity pervades the temporal manifold within which it is situated: this *trans-temporality* bespeaks *omni-temporality.* [152]

Ideality is understood in genetic analysis as a *scheme of repeatability across time.* This gives not only a certain "occasionality" but also a definable "historicality" to "objective" discourse.

All active synthesis, however, is interwoven with what is not spontaneously produced. The final level to which active synthesis points is passive synthesis. This level might itself be the result of previous acts of active production that have become sedimented into the horizon and, as a result, form a "secondary sensibility." Or it might be a level of embodied perception through which things are presented without active construction or interpretation, a level of "originary sensibility."

Husserl's account of passive synthesis moved through his constitutive to his genetic analysis. He turned, for example, to the presence of similarity and contrast played out in the relationship between profiles and objects, recurring across a number of different regional fields, and undertook a clarification of their "origin." In doing so he studied the differential interplay of associative, spatial, and temporal syntheses that accounts for the transfer of sense involved in our recognition of something as familiar, and for the transformation of sense that arises either as a result of becoming acquainted with new features or of being disappointed in our anticipations. Transformation has not only a structural but also a temporal dimension. Protention, to the extent that it directs experience and cuts a certain "line" of anticipation through the multiple possibilities thrown up by a given object, even links us to the motility of the lived-body and a certain affectivity that draws our intentions into a nexus of involvement. Ultimately, all passive syntheses rest upon the interplay of retention and protention, which allowed Husserl to then treat the basic laws of genesis as laws of time-consciousness. "The universal and essential form of intentional genesis, to which all others are related back, is that of the constitution of immanent temporality." [153]

The account of passive synthesis belongs to a discipline that Husserl, echoing but greatly expanding Kant, called transcendental aesthetics. Husserl took originary perception as his paradigm case here, which he set in contrast to the active production of propositional claims studied by what he called transcendental logic. Yet it also seems that the usual contrasts between active and passive begin to come apart in a genetic analysis of perception and speech. Perception is now understood in terms of multiple syntheses that are integrated through their protentions into the actions of the body, only to then find a new passivity in the phenomenon of affection. Speech, thought of as active synthesis, takes place against a passive context of an acquired language and prior established meanings fixed by a community of speakers, who, for their part, stake active claims of their own. Previously active constructions become sedimented and thus part of our sensibility; our sense of things falls under their spell as well. Transcendental aesthetics, then, covers not just perceptual senses but, with modification, the acquired and habitual meanings that also shape our concrete life-world. [154]

This gives us our final way of understanding the difference between constitutive and genetic analysis. We can say that constitutive phenomenology schematizes the structural transformations making phenomenal fields possible according to transcendental *space*. They are framed as layers or strata beneath each field, providing each with its supporting ground. Genetic phenomenology schematizes those transformations in terms of transcendental *time,* and thus as a process of development in which the earlier gives rise to the later and in which the later draws and gives direction to the now. Not only is the ideality of sense and meaning clarified through the notion of repeatability over time, but their transference and transformation rest upon the interlacing of retentions and protentions across a living present.

At yet a deeper and final level of genetic analysis Husserl discovers that space and time themselves are not just "forms" but are generated, on the one hand, by the interplay of position, motility, and place, and on the other, by the standing-streaming flow of the process of self-temporalization itself. Husserl's studies of the self-generation of space and time are clearly the most difficult of all his genetic studies. I am more than happy to leave their account to others. I will be content if this essay has been able to show Husserl as developing not a system of philosophy but a systematic method, and has been able to connect his contrast between static and genetic analysis to his claim that "time, seem from within, is the form of intentional genesis." [155] In 1934, only four years before his death, he tells Adelgundis Jaegerschmid: "Everything I have written so far is only preparatory work; it is only the setting down of methods." [156]

Notes

1. Letter to Bell, 22 September 1920, *Briefwechsel,* 3/3, 20.

2. In 1924 and 1925 Landgrebe revised the original editing that Edith Stein had done on these manuscripts, but even then, as Landgrebe reports it, Husserl viewed them only as "materials." As reported in Iso Kern, "Einleitung des Herausgebers," *Intersubjektivität II,* xvii.

3. Letter to Ingarden, 25 November 1921, *Briefwechsel,* 3/3, 213.

4. Letter to Ingarden, 24 December 1921, *Briefwechsel,* 3/3, 215.

5. The WS 1920/21 lecture course bore the title *Logik,* the SS 1923 course the title *Ausgewählte phänomenologische Probleme,* and the WS 1925/26 course the title *Grundprobleme der Logik.* Other labels that he applied to the lectures seemed more appropriate, such as *Urkonstitution, Genetische Logik,* and in the course of the lectures *transzendentale Ästhetik.* See "Editor's Introduction," *Passive Synthesis,* xiii–xiv.

6. Letter to Husserl, 21 March 1921, *Briefwechsel,* 3/2, 165.

7. Letter to Husserl, 1 January 1921, *Briefwechsel,* 3/2, 239.

8. Letter to Bell, 22 September 1920, *Briefwechsel,* 3/3, 20.

9. Letter to Ingarden, 12 December 1920, *Briefwechsel,* 3/3, 206.

10. Letter to Mahnke, 21 February 1926, *Briefwechsel,* 3/3, 453.

11. A course with this title had been offered several times before, but this time it is the London lectures, and then his interventions into them, that formed his text. This is traced in Donn Welton, *The Other Husserl: The Horizons of Transcendental Phenomenology* (Bloomington: Indiana University Press, 2001), chap. 6.

12. Letter to Bell, 13 December 1922, *Briefwechsel,* 3/3, 43.

13. Letter to Bell, 13 December 1922, *Briefwechsel,* 3/3, 43–44.

14. The first was published in 1923. See editor's introduction, *Aufsätze III,* xi.

15. Published as *Erste Philosophie I* and *II.*

16. This takes place in *Formal and Transcendental Logic,* in the manuscripts surrounding the *Crisis,* and in the text of the *Crisis* itself.

17. An extensive account of the ideas in this essay is found in Donn Welton, *The Other Husserl,* chaps. 1–9. The material in Section 3, however, is not covered there. See also Donn Welton, "Genetic Phenomenology," in *Encyclopedia of Phenomenology* (Dordrecht: Kluwer,

1997), 266–70, for a highly distilled account of the difference between static and genetic phenomenology.

18. For an elaboration of the ideas in this section see Welton, *The Other Husserl,* chaps. 2–4.

19. *Ideen I,* 163; *Ideas I,* 193–94 modified.

20. See Section 3 below.

21. *Ideen I,* 43–44; *Ideas I,* 44.

22. *Ideen I,* 43; after *Ideas I,* 44; italics removed.

23. *Ideen I; Ideas I,* §44.

24. *Erste Philosophie II,* 434.

25. Notice that he goes to lengths to correct the *Logical Investigations* by emphasizing the "parallelism" of noetic and noematic structures and the importance of attending to both. *Ideen I,* 266; *Ideas I,* 306.

26. *Ideen I,* 163; *Ideas I,* 193–94 modified.

27. *Ideen I,* 141; *Ideas I,* 171.

28. *Einleitung in die Logik,* 209.

29. For an elaboration of the ideas in this section see Welton, *The Other Husserl,* chap. 7.

30. At this time Husserl was in the throes of writing his Bernauer manuscripts on time.

31. Letter to Ingarden, 5 April 1918, *Briefwechsel,* 3/3, 182.

32. Ms. B III 10 (1921), 22–30a, published in *Passiven Synthesis,* 336–45.

33. *Passiven Synthesis,* 340.

34. *Passiven Synthesis,* 340.

35. *Passiven Synthesis,* 340

36. Letter to Boyce Gibson, 7 January 1932, *Briefwechsel,* 3/6, 142.

37. *Passiven Synthesis,* 345.

38. *Passiven Synthesis,* 340.

39. *Passiven Synthesis,* 340.

40. *Krisis,* 173f.; *Crisis,* 170f.

41. *Passiven Synthesis,* 340.

42. *Passiven Synthesis,* 303.

43. *Intersubjektivität,* II, 38.

44. *Passiven Synthesis,* 340.

45. *Passiven Synthesis,* 340.

46. *Passiven Synthesis,* 344, 347.

47. *Intersubjektivität,* II: 41.

48. *Passiven Synthesis,* 40.

49. *Intersubjektivität,* II: 41.

50. Husserl's constitutive account of perception in terms of interlocking associative, spatial, and temporal syntheses displaced his first static characterization of perception as an interpretative animating (*beseelen*) or apprehension (*Auffassung*) of data by meaning; it also introduced a proper notion of perceptual sense (*Wahrnehmungssinn*). The debate in the secondary literature over Husserl's notion of the noema has centered around *Ideas I* and for the most part has not looked into his rethinking the problem of "individuation" during the 1920s. In so doing, it has overlooked the way in which these studies, with their displacement of the form-content account of perception, transformed the concept of the perceptual noema. And it has confused what might count as a legitimate characterization of the contents of speech-acts with the noema of perceptual acts. See Welton, *The Origins of Meaning* (The Hague: M. Nijhoff, 1983), parts II and III. In this late period, I would suggest, perceptual senses are not Fregian-like ideal intensional [*sic*] entities, but *schemata* that organize, as they themselves are configured by, the relationship between perceptual syntheses and perceptual fields. They

are structures embodied in perceptual intentionality as a whole and account for (preconceptual) aesthetic, spatial, and temporal features which are anticipated, as they are constituted, in the course of perception. They coordinate the relationship between different passive syntheses and then between those syntheses and various field properties. On the question of the noema see John Drummond's essay in this volume; his "Noema," *Encyclopedia of Phenomenology,* 494–99; and his *Husserlian Intentionality and Non-foundational Realism: Noema and Object* (Dordrecht: Kluwer, 1990).

51. John Brough, "The Emergence of an Absolute Consciousness in Husserl's Early Writings on Time-Consciousness," *Man and World* 5 (1972): 298–326; reprinted in *Husserl: Expositions and Appraisals,* ed. Frederick Elliston and Peter McCormick (Notre Dame, Ind.: University of Notre Dame Press, 1977), 83–100; Rudolf Bernet, "Die ungegenwärtige Gegenwart: Anwesenheit und Abwesenheit in Husserls Analyse des Zeitbewußtseins," *Phänomenologische Forschungen* 14 (1983): 16–57; "Einleitung," and "Editorischer Bericht," in Edmund Husserl, *Texte zur Phänomenologie des inneren Zeitbewusstseins (1893–1917),* ed. Rudolf Bernet (Hamburg: Felix Meiner Verlag, 1985), xi–lxvii, lxix–lxxiii.

52. *Passiven Synthesis,* 340.

53. *Passiven Synthesis,* 111.

54. *Passiven Synthesis,* 128.

55. *Passiven Synthesis,* 387; text dated between 1920 and 1926.

56. Cf. *Passiven Synthesis,* 409.

57. *Passiven Synthesis,* 128.

58. Letter to Natorp, 29 June 1918, *Briefwechsel,* 3/5, 137.

59. *Logische Untersuchungen* (1st ed.), II, 336. By the second edition Husserl claims that what he has really done in Section 6 is isolate the "phenomenological content" of "the empirical ego in the sense of the soulish subject" and to "broaden out" the notion of experience "from what is inwardly perceived . . . to the notion of the 'phenomenological ego,' by which the empirical ego is intentionally constituted," a claim that makes almost no sense at all. *Logische Untersuchungen,* II/1, 358–59; *Logical Investigations,* II, 545.

60. As far as I know, this text includes the third and last occurrence of "genetisch" in the *Investigations.* The first two are found in *Logische Untersuchungen* (1st ed.), II, 4, 8; contrast *Logische Untersuchungen,* II/1, 3, 6; *Logical Investigations,* I, 249, 252. Findlay's translation is of the second edition but often includes translations of important sections of the first edition. If there is a corresponding translation I will give the page references after "*Logical Investigations.*"

61. *Logische Untersuchungen* (1st ed.), 336; after *Logical Investigations,* II, 545f.

62. See *Logische Untersuchungen,* I, xiv; *Logical Investigations,* I, 48.

63. *Ideen I,* p. 110, n1; *Ideas I,* 131, n10. See also *Logische Untersuchungen,* I, xvi; *Logical Investigations,* I, 49.

64. Paul Natorp, *Einleitung in die Psychologie nach kritischer Methode* (Freiburg i.B.: J. C. B. Mohr, 1888).

65. Natorp, *Einleitung in die Psychologie,* p. 70.

66. Natorp, *Einleitung in die Psychologie,* p. 90.

67. Natorp, *Einleitung in die Psychologie,* p. 90.

68. This has an important consequence for the notion of reflection in Natorp, one that Husserl will reject. If consciousness cannot be directly and immediately given, then "each ostensive immediate observation of what is experienced is already *reflection;* as reflected in self-observation the immediate is already no longer the immediate." See his discussion for a sharp and interesting critique of the efficacy of direct reflection (Natorp, *Einleitung in die Psychologie,* p. 93). Natorp himself finally suggests that the immediate can be known only by "reconstruction," an idea that thinks of it in Kantian terms as a hypothetical construction

inferred on the basis of "what has been formed" by consciousness (Natorp, *Einleitung in die Psychologie*, p. 94).

69. *Einleitung in die Logik*, 201–11.
70. *Einleitung in die Logik*, 205.
71. *Einleitung in die Logik*, 205.
72. *Einleitung in die Logik*, 205–6.
73. *Einleitung in die Logik*, 202.
74. Letter to Natorp, 29 June 1918, *Briefwechsel*, 3/5, 137.
75. Paul Natorp, *Allgemeine Psychologie nach kritischer Methode*. 1. Buch: *Objekt und Methode der Psychologie* (1912) (Amsterdam: E. J. Bonset, 1965).
76. *Ideen I*, 110, n1; *Ideas I*, 131, n10.
77. *Logische Untersuchungen*, I, xvi; *Logical Investigations*, I, 49. Husserl gives 1913 as the date of publication of *Allgemeine Psychologie nach kritischer Methode*, whereas it seems to have been 1912. Both Natorp's *Einleitung in die Psychologie* and his *Allgemeine Psychologie* are in Husserl's library, and both are heavily annotated.
78. Natorp, *Allgemeine Psychologie*, 189.
79. Natorp, *Allgemeine Psychologie*, 189.
80. Natorp, *Allgemeine Psychologie*, 189.
81. Natorp, *Allgemeine Psychologie*, 190.
82. Natorp, *Allgemeine Psychologie*, 191.
83. Natorp, *Allgemeine Psychologie*, 191.
84. Natorp, *Allgemeine Psychologie*, 191.
85. Natorp, *Allgemeine Psychologie*, 241. He is referring not only to Husserl's *Logical Investigations* but also to the 1911 *Logos* article "Philosophy as Rigorous Science." See "Philosophie als strenge Wissenschaft," *Aufsätze II*, 3–62; "Philosophy as Rigorous Science," in *Phenomenology and the Crisis of Philosophy*, trans. Quentin Lauer (New York: Harper and Row, 1965), 71–147.
86. Natorp, *Allgemeine Psychologie*, 239–40.
87. Natorp, *Allgemeine Psychologie*, 243.
88. Natorp, *Allgemeine Psychologie*, 248.
89. Natorp, *Allgemeine Psychologie*, 249.
90. Natorp, *Allgemeine Psychologie*, 249.
91. Natorp, *Allgemeine Psychologie*, 249.
92. Natorp, *Allgemeine Psychologie*, 251.
93. Natorp, *Allgemeine Psychologie*, 251.
94. Natorp, *Allgemeine Psychologie*, 252.
95. Natorp, *Allgemeine Psychologie*, 288.
96. Natorp, *Allgemeine Psychologie*, 254.
97. Natorp, *Allgemeine Psychologie*, 254.
98. The technical issue is that Natorp makes "discreteness within a continuum" a precondition for differences of time while Husserl thinks of the syntheses making discreteness possible as essentially temporal. This has the consequence for Natorp of making the consciousness of temporal differences itself a "transtemporal consciousness," a thesis that Husserl rejected and replaced with a notion of "self-temporalization." In the later work consciousness is fundamentally temporal. See Natorp, *Allgemeine Psychologie*, 255, for his view.
99. Natorp, *Allgemeine Psychologie*, 254.
100. He is referring directly to Husserl's "Philosophie als strenge Wissenschaft."
101. Natorp, *Allgemeine Psychologie*, 289.
102. *Erste Philosophie II*, 326. But in this text from 1925 Husserl is also convinced that theoretical rigor can be "awakened" by studying such figures.

103. *Krisis*, 204–5; *Crisis*, 201.

104. *Krisis*, 205; *Crisis*, 201.

105. Letter to Hocking, 7 September 1903, *Briefwechsel*, 3/3, 147. See the letter to Hocking of 4 June 1903, *Briefwechsel*, 3/3, 139 as well.

106. "Fichtes Menschheitsideal," *Aufsätze II*, 266–93; "Fichte's Ideal of Humanity," trans. James Hart, *Husserl Studies* 12 (1995): 111–33.

107. Letter to Ingarden, 5 April 1918, *Briefwechsel*, 3/3, 182.

108. He quotes it in his letter.

109. Letter to Grimme, 9 April 1918, *Briefwechsel*, 3/3, 81.

110. Fichte, *Erste Einleitung in die Wissenschaftslehre [1797]*, *Fichtes Werke* (Berlin: de Gruyter, 1971), 1: 440–41; *First Introduction to the Science of Knowledge [1797]*, ed. and trans. Peter Heath and John Lachs (Cambridge: Cambridge University Press, 1982), 21.

111. Fichte, *Erste Einleitung in die Wissenschaftslehre [1797]*, 463; *First Introduction to the Science of Knowledge [1797]*, 38.

112. Fichte, *Erste Einleitung in die Wissenschaftslehre [1797]*, 463; after *First Introduction to the Science of Knowledge [1797]*, 38.

113. Fichte, *Erste Einleitung in die Wissenschaftslehre [1797]*, 441; after *First Introduction to the Science of Knowledge [1797]*, 21–22.

114. Fichte, *Erste Einleitung in die Wissenschaftslehre [1797]*, 442; after *First Introduction to the Science of Knowledge [1797]*, 22.

115. Fichte, *Erste Einleitung in die Wissenschaftslehre [1797]*, 442; after *First Introduction to the Science of Knowledge [1797]*, 22.

116. Fichte, *Erste Einleitung in die Wissenschaftslehre [1797]*, 446; after *First Introduction to the Science of Knowledge [1797]*, 26.

117. Fichte, *Wissenschaftslehre nova methodo [1796/99]* (Kollegnachschrift K. Chr. Fr. Krause 1798/99), ed. Erich Fuchs (Hamburg: Felix Meiner Verlag, 1982), 15; Fichte, *Foundations of Transcendental Philosophy; Wissenschaftslehre nova methodo (1796/99)*, trans. Daniel Breazeale (Ithaca, N.Y.: Cornell University Press, 1992), 92.

118. Fichte, *Wissenschaftslehre nova methodo [1796/99]*, 94; after Fichte, *Foundations of Transcendental Philosophy [1796/99]*, 213.

119. Breazeale's note in Fichte, *Foundations of Transcendental Philosophy [1796/99]*, 214.

120. Fichte, *Wissenschaftslehre nova methodo [1796/99]*, 185; Fichte, *Foundations of Transcendental Philosophy [1796/99]*, 366.

121. "The sense of the world must lie outside the world"; Ludwig Wittgenstein, *Tractatus logico-philosophicus* [1921], *Werkausgabe* (Frankfurt am Main: Suhrkamp, 1984), I: §6.41; *Tractatus Logico-Philosophicus*, trans. D. Pears and B. McGuinness (London: Routledge & Kegan Paul, 1961), §6.41.

122. Fichte, *Wissenschaftslehre nova methodo [1796/99]*, 192; after Fichte, *Foundations of Transcendental Philosophy [1796/99]*, 380.

123. Letter (draft) to Frischeisen-Köhler, ca. February 1908, *Briefwechsel*, VI: 126. I should also mention that the term "genetic" is found in Schelling as well at precisely the same time it occurs in Fichte, that is, 1795 onward. This is not surprising for his first works, written in his teens, placed him as a disciple of Fichte. Then as a young genius of twenty-two he won a teaching post beside Fichte at Jena in 1798.

124. The two alternatives of idealism and dogmatism, Fichte suggested, arise by an abstraction of one of the elements given as intertwined in the structure of experience, either intelligence or the thing. If we follow the first course, I abstract from the content of thought and observe myself alone, becoming to myself an object of a specific presentation. The fact that I am thinking depends upon my "self-determination" in the sense that I freely determine myself to think this or that. If I freely make myself into an object, however, I grasp only

an object, in this case a determinate presentation, of experience and have not yet reached the ground. I do not grasp "myself-in-itself." Since this is an activity of self-determination, however, I am "compelled to presuppose myself as that which is to be determined by self-determination." Fichte, *Erste Einleitung in die Wissenschaftslehre [1797]*, 427; cited after *First Introduction to the Science of Knowledge [1797]*, 10. This means that I am compelled to pre-suppose in and through the experience of the self (the phenomenal self) the existence of the self (self-in-itself). Implicit in this is the idea that the self is not a thing, not even a mental presentation, but the active, creative center of all cognition. In contrast to the "empirical ego" we have the "transcendental ego," as Husserl would say. As the source of all objectivation the transcendental ego transcends objectivation. (We just saw this theme repeatedly in Natorp. One could speculate that he took it from Fichte, though this is already a consequence of Kant's treatment of productive imagination as transcendental.)

125. Fichte, Der "Hallesche Nachschrift" of *Wissenschaftslehre nova methodo* (1796/99), *Gesamtausgabe der Bayerischen Akademie der Wissenschaften*, ed. Reinhard Lauth et al. (Stuttgart: Frommann, 1970), IV: 2, x; Fichte, *Foundations of Transcendental Philosophy [1796/99]*, x.

126. Fichte, *Über des Verhältniß der Logik zur Philosophie oder Transscendentale Logik* (Vorlesung vom Oktober bis Dezember 1812), ed. Reinhard Lauth et al. (Hamburg: Felix Meiner Verlag, 1982), 42.

127. For an elaboration of the ideas in this section see Welton, *The Other Husserl*, chaps. 8 and 9.

128. *Intersubjektivität II*, 41.

129. Of course, *Ideas I* did speak of the phenomenological reduction as yielding the field of absolute consciousness (*Ideen I*, 94; *Ideas I*, 113), but it was also characterized in Cartesian fashion as a "complex of being closed for itself" and as "absolute being" (*Ideen I*, 93; *Ideas I*, 112). The Cartesian epochē, as Husserl puts it in his last work, lands us in the sphere of immanence "in one leap" and "brings this ego into view as apparently empty of content" (*Krisis*, 158; *Crisis*, 155). As a result it confuses a reduction to my own stream of consciousness with a reduction to subjectivity. As Husserl puts it about 1924, "this difficulty is solved when we make it clear that the reduction does not, first of all simply lead to the *actual* stream of consciousness (and its ego-pole)." In a way that thinks of the reduction effecting static analysis as regressive, as *Abbau*, Husserl stresses that "each experienced thing and so the entire world" is "an 'index' for an infinite manifold of *possible* experiences" (*Erste Philosophie II*, 434). Static analysis, then, is supported by a regressive reduction, and it gives us transcendental subjectivity as a field. In fact, Husserl even says in this text that this involves an "'extension' of the phenomenological reduction to monadic intersubjectivity" and that this occurred in his lectures of 1910 (*Erste Philosophie II*, 434), a claim difficult to square with the fact that in *Ideas I* (1913) he repeatedly speaks of subjectivity as a stream of experience and argues that it is given absolutely, that is, without sides or profiles.

130. Notice that the later Husserl does not begin with the ego as "mine" but introduces "a pecular kind of epochē" that effects a "reduction to my transcendental sphere of ownness." See *Cartesianische Meditationen*, 124; *Cartesian Meditations*, 93.

131. *Ideen I*, 163; *Ideas I*, 193.

132. Husserl, *Aufsätze III*, 29, 55.

133. *Passive Synthesis*, 343.

134. Published in *Aufsätze III*, 3–94. For an analysis of them see Donn Welton, "Husserl and the Japanese," *Review of Metaphysics* 44, no. 3 (March 1991): 575–606; *The Other Husserl*, chap. 12.

135. *Einleitung in die Logik*, 209.

136. *Cartesianische Meditationen*, 100–101; *Cartesian Meditations*, 66–67.

137. *Cartesianische Meditationen*, 100; *Cartesian Meditations*, 66.

138. *Ideen I,* 93; *Ideas I,* 112.

139. *Ideen I,* 161; *Ideas I,* 192.

140. *Intersubjektivität II,* 221.

141. *Einleitung in die Logik,* 209.

142. This means that to the extent that it does thematize the horizon, as we find in *Ideas I,* to that extent we are carried from within Husserl's Cartesian way beyond the parameters of Cartesian evidence.

143. For a first account of the world as horizon and of the difference between background and context, see my essay "World as Horizon" (Chapter 9) in this collection. This is further developed in Welton, *The Other Husserl,* chaps. 13–15.

144. *Formale und transzendentale Logik,* 316; *Formal and Transcendental Logic,* 316; italics changed.

145. *Erfahrung und Urteil,* 78; *Experience and Judgement,* 74–75.

146. See the First Logical Investigation.

147. *Intersubjektivität II,* 41.

148. *Passive Synthesis,* 339.

149. *Erfahrung und Urteil,* 269–70; *Experience and Judgement,* 226–27.

150. *Erfahrung und Urteil,* 328–29; *Experience and Judgement,* 273–74.

151. *Erfahrung und Urteil,* 309; *Experience and Judgement,* 258.

152. *Erfahrung und Urteil,* 313; *Experience and Judgement,* 261; translation and italics modified.

153. *Formale und transzendentale Logik,* 318; *Formal and Transcendental Logic,* 318.

154. Once Husserl found a way of integrating the notion of development and transformation into his phenomenological method, and once he found a way of moving from his first starting point in the monologue and the individual ego to communal existence and the lifeworld, new horizons open for his phenomenology. For this reason we find Husserl's very late work moving in the direction of yet another type of analysis, called *generative* phenomenology, in which the parameters of life and death, homeworld and alienworld, and even of earth and world are used to expand his first notion of genetic analysis. See the next essay in this volume by Anthony Steinbock. Also see his *Home and Beyond* (Evanston, Ill.: Northwestern University Press, 1996). What holds these accounts together is that temporality is understood as the final source in terms of which all development, all becoming, including that interplay of conscious life and world constitutive of our essential historicity, is explained.

155. *Intersubjektivität,* II, 221.

156. "Conversations with Edmund Husserl, 1931–1938," *New Yearbook for Phenomenology and Phenomenological Philosophy* 1 (2001): 336.

12

Generativity and the Scope of Generative Phenomenology

Anthony J. Steinbock

HUSSERL'S CONCEPTION OF phenomenology is perhaps best captured by the shibboleth "back to the things themselves!" By going back to the things themselves, Husserl evoked a style of thinking, a change in perspective, that did not rely on commonly held prejudices about the world, on the formal manipulation of rules, or on philosophical theories detached from experience. Going back to the things themselves in terms of how those "things" or "matters" (*Sachen*) are given served a liberating function, namely, to open one to matters as they are lived in their self-givenness. But just what are these matters, and how do we dispose ourselves to them such that they can give themselves to us?

The response to these questions is not as conspicuous as it may seem at first glance. For what immediately comes into play is not only a variety of matters and a select number of ways of approaching them, but also what gets counted as a mode of "givenness."

For example, we might begin by defining the "things" or "matters" of phenomenology as "phenomena." And by phenomena we may understand those matters that are self-given in evidence correlative to an intending act. But just what counts as a "phenomenon"? Can it be given even if it is not intended? It is true that the world itself gives itself to us, even if only with pretensions of completeness, and that we open onto the matters themselves with a basic perceptual belief that amounts to our immediate acceptance of the being of things. Since the things themselves are accessible without depriving them of their transcendence, and since our finite openness to the world is a participation in the disclosure of the world's inexhaustible meaning—a participation phenomenology calls "experience"—phenomenology emerges as a descriptive interrogation of that experience. But just what gets qualified as an experience, and what does this descriptive inquiry of experience entail?

When responding to these questions it is important to remember that one cannot ask what phenomena are, or even which phenomena get taken as phenomena, without asking how they are given to those experiencing and reflecting on that experience. There is a certain intimacy between how one approaches matters and the matters disclosed or revealed in those approaches—matters that in their own right demand a certain method. For the very ways in which the phenomena give themselves are solicited by our paths to them, and our dispositions toward them—our methods—are evoked by the very givenness of the things themselves, as Husserl himself has noted.[1]

Depending upon the way we dispose ourselves to the matters and the way the matters give themselves, certain phenomena will be on the limit of givenness. I call these phenomena *limit-phenomena*. By limit-phenomena, I understand those matters that are on the edge of accessibility in a phenomenological approach to experience, and not simply those matters that have historically been at the border of phenomenological discourse. For the purposes of this presentation, I will characterize limit-phenomena as those "phenomena" that are given as not being able to be given. According to this general understanding of limit-phenomena, limit-phenomena can include the unconscious, sleep, birth and death, temporality, the other person, other worlds, animal and plant life, the Earth, God, etc.

But doesn't claiming that these "phenomena" are limit-phenomena already claim too much, too soon? For it presupposes that they do in fact "appear" in some way to the phenomenologist, and further, to grant them the status of "limit"-phenomena presupposes not only the being but the very constitution of those limits.

It is recognized today that phenomenology is not an amorphous philosophical style of reflection, a univocal manner of entering experience. It is well known, for instance, that between the years 1917 and 1921 Husserl distinguished between two methodological approaches: "static" and "genetic."[2] What is less known is that Husserl also broached a third methodological perspective responding to different phenomena, a methodology I have formulated elsewhere as "generative phenomenology."[3] Before describing the scope and import of a generative phenomenology, and the relation between generativity and genesis, let me briefly describe the significance of static and genetic methods.

By static phenomenology, we understand two methodological approaches. First, static method can entail an *ontological* enterprise since it can analyze what something is, "structures" like formal and material essences, regions of being, morphological types, structures like intentionality, relations of foundation, etc. Second, static method can entail a *constitutive* analysis since it inquires into the way in which something is given, examining the roles of intention and fulfillment, modalization, etc. Accordingly, even though the analyses concerning the essential correlations of noesis and noema, subject and object, are static, because we inquire after *modes* of givenness, the questions raised in a static method can be "overall constitutive questions." But while static analysis can be both constitutive and ontological, in either case, there is no question of temporal development.

While I can grasp experiences in terms of their essential possibilities for a subject who emerges in and through them, Husserl insists that I still do not inquire into the genesis of the monad within a static approach.[4] For instance, I can vary myself as monad *qua* correlate of objects and the genesis belonging to the monad, but I do not inquire into its genesis as *self-temporalization*. Here the monad is treated simply as a "fixed" essential possibility, as an already developed subjectivity. It is for this reason that Husserl is able to maintain that a static analysis can be a constitutive analysis without being an inquiry into genesis.[5]

A genetic phenomenology concerns the temporal becoming of sense; it can trace the genesis of sense of the "passive," "aesthetic," or lived-bodily perceptual level, on the "active," judicative level, and the transition from passive perception to active egoic rationality. Prior to 1913, Husserl employed the term "genesis" primarily in a negative manner. In the *Logische Untersuchungen*, for example, Husserl criticized empirical psychology for imputing to ideal objects a subjective genesis in consciousness rather than understanding mathematical and logical entities as self-given to consciousness in intuition.[6] In *Ideen III* (1913), Husserl used the expression positively in an effort both to distinguish an ontological investigation into essences, which remains mundane, from a constitutive or phenomenological analysis of the noema in terms of intention and fulfillment, and to describe the relations of foundation obtaining between the categorial affair-complexes that presuppose sheer objects of perception.[7]

It was not until after 1917 that Husserl used the concept of genesis in its, now, proper sense. It was precisely this new, proper sense that demanded the formulation of a genetic method in distinction to a static method. In this respect, one would have to say that the concepts of stasis and genesis, as well as static and genetic methods, are co-eval. After this time, genetic analyses are understood as explicating monadic becoming for the full concretion and individuality of experience, that is, the concrete ego as a process of becoming in which its present experiences point back to previous ones (having become sedimented as habitualities) and predisposing the "I can" to future acquisitions that are "typical" and "familiar."

Because genetic analyses concern the concrete, factical, self-temporalizing monad, the investigations undertaken in *Zur Phänomenologie des inneren Zeitbewußtseins* (1905) are not by themselves genetic in the strict sense; at best they are transitional. True, these lectures do mention genetic themes, and the so-called time lectures do go beyond treating consciousness as a series of Nows by explicating the transition between those Nows,[8] but they are not fully genetic because they are still too abstract, treating the ego only as a temporal form, that is, as the form of time in terms of impression, retention, and protention as well as the forms of temporal connection: succession and coexistence. In his *Analyses Concerning Passive and Active Synthesis*, in which the distinction between the static and the genetic are fully in play, Husserl recognizes that "mere form is admittedly an abstraction, and thus from the very beginning the analysis of the intentionality of time-consciousness and its accomplishment is an abstractive analysis."[9] I will return to the significance of "abstraction" below when I discuss the relations obtaining between matters and methods.

While genetic phenomenology does broaden the scope of the phenomeno-logical field of experience, it too has its own restrictions, or as I will also discuss below, its "limits" concerning the constitution of normality and abnormality, human beings' relation to animality, birth and death, and the I–Other relation of intersubjectivity; ultimately, however, genetic analyses rest within the con-fines of egological constitution, *self*-temporalization, and individual facticity where the sphere of intersubjectivity extends only to a transcendental sociology, that is, to a synchronic field of contemporaries. I will return in more detail to genetic phenomena below. Here let me introduce the third dimension of expe-rience peculiar to phenomenology, what I call a generative phenomenology.

Let me emphasize that Husserl did not explicitly formulate this dimension of phenomenology as generative. But on the basis of a wide range of texts that evoke "generative problems" and that describe phenomena as "generative," and given Husserl's liberal use of expressions like "generative" and "generativity" in the later manuscripts, I find the formulation of this dimension not only jus-tified but demanded. In order to formulate the reasons for these assertions, I will have to articulate the role of "leading clue" or the dynamic interconnection between various dimensions of phenomenology, and this will be part of a more extended discussion of generativity. This is how I will proceed. First, I will give a brief description of phenomenological notions of normality and abnormality and then of the generative structure, homeworld/alienworld. I will then take up the issue of the very generation of generative phenomenology, considering various phenomena that are at once on the limits of phenomenality and that become phenomena for generative phenomenology. This will yield a brief but important discussion of the difference between "Generative" phenomenology and "generative" phenomenology. I will conclude with a note on the generative phenomenologist and phenomenological givenness.

1. Generative Phenomena

In distinction to genetic analysis, which is restricted to the becoming of individual subjectivity, a synchronic field of contemporary individuals, and intersubjectivity founded in an egology, generative phenomenology treats phe-nomena that are geo-historical, cultural, intersubjective, and normative. For Husserl, generativity suggests both the process of becoming, hence the pro-cess of generation, and a process that occurs over the generations as socio-geo-historical movement. Generativity becomes Husserl's new "Absolute," and in this sense, ultimately, the matter of generative phenomenology.[10]

Already by 1929, Husserl began addressing generative themes, distinguish-ing them from genetic ones,[11] but he took them up in a more concerted and consistent manner from 1930 to 1937 in manuscripts concerning "mundane

phenomenology" (the "A" manuscripts), "time constitution as formal constitution" (the "C" manuscripts), and "intersubjective constitution" (the "E"
manuscripts). Let me now turn to normality and abnormality in order to show
how genetic phenomenology and genetic matters can function as leading clues
to generative phenomenology and generative matters.

1.1. Normality and Abnormality: From Description to Teleology

Since the *Logische Untersuchungen*, Husserlian phenomenology has been
renowned as a *descriptive* science.[12] In this respect, Husserl understood phenomenological method very much the way Hegel did, namely, as a faithfulness
to the way in which the things themselves present themselves. This descriptive
enterprise began for Husserl as a static endeavor, focusing on the structures of
things and the constitution of meaning; only gradually did the static descriptive
pursuit yield the temporal dimensions implicit in the phenomena's structure.
When Husserl did make his explicit "genetic turn," he did so with an attentiveness to the problems of development: The phenomena of style, pattern,
habit, affectivity, and especially teleology become prominent. For when one describes the thing's structures, one also describes, even if implicitly, its internal
teleological movement: "Classification," observes Husserl, "is not merely a logical play of concepts, but a law of teleology."[13]

Due to the teleology inherent in structure, Husserl wants to maintain that
all descriptive sciences, whether botany, biology, anthropology, or philosophy,
belong on the side of history.[14] Within an "outer" history of facts and essences,
there lies an inner teleological coherence or "immanent historicity."[15] What
Husserl did in his later work was to make this historical-teleological dimension
explicit in his reflections.

It was as early as 1912, but especially in the years following 1917, that Husserl
connected the notion of teleology with the phenomenological concepts of normality and abnormality in his "genetic" method.[16] Normality and abnormality
are relational notions whose broadest parameters are a species and whose nar-
rowest are an act or a function. In describing, say, a particular act, the phenomenologist can detect what is functioning as a norm or a telos, which is to
say, an inner teleological sense. This sense is constitutionally normal (or abnormal) depending upon whether it is concordant, optimal, typical, or familiar in
relation to other acts (past or present), to a task, to an event, or within the
context of an individual's environing-world or community. Without exploring
all the facets of normality and abnormality here, it is important to note two
things. First, normality and abnormality are not in the first instance psychological, therapeutic, or medicinal notions, but constitutive ones since they concern
the very becoming of sense. A phenomenology of normality and abnormality
can avoid the "natural" and naturalistic pitfalls of presupposing normality to
be derivative of averageness or *ta kata physis*, and abnormality to be simply a
matter of deviance, unnaturalness, or artificiality. Second, within a genetic

method they can apply to something as minute as the functioning of a sense organ (as in eye movement, sight, touch, smell) or as expansive as a species. (While Husserl's genetic descriptions focus on individual acts, the function of sense organs, and lived-bodies, his generative descriptions take up the social and historical dimensions of constitution in life-world communities, specifically, in terms of homeworlds and alienworlds. In the latter case, Husserl is concerned not merely with primordial institution of sense, but with "primordial generation" and creative, historical emergence.)

When modes of comportment veer from what is concordant, optimal, or typically familiar, they can be called "abnormal" with respect to the constitution of sense (and not, for example, with respect to psychopathology). The simplest case of such an abnormality is an anomalous deviation, constituted as such by its reference back to the "normal" (the concordant, the optimal, etc.) as *its telos*. Husserl notes, however, that this constitutional deviation does not mean simply and unequivocally that it *must* only refer back to the normal (teleological) order, or that the present normal order must remain a norm. Rather, an action or a pattern of action that actually occurs in fact can simultaneously *institute* or *generate* beyond itself a new "concrete teleological sense" and thus a new normality and a new telos.

In some instances this may mean that the previous normal order becomes now abnormal in relation to the new normative disclosure. Rather than the "abnormal" serving as an index to the norm, it actually subverts or inverts the relation such that the previous abnormal becomes *the new norm*. It is now normal, and the old norm in relation to the new normal now becomes abnormal. Husserl's examples of this transvaluation range from the institution of a new perceptual teleology (through, say, optical surgery) to the generation of a new species. In the latter case, Husserl writes that "the primordial institution of wolf means that this abnormality in the earlier generation of the species stably creates the new teleology 'wolf' through the stability of the new teleological circumstances."[17] Accordingly, there is a generation of a new normal teleological order, a new meaning structure which, in relation to the past concordant order, *was* abnormal and referred to another telos; now, however, it institutes a new norm and new teleology.

In the institution of a new order through what was previously an anomaly or an abnormality, it is possible to institute a new normality "*in spite of the reference back to the earlier norm.*"[18] In other words, the transcendence of old norms and old orders does not necessitate a monolithic replacement of a previous normality with a new one. Different normal orders may exist *simultaneously*, both pointing to their own telos and being implicated in another. In the case of the lived-body, but especially in the constellation of the social world, there may be more than one norm functioning at the same time for the same act, event, form of life, etc. Thus, Husserl accounts for the constitution of a conflict of normal orders in experience.

The way in which Husserl conceives descriptive sciences implicitly involved in history speaks more explicitly to the historical and normative role of generative phenomenology. In order to elucidate the historical-teleological dimension of philosophy, and in particular, of phenomenological philosophy, Husserl will discuss the descriptive sciences in general, which are ostensibly removed from the issues of normativity and teleology. Taking the example of botany, Husserl writes that when a botanist describes plants, he or she begins with the world at hand. But when the botanist actually describes plants in the present world, he or she also takes up botany in its primordial institution with the first botanists, and hence is implicitly involved with a broader historical community of botanists and in the experience of their world.[19]

Moreover, at least functioning implicitly in the descriptive work of the botanist is an appropriation of the initial telos *as valid or invalid*. As mentioned above, even when one classifies something, one also implicitly grasps its dynamic, internal sense, its teleological orientation. In accepting it, one assumes that the original sense of the project is appropriate, and thus affirms the norm. One takes a position with it. In not accepting the sense, or accepting it roughly, one is engaged in the process of redirecting its sense, doing things differently, reforming with contemporary contexts of meaning according to a different futural norm. In attempting to guide present experience from the anticipated norm, the future becomes determinative of the present, and thus implicitly opposes the primacy of the present in a putative pure structural description.

In reforming botany, for example, one is orientated not only toward the past and the present, but also toward the future from the future. What seems to be only a descriptive enterprise of the present implicitly has a historical communal dimension, meaning here, a directedness toward an open intersubjective framework.[20] But what distinguishes the phenomenologist from the botanist?

In order for botany to function as botany, it does not have to be explicitly aware of what it is doing. But the phenomenologist does. According to Husserl, the phenomenologist is not only involved in the descriptive situation communally, historically, and normatively, but in a *critical* manner. This critical manner can be described as *optimal* in the sense indicated above. The natural attitude is normal in the sense of concordant; phenomenological reflection is abnormal in relation to it, but institutes a new normality and a new teleology that brings it to expression in a creative way. Hence, phenomenological reflection is normatively significant from the perspective of the natural attitude as abnormal, but from the new normality, as optimal.

In light of Husserl's sensitivity to the teleological-historical dimension of transcendental philosophy, Husserl grew critical of his earlier approaches to phenomenology, especially in *Ideen I*, for having utilized the implicit teleological sense of philosophy that was operating throughout his reflections, but without undertaking a special "historical-teleological reflection" making the primordial institution of philosophy and its communal historical sense an explicit problem.[21] By regarding the institution of sense historically (and by explicating it in terms of three modes of sense-institution—absolute primordial institution, relative primordial institution, and transformative institution), Husserl became much more attentive to the historical atmosphere in which he, as a transcendental phenomenologist, attempted to carry out philosophy.[22]

1.2. Homeworlds/Alienworlds

In these later years, Husserl had a way of getting at the sense of intercultural phenomena in which there are different paths of access from the realm of facts to the essential structures of reality, even those that are radically incommensurate through the description of normatively significant life-worlds, or what he called within a generative nexus, the interrelations of *"homeworlds"* and *"alienworlds."* Homeworlds and alienworlds are not merely "life-worlds," for the latter concept is still too abstract. Rather, they are normatively significant, geo-historical life-worlds formed by various modes of generative constitution. For example, the home is not one place among others, but a normatively special geo-historical place that is constituted with a certain asymmetrical privilege, and it can range from the smallest generative unit, "mother or parents and child," to a virtual cultural world. The home gets this asymmetrical privilege through modes of appropriation and disappropriation of sense that are bequeathed or historically sedimented and that extend historically over the generations.

In general, appropriating sense, or taking up sense which "stems" from a tradition, is a historical process of reawakening sedimented sense, the active taking up (thematic or pre-thematic) of previous acquisitions in a unique way.[23] These modes of appropriation and disappropriation express particular styles of access to reality, the ways of being guided by essential structures, and the ways in which connections are made, etc. For Husserl, these ways are selective/exclusive, a process that he calls "optimalization," which is a way of generating norms. The modes of accessibility and inaccessibility of home and alien are constituted and transmitted though such things as ritual, narrative, language, shared habits and customs, styles of movement and thinking, and so forth, that bring the essential structures to bear in *this* way rather than *that*. Accordingly, what gets constituted as "home" is not only a "ground-horizon" as a basis for living, but the very normatively significant life-world to which we return. The home becomes normatively significant to us as experience gets shaped concordantly and optimally, and over time typically, and with familiarity. In this way, Husserl understands the home to be constituted for the "homecompanions," generally speaking, in the mode of "accessibility." Because appropriation can also be naive, it needs to be tempered by an ethical and "reasonable" appropriation, or what Husserl also calls "critique."[24]

Though constituted with an experiential and normative weight through the appropriative/disappropriative process as "our" (i.e., our world, etc.), the home is not a one-sided, independent original sphere independent of the alien. Through the generative constitution of the sense of "home," an alienworld or alienworlds are liminally co-constituted *as* alien, in the extreme case, *as* neither

concordant, nor optimal, nor typical, nor familiar. Accordingly, Husserl understands alienness to be constituted precisely as *accessibility in the mode of genuine
inaccessibility and incomprehensibility.*[25]

Through modes of appropriation and disappropriation of the home, which
home is always in the process of being constituted as home, the alien is co-
constituted as alien. Moreover, not only is the constitution of the home liminally co-constitutive of the alien, but the alien is co-constitutive of the home
through modes of transgressive experience.

While appropriation is an explicit relation to others *qua* homecompanions
of a homeworld, and is implicitly the constitution of the alien of an alienworld,
it is always more than merely understanding one's own tradition, for an alien
subject may also understand our tradition without taking it up.[26] Husserl hints
at two broad types of encounter with the alien: occupation and transgression.
Whereas occupation (such as conquest, conversion, etc.) merely extends the limits of the home and is not experienced as such, "transgression" is the encounter
of the alien from the perspective of the home where the limits of the encounter
are left intact. Here violence would be a violation of limit-claims. If we were
to examine transgressive experience *abstractly,* we might conclude that transgression would be an encounter with the alien that simply abandons the conditions of the home for the encounter. As opposed to occupation which remains
"within," it would simply cross over. But generatively considered, transgressive
experience does not leave home in going beyond; it is a *crossing over from within.*

By transgressive experience, then, I understand a relation with the alien
that crosses over the "limits" of the home, but from within the home, and such
that the limits of the home are only exposed in the encounter with the alien,
and are never encountered like an object. According to Husserl, the home does
not exist as an independent sphere of ownness, but is only constituted as home
through the alienworld(s). Transgression is the process of crossing over the
limits of the home while remaining rooted in the home, and thus bringing an
explicit experience of limits into being. The generative relation of home/alien
that has been invoked here is itself not a thing to be encountered; rather, it
emerges as such through the encounter of the home with the alien, through liminal experience. Through the alien, we gain the home as home. The structure,
home/alien, is a co-original, co-foundational structure: Because we are constituted as "home," we belong to the alien in the process of co-constitution, but
precisely as not belonging to the alien as being home; and because we can encounter the alien through processes that transgress the limits of the home from
within the home, we encounter the home as if "for the first time," through the
encounter of the alien. In short, the structure, home/alien, exhibits concretely
varying degrees of homeness and alienness, since it is co-constituted through
an optimalizing process of generativity.

The notion of home for Husserl is irreducible to the foundational status
attributed to the ego and is not an "original" sphere, as was the case in a genetic
phenomenology. The home, however, is from the very start intersubjective and
co-constituted by the alien and the abnormal. Through this co-constitutive co-

relativity, we experience a constant becoming alien of the home. Homeworld and alienworld coexist in a relation of axiological asymmetry: They are irreversible and not interchangeable. For this reason, Husserl's phenomenological descriptions of homeworld and alienworld and of their fundamental constitutive co-relativity forcefully challenge the conception of a "one world" that could supervene upon the irreducible co-generational structure, homeworld/alienworld.

Finally, the explicit co-constitutors of a homeworld are now termed "homecompanions" [*Heimgenossen*].[27] Homecompanions are "transcendental co-bearers of the world" and include not only humans, but as we will see below, animals as well. Members of an alienworld are liminally co-constitutors of a homeworld, but strictly speaking not homecompanions.

Generative phenomenology is concerned in part with identifying *essential, a priori* structures that bear on the *re-constitution* of homeworlds and alienworlds over the generations. In a generative phenomenology, language and communication become constitutive problems for the formation of an intersubjective nexus and eclipse the central role that intropathy [*Einfühlung*] played in the constitution of the social world. For intropathy cannot take place with our dead or unborn homecompanions, with our ancestors, with those unknown, but nevertheless familiar.[28] The generative dimension of this communication includes the form of the "function of language in the *chain of generations*," that is, narrative.[29] This is one way in which the sense of a tradition can be appropriated as "my own" or as "our own."

This brief mention of the generative structure, home/alien, is not intended to exhaust the elements peculiar to a generative phenomenology. My purpose has been to suggest the wealth and distinctiveness of phenomena that come to the fore in the move from genetic to generative analyses.

Having suggested that the "things themselves" depend upon the level of analysis, and having suggested what these different levels are, I now want to inquire into their interrelation. This will require taking a generative view itself on the matters of phenomenology. For this reason, I want to begin the next section by asking how Husserl's notion of generativity is generated.

2. The Generation of Phenomenology

How does the philosopher renowned for his assiduous attention to consciousness, egological subjectivity, and punctual presence anticipate a method for handling intersubjective and historical becoming? Let me approach this question in two stages: (1) in terms of possible historical influences on Husserl, and (2) with respect to the problem of generativity within phenomenology.

2.1. Historical Influences: Heidegger and Dilthey

It would not be wrong-headed to seek Husserl's engagement with generativity and generative problems in motivations that lie outside of the internal development of Husserl's own work as it was developed prior to the 1930s. After all, Husserl never considered phenomenology to be an undertaking accomplished by a single thinker, but rather an ongoing historical project in which one participated.

It is well known that Heidegger was Husserl's close assistant from 1919 to 1922, and that even after disappointed attempts at collaboration, Husserl still regarded Heidegger as the only qualified successor to his chair in Freiburg (1928).[30] Moreover, because the majority of Husserl's writings on generative themes occur around the years 1930 and following, and because Heidegger's new philosophical perspective was so appealing to many of Husserl's own students, it would not be surprising to cite Heidegger, following the publication of his *Sein und Zeit*, as a motivating factor in Husserl's reflections on the problem of historicity.[31] In fact, in the summer of 1929, Husserl devoted a two-month study to *Sein und Zeit* as well as to some of Heidegger's more recent writings in order to come to grips with Heidegger's philosophy.[32] Particularly important for the theme of this paper are the occurrence of the expressions "generation" (*Generation*) and "historicity" (*Geschictlichkeit*), which are found in the second chapter of the second division of Heidegger's *Sein und Zeit*.[33] Given this association, esteem, and even a possible rivalry as a backdrop, it has become almost commonplace to link themes found, for example, in Husserl's *Krisis* (which dealt with notions like the lifeworld and history) to Heidegger's groundbreaking work.

But if we are seeking so-called "external," historical influences on Husserl in this regard, then a much more likely source would be Dilthey.[34] One clue in this direction is Heidegger himself. For precisely at the places where Heidegger uses "generation" and "historicity," Heidegger himself refers to Dilthey.[35]

Certainly, Husserl knew and respected Dilthey long before Heidegger's appropriation of the latter's work. Indeed, a relationship between the two thinkers was already established in the first decade of the twentieth century and became particularly poignant on the touchy question of historicism. A lively and revealing exchange was provoked by Husserl's famous "*Logos*" article from 1911, "Philosophie als strenge Wissenschaft."[36]

Not only was Husserl indirectly occupied with Dilthey in the 1920s through his own students (for example, Landgrebe who received his doctorate under Husserl for a thesis entitled "Wilhelm Diltheys Theorie der Geisteswissenschaften" in 1927),[37] or through Dilthey's students (for example, Georg Misch's *Lebensphilosophie und Phänomenologie* from 1929),[38] but—if Husserl's acquisition of volumes V and VI of Dilthey's *Nachlaß* in July 1924 are any indication—Husserl continued to be occupied directly with Dilthey's work.[39] In particular, we find similar themes occurring in a generative phenomenology that are peculiar to Dilthey, especially the question of historicity and the historico-spiritual movement of intersubjective accomplishments evaluated in terms of the temporal-space (*Zeitraum*) of generations.

To the best of my knowledge, neither Dilthey nor Heidegger ever use the expressions "*generativ*" or "*Generativität*," and the theory of constitution as the reproduction of normatively significant homeworlds and alienworlds appears quite unique to Husserl's theory of intersubjectivity. In fact, generative notions like home, homeworld, and alienworld can already be found in Husserl's writings around 1920.[40] It was also during this period (1922–24) that Husserl wrote explicitly on the becoming of historically intersubjective phenomena.

To be sure, Dilthey did analyze ontological categories of society that affect our concrete understanding, as well as the actual structural differences obtaining between generations and life. For Dilthey, one must perform a hermeneutical operation on objectifications of life, a process of "understanding" in which living human historical experience is grasped. But the crucial point at which Husserl's method diverges from Dilthey's hermeneutics is that juncture where the social structures are still presupposed in the interpretation. That is, Dilthey does not inquire into *how* these social and historical structures take on sense or how they are themselves generated; although, according to Dilthey, the human being does not have a fixed nature and is in the process of becoming historically, the philosopher of the *Geisteswissenschaften* does not investigate the *structure of this becoming* or the *becoming of this structure*. By contrast, the task of a generative phenomenology is precisely to inquire after how historical and intersubjective structures themselves become meaningful at all, how these structures are and can be generated. Accordingly, not only the past and present dimensions are invoked here, but the future too becomes a "matter" of generative phenomenology, and to such an extent that the generative phenomenologist becomes involved in the generation of generativity.

The points of convergence between Dilthey, Heidegger, and Husserl are simply too vast to be covered here.[41] I wish only to submit that in seeking the development of the problem of generativity in Husserl, one should not underestimate the influence that both Dilthey and Heidegger did exert or could have exerted on Husserl's thought by the 1930s.[42]

While one is justified in seeking external motivations of the development of generative phenomenology, it would be misleading to look *only* to external sources for the generation of generative themes in Husserl's reflections. More precisely, I want to maintain in what follows that the dimension of a *generative phenomenology is generated as part of the self-explication of phenomenology itself*.[43] This disclosure has to do with the style of phenomenological reflection that Husserl undertook.

Having made these initial gestures toward the generation of method, let me advance more explicitly to the generation of phenomenology within phenomenology.

2.2. Generating Phenomenology

Explaining the generation of generative phenomenology entails examining the matters and methods of phenomenology that I explicated above: static, genetic, and generative dimensions of phenomenology *from a genetic and then generative* perspective. Husserl began with a genetic understanding of the relation between static and genetic method and matters. Let me begin there.

2.2.1. From the Static to the Genetic

Husserl hints at such a genetic connection with the notion of "*Leitfaden*" or "leading clue." The basic question, he writes, concerns "how the investigations are to be ordered"; that is, it "concerns the leading clues of the system."[44] The notion of leading clue for Husserl articulates neither the "structure" nor the "method," but the *relationship of motivation* obtaining between methods and matters.

Husserl's methodological strategy has the peculiar trait of privileging the "simple" over the "complex" as a way of easing into phenomenological descriptions. For example, he will begin with the object in rest as opposed to the object in motion in descriptions of spatiality and kinaesthesis; he will begin with monothetic acts and then proceed to synthetic ones; he will describe the constitution of normality and abnormality by beginning with individual senses rather than the whole lived-body; and he will take as his point of departure a slice of single conscious intentionality rather than the factical individual monad when describing the phenomenological notion of the "Absolute."[45]

When Husserl reflects back on the emergence of genetic and static methods, he orders them by understanding static method as providing a leading clue to constitutive phenomena and its method: "*Is not static phenomenology precisely the phenomenology of leading clues,* the phenomenology of the constitution of leading types of objects in their being, and the phenomenology of the constitution of their non-being?"[46]

For Husserl, one must first establish static matters: structures like intentionality, etc. They then guide the formulation of the matters in their becoming as well as the formulation of appropriate methods. In a manuscript composed in the 1930s, Husserl writes: "That is thus static phenomenology. I analyze *ontologically* the being-sense world and correlatively inquire into the certainties of being, namely, concretely into the modes of givenness. *Ontological analysis* is [the] leading clue for the analysis of correlative validities of being."[47] In this case, Husserl can understand a "static" formal ontological or regional analysis as providing a leading clue for a "static" constitutive analysis.[48]

But a static analysis in both senses can also function as a leading clue for a genetic constitutive analysis. For example, as leading clues, the structure noesis:noema and modes of intention and fulfillment point to how consciousness *develops* actively and passively through transitions in retention, impression, and protention, or through remembering and expectation. Once we become clear about *what* consciousness is as a structure and *how* this "what" is constituted, Husserl maintains, the results of our static analyses can function as guiding clues to *how* consciousness arises out of consciousness through genetically functioning modes of "motivation," that is, the relations of conditioning obtaining between the motivated and the motivating.[49] Thus, types of possible objects and subjects (natural, psychic, and cultural-spiritual) function as lead-ing clues for the constitutive becoming of individual life and monadic commu-nities.[50]

When Husserl thematizes the progression of method, what he describes as a foregone conclusion and necessity of connection is actually the description of *his own* philosophical progression, that is, the *genesis* of phenomenological method in *his* hands. For Husserl, a static phenomenology really did function as a leading clue or way into a genetic phenomenology before it became con-scious of itself as such.[51] This connection between methods and matters Husserl only glimpsed with the word "*Leitfaden.*"

Here is how a genetic method comes to be formulated. Husserl finds him-self already in the process of "describing" phenomena *that exceed the restrictions of the method propounded at that time.*[52] Now, to describe these new matters, Husserl must already be employing a new method in order for those phenomena to give themselves in this new way, but without being conscious exactly how it is a new method or when it became so. To be more specific, it is not uncommon for Husserl to advance a particular theme during a certain period of research and not treat it again systematically until a decade later. Or, during a given period of time, Husserl will experiment with incompatible approaches mixing themes and importing past conclusions into new methods of procedure. The result is that certain phenomena Husserl wants to take up in fact exceed the boundaries of the operative method. He may begin, for example, by describing phenomena that are "static" such as the structure of conscious intentionality. But by moving to the question of the form of temporal synthesis or habituality, new methodological assumptions and evolutions are in play implicitly. Perhaps they are not quite fully "genetic," but they are certainly beyond what static analyses were able to offer. Looking back, Husserl tends to formulate retrospec-tively what methodological advances must have taken place in order to be able to describe the phenomena he did. He then clarifies the method for future in-vestigations of those same themes and for the enrichment of phenomenological method as a whole.

Understanding the general development of method in this way is helpful because it can account for how Husserl was able to describe generative phe-nomena that exceeded the bounds of genetic phenomenology, how Husserl could implicitly carry out a *generative* phenomenological method *without explic-itly* distinguishing the latter from a genetic method or formulating this most concrete dimension of phenomenology *as* a generative phenomenology. Accord-ing to his own notion of *Leitfaden*, generative phenomenology is *anticipated* by the emergence of genetic phenomenology and generative problems because it was already functioning guidingly from the very start! This is actually the state of a generative phenomenology in the 1930s. What I have done is to take the next step and to formulate this generative dimension as a generative phe-nomenology on the basis of genetic leading clues and matters that exceed the bounds of genetic analysis.

Thus far I have only suggested the relation of leading clue that exists between static and genetic methods. Let me now do this for the relation between genetic and generative methods.

2.2.2. From the Genetic to the Generative

Following Husserl's understanding of leading clue as the relation of motivation obtaining between methods and matters, we could say that genetic phenomenology functions as a leading clue for generative phenomenology. We find at least three similarities that hold for genetic and generative dimensions which held for static and genetic ones, and one important difference.

First, just as Husserl treated genetic problems sometimes years prior to calling them genetic in their proper sense, or expounding upon a genetic as distinct from a static phenomenology, so too, Husserl took up generative problems such as homeworld and alienworld, birth and death, sense-constitution through appropriation, social ethics, etc., while still working within the context of a genetic analysis and burgeoning distinction between static and genetic phenomenologies. Second, just as the structure of essence, type, etc., becomes the leading clue for genesis, so too does genesis itself become an open structure as a leading clue for generativity. Third, just as static and genetic phenomena stand in a relation of the simple to the complex, so too does Husserl intimate (initially) that genetic and generative phenomena exist in a relation of the simple to the complex: The individual genesis must be worked out prior to intersubjective becoming or generation, self-temporalization and monadic facticity prior to communal historicity, the constitution of the unity of a life prior to the constitution of the unity of a tradition.

Finally the relation between genetic and generative analyses differ in relation to static and genetic methods in one important respect. Whereas static and genetic matters fall under different rubrics, that is, that which is "structural," and that which is "dynamic," genetic and generative phenomena, on the other hand, both come under the rubric of dynamism and temporalization: Genetic method is concerned with self-temporalization or facticity, and generative method with socio-historical temporalization or historicity. In this respect, there seems to be more of an affinity between genetic and generative phenomena—and hence more occasion for their conflation and ambiguity—than between static and genetic ones. Perhaps this is one reason it took Husserl some time to see the essential differences between genetic and generative phenomena.

2.3. Leading Clues

This latter assertion, namely, that *there is* a difference between genetic and generative (as well as static) matters should not be immune to closer scrutiny. The comparison I just made between static, genetic, and generative matters and methods provokes two important and interrelated questions. First, just how *distinct* are these phenomena of static, genetic, and generative methods? That is, in what sense are the "things themselves" irreducible and distinct matters peculiar to the methodology? Second, this same question can be posed dynamically. What is the *directionality* of phenomenological method? Does working by leading clues only function in one direction, from static to generative, or does it also move in the other direction, from generative to static?

2.3.1. Distinctions of Matters and Methods

Jacques Derrida, in his famous essay "'Genèse et structure' et la phénoménologie," responds to the first question by asserting that for Husserl there are some given matters (*données*) that must be described in terms of structure and others in terms of genesis. For example, there are layers of signification that appear as systems, complexes, and static configurations which must obey the legality proper to and the functional signification of the structure under consideration. Other layers, he continues, are given in the essential mode of creation and movement, of inaugural origin or becoming, which require one to speak of them in the language of genesis, "supposing that there is one or that there is only one."[53] To this we might also add that indeed there are other languages of becoming, that there are still other layers that are given or pregiven in the essential mode of social and historical generation, and these require being addressed in the language of "generativity."

What Derrida recognizes in this brief passage cited above is a fundamental phenomenological insight, namely, that the *way* something gives itself corresponds to the manner in which we turn to it.[54] For the matters will give themselves, for example, statically through a static methodology. This is why Derrida's expression "there are *some* given matters" (*il y a des données*) "that *must*" (*qui doivent*) be described in such and such a manner, is ambiguous: To the extent that the necessity is internal to the "opening toward" the phenomena, the matters "must" be described in one way or another.

But—proceeding from static toward generative as Husserl is initially wont to do—does "necessity" mean that the phenomena given in one way cannot be described any other way?

Let us begin with some examples. When it comes to phenomena like consciousness, I do not see a necessity of restriction. For instance, once consciousness is regarded statically in terms of the structure of intentionality, it can also be regarded genetically as a process of self-temporalization, etc. Or let us take the example of a musical tone. Certainly a tone can be described statically in terms of a structural field of differentiation. Or again, a tone can be examined according to a static constitutional schema as sensation or "hylē." But even here, the tone as hylē in a static schema can also be taken as a temporal matter and—as Derrida rightly puts it—"the possibility of genesis itself."[55] It would seem then that this matter of static analysis is also amenable to a novel genetic constitutional account in a theory of passive synthesis or "transcendental aesthetic."

Even numbers, insofar as they belong to systems of numbers, seem to avail themselves to the language of "inaugural origin," creation and movement. Witness, for example, Husserl's efforts in the "Origin of Geometry"; would we not speak the language of genesis or generativity when describing the constitutional transformations in our self-understanding and the development of non-Euclidean geometries or alternative logics?

I do not want to suggest that static analysis cannot have a certain *advantage* in relation to other methodological approaches, since it can deal with stable laws and structural relations that provide a certain "clarity and distinctness" that we lack in genetic and generative analyses. Moreover, in Derrida's words a static analysis can provide an analysis of the very "structure" of opening, "structural a prioris" of genesis itself.[56] This structural aspect, along with constitutional considerations, are certainly integral to what Husserl understands by *transcendental* phenomenology.

But my interest goes much further than asserting that peculiar phenomena are opened up through different methods; this would merely be a "structural" view. Rather, it bears directly on the possibility of generativity, in the sense of both the phenomenology of generation and the generation of phenomenology. For we are addressing the movement between the methods and matters. Before avowing his own view, Derrida asserts that, for Husserl, the movement from the structural analyses of static constitution to analyses of genetic constitution is "nevertheless . . . a simple progress which does *not imply at all a 'surpassing'* . . . and still less an option and especially not repentance. It is a deepening of a work that *leaves intact* what has been discovered" (my emphasis). Derrida continues in this vein comparing the movement to Husserl's own metaphors of archaeology: One excavates genetic foundations and originary productivity *without* destroying or disturbing any of the more superficial structures already exposed.[57]

It is on these points that we would have to challenge the assumptions that Derrida attributes to Husserl about phenomenological method, and maintain instead—in the spirit of much of Derrida's work on Husserl—that in many if not most cases, static structures *are* surpassed, "rattled," or "ruined" through "deeper" genetic analyses, or even deeper, generative ones, such that new phenomena can flash forth as such. Let me take a deeper look into this issue by examining two sets of so-called limit-phenomena: birth and death, and animality.

2.3.1.1. Birth and Death. Let me take as a first example the matters of birth and death. To be sure, birth and death are everyday occurrences. We see them in hospitals, in homes, on the streets, read of them in the papers, see them on the news, watch them from a distance or empathically in movies. More intimately, perhaps, we experience joy at the birth of a child, celebrate another's or even our own birthday; we are grieved over the death of a loved one or a friend, and come together for memorial services. Birth and death are even encountered from a remote objective stance: Hospital staff record the time of birth, and physicians document the time of death; in some circumstances interns "assist" at a birth, a doctor performs a cesarean; in other cases emergency medical personal attempt to resuscitate a person who has just "died."

But if these everyday encounters with birth and death are to be anything more than occurrences we take for granted in either natural or naturalistic attitudes, or again, simply celebrated or mourned, and are instead to be clarified in terms of their very meaning they have for us in that celebrating or that mourning, they have to be elucidated according to the way in which they are given to us. It is here that phenomenology becomes significant precisely because it is a style of openness to these experiences that is concerned with the modes of givenness of what we take for granted in our lives.

How are we to approach phenomena like birth and death phenomenologically? One could try to approach birth and death from a static phenomenological perspective. A static phenomenology will look at how sense is constituted within a cross section of experience. Where birth and death are concerned, however, it is not even possible to broach these issues from a static phenomenological perspective because it does not and cannot take any account of temporal genesis. Birth and death remain here literally "sub-liminal." Static phenomenology (and I think, quite deliberately) can only take as its theme something like the modalities of the "present" of consciousness. In this case, what comes into focus is the impressional present, constituted liminally by the past and future, where past and future are constituted as limit-phenomena. In a static phenomenology, past and future are on the limits of givenness, given as not being able to be given, and as such co-constituting the present as being able to be given, accessible. Certainly, one can speak of retention and protention within a static phenomenology, but their givenness already presupposes a genetic insight into the genesis of the living present, though it never becomes an explicit theme.

While it is no coincidence that in his early static phenomenology expressed in *Ideen I* Husserl identified "the being of consciousness" as the *absolute*,[58] matters change significantly when phenomenology broaches a genetic perspective. Genetic phenomenology will examine not mere "consciousness," but the process of becoming as it concerns monadic self-temporalization, the continual process of becoming in time, a "unity of life" that has a habitual, sedimented heritage of the past and projection into the future. From this perspective, consciousness or the phases of consciousness are identified by Husserl now as "abstract" such that not consciousness,[59] but instead monadic facticity, becomes the true absolute.

It is precisely at this juncture, within a genetic phenomenology, that birth and death become issues for phenomenology, precisely as "limit-phenomena." These limit-phenomena are not arbitrary in the sense that they could arise just anywhere in phenomenology (for example, they could not become issues for a static phenomenology of consciousness). Rather, they are *relative* to a genetic phenomenology, and *necessarily* called forth by this particular methodology.

The parameters of genetic phenomenology, be it concerned with passive or active genesis, are the *individual life*. This is the scope of "first genesis," of which Husserl speaks in a later manuscript:[60] Everything prior to human childhood (and up to the point of death) remains unquestioned. And it must necessarily remain a kind of presupposition for phenomenology, on the limits of phenomenology. Why?

According to Husserl's work on a transcendental aesthetic as the preparation for a transcendental logic, monadic facticity is described as constitutive of space and time. As self-temporalizing, the individual cannot be exhaustively present "in time" at its own birth or present at its own death. While it constitutes a past and a future and lives through them with an abiding density, transcendental subjectivity—the human being clarified according to its sense and meaning constitutive possibilities (and the limits to those possibilities)—cannot constitute its own birth and death. For this reason, Husserl suggests in a provocative note to his lectures concerning passive synthesis that transcendental life cannot die and cannot be born.[61] But again, this can only be asserted from a phenomenological or constitutive perspective that is concerned with genesis. The individual being is constituted as a genetically dense life, and whose birth and death are only able to be constituted as the limits of that life, given as not being able to be given to that very constituting subject.

Certainly, this is not to say that one could not find, phenomenologically, constitutive echoes of birth and death within that life that seem to share the same sense: beginning and ending a project, conversions and rebirths, renewal, being "born again," "dying to the old self," etc. But this would still not be the strict sense of birth and death of the individual given to the phenomenologist as a *transcendental* event. For this to occur, birth and death could not remain on the limits of phenomenal givenness, but would themselves have to become phenomenal without taking birth and death as mere starting points or end points, and without taking their meanings as exhausted by the historian or the journalist.

The transcendental event of birth and death is precisely what appears within a generative phenomenology. As noted above, when Husserl turns to generative themes, and to generativity itself, he no longer speaks of static phenomena being the independent basis for "higher level" analyses or even of self-temporalization as being the foundation for historicity:[62] These are actually *pedagogical* statements suggesting a procedure of analysis. Instead, once generativity is "reached" explicitly, Husserl modifies his vocabulary and regards the former steps not as independent or founding, but now as abstractions from what is most concrete.[63]

As noted, one of the principal generative themes of a generative phenomenology is the relation of homeworld(s) to alienworld(s). Generative phenomenology takes as its ontological leading clue not psychology, but anthropology, and constitutively or phenomenologically examines not only sense-givenness in relation to the lived-body or even the concrete monad, but the generation of

sense primarily through the constitutive modes of appropriation and disappropriation.

It is within this generative dimension that Husserl reexamines the transcendental features of birth and death for phenomenology. The birth and death of
an individual (or even of a culture or a community!) do not have to remain
presupposed occurrences in the natural attitude or punctuations in objective
time. Rather, birth and death are grasped as transcendental (and not merely
mundane) events that are involved in the constitution of sense when that sense
is constituted as stemming from an intergenerational homeworld or alienworld
(and not from an *individual* consciousness or self-temporalizing subjectivity,
merely). Now Husserl can write, as he does in a manuscript from 1930, that
birth and death are *essential* occurrences for the *constitution* of the world.[64]

If phenomenological givenness is restricted to the confines of my self-
temporalization, the process of being born into a homeworld is admittedly beyond *my* immediate experience, since in this case my birth and death would be
constitutively at the limits of that individual experience. But at least my own
birth can be experienced by me another way, generatively, through my homecompanions, for example, my mother, father, guardian, siblings, neighbors, etc.
Moreover, since the "home" is really what is at issue here as a socio-historical
constellation, generatively speaking, one's own death can be experienced generatively, and become a transcendental feature, because it is integrated into
the very generation of meaning. For from a generative phenomenological perspective, it no longer "makes sense" to restrict the responsibility of sense-
constitution merely to the individual (actively or passively). For example, when
I have a child, "I" or even "We" do not merely constitute this child as son or
daughter; this child generatively constitutes me as "father"—a dimension of
constitution to which a genetic phenomenology is essential blind. The latter
cannot account for phenomenological ancestors or successors. Generative phenomenology also allows us to account, constitutively, for how an individual can
take responsibility for the actions of a "home"—be it a family, a city, a state, a
culture—and how a "home" can take responsibility for the actions of an individual.

Similarly, in a generative phenomenology, one is not only concerned with
a self-affective constitution and association as a temporal opening to the individual and to the world by the body (yielding a phenomenology of association,
of the unconscious, of instinct and drive); rather, one is historicized as an
"our," as a homecompanion constitutive of and constituted through others in
homeworlds as these homeworlds are co-founded in alienworlds. The processes
of being born and dying as they are involved in the generative transmission of
sense are integrated into the appropriation and disappropriation of normative
structures that are anticipated by ancestors and surpassed by successors through
traditions, stories, rituals, rebellions, generation gaps, renewals, rites of passage,
and so forth. This is another way in which one can speak of the generative birth
and death of individuals in a home. In short, it has to do with the very process

of becoming "home" as a homecompanion and of the becoming of a home. Further, because the processes of appropriation and disappropriation of sense need not be judicative, they can still be regarded as a type of original passivity.[65]

It is not possible to go into detail here regarding the constitutive roles that normality and abnormality can and do play in phenomenology.[66] Suffice it so say that the generative senses of birth and death *both* would be the process of becoming constitutively normal in the appropriation of the homeworld, which is actually a lifelong process and not anything one putatively reaches in adult-hood, *and* would be the process of becoming constitutively abnormal in either surpassing the established norms and traditions of the home (a process Husserl refers to as "optimalization") or in rupturing or rejecting norms and traditions. Accordingly, one can also speak of the generative birth and death of home-worlds themselves. One could account generatively for the birth of "Europe" as a spiritual formation, as Husserl does, for the constitution of a "promised land," for the "Renaissance" as a cultural rebirth after a period of dormancy, or for even a death of culture, when for example, the values that once animated the home no longer function guidingly or are no longer relevant. Thus, this death of a homeworld does not require that there are no longer biological de-scendants. What is lost here is the concrete generative density. This is the case with so-called "lost civilizations."

My point in giving these examples is to show how birth and death (1) do not even surface as phenomena, let alone limit-phenomena within a static phe-nomenology, (2) are constituted as limit-phenomena within a genetic phenome-nology in and through which "life" is constituted liminally with birth and death as limit-phenomena, and (3) undergo certain constitutive mutations within a generative phenomenology. These mutations can be stated as fol-lows. In the first place, the birth and death of the individual are no longer limit-phenomena, since the limits themselves become phenomenal within gen-erativity. This does not mean that birth and death lose their meaning, but are seen as abstract limits—which is to say—they are operative markers or distinc-tions within generativity. Second, generatively speaking, birth and death apply to the generation of homeworlds and alienworlds, and not just to individuals, and here birth and death also have constitutive significance. Because they are integrated into a constitutive account in which these very (former) limits appear as such, birth and death are *not essentially* limit-phenomena, but become phe-nomena for phenomenology.

2.3.1.2. Animality. So far I have been implicitly considering phenomena as they bear specifically on human life; but we could also undertake a similar line of inquiry as it relates to animality. Are animals, in their own way, constituted as phenomena for phenomenology? I would say that within both static and genetic methodologies, animality "appears" as a limit-phenomenon, on the limit of experience and phenomenological reflection. In a static phenomenology, animals are on the limit of phenomenology insofar as they are on the limits of what can be appresented in *Einfühlung* or intropathy in analogizing apperception. But I would also have to say that this problem is more peculiar to the phenomenological theory of *Einfühlung* than it is to animality itself. For example, assuming that *Einfühlung* functions by means of a positional presentation and a quasi-positional imagination, through which a passive analogizing transference of sense takes place constituting the sense "lived-body" and "psychic life" of the other—all on the basis of the originary givenness of another physical-body—one would be hard pressed to see how *Einfühlung* could function across gender lines, between radically different cultures, between adults and children, among children at different stages, let alone between human beings and animals. It is perhaps for this reason that in the 1930s Husserl writes that there must be essentially different concepts of *Einfühlung* for relations between adults and children, for children and animals, for adults and animals, even for humans and plants. Indeed, one might ask if intropathy is really functional when a young child sees adults "making love," when this action does not "make sense" bodily to the child. Would one not have to bring in a different dimension of phenomenology (a generative phenomenology!) to account for the constitution of intersubjectivity in a case like this?

Be that as it may, the point I would like to emphasize here is that not only animality, but many other phenomena as well become "limit-phenomena" from the perspective of a static phenomenology of *Einfühlung*. In some respects, animality seems to be just a different case. Of course, one could always find various "similarities" shared by animals and humans like kinaestheses, psychophysical subjectivity, and so on, but this would be "mundane" insofar as one would presuppose certain characteristics as ready-made and then point out how they are different or even incompatible. Furthermore, in this regard, the liminality of animals would consist in the surplus of human reason or human emotions, etc., over animals.

But from a genetic *phenomenological* perspective the liminality of animals and humans would be seen in a different regard. This requires exposing the liminality of animal life through the *constitutive* notions of normality and abnormality peculiar to a phenomenology of primordial constitution. As noted, Husserl distinguishes between four notions of normality: concordance and discordance, optimality and non-optimality, typicality and a-typicality, and familiarity and unfamiliarity. In the first instance, an organ could be constitutively normal by yielding a concordant series of appearances, or alternately by giving an object "maximally" with the best possible richness and differentiation in a unity, like when viewing an object from a certain privileged standpoint. In the second, while one would be able to distinguish a range of normality and abnormality from newborns to adults. Normality and abnormality find their limits at the species: we could not call different beings either normal or abnormal in relation to other species.[67] Thus, animality, understood phenomenologically within a *genetic* register, could only be **constituted at the limits of human life**. And it is here that animality is constituted **as a limit** phenomenologically.

For example, given the constitution of a certain optimal olfactory given-ness and sense-giving within humans, one could not say within a genetic phenomenology that the constitution of sense for a dog would be better or worse, normal or abnormal in comparison to humans, even though "objectively" speaking, we might say that a dog has a better sense of smell. Likewise, the eagle's or the mole's sight is constituted only at the limit of humanity's, genetically speaking, so that one could not speak of a human's sight being abnormal in relation to the "optimal" sight of a raptor's, or again, that a human's sight is more optimal than a mole's.

Insofar as Husserl maintains that animals are not generative—or rather, insofar as Husserl's assertions are correct—one could maintain that animality remains essentially a limit phenomenon, even when we move to a generative phenomenology.[68] Husserl makes this claim not because animals do not live intergenerationally, but first, because generativity is not for him merely a biological notion or a matter of reproduction, and second, because he thinks of animals as not being able to generate, historically or purposefully, new structures by renewing normative structures. According to Husserl, animals only engage in the mere repetition of their specific environing-world, and not the generation or renewal of its meaning. If this were as far as a phenomenological scheme of constitution went, we could not account fully for the constitution of intersubjectivity between humans and animals. Animality would be constituted only on the limits of phenomenal givenness. And if this is the extent to which generative phenomenology could take us, it would go no further than Heidegger's assertion that "the animal is world-poor" and that "the human being is world-forming" or world-constituting.[69] Realizing that within Heidegger there are perhaps resources that may take him beyond a rigid distinction between animality and human being, it is nevertheless along *generative* lines forged by Husserlian phenomenology that the liminality of human and animal life can be seen such that the limits are exposed as inessential limits.

Within the natural attitude we could distinguish between wild animals, domesticated animals, and animals that are pets. To some extent these distinctions could hold within a genetic phenomenology, but they do not entirely suffice for generative phenomenological distinctions. Certainly, animals can and do have the constitutional sense for us as "alien," especially in our experiences of a lion or a dolphin, an alienness that is not mitigated by finding similarities between them and us or by training them for circus or aquatic shows. And, of course, we can feel quite attached to a pet pig or goldfish.

But generatively speaking animals can also take on new sense as a "*home-companion*," not only taking on a sense of "home-animal" in which they would be familiar and typical (two other modes of normality) to our territories and ways of life; as homecompanions they would also co-constitute a world with us, "our" homeworld. Since a generative phenomenology is concerned with generative constitution, most concretely in terms of home and alien, generative phenomenology does not leave any room for speaking simplistically of a "human world" versus an "animal world" (as if one could speak of an overarching "one" human world that would not be modulated through the processes of normalization *qua* optimalization, ultimately in terms of homeworlds and alienworlds).

Although Husserl writes that the animal does not pose any questions and therefore does not give any answers[70]—on the one hand excluding the animal from the linguistically communicative sphere—he does on the other hand keep open the possibility of regarding animals as homecompanions and thus as *world-constituting*. An animal becomes a homecompanion when it contributes along with human homecompanions to the co-generation of a sense of a homeworld, for instance, in expanding concordantly and optimally (hence "normally") our world.[71] An eagle, through its extraordinary sight, a dog through its ability to smell, or again, black bears that eat certain fruits and not others, etc., can teach us something of "our" world that we never knew before, and even in a narrower epistemological regard can expand our world-horizons, contributing to the generation of meaning in the homeworld. This takes place without the animals being tamed, domesticated, or being merely of use value. They become co-constitutors of our "same" homeworld in and through their unique optimalities. Or even more prosaically, the dog through its sense of sight and smell can contribute to the constitution of a homeworld and, becoming a guide dog for the blind, co-constitute our world as a homecompanion.[72]

Such a generative constitutive perspective on the relation between animality and humanity makes us reflect on our own assumptions and precariousness of being world-constituting, for the questions and analyses can be posed and conducted with respect to infants, children, and adults in the tenuous undertaking of *becoming* homecompanions in homeworlds. We also encounter once more the generative issues of birth and death since even here we are concerned with how one is born into, maintained, and passes out of homeworlds as homecompanions. This is a process that is never finished, even after death, since a homeworld (no matter how large or small) could still appropriate someone into its "world" (a saint, a hero, a mascot), or disappropriate one (a traitor, etc.).

What conclusions do we reach, then, about animality? First, within a static phenomenology, the question about animality remains literally "sub-liminal" in the sense that its limits are not constituted as such. It is only in a genetic phenomenology, and more precisely, through the genetic constitutive notions of normality and abnormality that animality becomes constituted for humans as a limit-phenomenon, since animals' optimalities are given as not being able to be given for and to us. It is here that human and animal become liminal notions. Indeed, it is through a genetic phenomenology that these limits "appear" as a relative necessity to this method, that animality appears here as a limit-phenomenon and not elsewhere. Finally, despite its genetic liminality, animality was seen not to be an essential limit-phenomenon. Though there are some features that would retain animals on the limit of phenomenal givenness, within a generative phenomenology there are sufficient constitutive elements that call the limits themselves into question, since generatively speaking, animals can become *for us* co-world-constitutors precisely as homecompanions, contributing to the generative sense of a homeworld. Thus, even animality is seen from a generative perspective as not being an essential limit-phenomenon, but as a phenomenon for phenomenology.

These examples are sufficient to provoke the following considerations. If the progression from static to genetic phenomenology does not "damage" the earlier results as we proceed, then phenomenology can reach closure; it could not be generative. But if the results of the former analyses can be called into question, then phenomenology cannot and must not only proceed in one direction, from static to generative; it can and must also double back on itself, so to speak, in a critical manner, moving from generative to static dimensions. Would this reevaluation in the very progression of phenomenology not also suggest that static method might lose its privileged role for Husserl as the sole leading clue for phenomenology? Would not the dual movement from static to generative and generative to static, etc., open the possibility for phenomenology itself to become generative? Does it not give new meaning to Husserl's promulgation that the phenomenologist is a "perpetual beginner"? These considerations lead me to my second point under the problematic of leading clues.

2.3.2. Directionality

When Husserl begins to describe genetic phenomena, he implicitly abandons his strategy—so long a mark of his philosophizing—of ordering the movement of leading clue from the simple to the complex. Instead, the operative concepts now become the "abstract" and the "concrete." For example, when evaluating the process of self-temporalization from his time lectures, Husserl judges them to be merely "formal" and abstract.[73] Or again, from the perspective of the "*concrete* I" as unity of becoming, the "pure I" is only "*abstractly* identical."[74] In view of a genetic method, Husserl will even go so far as to question whether it is even possible to undertake phenomenology systematically in a static framework, that is, where genesis is fully ignored.[75]

Now, rather than the "complex" (say, the process of passive synthesis of temporal horizons) being presupposed by the "simple" (e.g., the impressional present), the latter as "abstract" presupposes the "concrete," factical monadic becoming. Confirming this view, Husserl charges that a static clarification, which at first functioned as a leading clue to a genetic analysis, now presupposes a genetic analysis.[76] On such a view it is possible to assert provisionally that even when one is undertaking static analysis, one is *already* at the level of genetic method, only abstractly. Thus Husserl writes: "Every such [static] analysis is in itself already to a certain extent genetic analysis."[77]

When Husserl begins to describe generative phenomena in the 1930s, we witness a similar strategy in play.[78] For example, Husserl adumbrates two distinct dimensions of phenomena. On the one hand, we have genetic matters which are referred to as phenomena "prior to generation," that is, a field of synchronic contemporaries which are in the process of becoming through "personal" or "self"-temporalization; this is the dimension of "abstract historicity." On the other hand, Husserl describes generative matters which, as he intimates, are in the process of becoming over the generations. These matters include intersubjective and cultural temporalization, a concrete, generatively formed temporality or historicity. Moreover, the movement from genetic to generative dimensions is depicted as a removal of abstraction or a "concretization" of matters. Here the concrete matter of phenomenology is not genesis but generativity, that is, the matter of phenomenology as emerging generatively.

What methodological assumptions are in play in order for Husserl to describe genetic and generative matters in this way? First, the "simple," that is, static can no longer be the concrete because now the putative "simple" is that which is more abstract.[79] Similarly, "generative problems" cannot be understood as belonging to a "higher" dimension which presupposes the "lower" spheres. The case now is just the reverse. Notice in this text, for example, that the individual is not described as a foundation for the community or self-temporalization as foundational for historicity; rather, self-temporalization is portrayed as an abstraction from and hence "presupposing" concrete historicity. But precisely as concrete, it cannot function as a "foundation" upon which other layers are built. Second, and related to the former point, the genetic sphere does not function merely as a leading clue to the generative domain; rather, the generative becomes implicitly a leading clue for genetic phenomena. This is a more specific way of expressing the general possibility for generative phenomenology: the movement is not from the simple to the complex, but from the concrete to the abstract.

In other words, in order to characterize genetic temporalization as "abstract" historicity, Husserl has to be *already* at a generative level of phenomenology, as concrete, when undertaking, say, genetic analyses. In the same way, as we saw above, Husserl labeled his earlier phenomenology of time- consciousness "abstract" from the perspective of concrete genetic analyses which he embarked upon through his analyses of "passive synthesis." This means, further, that even when one is pursuing static analyses, one is already at the farthest reaches of phenomenology; doing static phenomenology means that generativity is already there on the horizon and is implicitly qualifying other endeavors in terms of levels of abstraction *from* generativity. Undertaking static analyses is doing generative phenomenology, only abstractly; or put still differently, static analysis is already situated in generativity.

The various methods and matters of phenomenology would be characterized now in the following way: (1) Generative phenomenology whose matter is generativity is the most concrete dimension of phenomenology; it concerns intersubjective, historical movement. (2) Genetic phenomenology treats generativity shorn of its historical/generational dimension. The movement between levels here would be from generational temporalization or historicity to individual, self-temporalization or facticity. (3) Finally, generativity can be addressed statically through yet another level of abstraction, shorn of all temporal becoming. This would be a static analysis that treats generativity in terms of structure, or again, the structure of generativity.

3. Generative Phenomenology and generative phenomenology

What I have just said about leading clue and directionality requires an immediate qualification. Working provisionally, by way of leading clues, generativity and generative phenomenology were taken, respectively, as one dimension of experience and one dimension of method among others, namely, static and genetic. But this is not entirely accurate. For generativity and generative phenomenology have also emerged as encompassing, as it were, all of these dimensions. Thus, there are two ways of speaking of generativity, as intra-historical within the generation of homeworld and alienworlds, and Generativity as "historicity itself," or again, as a new kind of originating-Absolute. I will discuss how this Absolute needs to be treated phenomenologically in my last section. Here I wish to note that although these two senses of generativity *cannot* be separate, they are distinct. On the contrary, Generativity gets expressed only in and through the interrelation of home and alien; history is this working out of Generativity. Thus what Generativity is becomes what it is historically, but without being reduced to historical events.

Similarly, we can speak of "generative phenomenology" as a type of method that covers various historical phenomena, for example, ritual, generation gaps, cultural traditions, rites of passage, linguistic phenomena, etc. Here we would mean by generative phenomenology a dimension of experience that is peculiarly historical. But there is still another sense of this term, namely, as Generative phenomenology that includes all these aspects. It is in this sense that when one is doing genetic phenomenology, one is doing generative phenomenology, only abstractly within the context of generativity. If we take Generativity seriously, I do not see any way of avoiding this way of speaking.

What does this mean more concretely for the relation between genetic and generative/Generative methods? If genetic phenomenology covers genesis, most concretely, individual self-temporalization, how is the individual to be conceived within Generativity? Certainly, it does mean to situate the individual historically. It also means that the individual cannot be taken as self-grounding. For even situating the individual within the historical framework could still presuppose the historical framework to be self-grounding. Within Generativity, however, the individual(s) or even "homes" in relation to "aliens" are grounded in Generativity. Thus, one does not do away with the individual in a Generative phenomenology, but situates the individual within the Generative nexus. Accordingly, when one goes "back to" the individual within a Generative phenomenology, one not only does not lose the individual, one does not lose the ground of the individual either. One takes up the individual in its richness.

Moreover, it is still possible to do "genetic" phenomenology, say, if one wants to focus on contemporaneous individuals, the lived-body, self-temporalization, my perception of this piece of music, etc. But undertaken from a Generative phenomenological perspective, *this* genetic phenomenology will be "restrictive"; it will not be abstract, but restrictive because it will be carried out on the basis of Generativity phenomenology and its insight into Generativity.

4. Situatedness of the Generative Phenomenologist

How is the phenomenologist situated in Generativity, and how is phenomenology able to handle something like "Generativity"?

4.1. Generativity and Generative Structure

In order to understand how the phenomenologist, the Generative phenomenologist to be precise, is situated in Generativity, one cannot avoid claiming both that Generativity—that gets expressed in terms of home/alien—is an "essential" structure *and* that it is peculiar to a certain cultural and historical tradition, namely, of the West.

Generativity was indeed "discovered" in the West and is the very process by which there are normatively significant structures that have a unique and irreducible orientation, and that through their difference make a difference, permitting not only the experiences of anticipation, disappointment, crises, but also of overcoming them. As noted, Generativity becomes articulated normatively, socially, and geo-historically in the very structure home/alien. When we speak of the Generative nexus as home/alien, we are describing the movement of Generativity, and hence the "whole" generative framework. The whole Generative framework, however, is not described from an objective, third-person perspective, but from within the home, in this case, within Generativity. Accordingly, the structure of generativity as I have expressed it here does not merely account for differences that would be alien to a particular home, but for the possibility of something radically alien even to Generativity itself!

When speaking of the "whole" structure from within a Generative perspective, we are placed in the peculiar situation of describing the whole from within the home as in relation to the alien. In this respect, Generativity is a structure of the whole. But directly related to this, and for the same reasons, one must also say that the Generative structure of home/alien arises from the insight into reality as Generativity, and is thus peculiar to the West. So, from the Western point of view, Generativity takes the form of home/alien and "defines" this perspective as "home." This is the whole structure interpersonally and historically clarifying itself in terms of home/alien. For the East, however, the so-called whole structure is clarified, in Kitaro Nishida's terms, as the self-identity of absolute contradictories.[80] On the one hand, this means the East in relation to the West; but its "point" would be emptiness, whereas for the West it would be Generativity.

The challenge here, for us in the West, is having to speak of the whole Generative framework expressed in terms of homeworld and alienworld from within the perspective of the home *but without resolving the tension of home/alien and thus closing off the unique modes of expression peculiar to the alien which may call the home (e.g., Generativity) into question.* This is further complicated by the fact that for us the *only access to the whole is precisely in the encounter with the alien within Generativity:* The Generative framework is given only in this incongruous, absolutely irreducible relation and not outside of it. Because we bring the generative density of the home with us, we speak through the home toward the alien. This exemplifies the structure of "transgressive experience" that I alluded to above.

If Generativity is to be sensitive to its own generative situatedness, it cannot take itself for granted, and we cannot address Generativity as if, for example, the problem of "emptiness" were of no consequence to the East and as if emptiness could simply be integrated by Generativity.

This is not the same as asserting, as a Westerner, that Generativity is simply a "narrative" of the West. To put it forth as one narrative among others would be *to relativize* the home (and the alien) and to presuppose that I could somehow abstract the home from the relation, comparing it to the East by some overarching supposed neutral term. Instead, it is precisely in the face of emptiness that Generative phenomenology can describe generativity, for to communicate generativity cross-culturally demands doing so within Generativity in the face of emptiness. Cross-cultural communication as a crossing over from within entails describing the Generative framework *fully* from the home as it is open to being called into question by the alien in and through the liminal encounter with the alien. In its own way, Generativity allows the full incommensurability of emptiness, even if emptiness calls Generativity into question.

That the Generative phenomenologist participates in Generativity means several things. First, the particularity of the Generative phenomenologist is essential; as the historical situations unfold, the phenomenologist must critically describe and normatively participate in the generation of interpersonal life. And the phenomenologist must continually account for the changes that he or she introduces into Generativity. Generative phenomenology is still my reflection and my intervention in the things themselves. But it is not as if I am self-grounding. I do not describe as if I were we, but I do undertake phenomenology with the full, though not exhaustive, responsibility of the interpersonal nexus.

Second, because the project of a Generative phenomenology is situated within Generativity, Generative phenomenology cannot end with Husserl. That is, phenomenology becomes a communal effort, not just among contemporary phenomenologists, but as a project handed down and appropriated over the generations. Phenomenology is itself modified according to the historicity of the times and in terms of the facticity of the individual phenomenologists.

Third, generative phenomenology was never contained fully within Husserl's writings. But more importantly, in order for generative phenomenology to be *Generative* phenomenology, it must go beyond being "Husserlian" phenomenology. I do not mean this in the sense that Husserlian phenomenology is defective, in the sense that Schutz, Habermas, or Adorno might understand. Rather, it belongs to the very structure of Generative phenomenology that it goes beyond itself.

Finally, how does Generative phenomenology go beyond itself? Is there any motivation? One way of describing this motivation would be to recognize that Generative phenomenology has to identify and address identified crises that are produced by the very fact that history can never outrun Generativity. The structure of Generativity precludes closure, either conceived as an overcoming of alienness, or as an exhaustion of meaning structures. The Generative phenomenologist in his or her particularity experiences crises according to future possibilities and is consequently involved in the critical project of generating, and not merely repeating, meaning-structures.

But this presupposes something still more. The crises are only experienced as crises because something else is guiding the Generative phenomenologist that allows the crises to show up as such. In the terminology of revelation, this would have to be understood as the absolute value of persons and of Person, who in their absoluteness, that is, uniqueness, solicit our interventions and consequently the generativity of new meaning.

4.2. Disclosure and Revelation

There is nevertheless already apparent a certain limitation to and within these descriptions, limitations that are not easily apparent. The difficulty with a Generative phenomenology if it only goes this far—a difficulty inasmuch as it is conceived along the lines of Husserlian phenomenology (but not exclusively Husserlian phenomenology)—is that it has been traditionally restricted to one mode of givenness, *though this need not be the case*. This mode of givenness I call "disclosure."

Disclosure is a type of givenness that is more or less dependent upon my power to usher things into appearance, either through the power of my "I can" or my "I think." When I intend an object, an object gives itself (whether or not it is the object I intended) in such a way that it points further on to new ontic themes and new horizons. However, disclosure is not at all tied one-sidedly to the subjective aim, since it encompasses the givenness instigated by the object: The affective force of the object can provoke my intending; *the object itself* can function as a lure that guides experience. What appears does so within the economy of concealment and disclosure, provoked by either the subject or the object.

There is, of course, nothing wrong with this mode of givenness; it describes a genuine dimension of our experience that concerns the relative givenness of things in the economy of disclosure and concealment. And it describes our relation to the world as one of immediate or mitigated belief in its being.

The problem is that disclosure has become the dominant model of givenness. When, for example, disclosure is the ruling mode of givenness, the other person, the "alien," or even "alienworlds" can only be described negatively, given as not being able to be given, accessible in the mode of inaccessibility. In fact, this seems to be the precise limit of Husserl's characterization of the alien (cf. CM and XV 631). By limiting ourselves to disclosure we miss the moral and religious dimensions of experience, and we limit the very givenness of the so-called "Other." This constant limitation has been allowed virtually to efface another mode of givenness, *revelation*.[81]

By revelation I understand an "infusion" into the relation of Being and being, into the horizon of Being, an infusion which is not dependent upon our efforts and which exceeds, in principle, our perceptual and cognitive abilities understood as the power to disclose. Unlike the economy of disclosure, what is revealed does not point to another being within the horizon of Being, but to the *giving that gives itself* in being.

If we allow this other mode of givenness to come into play, then the "alien" will be qualified positively now as "person." Only "person" is given in the mode of revelation. Person *reveals* him- or herself as person most deeply in the emotional life in loving. As revealed, person is given as *absolute*, where the mode of access is itself absolute; in this sense revelation is an absolute relation to an absolute. The absoluteness of person is revealed in the quality of its directedness, ultimately in the uniqueness of the style of loving. For Max Scheler (an early phenomenologist who already described both disclosive and revelatory modes of givenness), absolute person is revealed either as *infinite* or as *finite*. Employing these distinctions we can say that if absolute person is given through *irreversible* uneconomic giving, absolute person is qualified *as* infinite, *as* Holy. The sphere of experience here is religious. If absolute person is revealed through *reversible* uneconomic giving, absolute person is qualified *as* finite person. The sphere of experience here is moral. The religious and moral spheres of experience have their own regularity and their own essential interconnections pertaining to "evidence" and "illusion." This gift-giving motivates faith, moral or religious, and takes us beyond limits of givenness as disclosure peculiar to the sphere of belief.

By this brief introduction to the distinction between disclosive and revelatory modes of givenness, I want to make the following two points. First, in contrast to *Husserl's* genetic and even generative descriptions, the other person or even alienworld(s) need not be described merely negatively as an interruptive force, calling into question my power to disclose, my power to comprehend, or my ability-to-be. The other person is not merely given as not being able to be given, accessible in the mode of inaccessibility, on the limit of my experience. *This is only a description yielded when disclosure is our model of givenness.* Rather, when givenness is opened to revelation, to the givenness of absolute person that cannot be contained by disclosure, the other is "revealed" not as a limit to my experience, but as a *moral invitational force,* simultaneously revealing and revealed, exemplary of absolute, infinite giving.[82] Such a revelatory givenness would, in general, make up the sphere of moral experience.

Second, Generativity could not be something described merely in terms of disclosive givenness. Rather, Generativity would be qualified in terms of revelatory givenness as absolute infinite Person, or "Holy." This is, of course, not to say that now we would "know" the Holy exhausting cognitive limits, since the style of openness here is not epistemological but religious. The Holy is only given, that is, *revealed* in and through religious experiencing, and not outside of it. The ineffability of the Holy here would not be an epistemological trait, but an over-abundance of gift-giving which is beyond our power of disposal. Hence, revelatory givenness is "infused," literally a givenness or grace, and not acquired.

Revelatory givenness of infinite person is religious experiencing. Because this kind of givenness is not anything we can produce of our own accord, *phenomenologically* the task is to cultivate a type of openness in which the Holy can reveal itself to us. The decisive point here is that in opening oneself in order to describe phenomenologically the givenness of the infinite absolute, we are also open to being struck by this revelatory givenness, instigating a religious and moral life that is then articulated in terms of religious or moral faith. In this respect, even the Holy could not be constituted as a limit-phenomenon.

Where revelatory givenness is concerned, what is entailed here is not merely a conversion from the natural to the phenomenological attitude, which Husserl *likens* in the *Krisis* to a religious conversion, but a shift from disclosive to revelatory givenness that is a religious and moral conversion. In this respect, the disclosive aesthetic and cognitive structures of experience are modified within religious and moral revelation. This is the way Scheler writes that one can begin with art, philosophy, science, education, politics, law, etc., and, being guided by the inherent inspirational value of the particular field, can be guided implicitly to the religious dimension of experience; if and when experienced, the former would appear pedagogically as steps to religious experience from the perspective of religious experience, a dimension of experience that in no way could have been derived from them.[83] In different terms, just as stasis and genesis are understood as leading clues to generativity, and from this point of view, as abstractions from it, the particular value fields can be seen as leading clues to the religious dimension of experience, but from this perspective, as relative limitations within it. Because of the absoluteness of infinite and finite person, an absoluteness that cannot be equated with universality, revelatory experience of Holy does not imply pantheism.

Finally, from a Generative phenomenological perspective, Generativity becomes a call to each one of us personally, uniquely. If the "response" to that call is philosophical in nature, then the Generative phenomenologist must not

only "describe" the Generative movement as it is taking place, but also participate in the co-constitution of the co-relation home/alien, directing the latter's
movement as conforming to the movement of Generativity. But within Generativity, this can only be done by assuming responsibility for the history of
Generativity through inter-*personal* relations. It is in this respect that the matter
of "phenomenology" is Generativity, and what ultimately allows phenomenology to be called Generative.

Notes

This article draws on a few previously published articles that I have written concerning generative phenomenology. While I do cover similar material here in terms of the exegesis of
generativity and generative phenomenology, I have taken this occasion to respond, at least
implicitly, to various questions concerning generative phenomenology that have arisen since
the publication of *Home and Beyond: Generative Phenomenology after Husserl* in 1995. I ask
indulgence on the part of the reader for those portions that appear familiar, and hope that
they will serve the new themes and insights addressed here as well as facilitate a deeper understanding of generativity and the project of a generative phenomenology.

   1. *Logische Untersuchungen*, 535; *Logical Investigations*, 663: "Die Mühen sind aber
durch die Natur der Sachen selbst gefordert."

   2. See Donn Welton's second essay (Chapter 11) in this collection.

   3. See my *Home and Beyond: Generative Phenomenology after Husserl* (Evanston, Ill.:
Northwestern University Press, 1995).

   4. *Intersubjektivität II*, 40. An English translation of this text, along with another one
on "static and genetic" methods, is available in *Continental Philosophy Review (CPR)* 31, no. 2
(April 1998), trans. Anthony J. Steinbock, 127–52. These texts are also in Edmund Husserl,
Analyses Concerning Passive and Active Synthesis: Lectures on Transcendental Logic, trans.
Anthony J. Steinbock (Dordrecht: Kluwer, 2001).

   5. *Intersubjektivität II*, 41; *CPR* 31, no. 2, 149. And see *Passive Synthesis*, 340: "Bei
diesen Beschreibungen, den konstitutiven, ist keine Frage nach einer erklärenden Genesis"
(*CPR* 31, no. 2, 137). Note also that in the section of this manuscript appended to the volume
on passive synthesis, Husserl explicitly distinguishes between a level of "constitutive phenomenology" and the "phenomenology of genesis" (*Passive Synthesis*, 340, n1; *CPR* 31, no.
2, 152 n28), and likewise distinguishes between two modes of constitutive analysis (*Passive
Synthesis*, 345; *CPR* 31, no. 2, 137).

   6. Cf. Rudolf Bernet, Iso Kern, and Eduard Marbach, *Edmund Husserl: Darstellung
seines Denkens* (Hamburg: Meiner, 1989), 180, hereafter cited as *Darstellung*.

   7. See *Ideen III*, 125, 129. See also *Logische Untersuchungen*, §§40–52. Cf. Bernet et
al., *Darstellung*, 182–83.

   8. Cf. Donn Welton, *The Origins of Meaning: A Critical Study of the Thresholds of
Husserlan Phenomenology* (The Hague: Nijhoff, 1983), 172.

   9. *Passive Synthesis*, 128.

   10. In the third section of this article I suggest that there are really two different senses

of generativity, and that there are certain prejudices within Husserl's own undertaking that cannot ultimately do justice to the strong sense of "Generativity" as the new Absolute; for it demands the recognition of a unique mode of givenness, not disclosure, but revelation; in this respect, Generative phenomenology indeed has to be taken up "after" Husserl.

11. See, for example, the context of discussion in Husserl's "Cartesian Meditations": *Cartesianische Meditationen*, 169; *Cartesian Meditations*, 142. (There is an unfortunate mistranslation in the English edition that blurs the distinction between generative and genetic themes.)

12. See, for example, Husserl's "Einleitung" to *Logische Untersuchungen*.

13. *Krisis*, 320.

14. *Krisis*, text 26.

15. *Krisis*, 396, 405, 417.

16. See my "The Phenomenological Concepts of Normality and Abnormality," in *Man and World* 28 (1995): 241–60.

17. *Krisis*, 319.

18. "(Doch ist es denkbar, daß die leibliche Änderung auch 'bessere' Erscheinungen ergibt.) Wer ein pathologische Sinnesorgan *ursprünglich* hatte, wer seine erste Konstitution mit Erscheinungen geleistet hat, die anomal sind,—aber bei nachträglicher Gesundung des Organs wird eine *neue optimale* Erscheinungsgruppe derselben Dinge konstituiert, und die bestimmt nun *trotz der Rückbeziehung* auf die *frühere Norm,* die für die Durchhaltung desselben Dinges notwendig ist, im weiteren Leben, (was das Ding selbst ist)" (Ms. D 13 I, 175a, my emphasis).

19. See *Krisis*, 312.

20. See *Krisis*, 312–14.

21. See *Krisis*, text 34, "Zur Kritik an den *Ideen I*."

22. See *Krisis*, text 34 and 399–403.

23. See, for example, *Intersubjektivität III*, 463f.

24. See *Aufsätze II*, 4, 33ff., 63ff. Also see my "The Project of Ethical Renewal and Critique: Edmund Husserl's Early Phenomenology of Culture," in *Southern Journal of Philosophy* 32, no. 4 (winter 1994): 449–64. See also Donn Welton, "Husserl and the Japanese," *Review of Metaphysics* 44 (March 1991): 575–606; *The Other Husserl*, chap. 12.

25. *Intersubjektivität III*, 631.

26. See *Krisis*, 13–14, 40, 373.

27. See, for example, *Intersubjektivität III,* text 11, 148–70, or text 14, 196–214, or again text 27, 428–37, as well as their accompanying appendices.

28. Cf. *Intersubjektivität III*, 472–75, 218ff.

29. See *Intersubjektivität III*, 145.

30. See Herbert Spiegelberg, *The Phenomenological Movement: A Historical Introduction* (The Hague: Nijhoff, 1984), 340–47, hereafter *Phenomenological Movement*.

31. Heidegger dedicated and presented a copy of *Sein und Zeit* to Husserl on his (Husserl's) birthday (8 April 1926). See, for example, Georg Misch's "Nachwort" in his *Lebensphilosophie und Phänomenologie: Eine Auseinandersetzung der Diltheyschen Richtung mit Heidegger und Husserl* (Darmstadt: Wissenschaftliche Buchgesellschaft, 1975), 328, hereafter *Lebensphilosophie und Phänomenologie*.

32. *Husserl-Chronik: Denk- und Lebensweg Edmund Husserls,* ed. Karl Schuhmann (The Hague: Nijhoff, 1977), 303–4 and 349, hereafter *Husserl-Chronik*.

33. It would be an interesting project to consult Husserl's marginal notes on *Sein und Zeit* in order to understand the influence of Heidegger on Husserl. One would find, however, expressions of incredulity on Husserl's part, that is, statements protesting that he (Husserl) had already done what Heidegger claimed to do, and that Heidegger, instead, is simply appropriating Husserl's work only without deep thinking.

Early comments by Husserl on Heidegger's *Sein und Zeit* can be found in Husserl's dedicated copy of this work. See D. Souche-Dagues's Herculean task of interpreting Husserl's marginal responses to Heidegger's *Sein und Zeit* in "La lecture husserlienne de Sein und Zeit," *Philosophie* 21: 7–36.

34. See David Carr, *Time, Narrative, and History* (Bloomington: Indiana University Press, 1986), 102–10, hereafter *Narrative*.

35. See Martin Heidegger, *Sein und Zeit* (Tübingen: Niemeyer, 1977), 377 and passim. And for Heidegger's relation to Dilthey see Spiegelberg, *Phenomenological Movement*, 395f.

36. Their personal contact seems to have been instigated by Husserl's discovery that Dilthey was lecturing on his own (i.e., Husserl's) second volume of the *Logische Untersuchungen*. At this point, Husserl traveled to Berlin to see Dilthey. By December 1910, Dilthey sent Husserl a copy of his work *Der Aufbau der geschichtlichen Welt in den Geisteswissenschaften*. But it was only after Husserl completed his *Logos* article (February 1911) and Dilthey's objection to Husserl's intimation of Dilthey's philosophy as "historicism" that Husserl gave a thorough reading of Dilthey's book (September/October 1911). See *Husserl-Chronik*, 87–88, 151, 159, 161. See also Husserl's correspondence with Dilthey, *Man and World* 1, no. 3 (1969): 428–46, esp. the letter from 29 June and 5/6 July 1911.

37. See *Husserl-Chronik*, 321.

38. See *Edmund Husserl und die phänomenologische Bewegung*, ed. Hans Rainer Sepp (Freiburg: Alber, 1988), 344. Apparently, Misch initiated a correspondence with Husserl by sending Husserl the first part of his work. See *Husserl-Chronik*, 346.

39. *Husserl-Chronik*, 282. David Carr also reminds us that 1927 was the year volume VII appeared containing the piece Husserl had originally received from Dilthey, namely, *Der Aufbau der geschichtlichen Welt in den Geisteswissenschaften*. See *Narrative*, 103.

40. Although they are unaccompanied at this time by the expression "generative." See Ms. A V 10/I, entitled "Umwelt, Heimwelt." See, for example, 127–28: "Diese Heimwelt ist Korrelat seines eigenen Daseins, er ist personales Subjekt seines 'Lebens'—das hier nicht eine momentane Lebens—gegenwart bezeichnet, sondern das Leben in weitem Horizont (schließlich, mindest auf höherer Stufe des Menschentums: sein gesamtes Leben als Ganzheit), das Leben, das ihm 'vergönnt ist,' oder ihm schicksalsmäßig 'auferlegt' ist."

41. On Dilthey and Husserl see *Dilthey and Phenomenology*, ed. Rudolf A. Makkreel and John Scanlon (Washington, D.C.: University Press of America, 1987). *Dilthey und der Wandel des Philosophiebegriffs seit dem 19. Jahrhundert*, ed. Ernst Wolfgang Orth (Freiburg: Alber, 1984). See also Rudolf A. Makkreel, "Husserl, Dilthey, and the Relation of the Life-World to History," in *Husserl and Contemporary Thought*, ed. John Sallis (Atlantic Highlands, N.J.: Humanities Press, 1983), 39–58. And see Peter Borsen, *Zur Phänomenologie des Bewußtseinsstromes: Bergson, Dilthey, Husserl, Simmel und die lebensphilosophischen Antinomien* (Bonn: Bouvier, 1966).

42. If we were to look for influences more "internal" to Husserlian phenomenology, one would have to cite Husserl's assistant Eugen Fink during the 1930s. See, for example, Eugen Fink, *VI. Cartesianische Meditation. Teil I. Die Idee einer transzendentalen Methodenlehre*, ed. Hans Ebeling, Jann Holl, and Guy van Kerckhoven (Dordrecht: Kluwer, 1988). And see Ronald Bruzina's introduction to his translation of this text, Eugen Fink, *Sixth Cartesian Meditation: The Idea of a Transcendental Theory of Method*, trans. Ronald Bruzina (Bloomington: Indiana University Press, 1995), vii–xcii.

43. David Carr makes a similar point concerning the question of history in his *Phenomenology and the Problem of History* (Evanston, Ill.: Northwestern University Press, 1974), chap. II.

44. *Passive Synthesis*, 344; *CPR* 31, no. 2, 141.

45. He explains: "All of this sketches a certain path of phenomenological considerations —after one carries out the phenomenological reduction, which forms the point of departure.

I must proceed step by step; at first I still do not even see that a stream of lived-experience is constituted internally; I have still not fixed it scientifically at all, to say nothing of monadic individuality [or] the ego of abilities constituted in it, etc." (*Intersubjektivität II,* 35; CPR 31, no. 2, 144).

46. *Intersubjektivität II,* 41, cf. 40; CPR 31, no. 2, 149–50.

47. *Intersubjektivität III,* 616, my emphases; and see *Ideen I (Hua),* 359; *Ideas I,* 369, 360ff., 371ff.

48. As he did for example with respect to psychology, biology, and anthropology. See *Ideen I (Hua),* 379f. And see *Krisis.* For a critical interpretation of this edition, see my "The New 'Crisis' Contribution: A Supplementary Edition of Edmund Husserl's *Crisis* Texts," *Review of Metaphysics* 47 (March 1994): 557–84.

49. *Intersubjektivität II,* 41; CPR 31, no. 2, 149–50.

50. It is precisely this progression from static to genetic, from an ontology of constituted structures to dynamic becoming, that also issues in the style of transcendental inquiry Husserl calls "questioning back" (*Rückfrage*) or what becomes Husserl's own style of "regressive" procedure. Husserl understands this process later as a method of questioning back (*Rückfrage*) into the founding layers of validity "and therefore a questioning back into genesis" (*Intersubjektivität III,* 614).

51. It is also from the possibility of a genetic analysis that Husserl can explicitly identify his *Ideen* as a piece of *static* phenomenology (*Passive Synthesis,* 345; *Intersubjektivität II,* 41; CPR 31, no. 2, 138ff., 148ff.).

52. As Larrabee has shown, apperception is a splendid example of a phenomenon that exceeds the boundaries of a static analysis. Cf. Mary Jeanne Larrabee, "Husserl's Static and Genetic Phenomenology," *Man and World* 9, no. 2 (June 1976), 167–68.

53. Jacques Derrida, in *L'écriture et la différence* (Paris: Seuil, 1967), 230, hereafter *L'écriture.*

54. See *Ideen I (Hua),* 362.

55. See Derrida, *L'écriture,* 243–44.

56. Derrida, *L'écriture,* 231.

57. Derrida, *L'écriture,* 231: "C'est l'approfondissement d'un travail qui laisse intact ce qui a été découvert, un travail de fouille où la mise au jour des fondations génétiques et de la productivité originaire non seulement n'ébranle ni ne ruine aucune des structures superficielles déjà exposées."

58. Cf. *Ideen I (Hua),* §§54, 76.

59. *Ideen I (Hua),* §81.

60. See *Intersubjektivität III,* 619.

61. *Passive Synthesis,* 377–81.

62. Cf. *Ideen I (Hua),* 169; *Ideas I,* 181.

63. See *Intersubjektivität III,* 138 n. 2; *Passive Synthesis,* 126ff.

64. See *Intersubjektivität III,* 171: "Problem: Generativität—Geburt und Tod als Wesensvorkommnisse für die Weltkonstitution."

65. See Husserl, Ms. C 17 84b: "so Vererbung ursprünglich generativ und Vererbung der gewöhnlichen Tradition, historisch. Alles Assoziation. Deckung ist Sinnübertragung. Da kommen wir auf Merkwürdigkeiten." See also Ms. A VII o, 2a: "Die Weckung der fernen Vergangenheiten—generativ." See too Ms. C 17 85b: "Dazu kommt die transzendentale Aufklärung der generativen Erbschaften, nicht der biophysischen, sondern der psychischen und somit transzendentalen."

66. See my *Home and Beyond,* especially §§3 and 4.

67. Husserl, Ms. D 13 I, 161a: "Die Normalität bezieht sich auf die Spezies"; *Intersubjektivität III,* 167, 173.

68. *Intersubjektivität III,* 174–85.

69. See Martin Heidegger, *Die Grundbegriffe der Metaphysik* GA 29/30 (Frankfurt am Main: Klostermann, 1983), esp. §§42–63.

70. Ms. C 11 II (1934): "das Tier hat keine Fragen und somit keine Antworten."

71. See Husserl, *Intersubjektivität III,* 167: "Doch es fragt sich, ob das wirklich so richtig ist, da man einwenden könnte, daß, wenn die Tiere verstanden sind als sich auf die Welt beziehend, dieselbe, die die unsere ist, sie auch gelegentlich als Welt mitkonstituierend fungieren können. Wenn der Hund als ein Wild witternd verstanden wird, so belehrt er uns gleichsam von dem, was wir noch nicht wußten. Er erweitert unsere Erfahrungswelt." See also *Krisis,* 87; *Crisis,* 85.

72. In a different context, Junichi Murata has also pointed out that even though the perception of colors unique to a species other than human, a species like bumblebees, would be radically incommensurate with the perception of colors as they are given to humans (e.g., ultraviolet colors), and cannot be considered to be other aspects of *our* visible colors, the colors of flowers that have co-developed with the perceptual organs of bees can be given, and indeed enjoyed by us, from our perspectives, since they are still aspects of the "invisible" color. See Junichi Murata, "Colors of the Lifeworld," in *Phenomenology in Japan,* guest ed. Anthony J. Steinbock, *Continental Philosophy Review* (formerly *Man and World*) 31, no. 3 (1998): 293–305.

73. *Passive Synthesis,* 126ff.

74. *Intersubjektivität II,* 34ff.; *CPR* 31, no. 2, 145ff.

75. *Passive Synthesis,* 344; *CPR* 31, no. 2, 141.

76. *Passive Synthesis,* 343; *CPR* 31, no. 2, 140.

77. *Intersubjektivität II,* 480.

78. *Intersubjektivität III,* 138 n2: "The constitution of an abiding co-humanity, of a general sociality referring co-relatively to a practical environing-world, can be treated *abstractly* already *prior to generation;* and, thus, by virtue of the type of temporalization of this practical environing-world as *personally* significant, there lies already *an abstract historicity* enclosed within it. If we put into play *generation,* then this progression in terms of *concretion* is also a *concretization* of the remaining co-humanity, mother, i.e., parents and child, etc.; and at the same time we have a *more concrete, generatively* formed temporalization and *historical* environing-world." My emphases.

79. Compare *Logische Untersuchungen* (Third Logical Investigation), §17 and *Ideen I (Hua),* §15. Here that which is non-independent was considered abstract, and independent or simple, concrete.

80. Concerning the aforementioned "point," see Luther, *A Dialectics of Finite Existence.*

81. This is a problem I addressed in another essay entitled "Idolatry and the Phenomenology of the Holy: Reversing the Reversal," in *Phänomenologische Philosophie in Japan: Beiträge zur interkulturellen Gespräch,* ed. T. Ogawa, M. Lazarin, and G. Rappe (Munich: Iudicium, 1998), 385–406.

82. I have developed this position in an essay entitled "The Face and Revelation: Levinas on Teaching as Way-faring."

83. Max Scheler, *Gesammelte Werke,* vol. 5 (Bern: Francke 1954), 324–25.

Contributors

Rudolf Bernet is Professor of Philosophy at the University of Leuven (Belgium) and Director of the Husserl-Archives. He is the editor of Husserl's *Collected Works* and *Husserliana* and of the series *Phaenomenologica*. He has published Husserl's posthumous writings on time and numerous articles in the fields of phenomenology, psychoanalysis, and contemporary philosophy. His books include *An Introduction to Husserlian Phenomenology* and *La vie du sujet*.

David Carr is Charles Howard Candler Professor of Philosophy at Emory University. He is the author of *Phenomenology and the Problem of History; Time, Narrative, and History; Interpreting Husserl;* and *The Paradox of Subjectivity*. He has written numerous essays on phenomenology, transcendental philosophy, and the philosophy of history.

Paul Crowe obtained his Ph.D. from the University of Louvain, Belgium, in 1999. He is currently Assistant Professor of Philosophy at Temple University.

John J. Drummond is Professor of Philosophy and departmental Director of Graduate Studies at Fordham University. He is the author of *Husserlian Intentionality and Non-foundational Realism: Noema and Object*. In addition to editing or co-editing four volumes of essays, he has published numerous articles on Husserl's theories of intentionality, pure grammar and pure logic, moral experience, and community.

Klaus Held, Professor Emeritus of Philosophy at the Bergische Universität in Wuppertal, has served as president of the Deutschen Gesellschaft für phänomenologische Forschung from 1987 to 1994. He is the author of *Lebendige Gegenwart*, which is on the problem of time in Husserl's later manuscripts and will be coming out in English translation. In addition to editing his own selection of Husserl's writing, published by Reclam Verlag, he is also the author of many articles on the phenomenology of Husserl and Heidegger, Greek philosophy, and political philosophy.

Christopher Jupp is currently completing his doctoral dissertation on the phenomenology of imagination and aesthetic experience in Husserl, Merleau-Ponty, and Levinas at the University of Edinburgh. He has tutored in philosophy at the Universities of Memphis, Edinburgh, St. Andrews, Stoke-on-Trent, and Stirling.

Dieter Lohmar teaches philosophy at the University of Cologne. He is working on the critical edition of *Husserliana,* Associate Editor of *Husserl Studies,* member of the scientific committee of the series *Phaenomenologica,* and member of the *Conceil Scientifique.* Among his publications are *Phänomenologie der Mathematik: Elemente einer phänomenologischen Theorie der mathematischen Erkenntnis; Erfahrung und kategoriales Denken: Hume, Kant und Husserl über vorprädikative Erfahrung und prädikative Erkenntnis;* and a commentary, *E. Husserls Formale und transzendentale Logik.* His focus is on the transcendental philosophy of Kant and Husserl, empiricism, philosophy of formal sciences, and intercultural philosophy.

Lanei Rodemeyer is Assistant Professor in the Philosophy Department at Duquesne University. Her most notable published article is "Dasein gets Pregnant" (*Philosophy Today*). She is currently working on a book centered in Husserlian phenomenology, entitled *Intersubjective Temporality: It's about Time.* Besides scholarly work focusing on Husserl and temporality, Rodemeyer's interests turn to applying phenomenology to areas such as race and gender studies.

Anthony J. Steinbock is Professor of Philosophy at Southern Illinois University at Carbondale. In addition to articles in social, political, and phenomenological philosophy, he has published *Home and Beyond: Generative Phenomenology after Husserl,* and edited *Phenomenology in Japan* and *The Philosophy of Michel Henry* for *Continental Philosophy Review.* He has also published a translation of Edmund Husserl's *Analyses Concerning Passive and Active Synthesis: Lectures on Transcendental Logic.* His recent work deals with issues of verticality and idolatry, and religious, moral, and ecological experience.

Donn Welton is Professor of Philosophy at the State University of New York at Stony Brook. He is author of *The Origins of Meaning: A Critical Study of the Thresholds of Husserlian Phenomenology* and *The Other Husserl: The Horizons of Transcendental Phenomenology,* and the editor of *The Essential Husserl: Basic Writings in Transcendental Phenomenology.* He has also edited and contributed to two collections on the concept of the body: *Body and Flesh: A Philosophical Reader,* and *The Body: Classic and Contemporary Readings.*

Dan Zahavi is Professor and Director of the Center for Subjectivity Research at the University of Copenhagen, sponsored by the Danish National Research Foundation. His publications include four authored books: *Intentionalität und Konstitution, Husserl und die transzendentale Intersubjektivität, Self-awareness and Alterity,* and *Husserl's Phenomenology,* as well as more than sixty articles. He has also edited or co-edited six volumes, including *Alterity and Facticity: New Perspectives on Husserl,* and *One Hundred Years of Phenomenology: Husserl's Logical Investigations Revisited.*

Gina Zavota will be completing her Ph.D. in Philosophy at the State University of New York at Stony Brook in 2003. She has also studied at the Bergische Universität in Wuppertal. In her dissertation she undertakes a phenomenological reading of Plotinus's *On Eternity and Time*. She has published several German translations and has articles forthcoming on Husserl and Gothic architecture.

Index

Abstraction
  ideational, 106
Achievement, 40
Acts
  founded, 83
  founding, 83
Adumbration, 18, 20, 25–27, 38
Affection, 126, 141–142
Alienworld, 296
Angst, 200, 211–213, 215, 217
Animality, 309, 311
  and limit-phenomena, 312
  and the sub-liminal, 312
Anxiety, 193–196
Apperception, 39, 141–142, 145
  vs. appresentation, 144
  and protention, 142
  typifying, 107, 109–112
Apprehension, 39–40
  intuitive, 108
Appresentation, 39, 143–145
Association, 43
Attitude
  natural, 18–20, 23, 34, 70, 84, 188, 193, 196, 223, 295
  phenomenological, 84, 188
  philosophical, 70
Awakening association, 112–113

Background, 230, 279
  horizonal, 263
Birth and death, 305–307
  and limit-phenomena, 309
  as transcendental event, 307
Botany, 295

Cartesian dualism, 27–28, 40–41
Cartesian way, 260, 273–274, 276
Causality, 104, 183
Claims, 225–227
  vs. descriptions, 226–227, 229
Cogito, 147
Community and sociality, 240

Complexes
  ideal vs. real, 279
Concepts, 226
  discursive, 96
  empirical, 97, 100–101, 103–104, 109–110
  geometrical, 99
  of the a priori, 106
  of the understanding, 99
  scientific, 111
Consciousness, 269
  of existence, 191
  horizonal, 19–20, 59
  imaginative pictorial, 204
  intentional, 13–14, 16, 35
  internal, 168
  perceptive-pictorial, 203–204
  pictorial, 206
  transcendental, 186
  world, 52
Constitution, 30, 32, 35, 40, 46, 113, 234, 259
Contents, 65–66
  intentional, 70
Context, 229
Correlation, 9–10, 13–14, 73, 262

Déjà vu, 209
Differential implication, 228
Discharge (Abfuhr), 206
Disclosure, 318
  as moral and religious, 319
Dissonance, 225
Doxa (opinion), 7
Dreaming, 210, 214, 216
Drive (Trieb), 205–206, 215–216

Expectation, 125
Ego, 187, 191, 272–273, 276
  foreign, 49, 51
  performing, 29
  primordial, 47, 241–242
  pure, 29
  transcendental, xiv, 29
Egological constitution, 292

Printed in the United States
95279LV00002B/9/A

9 780253 216014